LAND SCAPE APPROACH

Published by
Applied Research and Design Publishing,
an imprint of ORO Editions.
Gordon Goff: Publisher

www.appliedresearchanddesign.com
info@appliedresearchanddesign.com

Authors: Hannes Zander, Shelagh McCartney, Samantha Solano, Sonja Vangjeli
Project Manager: Jake Anderson
Book Design: Pablo Mandel / circularstudio.com

Typeset in Avenir

10 9 8 7 6 5 4 3 2 1 First Edition

ISBN: 978-1-954081-23-9

Library of Congress Control Number: 2021925264

Color Separations and Printing: ORO Group Ltd.
Printed in China.

We acknowledge and thank all of our ancestors that have gone before us, mentors that have guided us and friends, families and colleagues that have supported the realization of this book.

We acknowledge the support for *Landscape Approach: From Local Communities to Territorial Systems* from:

Canada Council for the Arts | Conseil des arts du Canada

LACF FAPC

Canada Council for the Arts.

Annual Grant from the Landscape Architecture Canada Foundation (LACF).

SRC Publication Grant, Faculty of Community Services, Toronto Metropolitan University § Canada.

Social Sciences and Humanities Research Council of Canada (SSHRC).

AR+D Publishing makes a continuous effort to minimize the overall carbon footprint of its publications. As part of this goal, AR+D, in association with Global ReLeaf, arranges to plant trees to replace those used in the manufacturing of the paper produced for its books. Global ReLeaf is an international campaign run by American Forests, one of the world's oldest nonprofit conservation organizations. Global ReLeaf is American Forests' education and action program that helps individuals, organizations, agencies, and corporations improve the local and global environment by planting and caring for trees.

LANDSCAPE APPROACH

From Local Communities to Territorial Systems

HANNES ZANDER
SHELAGH MCCARTNEY
SAMANTHA SOLANO
SONJA VANGJELI

a r +d
APPLIED RESEARCH +DESIGN PUBLISHING

Contents

2.3/5.4 Cape Town, South Africa
4.4 Inner Niger Delta, Mali
1.2 Toulouse, France
2.4 Yazd, Iran
3.4 Northern Norway
3.3 Northern Sweden
1.3 Jalalabad, Afghanistan
5.5 Chennai / Kochi, India
3.2 Singapore
1.4 Guangzhou, China
4.2 Inner Australia

4.1 Newfoundland
5.2 New York / Boston, USA
4.3 Williams Treaty Area
1.5 Baltimore / Atlanta, USA
1.1/2.1 Toronto, Canada
3.1/5.1 Ontario
2.2 Mexico City
2.5 Uros, Peru
5.3 Chile

Foreword

Landscape as Approach: Engaging Medium-as-Method

Nina-Marie E. Lister

Here in the relative dawn of the Anthropocene, on the edge of climate change, with biodiversity in free-fall, landscape has been *leaning in*: to ecology, urbanism, infrastructure, activism. No longer chained to a staid and picturesque past (nor, as Ellison wryly observed, suffocated by its embrace),[1] landscape has busted out—reframed and reinterpreted in a grittier, messier, dynamic, performative, post-industrial, even post-human condition. In the twenty-first-century context of global crises, landscape is spoiling for the good fight, as a collective approach—a set of approaches—to design for resilience, for diversity, for *better*. The medium of landscape itself is now complicit, as a mode of working, as an ally in change-making, and finally, firmly engaged as *method* (and yes, as Anderson warns, there is madness in it too).[2]

Long acknowledged as both a cultural construct and artifact, landscapes made and remade reveal a dynamic intersection of culture and nature, and the interstitial but blurry space between them—reflecting novelty, emergence, and adaptation. Once predominately cultural, fixed in intention and construction, today's public landscapes and their attendant designs are more likely performative, dynamic, and flexible; some are explicit in their unfolding and becoming, sometimes in tension and dialogue with the disappearance of the "natural," the injustice of displacement and loss, the unlearning of colonialism, and the claiming of novelty. They may lament absence as much as they celebrate diversity. What is pivotal and critical, is that landscape has become a medium for revelation, learning (and unlearning), and advocacy, even activism in the face of the twin crises of climate change and biodiversity loss; and with these, growing economic disparities and their deepening socio-political injustices. At the same time, the medium of landscape—at the fertile intersection of art and science—is also the birthplace for emergent and transdisciplinary methods of seeing, revealing, knowing, and making.

This timely collection offers a global perspective of the growing agency of landscape-based design, grounded in projects and reflected in case studies that connect culture and nature, engaging people, places, and power in the making of contemporary landscapes. To be clear, landscape-based approaches to applied research, representation, planning, and design are far from new: they follow an evolutionary trajectory from (to name only a few) Olmsted to McHarg, Steinitz to Steiner, Spirn, Corner, Reed, and Orff; they build on and from a century of foundations in ecological systems, laid by Haeckel, Clements, Gleason, Odum, Holling, and Forman; and are influenced in representation by myriad visual arts and their associated technologies. What is different with this collection and its resulting approach is its global perspective and the editors' timely emphases on collaboration, co-creation, and connectivity, between people, places, and power.

As editors and leaders of the nascent International Landscape Collaborative (ILC), McCartney, Solano, Vangjeli, and Zander reflect the ILC's emerging voices and the strength of its diversity across disciplines, geographies, cultures, and practices. McCartney's leadership is reflected through a deeply collaborative, land-based, decolonizing design-research practice while Vangjeli's experience is grounded in complex socio-ecological urban infrastructural projects. Solano's public work in gender-equity and Black Urbanism brings a timely equity lens to landscape discourse and approaches, while Zander's scholarship in territorial systems of extraction and consumption lend a contemporary geo-political context to the work. Collectively, the editors reflect and project the ILC's emerging voices: through this volume, the ILC captures and capitalizes on landscape's next turn, fueled by the zeitgeist of urgency, with growing resistance to colonial norms, and cultural awakening to the power of people *with-and-in* the places and systems sustained by landscapes. The resulting approach is timely, necessary, and rightly in the hands of the next generation of scholars, practitioners, and activists.

In this, the bright lights of the International Landscape Collaborative shine on landscape itself as medium and method—a collective approach—to integrated and novel solutions born of design agency and hopeful co-creation for resilience in turbulent times. With them, I take courage.

—Nina-Marie Lister, Toronto, October 2021

Nina-Marie Lister,
MCIP RPP Hon. ASLA

Professor & Director, Ecological Design Lab, School of Urban & Regional Planning, Toronto Metropolitan University

Winner of the 2021 Margolese National Design for Living Prize
Editor, The Ecosystem Approach: Complexity, Uncertainty and Managing for Sustainability (2008), Projective Ecologies (2014, 2020).

1. Ellison, Aaron M. (2013), "The suffocating embrace of landscape and the picturesque conditioning of ecology." *Landscape Journal* 32:1 pp 79–94.

2. Anderson, Pippin. (2015) "Though there is method, *there is madness in it: How silos of methods impede cross-cutting research." The Nature of Cities,* May 15. https://www.thenatureofcities.com/2013/05/15/though-there-is-method-there-is-madness-in-it-how-silos-of-methods-impede-cross-cutting-research/

Preface

Crafting Socio-Environmental Entanglements in a World of Growing Uncertainties

Hannes Zander

Landscape Approach is the second book publication by the International Landscape Collaborative. The book continues to define a landscape approach through a selection of case studies, proposals, and built work in different geographic and cultural contexts. It presents different ways of reading, understanding, envisioning, and designing the built environment which are all informed by the medium of landscape.

The cultural geographer Denis Cosgrove understands landscape as a cultural artifact. It is the "collective human transformation of nature,"[1] created through the adaptation of a society to its natural environment which has been transformed over time in order to make the land productive to sustain itself and develop collectively. Landscape is the unity of people and their environment, the collective making of a place, the creation of a local identity, and thus the physical expression of a society, including its organization and power structures, and its relationship to the extra-human nature.[2]

Landscape is inherently interdisciplinary as it lies at the intersection of social and environmental studies, between the abstract, mental, and the tangible, geo-physical; between arts, humanities, geography, and natural science. Landscape is also inter-scalar. It is concerned with the insider's perspective of an individual site, person, species, material, or technology. At the same time, landscape is the outsider's conception of a cohesive, territorial system, a cultural, socio-environmental formation. And while landscape "is a way of seeing the world,"[3] it is also a medium to represent the world. It provides the tools to visualize multi-layered ecosystems, complex interrelationships, and convey conflicts, challenges, and opportunities in the intricate web of life. What this book argues is that the medium of landscape—and with that landscape architects, landscape planners, and landscape thinkers—finds itself in an opportune position to tackle some of the most pressing environmental, but also socio-political, issues the world is facing today.

The book promotes a landscape approach as a framework to ground individual places, communities, and habitats in a broad, territorial context that is informed simultaneously by social, political, and economic, in addition to environmental, systems and interrelationships. A landscape approach allows the ability to manage complex, challenging,

OPPOSITE PAGE Polders (detail), Grootschermer, The Netherlands, 2011. Edward Burtynsky

and contested anthropogenic ecosystems holistically—both in urban and rural contexts—by balancing competing demands of socio-economic, legal, and political actors and interests that affect land uses. The approach provides adaptive and integrated management strategies to ensure equitable and sustainable processes, yet, within these systems, also envision and design new and innovative uses, technologies, and built forms. Considering the holistic, inclusive, and multidimensional perspectives which landscape-informed narratives provide allows for development of nature-based solutions that integrate human societies, their needs and cultures, into cohesive systems of water, energy, soil, and non-human species.

A Human-Shaped Planet of Uncertainties as Context

Two conditions are characteristic for the Earth system in which we operate and live in today: First, the realization that the vast majority of the terrestrial biosphere is either actively used by humans or has been transformed into novel ecosystems,[4] forming complex mosaics of anthropogenic biomes.[5] And second, the notion of instability and uncertainty: The world has entered a new era that broke with the unusually stable ecological conditions that characterized the interglacial, moderately warm period of the Holocene and which provided the ecological conditions that allowed humans to thrive and develop our modern human civilization.[6] The resilient and relatively stable Earth system has been shaken up through the way the global population has multiplied in number and expanded activities and their imprint across the world. Once the transformation of biophysical systems reaches certain thresholds, they can become highly sensitive and unstable, creating conditions that are not only far less conducive for our current human development but potentially lead to abrupt environmental transformations with results that can be irreversible.[7]

Symptoms of the growing impact of human activity on the world have become increasingly obvious across planetary scales. In recent years, the world has experienced record rates of global environmental transformations with global warming and changing climates being the most prominent. These environmental changes, leading in some cases to existential crises, need to be understood as integral parts and an expression of humanity's behavior and way of organizing nature. Social development is dominated by an exploitative regime characterized by the separation of humans from the extra-human nature, the commodification of natural resources and markets of capitalist accumulation. This human-dominated world ecology has disrupted and degraded ecosystems but additionally created social conflicts such as economic, race, and gender inequalities, expropriation and forced migration, issues of public health, and shortages of food and drinking water.

Landscape as Common Ground

This complex and increasingly unstable condition of today's world with its planetary environmental transformations is the context in which we operate. The predominant view of seeing humans as separated from nature and modern civilization as having been built out of nature, grown in accelerated pace at the cost of exploiting and materializing the extra-human environment, is essentially a dualist view of the world that is constraining humanity of fundamentally resolving the destructive consequences of this regime. Instead, as scholars in humanities suggest, humans and nature need to be seen deeply entangled and unified in a holistic Earth system, and human history as having been co-produced together with the extra-human nature.[8]

Landscape has the capacity to anticipate models of human-environmental entanglement that addresses their intricate interactions and interdependencies.[9] It has the ability to mediate between different interests and can serve as a common ground for interdisciplinary discourse and negotiation, offering insights into complexities that cannot be gained from one sector's perspective alone. Landscape can guide holistic frameworks and strategies to restore natural ecosystems, and yet it can also inform the built environment and thus mediate between conservation and societal development. The extra-human environment bears tremendous energy and potential to clean, restore, and rebuild degraded ecosystems. Nature-based solutions take advantage of these restorative qualities and work together with the land, with non-human life, soil, and water systems as allies, giving nature space and time to heal.[10] The coupling of human and environmental systems can restore, improve, and envision landscape systems that benefit both the people who inhabit and maintain the landscape and the extra-human environment. A holistic landscape thinking is simultaneously context-specific and longitudinal over scales of space and time to incorporate spatial and temporal dynamics. A landscape-informed approach to planning practices provides the tools to not just critically observe and analyze complex geographic systems of human-environmental entanglement but, in addition, to envision possible futures and design with sensitivity in that multi-layered context across different scales. Landscape thinkers should thus be part of planning teams that work on large-scale projects for land restoration, environmental adaptation, or the implementation of regional infrastructures. They can act as mediators between different disciplines and project agencies and can negotiate different interests of both the extra-human environment and the communities that inhabit, cultivate, and co-produce shared ecosystems.

A Brief Review of Landscape Approaches

According to Cosgrove, the origin of landscape coincides with the emerging of early capitalism in Europe in the 15th-century Northern Italian Renaissance. Landscape can therefore be understood as the manifestation of exactly the separation of humans from nature, which later intensified with Cartesian thought and the colonial expansion of European societies, and which has been described above as constraining holistic thinking. However, Cosgrove dates the end of this traditional conception of landscape in the 19th century when "features of pure market capitalism [...] were distinctly blurred by the intervention of the state."[11] At that time, the society became increasingly concerned with collective issues of sanitation, housing, public health, and general well-being. And it is at that time, in the second half of the 19th century, when the idea of landscape was turned into a medium of anticipatory design for the public realm.

While landscape architecture started to be formalized as a profession in the second half of the 19th century, landscape became a physical medium—no longer as the unintended expression of a society's geographic shaping of their environment but as an active catalyst for the creation and management of cities and the built environment. Early systematic landscape thinkers, such as Frederick Law Olmsted, Charles Eliot, or Warren Manning, were concerned with issues of public health and sanitation, drinking water and fresh air, land conservation, nationwide resource management, as well as institutional strategies and policies for long-term land management. While this first generation of landscape architects followed a pastoral ideal in their designs that was rooted in a strong binary, urban-rural divide, they laid the foundation for the use of landscape as a medium to give form and meaning to growing cities, and, most importantly, think landscapes holistically as cultural products and socio-environmental formations. Revisiting the origins of landscape architecture and regional planning reveals a strong legacy of engaging with different agencies and designing with sensitivity to enable development for balanced socio-cultural, economic, and environmental processes.

At the end of the 19th century, legal planning began to become more dominant. This led to rather authoritarian and later modernist urban planning schemes which eventually pushed landscape to a mere backdrop in and around cities, no longer aligning with the integrative thinking of early landscape architecture projects. Ecologically informed planning and interests in the region as a new scale added nuance to landscape architecture in the first half of the 20th century. But it required a wave of serious environmental concerns in the 1960s until the idea of landscape as a unifying design medium returned. Books such as *Silent Spring* (1962) or *Limits of Growth* (1972) sent alarming messages and created awareness for the far-reaching impacts of rapid, industrial growth and the limitation of natural resources in an increasingly globalized world economy. A novel landscape approach became popular through Ian McHarg's work with his seminal book *Design with Nature* (1969). Influenced by Lewis Mumford and Patrick Geddes, he described scientific approaches of spatial, ecological planning, including innovative mapping and the use of early computer technologies, to be integrated into decision-making processes of modern development and as the basis for design. McHarg's work can be criticized for its anti-urban approach,[12] concerned with land conservation and essentially the identifying of places that should *not* be built. However, the ecological shift in the 1960s broadened the scope to more holistic and systematic thinking which was fundamental for later theories and practices such as landscape ecology.

In the late 20th century, landscape was increasingly thought of as pervasive networks, complex mosaics, and highly dynamic systems. Landscape ecology added a spatial dimension to ecological processes, providing the theoretic vocabulary to effectively ground ecological principles in planning.[13] Several landscape planning frameworks have been developed as operational tools in the United States and Europe.[14] Since the 1990s, a landscape approach has become more prominent in the international institutional discourse, urging for cross-sectoral integration of science, policy, and multiple stakeholders, including NGOs and local communities in participatory planning, with the aim of sustainable development and the conservation of resources.[15] With broadening sets of Earth science data representing wider ranges of species, biodiversity, and ecosystems, computer models and landscape concepts became more cohesive and accurate.[16] Conservation strategies started to include ecology and society more consciously, embracing a social-ecological system approach in which conservation was thought in a more dynamic and less restrictive manner.[17] More recently, a landscape approach was promoted in policies addressing climate change, concerned with natural resource management and integrated land-use planning as a way to reduce levels of greenhouse gases and to mitigate climate change—specifically in agriculture and forestry.[18] Contemporary conservation proposals are increasingly ambitious, bold, and large in scale, most prominently in the *Half Earth Project*.[19]

In the urban realm, landscape approaches were less concerned with conservation, natural resource management, land-use planning, and sustainable development. However, as in rural environments, they were in the same manner led by the inherent logic of the geophysical conditions, natural forces, and larger contexts at the spatial unit of watersheds. Influenced by McHarg's work, theories for how to design with nature in cities were defined, such as in Anne Wiston Spirn's *The Granite Garden* (1984). Landscape urbanism emerged in the late 1990s. It promotes the landscape as a performative medium that can serve as a catalyst for urban revitalization, particularly in the context of post-industrial cities. The beginning of landscape urbanism can be traced to postmodern critiques of modernist architecture and planning in the U.S. and Europe, an economic restructuring, shifts toward a diversification of consumer markets, and the resulting transformation of urban centers starting in the 1960s with many industrial and logistic sites that were abandoned and left as inner-city brownfields, offering opportunities for cities to be restructured, rethought, and redesigned.[20]

Landscape urbanism recognized the potential in landscape-informed solutions to provide highly adaptive and flexible qualities to revitalize the urban realm where urban design and architecture failed to effectively respond to the spatial decentralization of cities, and large, vacant, and contaminated sites that were left behind. Landscape in urban contexts offers powerful tools and design interventions to develop programs that are not only ecologically productive, but also socio-culturally and economically. Landscapes can also act as instrumental, highly effective infrastructural systems, providing essential resources and services that can react to environmental hazards such as flooding, as well as generate and support urban economies.[21] While landscape urbanism and environmental planning share the same roots in the tradition of scientific and systematic McHargian analysis, the outcome in landscape urbanism is a cultural product that evolved from architectural design theory, operates at the scale of a specific intervention and site, and is the result of urban restructuring.

Urban ecology also began in the 1990s but is rooted in a more traditional idea of ecology, evolving from science-based research, and operating at larger scales of metropolitan regions.[22] Ecology has continued to be promoted as a concept for urbanism. However, its meaning has shifted from being a science, primarily concerned with environmental systems, to a cultural term that has become integrated in the daily life of people and across the design practices, equally including social, economic, and political dimensions in addition to environmental.[23]

Ambitions of the Book

This brief review shows that there are different landscape approaches across different sciences and responding to different geographic contexts. Therefore, this book does not want to define one landscape approach as a universal concept or method. Rather, it aims to offer a selection of texts, visual representations, and built examples that describe a certain culture of thinking and ways to approach complex and multifunctional social-environmental systems across different scales. *Landscape Approach* includes interdisciplinary narratives which differ in scale, geographic, and cultural context, but are all grounded in a rich landscape reading and use the conception of landscape as guiding framework. They equally discuss the designs of urban sites and strategies for rural environments. They are concerned with both individual members of local communities and global forces of environmental and political processes. The book suggests to weave such different scales and dimensions together in order to address the complex interdependent issues of environmental change, ecological degradation, and socio-cultural inequalities.

Thinking broadly and encouraging a discourse across geographic, disciplinary, and cultural boundaries requires an effort to reach out to unknown territories. In that regard, *Landscape Approach* is radical and highly ambitious. There is an evident threat of such an inclusive, multidisciplinary approach to being dismissed as overly vague, ambiguous, and general. However, we believe that such broad perspectives are not a weakness. On the contrary, being able to think holistically, to see the individual human as closely entangled with diverse communities and the extra-human environment, to encourage a discourse outside of disciplinary silos, and being able to connect seemingly local issues to regional and even planetary complexities is not only a powerful ability but a necessity in order to address current and future challenges that humanity is facing.

The International Landscape Collaborative

The International Landscape Collaborative (ILC) is an independent group of landscape architects, planners, and designers that started to form in 2017. In the context of environmental degradation at a global scale, the members share a common interest in using the landscape as a catalyst to productively address pressing environmental and social challenges of our time. This mission also aims to broaden the scope of landscape practices to engage with other disciplines and promote an inclusive discourse across sectors. The landscape approach, grounded in the legacy of landscape architecture and regional planning as well as holistic, nature-based solutions, thereby serves as a guiding principle.

While landscape is traditionally a distinctly Western concept, the parallel reading of landscape themes and issues across different world geographies allows to reveal similarities but also distinct regional differences. The landscape approach is promoted particularly in contexts where planned infrastructural systems are not yet codified or consolidated. Such emerging regions and remote territories generally lie outside the traditional disciplinary discourse, yet they offer challenging fields of research and practice. Including them in the discourse reveals socio-environmental inequalities and gives a voice to marginalized groups such as Indigenous communities, that would otherwise go unnoticed. As a network of like-minded scholars and practitioners, the ILC wants to collectively learn through the sharing of case studies, project proposals, and built work in different geographic and cultural contexts and across disciplinary boundaries.

In 2019, the ILC published their first book, *From the South: Global Perspectives on Landscape and Territory*.[24] The book aimed to foster a dialogue of landscape work that is happening outside the traditional centers of the landscape discourse which allowed to reframe the predominant north-to-south vector of transferring theory and practice in landscape architecture and planning. This second book, *Landscape Approach*, continues the same goal of expanding the design and planning discourse to engage larger scales, broader topics, and groups of the society that are usually left outside such conversations. The ILC hopes to grow as an active network through which productive collaborations can emerge with the goal of using the landscape approach to envision and plan for a more sustainable, just, and inclusive world. The group provides a forum to discuss and present work in printed and online publications, as well as at periodic conferences, seminars, and site visits. The ILC aims specifically to provide a platform for emerging voices of young scholars, planners, and designers to connect and learn from each other across disciplinary, cultural, and geographic boundaries.

Endnotes

1. Denis Cosgrove, *Social Formation and Symbolic Landscape*, 2nd ed. (Madison, WI: University of Wisconsin Press, 1998), 14.
2. John Brinckerhoff Jackson, *Discovering the Vernacular Landscape* (New Haven: Yale University Press, 1986).
3. Cosgrove, *Social Formation and Symbolic Landscape*, 13.
4. Richard J. Hobbs et al., "Novel Ecosystems: Theoretical and Management Aspects of the New Ecological World Order," *Global Ecology and Biogeography* 15, no. 1 (2006): 1–7.
5. Erle C. Ellis, "Ecology in an Anthropogenic Biosphere," *Ecological Monographs* 85, no. 3 (2015): 287-331.
6. Will Steffen et al., "Planetary Boundaries: Guiding Human Development on a Changing Planet," *Science* 347, no. 6223 (February 13, 2015): 1259855.
7. Johan Rockström et al., "Planetary Boundaries: Exploring the Safe Operating Space for Humanity," *Ecology and Society* 14, no. 2 (November 18, 2009): 32.
8. See for example: Donna J. Haraway, *Staying with the Trouble: Making Kin in the Chthulucene*, (Durham, NC: Duke University Press, 2016); Anna Tsing et al., eds., *Arts of Living on a Damaged Planet: Ghosts and Monsters of the Anthropocene*, (Minneapolis: University of Minnesota Press, 2017); Jason W. Moore, *Capitalism in the Web of Life: Ecology and the Accumulation of Capital* (London: Verso, 2015).
9. Jianguo Liu et al., "Coupled Human and Natural Systems," *AMBIO: A Journal of the Human Environment* 36, no. 8 (December 2007): 639–49.
10. E. Cohen-Shacham et al., "Nature-Based Solutions to Address Global Societal Challenges" (IUCN, 2016); Christian Albert et al., "Addressing Societal Challenges Through Nature-Based Solutions: How Can Landscape Planning and Governance Research Contribute?," *Landscape and Urban Planning* 182 (February 1, 2019): 12–21.
11. Cosgrove, *Social Formation and Symbolic Landscape*, 3; 254-256.
12. Charles Waldheim, *Landscape as Urbanism: A General Theory* (Princeton, NJ; Oxford: Princeton University Press, 2016), 53.
13. Richard T. T. Forman and Michel Godron, *Landscape Ecology* (New York: Wiley, 1986).
14. Carl Steinitz, "A Framework for Theory Applicable to the Education of Landscape Architects (and Other Environmental Design Professionals)," *Landscape Journal* 9, no. 2 (1990): 136–43; Richard T. T. Forman, *Land Mosaics: The Ecology of Landscapes and Regions* (Cambridge: Cambridge University Press, 1995); Frederick Steiner, *The Living Landscape: An Ecological Approach to Landscape Planning* (New York: McGraw-Hill, 2000).
15. Jianguo Wu and Richard Hobbs, "Landscape Ecology: The State-of-The-Science," in *Key Topics in Landscape Ecology*, ed. Jianguo Wu and Richard J. Hobbs (Cambridge: Cambridge University Press, 2007), 271–87; Ruth S Defries and Cynthia E. Rosenzweig, "Toward a Whole-Landscape Approach for Sustainable Land Use in the Tropics," *Proceedings of the National Academy of Sciences* 107, no. 46 (November 16, 2010): 19627–32.
16. Katherine A. Zeller, Kevin McGarigal, and Andrew R. Whiteley, "Estimating Landscape Resistance to Movement: A Review," *Landscape Ecology* 27, no. 6 (July 1, 2012): 777–97; Claire Vos et al., "Toward Ecologically Scaled Landscape Indices," *The American Naturalist* 157, no. 1 (January 1, 2001): 24–41.
17. Fikret Berkes and Carl Folke, *Linking Social and Ecological Systems: Management Practices and Social Mechanisms for Building Resilience* (Cambridge University Press, 2000).
18. See as an example of a cohesive report by an intergovernmental organization: IPCC, "Climate Change and Land: An IPCC Special Report on Climate Change, Desertification, Land Degradation, Sustainable Land Management, Food Security, and Greenhouse Gas Fluxes in Terrestrial Ecosystems" (In Press: IPCC, 2019). https://www.ipcc.ch/srccl/.
19. Edward O. Wilson, *Half-Earth: Our Planet's Fight for Life*, (New York: Liveright, 2016), https://www.half-earthproject.org/.
20. Waldheim, *Landscape as Urbanism*.
21. Pierre Bélanger, "Landscape As Infrastructure," *Landscape Journal* 28, no. 1 (January 1, 2009): 79–95.
22. Frederick Steiner, "Landscape Ecological Urbanism: Origins and Trajectories" 100, no. 4 (2011): 333–37.
23. Mohsen Mostafavi, "Why Ecological Urbanism? Why Now?," in *Ecological Urbanism*, ed. Mohsen Mostafavi and Gareth Doherty, Revised Edition (Zurich: Lars Muller Publishers, 2016), 12–55.
24. Flavio Sciaraffia, Sourav Kumar Biswas, Thomas Nideroest, Hannes Zander, eds., *From the South: Global Perspectives on Landscape and Territory* (Santiago, Chile: Ediciones Universidad del Desarrollo, 2019). The book resulted from the group's inaugural symposium organized by the ILC in January 2018 in Santiago, Chile and includes 18 chapters that are discussing different world geographies through the lens of landscape with a regional focus that is laid on Chile and southern hemispheres more generally.

Introduction

Hannes Zander, Shelagh McCartney,
Samantha Solano, Sonja Vangjeli

Landscape Approach is a collection of twenty-three essays that promote the medium of landscape through a diverse array of narratives, projects, identities, and geographies. It is structured into five sections that organize the argument for a landscape approach around concepts of urban landscape systems, ecology, politics, territory, and practice. Together, the sections traverse multiple geographical contexts and provide an international dialogue that can be read in response to each other. This particular framing offers a distinct lens that creates new conversations and identities of landscape divergent from mainstream discourse. Throughout the book, authors discuss issues that occur in sites of: urban growth and development, remote areas of extraction and production, environmental degradation and transformation, and social inequality and discrimination. The texts each articulate a strong sense of urgency in addressing such conflicts, spanning from local communities to territorial systems, that demand a multi-scalar, cross-boundary integration that acknowledges the complexities and interrelationships of politics, economy, ecology, and culture.

As the second book publication from the International Landscape Collaborative (ILC), *Landscape Approach* shifts the regional focus "To the North," from the first volume's focus "From the South" which centered on Chile and a global Southern reading. Even though the chapters are geographically diverse, this book focuses on Northern narratives throughout Canada and includes at least one Canadian territory per section. This is important because the vast territories in northern parts of Canada, and the far North in general, are experiencing rapid environmental transformation and shifting geo-political interests. Large land masses in the northern territories are dramatically affected by long-term environmental change such as global warming. This compromises vital wildlife habitats, ecosystems, and freshwater reserves, making their preservation and careful, sustainable management crucial for the future of the world. Simultaneously, many prime zones for material extraction are located in the far reaches of the northern hemisphere and the fast-progressing thawing of Arctic ice and permafrost opens up new grounds for these destructive processes to occur. A question becomes, with these "new" territories emerging as fertile grounds for resources, how can we

OPPOSITE PAGE Relocation of a nomadic Nenets camp along the Yenisei River near Dudinka, Krasnoyarsk Krai, northern Siberia, Russia. Yann Arthus-Bertrand

be strategic in its inevitable development that centers on the landscape and its inhabitants first.

In parallel to the Northern focus of this book was the integration of Indigenous knowledge, experience, and storytelling throughout several of the chapters. The book highlights and learns from traditional ecological knowledge, sustainable technologies, and alternative worldviews which offer a critical lens for designers, planners, policymakers to not only consider but partner with the communities affected by our professional outcomes. Several chapters demonstrate how Indigenous societies preserve a precious wisdom of living in harmony with cycles of nature which bears the potential to influence future societal development. While Indigenous communities make up just four percent of the global population, they are stewards of up to 80 percent of the planet's biodiversity.[1] However, they are in many cases exposed to conflicting geo-political interests with short-term economic gains. It is key to recognize the deep-rooted landscape wisdom, traditional ecological practices, art, and innovative technologies of Indigenous peoples. The book simply doesn't discuss Indigenous issues and people, rather it is a demonstration of talking with them, learning from them, and letting them tell their stories. Three of the chapters are written by members of Indigenous communities and offer an invaluable opportunity to listen. Overall, the book highlights eight chapters influenced and informed by Indigenous narratives which, if not as an author, have been developed in close collaboration with members of those communities.

There are several additional themes that can be recognized throughout the book that more closely align within the individual sections, outlined below. There are instances where parallels can jump sections and it is the intention of this book that the sections and their chapters can be read independently as well as together. Collectively, the book draws lessons that can be gleaned from several propositions grounded in inclusive, contextual, and multi-scalar readings. All contributions aim to be projective and push boundaries of landscape-informed practices that are socially and environmentally resilient, just, and sustainable.

Planning Metropolitan Landscape Systems

Planning Metropolitan Landscape Systems focuses on planning approaches and policy frameworks at the scale of urban regions to establish regional green-blue landscape systems that support ecological functions and resilience, the health and wellbeing of urban populations, as well as guide urban growth and identity. An understanding of cities as part of nature and the socio-ecological linkages that bind urban and regional landscapes

---

1 Claudia Sobrevilla, *The Role of Indigenous Peoples in Biodiversity Conservation* (Washington, D.C.: World Bank, 2008).

are at the core of the planning processes examined in the five chapters. The papers look at six very different city-regions in Canada, the U.S., France, China, and Afghanistan, each with its own unique issues and opportunities, different cultures, climate, growth patterns and institutional frameworks. The first two chapters focus on urban planning and heritage conservation policies aimed at preserving and growing landscape systems from a public sector perspective, while three others offer perspectives from design practices proposing new approaches and methodologies for planning growing urban regions around landscape frameworks. Drawing from principles of urban ecology as well as local knowledge and traditions, each of the proposals presented offers alternatives to typical technocratic planning frameworks, working toward more holistic, site-specific, landscape-led approaches for planning dynamic urban regions that can adapt to future change.

The first chapter, *Wild, Connected and Diverse – the Role of Landscape Architects in Establishing the Natural Ecosystem of Canada's Largest City*, focuses on Toronto's system of natural parklands and the legacy of past and current conservation policies and planning initiatives that have contributed to the preservation, restoration, and enhancement of the urban ecosystem. Landscape architects have played a critical role in the establishment of policy frameworks and plans that prioritize the city's unique landscape system of ravines and lakefronts. As the city grows into a metropolis, renewed efforts, strategic policies, and stewardship are needed to protect and expand Toronto's landscape system as a vital armature.

Perspectives on Heritage Conservation and Sustainable Development looks at the challenges of implementing urban development policy tools that try to reconcile urban ecology with heritage conservation in the highly regulated historic city of Toulouse, which is vying for UNESCO World Heritage City status. The shift in scope of urban heritage conservation from monuments and built fabric to landscape and territory, based on the UNESCO Historic Urban Landscape Approach, is leading cities like Toulouse, Bordeaux, and Seville to take a more holistic planning approach to reintegrating nature in the city and reconnecting with urban rivers and their watersheds.

A Reflexive Approach to Uncertainty: Situating Planning Practice in the Landscape of Afghanistan's City-Regions examines the legacy of imported technocratic master planning in the contested urban regions of Afghanistan and proposes an alternative landscape-based strategic planning approach grounded in the realities of the specific context to guide urban expansion in the Jalalabad city region. The interdisciplinary approach is based on the understanding of socio-ecological links between Afghan livelihoods and their landscape, the interdependency between the city and its rural hinterland, and the understanding of the landscape as a changing medium. The planning framework proposed by the Sasaki team anticipates uncertainty by proposing toolkits and development scenarios that allow for nimble adaptation to political, social, and environmental change.

Ecological Infrastructure as a Systematic Approach to Water Issues focuses on Guangzhou and explores Turenscape's "sponge city" planning approach, making the case for ecological infrastructure (EI) across three scales—city, district, and community—as security patterns to mitigate the region's water issues and increasing vulnerability due to climate change. The chapter draws from the traditional agricultural knowledge of the Pearl River Delta to propose a nature-based approach to regional water management. In contrast to the strategic approach in Afghanistan, the sponge city framework represents more of a top-down centralized approach, well integrated in planning policy.

The last chapter, *Anchoring Our Cities in Ecological Identity*, illustrates an interdisciplinary socio-ecological planning approach through the work of the planning and design firm Biohabitats—based in Atlanta, Georgia and Baltimore, Maryland—to establish green networks that can structure urban growth and change. Their collaborative interdisciplinary approach is grounded in principles of urban ecology and close community collaboration, drawing from personal narratives and experiences to establish strong relationships to place and encourage long-term stewardship. Working across scales—from a pocket park to the neighborhood and habitat corridor—they work toward landscape systems that provide ecosystem functions, support biodiversity and human health, and contribute to the city's identity.

Building Ecological Infrastructures

Water as the lifeblood of culture is a unifying theme of the chapters gathered together in the *Building Ecological Infrastructures* section. For the societies discussed in these chapters, water is an ordering element, taking on a cultural role to bring equity, as well as regenerate and heal communities. These case studies demonstrate the potential of designed or natural landscape systems to serve as performative urban infrastructures by cleansing water, regulating floods, bringing equity to unequal cities by offering recreational opportunities and green space, and restoring culture through a transdisciplinary landscape approach that offers ecologically rich environments that mitigate environmental degradation while sparking new socio-economic processes that strengthen metropolitan resilience. The cases also highlight the limitations of an overly engineered approach to infrastructure planning that works against natural systems rather than with them. Instead, these built projects and programs can improve livability in their urban environments through the use of hybrid, nature-based solutions facilitated by innovative technologies—technologies that are either born out of imitating landscape ecologies with little disruption to the systems they are engaging with, as outlined in de Salvatierra's chapter on *Eternal Ephemera*, or through complex engineering which works to mirror the systems that were removed as a result of human inhabitation, as discussed in Baker and Vangjeli's *Port Lands Flood Protection*. Each of the case studies presented in this section focus on layers of the ecosystem that reflect a landscape approach to urban infrastructure, an approach that reconnects nature-based systems in each project.

Beginning in Toronto, Canada with *Port Lands Flood Protection: A Landscape Infrastructural Approach*, Baker and Vangjeli describe the design process of a large transdisciplinary landscape infrastructural project in which a balance of ecology and complex engineering inform each other to recreate a naturalized river outlet on a post-industrial site to protect the city from floods. Very much a product of the current environment, this case establishes that built mega projects can be led by a landscape approach to address the impacts of past engineering, restore the ecological functions of natural systems that were once using landscape infrastructure that mirrored nature-based systems, while at the same time creating iconic parks and public realms.

The landscape approach is particularly relevant to urban regions within developing economies as ecological systems can be strategically leveraged to serve as subsidized and resilient forms of infrastructure. The cases of Mexico City and Cape Town embody expensive engineering responses to water that work against the natural systems, and thus make the relationship between water and their respective cities worse with every passing day. Rather than using a landscape approach and learning from Indigenous ways of knowing how to work with a landscape that varies, Mexico City is trying to out-engineer nature instead of working with natural hydraulic systems, such as in the prospective Hydric District outlined by Chávez, Rico, and Tudela in *Urban Water as a Resource, Not as Waste: The Case for Medium-Scale Hydric Districts in Mexico City*. A similar natural solution presents itself to Cape Town through the Livable Urban Waterways (LUW) program, as described by Faragher in *Livable Waterways for a Water-Sensitive Transition for Cape Town*. Both Mexico City and Cape Town are unequal cities—one dry, one wet—and both are struggling against natural water systems using over-engineered approaches to try to provide potable water for their inhabitants. Yet in both cases, bottom-up, small-scale initiatives that can make large-scale change are framed as opportunities for transdisciplinary projects and implementation of nature-based solutions. Such solutions lay the groundwork, through a project or a program, for what could be a turning point in both Mexico City's and Cape Town's relationship with water and a move towards resilience. For Mexico City, Chávez, Rico, and Tudela outline a project that looks for ways to work with ecosystems rather than imposing conventional engineering solutions; similarly, for Cape Town, Faragher outlines a program with policies that revitalize waterways in order to integrate divided communities, resulting in healthier, water-sensitive cities through new partnerships in cities with failed relationships to water.

In *Qanatscape: Revealing the Historic Water Landscape of the "Qanat" to Inform Future Green Infrastructure in Cities of Arid Iran*, Chamani explores a historic water infrastructure system, one that positively established a water landscape through the system of the landscape itself, as a site of cultural resurgence. Qanatscapes coexist with other living systems that depend on that water source; from this observation, Chamani argues that, in building with the landscape approach by imitating nature-based systems, a sustainable urbanism can be created that is specific to the localized water conditions—an urbanism that can both reinvigorate culture and offer the value of looking within rather than importing solutions.

In *Eternal Ephemera: Soft Infrastructures in the Floating City of Uros, Peru*, de Salvatierra examines culture at the building scale rather than the urban scale and pushes the boundaries of where urbanization begins, the materials used to construct cities, and how to build a sustainable urbanism. De Salvatierra opens up a discussion on the methods of how we study and examine urbanism using the case of Uros, extending Indigenous ideas of building and blurring the boundary of where water ends and urbanization begins. The shift from mega project to handmade project in this section highlights the Indigenous technologies used to create a sustainable urbanism on water, as well as the benefits that a landscape approach can bring to projects and programs in urban environments.

Reading Socio-Political Landscapes

Every place, person, or non-human species is part of a large web of social, political, economic, and environmental relationships. Virtually every ecosystem is affected by the impact of human processes. In a world that is dominated by a globalized market economy, every place, resource, and commodity can be connected to global, socio-political forces and interdependencies. The third section *Reading Socio-Political Landscapes* provides such narratives of complex entanglements across multiple scales. Four chapters identify different institutional, political, social, and economic actors in different geographies and describe in each case how these actors—with often conflicting goals and interests—shape and co-produce physical environments. Such processes generate multi-layered landscapes that operate across scales and create complex ecologies that have in many cases been reshaped multiple times over time.

Instead of looking at isolated, contemporary sites, the chapters aim to discuss cohesive studies of large, territorial contexts and their inherent histories of social-environmental co-production. The ability to connect individual places and their users to such complex, multi-spatial, and temporal contexts, provides a rich and holistic understanding of specific issues, conflicts, and opposing interests. A landscape-informed reading of such territorial complexities allows us to identify the different stakeholders, establish a mutual dialogue to engage with them, negotiate between different interests, and eventually, to effectively intervene in these systems across multiple scales and time frames.

The four chapters in this section present narratives of very different geographic and cultural contexts. The first text, *Forest Plantations as Spatiotemporal Reclamation Strategy*, reveals how forests in Southern Ontario are by no means "natural" but have been consciously developed as a reaction to the devastating environmental consequences of exploitative logging practices in the 19th and early 20th century. They form today a highly managed and institutionalized landscape that is constantly adapting to changing environmental conditions.

Earth Moves: Singapore's Land Reclamation Projects and the Construction of Territory discusses the material of sand as a narrative to describe geo-political interests that connect Singapore's ambitious plans of rapid urban and economic growth to remote hinterlands. Cycles of sand as a crucial commodity are traced from the individual building on Singapore's waterfront as the iconic manifestation of a ubiquitous trend of urbanization, to the property of reclaimed land as a mode of speculative investment, to sites of sand mining as contested foreign territories of material extraction, and across the transportation and trading network of global markets.

The final two chapters of this section discuss vast geographies in far northern Europe. *"Hic et Nunc" Palimpsests: Reconstructing Historical Natures Through the Malm Territory of Extraction* presents the Malm territory in Northern Sweden, a geography that is characterized by large-scale processes of material extraction and energy production. It is described in a historical, colonial narrative across multiple scales that reveals how the socio-environmental context has been transformed over time through the institutionalization of the Swedish state, through capitalist markets' endless need of accumulation and spatial expansion, and the appropriation of the extra-human environment, of women, and Indigenous communities.

The Living and Breathing Map of Sámi Reindeer Herding provides insights into Sámi herding communities in Northern Norway. It describes their deeply rooted and collectively shared understanding of the natural environment through a narrative of earmarks relating to semi-domesticated reindeer herds. This offers an alternative reading and mental mapping of the traditional landscape as a highly dynamic system of social-environmental interdependencies that is sensitive to forces of changing environmental conditions, economic growth and development, as well as institutional plans of modernization.

Planning for Territorial Systems

Planning for Territorial Systems discusses sites and regional contexts that are influenced by territorial resources, economies, infrastructures, livelihoods, and local- and Indigenous-knowledge systems. Here the term "territory" is openly understood and defined, operating through several scales and limits that have critical attachments to hydrological narratives. This section presents speculative visions of new relationships to engage with the territory through cultural storytelling, mapping, policy shifts, and projective landscape projects. What emerges from these unique perspectives that alter the framing of territory, is an overall realignment of territorial actors—where the drivers of a landscape approach come from the people, the ground, and planning and design are secondary, and not necessarily the intervention required. Through four very different but aligned lenses, the chapters in this section are organized to read in conversation with each other through scale, location, and narrative.

Starting in the northern territorial waters of Newfoundland, the first chapter calls for a new way to describe territory in the context of local, self-sufficient land and water-based economies. The over exertion of large-scale infrastructural connections based solely on resource extraction opportunities, destroyed several critical settlements and livelihoods throughout the region. *On the Edge: Re-Framing Our Understanding of a Nissological Territory* reclaims these lost relationships and economies through speculative studio-based research projects and opens up the section's goal of reconsidering who has the agency to impact territorial operations and success.

From the coasts and oceans of Newfoundland to the inland drylands of Western Australia, the second chapter builds on territorial agency from Indigenous concepts of cultural water that were also impacted by extractive infrastructures and planning. Through a series of critical mappings, *WaterLore for the Drylands: Strategies for Activating Cultural Waters in Regimes of Extraction* deploys the power of representation to shift the collective understanding away from the known top-down tracings of land and value. The chapter focuses on Aboriginal and non-Aboriginal cultural stories and practices as a way to learn from people who already know how to work with less reliable water regimes in dryland territories. These new cultural mappings aim to present new realities and possibilities for speculative designed management systems for human and ecological communities.

The next chapter brings us back to Canada in the Duffins Creek, Williams Treaty territory in Ontario. The authors offer a unique approach that keeps with the Indigenous methods of teaching and learning through storytelling. They present the story of the Duffins Creek wetland that was threatened due to urbanization wherein a landscape approach of conservation through First Nation rights, knowledge, and

Treaty obligations led to an inclusive process of landscape change and respect. *Conservation Through Indigenous Treaty Revival: The Duffins Creek, Williams Treaties Area* shifts the focus again away from the top-down, planning, design, policy professional and calls for space and agency for the peoples most impacted by and knowledgeable of the extents of their territorial landscape systems.

The last chapter in this section, like its counterparts, centers around local understandings of context and cultural traditions. In the Sahel territory of Africa, the chapter focuses on a hydro-agricultural infrastructure found in Mali. With the urgencies of a shifting climate and its impacts on land productivity and livelihoods, *Blue Gold: Hydro-Agricultural Infrastructure & Climate Change in the Sahel* proposes a means for design to leverage existing infrastructural systems to instill ecological function within productive agricultural areas—land uses usually in conflict with each other. The speculative design project presented not only addresses these landscape systems, but also addresses local food insecurity and the creation of additional economic opportunities for the community, especially for women.

New Models of Practice

This last section of the book presents five cases of groups or individuals who built their own models of practice and research that are informed by landscape, collaboration, and nature-based solutions. The practices all operate in different cultural, political, and environmental contexts. They use distinct facets of design and planning to approach issues of socio-environmental conflicts but also to recognize, identify, and convey the potentials and opportunities which they bear. The chapters present strategies of collaboration to reach out and communicate across cultural and disciplinary boundaries. They are informed by the realization that the creation and development of the built environment is never a zero-sum game and that it includes opposing interests such as economic growth and environmental protection. The five chapters, however, demonstrate how these opposing interests can provide opportunities to engage with a diverse array of stakeholders—including social groups and communities, political institutions, different sciences, arts, academics, and practitioners—to come together and negotiate over their different, often conflicting interests, aiming to find balanced, nature-based solutions that are both socially and environmentally positive.

The different cases of practice build a showcase of how a landscape-informed approach allows designers, architects, and planners to engage with new scales and territories that are not traditionally in their disciplinary domain. Instead of conventional and one-dimensional modes of problem-solving, the texts present strategies of actively searching for opportunities to intervene across scales, using the multi-layered readings of landscape as a catalyst to facilitate new dialogues, change mindsets, and make long-lasting impacts in the built environment. Some of the chapters also demonstrate how a landscape approach was able to be successfully established in institutional contexts where multi-disciplinary, socio-environmental thinking is often absent, leading to paradigm shifts and offering holistic, widely accepted, and cost-effective solutions.

The first chapter, *Codesign, Collaboration and Systems Change,* establishes *partnership* as a critical method and relational ecosystem framework for addressing complex issues in contested landscapes in Canada's near and far North. Drawing from the experiences of Together Design Lab and Ecological Design Lab at Toronto Metropolitan University School of Urban and Regional Planning in Toronto, the chapter illustrates collaborative models of practice by exploring the potential of cross-cultural, multi-sectoral, transdisciplinary partnerships as forms of resistance to traditional power structures and silos of technical knowledge. From working with Indigenous peoples to develop community-based housing systems to co-creating green infrastructures that link people, wildlife, and landscapes across roads, the authors link praxis and research to demonstrate how community-based and participatory methods can be used across scales to create meaningful change through a landscape approach. The chapter also highlights the critical role of academia in training students in new models of collaborative place-based practice to enable long-term systemic change.

Resensitizing Urban Waterways and Their Publics is the story of how the collective Mare Liberum (ML) uses public art as a form of engagement to take part in the (un)planning and the shaping of public perception, attention, and environmental policy. Through the participatory process of boat building and water traversing, ML aims to physically connect people to water and facilitate a transdisciplinary dialogue that creates awareness for public space, urban waterways, and the environmental complexities of entire river systems. The chapter discusses the timelines of these issues and outlines the institutional collaborations and funding structures that made this type of work possible.

A Strategy-Driven Model for Sustainable Socio-Environmental Transformation in Chile describes how a holistic, landscape-informed approach has been able to influence public policy and high-level decision making in Chile. It presents the case of priority wetland conservation strategies that address socio-environmental challenges, guide the assessment of ecological qualities, and propose progressive avenues for nature conservation. It discusses how these tools have been developed, following a strategic, flexible, and long-term model, and successfully implemented across technocratic governmental institutions.

Lindsey Howe and Ben Mansfield in *Learning Development by Doing: The "Massive Small" Evolution of the Resilient Civic Design Collective* tell their story of building a practice that is invested in developing safe, healthy, and equitable environments for communities in marginalized neighborhoods in South Africa. Taking advantage of underutilized plots of land and mediating between local communities, landowners, and government agencies, they have developed a unique model of practice, project development, and fundraising, working between their base in Europe and local experts on site in African cities, and including collaborations with an international pool of designers and educational institutions.

The last chapter, *Collaborative and Strategic Approaches to Build Urban Resilience in India*, describes how the Sponge Collaborative aims to establish the landscape approach in Indian cities, engaging with local ministries, municipal corporations, city engineers, and other stakeholders. Several competition wins enabled the young collective to test new models of resilient urban development in the context of South Indian cities. Green infrastructures are productively implemented into the urban fabric to mitigate the effects of flooding and creating environmental as well as socio-economic benefits.

***

Landscape Approach draws on a variety of scholarly expertise, practical experience, and local wisdom to present a rich collection of chapters that are grounded in specific and complementary geographic and cultural contexts. The book spans from the scale of the metropolitan region where the landscape approach can build on a strong legacy of planning practice; to locally designed systems that act as performative infrastructures and help to sustain societies; to revealing the socio-political complexities of different actors and their often conflicting interests in the process of organizing nature; to discussing speculative planning schemes at the scale of the territory that include and benefit social and environmental systems; to, lastly, highlighting individual stories of building new models of working collaboratively and translating landscape thinking into practice.

The reading of these landscape-informed narratives across geographies, cultures, and disciplines leads to a new way of thinking about the role of design, policy, and planning in impacting and understanding our shared ecology. *Landscape Approach* offers a diverse range of pathways towards landscape-informed practices that will ultimately lead to environmentally sustainable and socially just futures—from local communities to territorial systems.

1 PLANNING METROPOLITAN LANDSCAPE SYSTEMS

Planning Metropolitan Landscape Systems presents planning and policy frameworks at the scale of urban regions which aim to establish regional green-blue networks that support ecological functions and resilience, improve the health and well-being of urban populations, and guide urban growth. Across six city-regions, each with its own unique cultures, climate, growth patterns and institutional frameworks, the chapters offer alternatives to typical technocratic planning frameworks, working toward more holistic, site-specific, landscape-led approaches for planning dynamic urban regions that can adapt to future change.

1.1

Wild, Connected, and Diverse

The Role of Landscape Architects in Establishing the Natural Ecosystem of Canada's Largest City

Jane Welsh

"Turn, look down: there is no city; this is the center of a forest."
— Margaret Atwood, 1970 *The Journals of Susanna Moodie.*

Toronto is a dynamically growing city of 2.9 million people, one of the fastest growing cities in North America. Located on the north shore of Lake Ontario and the intersection of the Carolinian and the Great Lakes-St. Lawrence Forest zones, Toronto has, surprisingly, a relatively robust and extensive natural ecosystem found within its many river valleys and along its waterfront.

Toronto, named after *Tkaronto*, the Mohawk word meaning "where there are trees in the water," describes a deep-rooted and meaningful relationship in natural stewardship between the people and the place.[1] This relationship has endured over thousands of years, however, the strength of this connection between the people and the natural landscape has ebbed and flowed. Prior to European settlement Toronto's landscape was defined by a mix of hardwood forests and shrub swamps, with extensive marshes at the mouths of the Don, Humber, and Rouge rivers. Over the last three centuries forests were cleared, rivers dammed, and most natural areas were converted to agriculture and then later to asphalt, brick, concrete, and glass as the city spread outwards and upwards from the shoreline. As ecologist John Riley described, after three centuries of conversion, the natural landscape of Toronto is a "shadow of its former self."[2] These changes to the natural system have not been without consequences, resulting in a gradual loss of species and sudden loss of life and property when Hurricane Hazel hit Toronto in 1954.

Toronto today has a robust and extensive system of natural areas. These natural areas, found in the ravines and along the waterfront, together with the city's parks and open spaces, tableland forests, street trees, back yards, and green roofs give Toronto its identity as a "city within a park." [FIG. 2-4] The system adds immeasurable beauty and liveability to the city, contributes to the health and wellbeing of residents, cleans the air, and consumes and moves stormwater.

The existence of Toronto's natural ecosystem is the result of several factors, including advocacy and recognition of the importance of the natural system through a number of forward-thinking plans enacted in

OPPOSITE PAGE Burke Brook, one of Toronto's forested ravines is a hidden gem in the urban fabric. Robert Burley, 2014

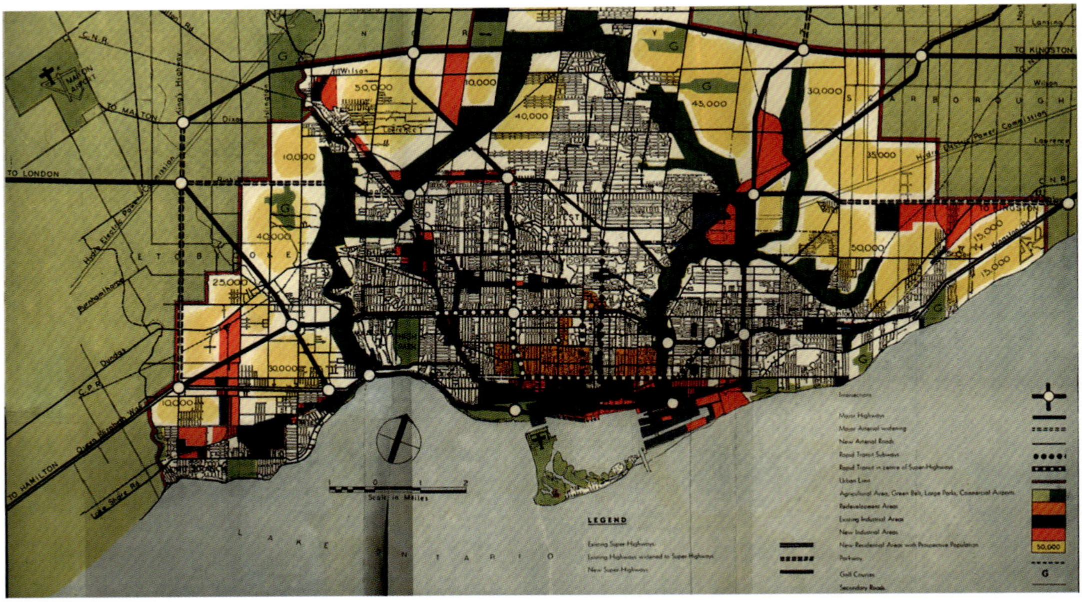

FIG.1 Map from the 1943 "Master Plan for the City of Toronto and Environs", as reproduced in the Royal Architectural Institute of Canada, Journal, June 1944.
City of Toronto

the early part of the 20th century. Over the past fifty years the efforts of landscape architects, in both the public and private sectors, to reconnect nature and city has been crucial to ensuring that the natural ecosystem in Toronto was not just protected, but restored and enhanced. As Toronto continues to grow, it is even more important that the quality and quantity of its urban ecosystem increases, adding to the city's resilience and the well-being of its residents.

Recognition of the Importance of the Natural System

> "As the years go on and the population increases, there will be a need for these lands and more, and in life where so much appears futile, this one thing will remain."
>
> — Charles Sauriol, renowned Canadian naturalist.

Early recognition of the importance of Toronto's natural landscape system was articulated in a 1909 plan by the Toronto Guild of Civic Art who advocated for the protection of Toronto's natural assets (the lakeshore, the island, the ravines) for their beauty and recreational opportunities "to develop the natural character we have, and make of Toronto not just a beautiful city, beautiful in a conventional way, after the model of some other city, but to bring out its own beauty. It is the character of the town that makes the dwellers love it."[3] The focus for protection was on the picturesque beauty of forest and ravines, rather than ecologically important but less beautiful marshes and wetlands, such as Ashbridges Bay, which were filled in to be used for other purposes.

The importance of a connected natural system was first set out in the 1943 *Master Plan for the City of Toronto and its Environs*[4] [FIG. 1] which laid out an inner green belt and the need for conservation of the Niagara Escarpment and Oak Ridges Moraine. In 1954 the Metropolitan Toronto's Planning Board recommended the establishment of a 2,700-hectare park system based on the major river valleys. At the time 40 percent of the system was vulnerable to urban development and Metro Council authorized the creation of an acquisition fund and directed the preparation of an Official Plan to address the river valleys and Toronto Island. As Parks Commissioner Tommy Thompson had the foresight to note in 1955 "the tempo of modern living and density of our population make it essential that nature be preserved in those areas where it still exists."[5]

Much of the initial protection of the ravine system was achieved through the acquisition of these lands by the public sector. However, by 1960 it was apparent that the lack of policy regulating private development had resulted in the loss of over 40 percent of the original ravine lands. While the higher tier Metro Official Plan had strong policies in place for the protection of the major river valleys and waterfront, local municipal plans were slower to follow suit until spurred on by the advocacy of environmental groups. In their 1976 "Toronto the Green" paper, the Toronto Field Naturalists recommended that all the municipal official plans "explicitly recognize the conservation of natural areas as an important aspect of planning" and that all municipalities adopt ravine protection bylaws.[6]

In 1998 Metro Toronto amalgamated with the municipalities of Toronto, Etobicoke, York, East York, and Scarborough providing new opportunities to protect the natural system. The new Official Plan included comprehensive policies for the protection of the natural system and a new Ravine Protection Bylaw required permission to remove or injure trees and vegetation. Landscape architects co-led the development of that first city-wide Ravine Protection Bylaw and supervised its implementation. In 2016 the updated Official Plan environment policies added further protection with the designation of an additional 68 Environmentally Significant Areas.

FIG.2 Scarborough Bluffs Park, 2014. Robert Burley

FIG.3 Humber Marshes at the mouth of the Humber River, 2016. Robert Burley

FIG.4 Highland Creek Park, 2016. Robert Burley

Influence of Landscape Architects

> "Viewing cities as part of the natural world, rather than separate from it to inspire a new aesthetic for urban design."
>
> — Anne Whiston Spirn, *The Granite Garden, 1984.*

Landscape architects design, plan, manage, and conserve the landscape, bridging the gap between the natural and built environment through innovative design solutions that work to protect the wild and to promote planning and design that benefits and sustains both ecosystems and society. Landscape architects depend on science-based and local knowledge to inform their decisions, working through constructive partnerships with scientists at a scale relevant to their work.[7] In Toronto, the work of landscape architects has been crucial to ensuring that the natural ecosystem was not just protected but restored and enhanced through thoughtful planning, regulations and policy, master plans, stewardship and importantly, sensitive design. Landscape architects have worked hard to reconnect nature and city leading to renewed interest and investment in the natural urban system.

The focus on understanding and protecting the natural ecosystem was carefully addressed in the 1976 report on Toronto's waterfront prepared by landscape architects Anne Whiston Spirn and Narendra Juneja to "ensure that environmental concern be given at least as much due as social, political, and economic concerns."[8]

Michael Hough's 1984 book *Cities and Natural Processes* and his 1991 paper "Bring Back the Don" as well as the considerable design influence of his firm on the restoration of natural areas, had a profound impact in shaping the protection of Toronto's natural spaces. His advocacy for "Ecosystem Planning"—the integration of ecology, social, and cultural ingredients into city planning was a major influence on the 1994 *Official Plan of the Municipality of Metropolitan Toronto: the liveable metropolis* which set a new baseline for the protection of the regional natural heritage system. His vision of a naturalized mouth of the Don River [FIG.5] is being realized almost 30 years later under the direction of another landscape architect, Michael Van Valkenburgh and the landscape architects working for Waterfront Toronto. The Port Lands Flood Protection project is intended to establish and sustain the form, features, and functions of a natural river mouth, providing critical flood protection to a 240-hectacre area of Toronto's eastern waterfront [FIG. 6].

Continuing with the legacy of Ian McHarg's *Design with Nature* and Hough's *Cities and Natural Processes*, landscape architects in Toronto have been leading innovative design solutions for natural spaces that not only enhance and restore natural systems, but use nature-based solutions to absorb, detain, allow for movement of water, reduce ambient temperature, provide conditions that support biodiversity, design to protect sensitive landscapes, and reduce erosion. Examples include the regenerative landscape of the former industrialized flood zones of Cotton Woods Flats and the design of Corktown Common which allows for flooding of the Don River with an extensive urban prairie and lowland meadow.

New approaches to connect and expand the natural system to Toronto's urban core are on-going. The recently approved plan for Toronto's downtown identified the Core Circle, envisioned by landscape architecture firm Public Work as a continuous network of natural features, green spaces, and the public realm around Downtown, linking the natural features of the Lake Ontario shoreline, the Toronto Islands, Garrison Creek, the ancient Lake Iroquois shoreline, Rosedale Valley Ravine, and

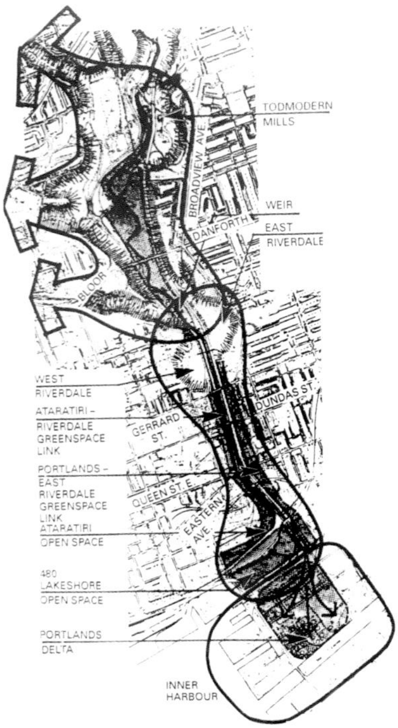

FIG.5 Lower Don Strategy Plan. Task Force to Bring Back the Don, 'Bringing Back the Don', Toronto, Hough Stansbury Woodland, Prime Consultants, 1991, City of Toronto

FIG.6 Don River Mouth Naturalization and Flood Protection Project. Michael Van Valkenburgh Associates, Waterfront Toronto

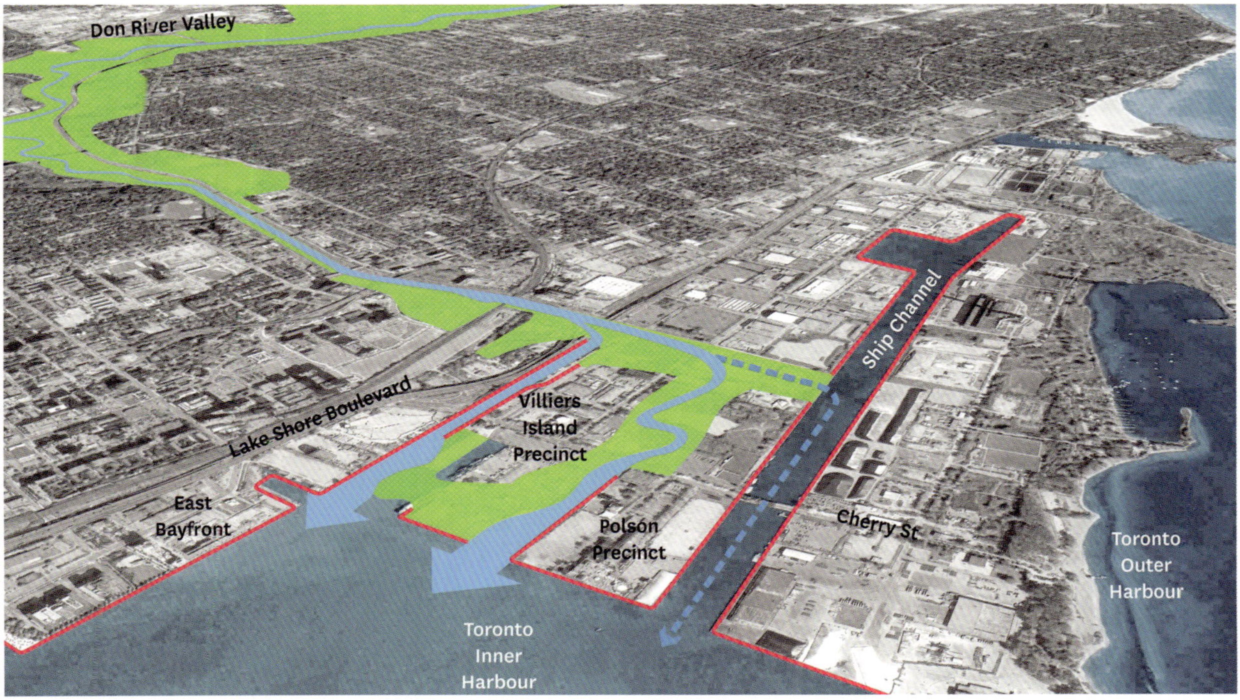

the Lower Don Valley. The Core Circle serves as a structure connecting parks to the city's natural features and to its "great streets" and the shoreline stitch, reconnecting the city to its waterfront [FIG. 7].

Protecting, Managing, and Investing in the Natural System

> "The ravines are to Toronto what canals are to Venice and hills are to San Francisco. They are the heart of the city's emotional geography, and understanding Toronto requires an understanding of the ravines."
> — Robert Fulford, *Accidental City*.

Toronto's remaining ravines and associated forests define the city's landscape, contain the majority of its natural areas, offer mental and physical respite for its residents, and play an important role in the resilience of the city. There have been strong policies in place for their protection. Despite all these efforts, Toronto's natural systems are slowly and incrementally being eroded through overuse, through small or large development adjacent to the system, or through the repair of critical public infrastructure. The City of Toronto's Tree Canopy Study (2019), which surveys the state of the city's urban forest every 10 years, provides some indicators of this. The study notes that there has been a decrease in the average overall condition of the urban forest, an increase of invasive species, and an increase

FIG.7 Downtown Core Circle. Public Work, City of Toronto

of impervious cover throughout the city. What was lacking was a strategic coordinated plan for management and on-going investment for the six rivers and 11,000 hectares that make up the city's ravines.

Toronto's first Ravine Strategy (2017) was led by landscape architects from the City and the Toronto and Region Conservation Authority. It provided, for the first time, an intentional and coordinated vision and approach to managing this natural system through a series of strategic actions to achieve a healthy, accessible, and vibrant ravine system. The Strategy was intended to balance the protection and restoration of the system with human use and enjoyment so that the ravines continue to bring nature to people and flourish for the next 100 years and beyond.

The Ravine Implementation Plan (adopted in January 2020) identified a number of strategic investment priorities, based on criteria including high ecological value; high levels of existing use; anticipated adjacent population growth; and/or limited access to green space. An analysis to identify the top priority areas was undertaken by landscape architecture firm Schollen & Co. using geospatial analysis of a matrix of data gathered for areas throughout all 105 ravine segments within the ravine system. These Priority Investment Areas were the basis for approval of an additional $2.4 million for invasive species and litter clean-up and $8.3 million for trails and ecosystem restoration. A total of $70.1 million was identified in the approved 2021 City budget for capital projects including reconstruction of ravine parks, storm damage repair, trails, watercourse erosion mitigation, and channel stabilization [FIG. 8]. This work set the stage for Toronto to take advantage of the July 2021 announcement of a new Natural Infrastructure Fund which will provide $120 million for investment in large natural infrastructure projects. Toronto's Ravine Strategy was cited as an example of leadership in natural infrastructure solutions in the federal Budget.

Toronto's first Biodiversity Strategy (2019) was intended to align and support the Ravine Strategy by addressing ecological integrity, management of invasive species, and the importance of local native plant material. The actions of the Strategy go beyond the ravine system to include the public realm and private spaces, considering education and a review of current policies and regulations (including bylaws). It aims to promote a livable city that supports biodiversity through increasing the quality and quantity of natural habitat throughout the city, designing the built environment to support biodiversity, and increasing access to and awareness of nature in the city.

The City's Natural Environment and Community Programs group designs and implements complex ecological restoration projects using an ecosystem approach and works with local stewardship groups to foster engagement and implement these projects. The challenge is how to encourage connection and access to nature while protecting the sensitive system. This was addressed in the Natural Environment Trail Strategy (2013 LEES+ASSOCIATES) and the Crothers Woods Trail Management Strategy (The Planning Partnership, 2007) which successfully applied sensitive design for recreational use while preserving and restoring the site's ecology.

Beyond the ravine system, initiatives such as the Green Streets Technical Guidelines support the system and help to integrate nature into the city. Prepared by landscape architectural firm Schollen & Co., they provide technical guidelines for building green infrastructure into our streets and public realm. The Guidelines take an innovative approach that uses a decision model to plan the right treatment based on soil type and local conditions, helping the designer determine the right approach.

One important tool that is often overlooked is increasing awareness through communication of the beauty of the landscape and its inhabitants.

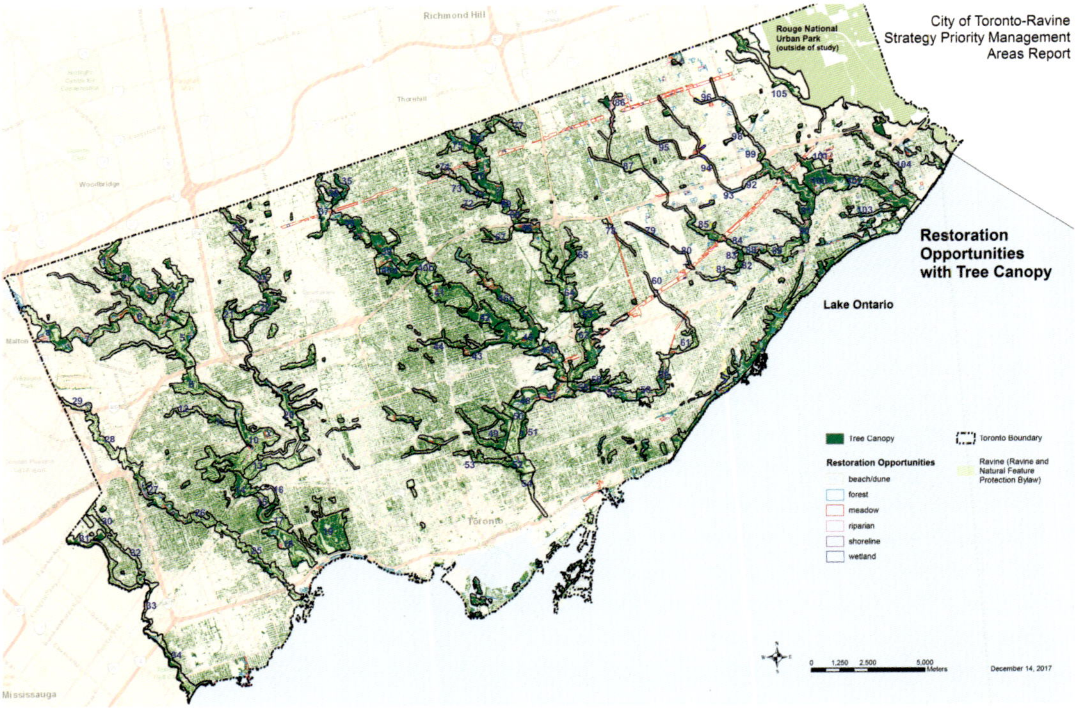

FIG.8 Ravine prioritization mapping-restoration opportunities. Schollen & Co., City of Toronto

In the book *An Enduring Wilderness,* the evolving and haunting beauty of Toronto's natural spaces in the ravines and waterfront are documented through a series of photographs and essays. Toronto's Biodiversity Booklet Series was created to help reconnect people with the natural world and raise awareness of the seriousness of biodiversity loss. There are nine booklets (including bees, butterflies, fishes) prepared through a collaboration of voluntary citizen scientists and local experts. In his book *Accidental Wilderness*, landscape architect Walter Kehm describes how his original design for Tommy Thompson Park evolved to become an "urban wilderness," home to over 350 bird species and animals and an important destination for resident's mental, physical, and spiritual health.

With approval of capital investment through the Ravine Strategy implementation, Toronto, together with the Toronto and Region Conservation Authority, has a committed budget for investment in capital projects and for outreach. Also, importantly, the City has a defined collaboration with stakeholders such as Evergreen (for the Loop Trail) and Parks People. This places the City in a good position to take advantage of federal funding opportunities such as the spring 2021 Natural Infrastructure Fund. This momentum needs to continue to achieve and maintain a healthy natural heritage system.

Expansion of the natural ecosystem in an urban area like Toronto can be difficult and requires many tools and creative approaches beyond regulation, policy, and investment to be successful in not only protecting and enhancing the existing system and ensuring its long-term health but also in integrating nature into the built form of the city. Outreach tools such as *Enduring Wilderness and the Biodiversity* booklet series, as well as engagement of volunteers in planting and restoring natural areas help to increase awareness of and advocacy for the natural system, an important ingredient of public influence on Council decisions.

Conclusion

> "Perhaps it will be the city that reawakens our understanding and appreciation of nature, in all its teeming, unpredictable complexity."
> —Jane Jacobs, "The Greening of the City," the *New York Times,* 2004.

For a city of 2.9 million people, Toronto has a surprising quantity of natural areas, a result of early recognition of the scenic beauty of its landscape and advocacy for the value of its environmental features. This led to a strong history of acquisition, planning, and policies and regulations for protection. What had been missing was a comprehensive strategy and targeted strategic investment in the ravines. This was addressed with the Ravine Strategy Implementation Plan and new ways of thinking about how to enhance the system through concepts such as the Core Circle to connect the parks, natural features, and great streets in Downtown Toronto. More recently the City has taken an innovative approach through communication tools such as *Enduring Wilderness* and through programs and policies using a different lens, such as the Biodiversity Strategy.

Toronto's dynamic growth makes protection of the quality and quantity of its urban ecosystem incredibly important. The continued role of landscape architects in both the public and private sectors is crucial to ensuring that the natural ecosystems are not just protected, but restored and enhanced through planning, regulations and policy, master plans, stewardship, and most importantly sensitive design.

Endnotes

1. Carolynne Crawley, "Foreword," in *Toronto Biodiversity Strategy* (Toronto: City of Toronto, 2019).
2. John Riley, *The Once and Future Great Lakes Country: An Ecological History* (Montreal, Quebec: McGill-Queen's University Press, 2013).
3. Wayne Reeves, "Imagining, Creating, and Sustaining Toronto's Natural Parklands: A Short History," in *An Enduring Wilderness, Toronto's Natural Parklands*, photographs by Robert Burley (Toronto, Ontario: ECW Press, 2017), 222-223.
4. Ibid., 224.
5. Ibid., 224-225.
6. Ibid., 226.
7. Colleen Mercer-Clarke, *Nature Based Solutions by Design* (Ottawa, Ontario: Canadian Society of Landscape Architects, 2021), 2.
8. Wallace McHarg Roberts & Todd, *Environmental Resources of the Toronto Central Waterfront*, 1976.

1.2

Perspectives on Heritage Conservation and Sustainable Development in Toulouse, France

Aliza Sovani

A Shift of Scale in Heritage Conservation Practice

For centuries, urban heritage and its management have been guided by the distinct aim to conserve—mainly architectural and archeological—resources for future generations. These resources were key to defining national cultural identities and values. Traditionally, a selective group of heritage resources would be conserved, while the rest could be neglected or destroyed without further accountability.[1] Today, as cities worldwide face unprecedented environmental destruction and social injustice, discourse in urbanism in historic cities has shifted towards more sustainable and inclusive models of resource management. The search for sustainable development processes that integrate environmental, social, and cultural concerns into the planning, design, and implementation of urban heritage management programs[2] has resulted in the definition of the UNESCO Historic Urban Landscape Approach (HUL) and the United Nations (UN) New Urban Agenda.[3]

The HUL approach was created in 2011 with the aim of providing updated guidelines and tools for the management of historic cities.[4] Its principal novelty was the adoption of a landscape view of heritage interpretation and heritage management. This was a distinct shift from monument to territory, whereby the historic urban landscape is the result of knowledge accumulated through the long-term sustainable use of space, natural resources, and the territorial network of the city.[5] The policy framework proposed by the New Urban Agenda, adopted at Habitat III in 2016, works as an accelerator of the UN Sustainable Development Goals (SDGs) which speak boldly about the role of heritage in development considering the UN's declaration that humanity had reached the urbanization threshold of 50 percent[6]: Target 11.4 calls for "making cities and human settlements inclusive, safe, resilient and sustainable by strengthening efforts to protect and safeguard the world's cultural and natural heritage."[7]

Despite broadening the scope of the historic urban environment, in practice the focus of sustainable development strategies and policies in

OPPOSITE PAGE Place de la Daurade constitutes one of the most important links between the city and the Garonne River. Aliza Sovani, 2021

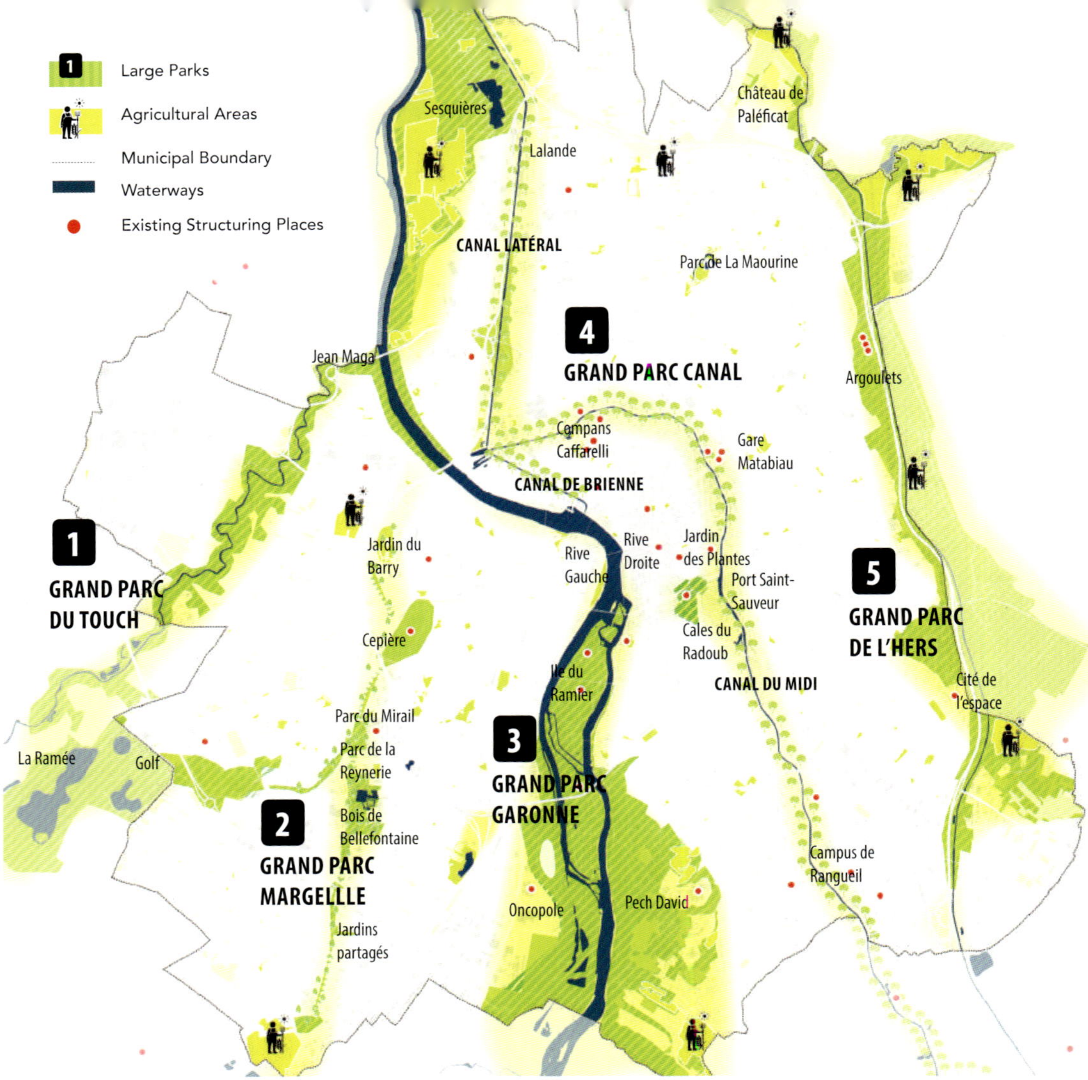

historic cities has largely been on how to prevent and mitigate the impacts of urban development on cultural heritage.[8] On this basis, the need to approach urban policy in a new way and with renewed—landscape led—tools is necessary in order to better integrate urban heritage conservation strategies within the larger goals of overall sustainable development. Through this lens, a central question emerges: How can landscape connectivity, ecological restoration and green infrastructure be achieved when it is at odds with preserving a fixed historic urban fabric and image?

Across the globe, the natural heritage of river corridors, canals, urban forests, parks, and public spaces, have shaped historic cities. This network of open space remains a foundational asset for urban life, ecology, and the economy.[9] Within this heritage landscape framework, this essay presents perspectives on existing strategies in heritage conservation and reflects on the implementation of a sustainable urban development approach in Toulouse, a hopeful World Heritage City, in south-west France. Efforts to conserve Toulouse's historic center have relied upon traditional

FIG. 1 Five "Grands Parcs" along key water corridors will structure the city. Mairie de Toulouse/AUAT, 2019

approaches and methodologies that are now being adapted to the new environmental paradigm.

Toulouse - Ville Rose, Ville Verte

Toulouse is the fourth largest city in France, located in the south-western region of Occitanie, with just over one million inhabitants in 2020. The uniqueness of the heritage of Toulouse is evident not only because it has 51 nationally classified heritage buildings and 154 registered historical monuments,[10] is home to three UNESCO World Heritage Sites and in the process of an application to become a World Heritage City, but because the geohistory of Toulouse is uniquely characterized by the presence of water courses that transect the city and continue to be tied to the contemporary cultural identity that favors quality of life[11]: In Toulouse, these are the Garonne River and the Canal du Midi. It is useful to provide a historical backdrop on urban development in Toulouse to describe the relationship between the city and the landscape; a landscape into which it is possible to place the current sustainable urban development strategies, and whereby the Garonne River and Canal du Midi appear as essential axes throughout all 37 metropolitan regions of Toulouse [FIG. 1].

Urban History

Historically, Toulouse was identified as La Ville Rose (The Pink City) due to the hue of the terra-cotta brick which continues to be used extensively in buildings and river embankments and is central to Toulouse's historic image and identity as a flood-prone riverfront city. Progressive degradation of the river landscape has created a system of urban and peri-urban concrete dikes and pink-brick embankments[12] [FIG. 2].

Over the past decades, many initiatives have relied on the architectural and cultural enhancement of city shores aimed to put the Garonne River back in the heart of the city center. The late 17th-century Canal du Midi is the initial part of the Deux-Mers Canal project which links the Mediterranean Sea and the Atlantic Ocean. UNESCO declared the canal a World Heritage Site in 1996 as one of the most extraordinary civil engineering achievements of modern times.[13]

Even with the existence of such a strong cultural identity tied to this hydrological landscape framework, advancements in construction techniques and new economies in the 20th century marked a pronounced transformation in the traditional way of life for Toulousians and as an effect in urban form.[14] With the industrialization that came along with the Second World War, the homogenous society that was very much still rural and connected to the countryside became submerged by a demographic shift: French from the north of the country, Italians, Spanish, Portuguese, and North Africans.[15] The significant economic

FIG.2 Toulouse, Ville Rose. Pink-hued brick river embankments are central to Toulouse's historic image and identity. Aliza Sovani, 2021

development and urban growth seen in Toulouse since World War II has led to the city of today as the center of the European Aerospace Industry. Urban development in Toulouse became a game of unregulated real-estate development built on the promotion of the North American dream of owning an individual property in the suburbs and has thus long been synonymous with urban sprawl without regard for the loss of natural spaces.[16 17]

The New Metropolitan Vision

Toulouse's urban history demonstrates that the transformation of the urban landscape has implicated pronounced social transformation. In response, in 2019, the City of Toulouse approved a new guiding Territorial Urban Development Plan for the Toulouse Metropolitan Urban Project: *Toulouse - Ville Rose, Ville Verte* (Toulouse - Pink City, Green City).[19] The vision for the urban future of Toulouse relies on the notion of a collective heritage identity based on eight critical resolutions that form a manifesto.[19] Of these eight resolutions it is worth expanding on two of them within the discussion on shifting contemporary heritage interpretation and management:

Résolution 1. Pour un projet urbain qui valorise notre patrimoine "For an urban project that values our heritage" concentrates exclusively on the plurality of architectural and urban forms, rural and urban, that make up the built heritage of Toulouse. The banks of the Garonne River and Canal du Midi are mentioned briefly within the scope of heritage areas in the historic core. The resolution goes on to state that in face of contemporary urban challenges, the heritage of historic value must be protected and enhanced as one of the fundamental cornerstones.[20]

Résolution 3. Pour un projet urbain qui favorise la nature en ville "For an urban project that promotes nature in the city" concentrates in large part on the necessity for a shift away from urban sprawl for the betterment of biodiversity, of the balance of the ecosystem and on lowering infrastructure expenditures. Bringing nature into the city concerns in large part the Garonne River and Canal du Midi, as well as their surroundings. It is envisioned as the construction of large urban parks, connected open space corridors, accessible neighborhood gardens and tree-lined cycling paths. The vision also prioritizes the preservation of private gardens, historically remarkable perspectives, and large trees of value to offset the urban heat island effect.[21]

Together, Resolutions 1 and 3 of the Urban Project Manifesto, as outlined above, are centered on the protection of built heritage, the environment, the economy, and quality of life—or in other words at the intersection of

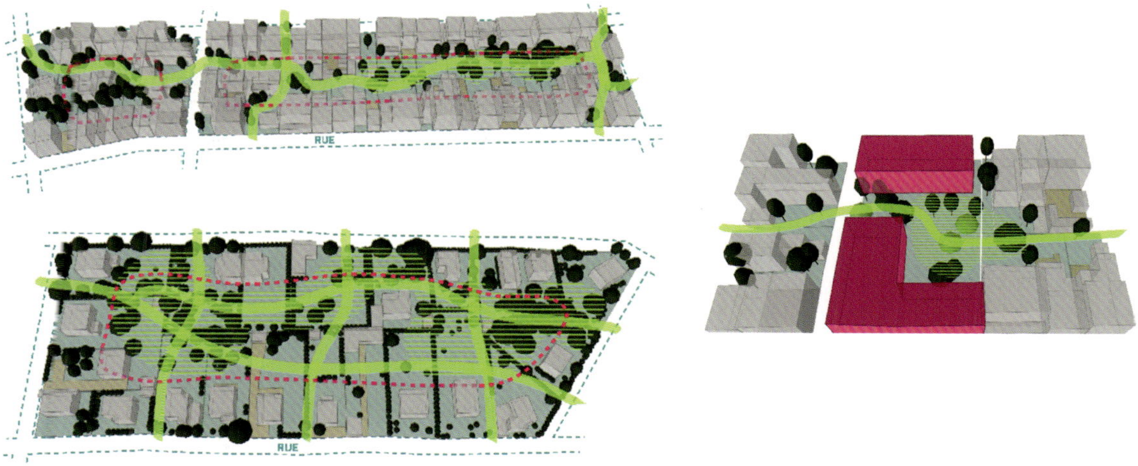

FIG.3 Notions of landscape continuity are operationalized in municipal policy tools in Toulouse. Mairie de Toulouse/AUAT, 2019

heritage conservation and sustainable development. Yet, the continued distinct separation of these two imperatives gives light into the opposition of existing defined structures of heritage and planning policy in France.

Perspectives on Urban Heritage Management in Toulouse

The strategies outlined in Toulouse – Ville Rose Ville Verte are being implemented within the following urban policy frameworks and heritage protection measures in accordance with existing legislation in France:

Remarkable Heritage Site (SPR), a town planning document to allow the development of the heart of the metropolis while protecting its remarkable heritage elements. This perimeter also relates to the core heritage assets that would enable Toulouse to succeed in a UNESCO World Heritage City inscription. The SPR is accompanied by its *Plan de Sauvegarde et de Mise en Valeur (PSMV),* a master plan imposing strict controls mandated by the State on all works undertaken in the designated area.

Local Intermunicipal Urban Planning Plan (PLUi-H), approved in April 2019, is a municipal urban policy and zoning regulatory document for land use, occupation, and all development planning authorization. This document does not modify the protected sector (PSMV) which continues to apply, and which integrates with the PLUi-H.

Historic Monuments and Historic Monuments Buffer Zone, the protected heritage buildings due to public interest and within a 500-meter radius from a historic monument protected on the idea of co-visibility and coherence with the urban surrounding imposing strict controls by the State heritage architects on all work undertaken.

From the perspective of a landscape architect working in development planning approvals with the City of Toulouse, I have observed both the coordination and opposition of policy tools with the core intent of increasing nature in the city within a heritage-led sustainable development framework. As seen in [FIG. 3], this coordination is operationalized by, for example, a move towards valorizing ecological corridors made possible through new integrated municipal policy tools in both the historic core and the metropolitan area, outlined in the 2019 Charte métropolitaine pour la qualité urbaine—an annex to the PLUi-H—on the quality of project integration with the conservation, enhancement, and/or creation of vegetated open spaces that structure the landscape and provide ecosystem services.[22] Even more, the PLUi-H dictates a green-space minimum area obligation for multi-unit residential developments with more than 10 dwellings. This common area must have real social and ecological function and value existing landscape groupings on-site that contribute to improving quality of life, stormwater management, the maintenance of urban biodiversity, and the elimination of the heat island effect.[23] These examples demonstrate a shift in urban policy in the historic urban environment of Toulouse that certainly addresses larger areas, including natural heritage assets, and goes beyond conservation values more traditionally associated with built heritage, by including ecological and social values.

At the same time, while there is coordination, a relatively traditional conceptualization of heritage values in the historic center is still common in heritage management operations in Toulouse. When looking at what is considered heritage in daily policy practice in Toulouse's historic center, the results reveal a focus on objects and areas. Most policy used in urban development approvals is directed at built assets and immediate areas and less at the entire urban landscape as a functioning system. Take for example the Grand Park Garonne and the Urban Forestry initiative. Today, the Grand Park Garonne project focuses largely on the historic center with a multitude of high-profile projects, including the restoration of several quays in the center of Toulouse completed between 2015 and 2020. However, the urban river landscape is marked by an evident secondary focus on restoring an ecologically functional river.[24] Philippe Valette, University of Toulouse Professor of Geography & Geohistory, expands on this reality through the following critical question: Can we imagine a higher level of ambition around an ecological reconquest of the riverbanks in the city?[25] Even more, peri-urban river landscapes in Toulouse are still under the pressure of a city seeking to expand, including in flood zones. As for most rivers, the low presence of natural riverbank restoration operations can be explained by interventions which often require a significant financial investment.[26] Therefore, the importance of a coordinated large-scale sustainable development vision is significant to ensure actions are designed and budgeted for with a view to targeting several objectives at the same time, in an integrated management approach. A similar issue arose around the urban forestry objective across the entire Toulouse Metropolitan territory. Strategies revealed that even though the objective to plant 100,000 trees over a 10-year period related to combatting the urban heat island effect, in practice, had no significant position in the dense heavily concreted areas in the city center and instead are set to be planted primarily in peri-urban settings.

Toulouse's urban policies on increasing nature in the city highlight a lack of tools to redefine the scope of heritage values beyond objects to the cultural value of landscape systems in the context of the territorial sustainable development plan. While Toulouse continues to battle the museification of the historic center, the neighboring city of Bordeaux is already pursuing a series of urban policies centered on sustainable development and urban heritage protection to balance these two imperatives. These cases reflect the uniquely French situation, where not only have laws become more ambitious in terms of sustainable development, but also heritage conservation has long been integrated into urban planning.

The Historic Urban Landscape (HUL) Approach in Bordeaux and Seville

When looking at the intense urban transformation process over the last twenty years of the UNESCO World Heritage City of Bordeaux, the results reveal that the success of the project is hinged in part on the spatial, perceptual, and cultural reconnection of the urban system with the Garonne River, focused primarily on public spaces but also on the notion of HUL as a guiding heritage conservation framework aligned to broader sustainable development goals. Alongside the PLU, the SPR and the PSMV, Bordeaux pioneered the development of Ville de Pierre, a specific HUL-integrated conservation tool, which analyzed more than 40,000 lots and public spaces and defined specific conservation actions to be implemented.[27] With the recent ambitious target of planting one million urban trees, the case of Bordeaux continues to be emblematic of a historic living city that demonstrates the possible adaptation of French heritage conservation tools to the HUL Approach towards the consideration of sustainable development aims.

Heritage leaders elsewhere in southern Europe, such as the historic city of Seville, Spain have managed to create a novel Guide for the Historic Urban Landscape of Seville (GHULS) as a planning support tool to help guide transformation not just for the city, but also for the territory in which the city lies through an administration and management of cultural heritage within a new governance framework.[28] The guide focuses both on the city and on other municipalities that form part of the fluvial landscape—the watershed—of the Guadalquivir River which also acts as the central matrix that generates the cultural landscape that houses Seville. The GHULS scope of study was delimited by means of a multiscale landscape analysis process which highlighted different geographical phenomena and cultural dynamics, and which together, have helped to characterize the HUL of the city. This has helped shift towards a new holistic paradigm that focuses on the capacity of culture to improve the quality of life of people and seeks to recover the historical link among culture, development, and sustainability. The protection of territorial resources by way of defining the HUL beyond the historic center of Seville is further made clear through the first objective of the guide: *(i) Restore the Environment, Urban and Peri-Urban Areas*. The measures associated with these objectives include riverbed regeneration, naturalization of artificial riverbanks, urban ornithology, trees in the city, river parks, and agricultural parks along the Guadalquivir River. However, in Spain, the legal framework and the current political system is characterized by the division of power among various administrations—national, regional, and local.[29] In the case of the GHULS, it was unfortunately never introduced into municipal urban policy and remained a research study conducted by the regional Andalusian Institute for Historical Heritage, leaving it up to the local administration to deduce the general interrelation between heritage and the concept of sustainable development for use in their daily practice.

In their own right, the Toulouse, Bordeaux, and Seville case-studies provide valuable examples of the conservation of urban heritage as no longer simply the freezing of a district with special characteristics, but rather the way in which heritage landscape systems strengthen cultural identity and become models for the broader process of urban growth.

Conclusion

The notion of sustainable development has evolved over time into a more complex and holistic concept, which explicitly recognizes cultural heritage as a driver of sustainability. In the historic urban environment—such as the cases of Toulouse, Bordeaux, and Seville—the key factor for the conservation of the historic city as a dynamic living organism relies on the full adoption of a landscape view of interpretation of heritage values definition formalized in national frameworks and codified in municipal urban policy. Through this lens, geographical phenomena and cultural dynamics collectively characterize the historic urban landscape of the city. This could mark the full shift from monument to territory in heritage management in the context of sustainable development whereby "urban heritage values are directly linked to the spirit of place in the landscape because it is from the cultural landscape that the original canvas of urban form springs."[30] The potential forthcoming label of Toulouse as a UNESCO World Heritage City, with the expected increase in levels of heritage conservation guidelines, will surely provide a valuable platform to discuss this concept further.

Endnotes

1. Ana Pereira Roders and Francesco Bandarin, eds., *Reshaping Urban Conservation – The Historic Urban Landscape Approach in Action*, 21–22 (Singapore: Springer, 2019).
2. Ana Pereira Roders and Ron van Oers, "Historic Cities as Model of Sustainability," *Journal of Cultural Heritage Management and Sustainable Development* 2, no. 1 (2012): 4–14.
3. Pereira Roders and Bandarin, *Reshaping Urban Conservation, 16–26.*
4. Joaquín Martínez Pino, "The New Holistic Paradigm and the Sustainability of Historic Cities in Spain: An Approach Based on the World Heritage Cities," *Sustainability* 10, no. 7 (2018): 2301.
5. Pereira Roders and Bandarin, *Reshaping Urban Conservation*, 17.
6. Ibid., 15.
7. "Sustainable Development Goal 11.4," UNESCO, accessed April, 2021, http://uis.unesco.org/en/topic/sustainable-development-goal-11-4/.
8. Kalliopi Fouseki, Torgrim Guttormsen, and Grete Swensen, *Heritage and Sustainable Urban Transformations: Deep Cities* (New York: Routledge, 2021).
9. Matthias Ripp and Dennis Rodwell. "The Geography of Urban Heritage," *The Historic Environment: Policy & Practice* 6, no. 3 (2015): 240–76.
10. S. R. "Toulouse Veut Le Classement Unesco." *LADEPECHE. fr*, February 7, 2015, https://www.ladepeche.fr/article/2015/02/07/2044838-unesco-toulouse-part-de-loin.html.
11. Philippe Valette, "La Garonne à Toulouse," *Norcis*, no. 237 (2015): 81–100.
12. Jean-Marc Antoine and Philippe Valette, "La Place Des Inondations Dans La Fabrique Des Paysages Fluviaux Urbains. Le Cas De La Garonne à Toulouse (Du Xviie Siècle à Aujourd'Hui)," *Sud-Ouest européen*, no. 44 (2017): 25–39.
13. "Canal du Midi," UNESCO World Heritage Centre, accessed February, 2021, https://whc.unesco.org/en/list/770/.
14. Pierre Barrère, "Le Rôle De Jean Borde Dans La Géographie Bordelaise," *Revue géographique des Pyrénées et du Sud-Ouest* 49, no. 1 (1978): 5–9.
15. Colette Zytnicki, "La Ville rose à l'épreuve de la modernisation," review of *Modernizing the Provincial City. Toulouse, 1945-1975, by* Rosemary Wakeman, *Annales du Midi,* 2001, 77–79.
16. Mairie de Toulouse and aua/T, "Plan Guide: Le Projet Urbain Toulousain: Ville Rose - Ville Verte," published March 2019 at Toulouse, pdf, https://www.toulouse.fr/web/projet-urbain/-/projet-urbain-toulousain-plan-guide.
17. Zytnicki, "La Ville rose."
18. "Plan Guide: Le Projet Urbain Toulousain."
19. "Pour un projet urbain qui affirme notre identité," Mairie de Toulouse, accessed February 2021, https://www.toulouse.fr/web/projet-urbain/manifeste/pour-un-projet-urbain-qui-affirme-notre-identite.
20. "Pour un projet urbain qui valorise notre patrimoine," Mairie de Toulouse, accessed February 2021, https://www.toulouse.fr/web/projet-urbain/manifeste/pour-un-projet-urbain-qui-valorise-notre-patrimoine.
21. "Pour un projet urbain qui favorise la nature en ville," Mairie de Toulouse, accessed February 2021, https://www.toulouse.fr/web/projet-urbain/manifeste/pour-un-projet-urbain-qui-favorise-la-nature-en-ville.
22. Toulouse Métropole and aua/T, "Charte Métropolitaine pour la Qualité Urbaine: Guide d'application du PLUi-H," published December 2019 at Toulouse, pdf, https://www.toulouse-metropole.fr/documents/10180/26915883/Charte_Metro_Qual_Urb_def.pdf.
23. Toulouse Métropole and aua/T, "PLUi-H: Plan local d'urbanisme intercommunal tenant lieu du programme local de l'habitat 2019," published April 2020 at Toulouse, pdf, https://www.toulouse-metropole.fr/documents/10180/26884518/3A_REG_ecrit_PEBE_20200304.pdf/be35bdb9-25ca-4491-bd46-55c688bdbb32.
24. Mélodie David, Philippe Valette, Jean-Michel Carozza, and Marylise Cottet, "La Restauration Des Services Écosystémiques Le Long De La Garonne Toulousaine: Premier État Des Lieux," *Sud-Ouest européen*, no. 44 (2017): 151–65.
25. Philippe Valette, "Les Noces De Toulouse Et De La Garonne," *Sud-Ouest européen*, no. 31 (2011): 201–2.
26. David, Valette, Carozza, and Cottet. "La Restauration."
27. Federica Appendino, "Balancing Heritage Conservation and Sustainable Development – The Case of Bordeaux," *IOP Conference Series: Materials Science and Engineering* 245 (2017): 062002.
28. Román Casares Fernández-Baca, Silvia Cacho Fernández and Pedro Escobar Salmerón, *Guide to the Historic Urban Landscape of Seville: Informative Document* (Sevilla: Instituto Andaluz del Patrimonio Histórico, 2017), 14–15.
29. Martínez Pino, "The New Holistic Paradigm," 10.
30. Ibid., 3.

1.3

A Reflexive Approach to Uncertainty

Situating Planning Practice in the Landscape of Afghanistan's City-Regions

Justin Kollar, Thomas Nideroest, Mirwais Rahimi

Economic crises, volatile politics, and the increasingly complex and unpredictable impacts of climate change have brought about new forms of uncertainty that challenge conventional planning approaches. As a result, this ever-expanding imperative to address added complexity stretches the scope of work beyond the horizon of our individual disciplinary expertise. Thus, some have advocated for more interdisciplinary collaboration to "address the increasingly complex and widespread environmental, economic, social, and political changes that typically transcend traditional management boundaries." Reed et al. argue for an "integrated landscape approach" for collaborative work to "ensure equitable and sustainable use of land while strengthening measures to mitigate and adapt to climate change."[1] But no matter how we, as practitioners, decide to intervene, we should be wary of the triumphalist assertions that often accompany technical solution-making—particularly when the variegated social and environmental complexities of the real world pose challenges to the translatability of expert-driven planning frameworks. We must acknowledge the continuing fact of uncertainty in our work and opt for a self-critical and reflexive approach. What impacts will this plan have? How will it be implemented? Whose needs and what values are missing?

This essay traces our reflections on uncertainty over the course of our multi-year work in Afghanistan by contextualizing it in the country's broader history of technocratic projects on the landscape. We write as members of both the consulting team which was led by Sasaki, a Boston-based planning firm, and the Ministry of Urban Development and Land (MUDL) which managed the project in Kabul. This work included the development of Strategic Development Frameworks (SDFs) for Five Provincial Capital Cities which was initiated by the Afghan government in 2019 with support from the World Bank.[2] The SDFs are designed as strategic tools that aim to reconcile the disjointed yet intimate connection between the urban and rural in Afghanistan's city regions, consolidating Afghanistan's key urban regions along the ring road linking Kabul to broader international trade networks. This project is just one part of a

This chapter includes work and data conducted under the Strategic Framework Development (SDF) for the Five Provincial Capital Cities of Herat, Jalalabad, Kandahar, Khost and Mazar-e-Sharif between 2019-20. While writing our reflections for this article in fall 2021, a new government has been established in Afghanistan, bringing a new set of priorities. This highlights the level of uncertainty involved in planning and development today. However, climate change and the need for adaptation remains a constant reality. In view of these ongoing challenges, we hope planning in Afghanistan centers on the dynamics of human and environmental processes rather than being too much of a technical exercise.

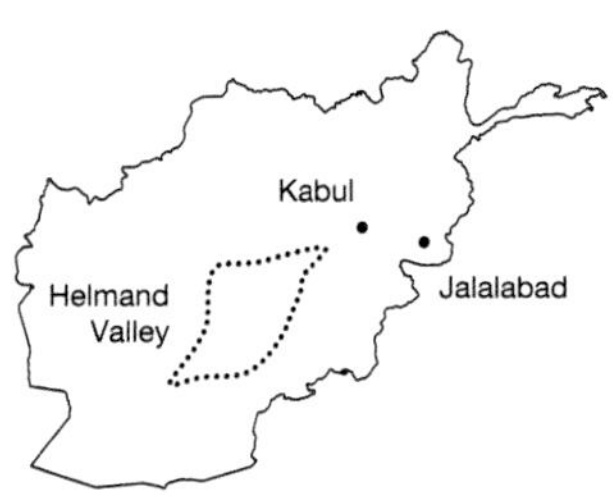

OPPOSITE PAGE Urban settlement patterns of Jalalab's District 7, showing Darunta Dam and Nangarhar University along the Kabul River and constructed irrigation canal. Digital Globe Satellite Imagery 2019

legacy of nation-building projects—each characterized by an idealism of an expert-driven approach that reduced complexity to a technical problem so that prescribed solutions could be engineered. We hoped to avert these pitfalls even as we acknowledged our familiar role vis-a-vis these past planning efforts. Relatedly, the formulation of a National Urban Policy in 2018 provided the basis for more "strategic tools" for planning to address the static nature of conventional master plans.[3] We illustrate this strategic turn through the content of an SDF created for the Jalalabad city region which aims to address the inherent challenges of rapidly growing urban areas while negotiating the evolving political, economic, social, and environmental challenges that have emerged.

Taming an Uncertain Landscape

Throughout modern history, nation-building in Afghanistan can be said to be a project to make legible an uncertain landscape—often with social and environmental ramifications.[4] As the Cold War had started to gear up between the Soviet Union and the U.S., one of the most ambitious nation-building projects was undertaken, which sought to modernize Afghanistan by transforming the Helmand River basin into an agricultural powerhouse. The project was modeled after the Tennessee River Valley Authority (TVA) which the American government eagerly promoted to counter the alternative version of developmentalism that the Soviets had undertaken in Afghanistan[5] [FIG. 1]. It was believed that, through such expertise, a modern network of dams and irrigation infrastructure coupled with a nomad settlement program could "make the desert bloom"[6] bringing with it political stability through economic development. However, major

FIG. 1 Display of the Helmand Valley Authority infrastructure projects at the Jeslyn Fair in 1956, Kabul, Afghanistan. Photograph by Joseph O'Donnell. Cudney Collection, Meridian International Center, Washington, DC and the US Department of State

challenges arose with the lack of serious considerations for the particularities of the climate, social dynamics, and lessons from centuries of water diversion projects in the region. For example, waterlogging and salinization plagued the project when, in 1965, a study revealed that crop yields had actually dropped since project initiation.[7] Resettlement programs reshaped the social landscape by increasing the number of smallholders resulting in many irregularly shaped plots leading to drainage problems. The chosen technical solution was to bulldoze the areas and redistribute land in "large, uniform, smooth land plots." Tired of the disruptive technical oversight, the farmers "met the bulldozers with rifles"[8]—foreshadowing the abolition of the monarchy in a coup in 1973 which led to the gradual end of American development aid in the Helmand Valley by 1975.

Even though subsequent evaluations of the Helmand project make it out to be a mix of success and failure,[9] it left an imprint on the landscape—the inheritance of which is a major driver of the political economy.[10] Rather than confronting social and environmental complexities reflexively, political and social issues were subordinated and the landscape itself was "flattened" into a technical object that could be engineered to suit national and geopolitical directives. In the face of repeated failure, the anticipation of uncertain outcomes was obscured both by political needs and a conviction that each new situation could be seen as a technical problem requiring a technical fix.

The capital city of Kabul has a special place within the broader context of nation-building. As with the Helmand Valley project, the history of planning in Kabul reflects the urge to tame an uncertain landscape without regard to the social and environmental consequences. The famous Afghan saying "let Kabul be without gold, but not without snow" emphasizes the dependence on the variable gifts of nature. Kabul's early Moghul gardens maintained and developed by Babur in the 16th and 17th centuries symbolized this urge by building on ages of water engineering knowledge that harmonized nature and culture. However, the introduction of modernist ideas into the national developmentalist bloodstream in the early 20th century[11] placed Kabul at the center of a national technocratic image, which ignored Kabul's historical development and exacerbated the deterioration of the socio-ecological conditions upon which the city is dependent.

After gaining independence from British influence in 1919, the new Emir, Amanullah Khan, embarked on a program of modernization at all costs.[12] An early plan for Kabul was rushed into implementation that extended the city to the southwest with the establishment of grand Parisian boulevards flanked by a dense rectangular network of streets. Little progress was made by the time the project was cast aside in 1938 for the development of "New Kabul" without any overall plan or vision. Starting from the central part of the city and moving west, the urban fabric began to take shape incrementally, absorbing land

with little regard to the environmental cost. By the 1960s, Western-style planning and architectural schemes had begun to marginalize history, culture, and tradition. Under King Zahir Shah, a new more expansive master plan was developed,[13] proposing the complete demolition of the historic old city. A guidebook on the new master plan reflects this cavalier attitude towards the modernization of Kabul: "Despite being the treasures, honors, and traditions of our ancestors, every corner, passage, market, house, yard, and monument representing 2,000 years of our people ... According to the 25 Year Master Plan of New Kabul, this area of the city will be demolished as soon as possible leaving no trace of those monuments, passages, and alleys to remain."[14]

Throughout this history, the disconnection between master plan and reality led to a patchwork of disinvestment and uneven spatial development patterns. Repeating these earlier attempts, a master plan in 2009[15] proposed an entirely new city which called for land dispossession lacking adequate environmental protection and failing to address water issues due to decades of poor planning.[16] Today, over 70 percent of the building stock has been built informally leading to the degradation of the natural environment. As planners translate experiences from Kabul to other parts of the country, the preference for a top-down, *tabula rasa* approach must be confronted in order for more foundational socio-ecological issues to be addressed head on.

Enacting a Strategic Development Process

Years of sluggish growth, few successes, and a failure to "win the hearts and minds" of the Afghan population is evidenced by poor service delivery in rural and urban areas alike. This prompted a move away from conventional master planning toward more open-ended, strategic planning tools to bridge the urban-rural divide. Thus, in our work on the SDF[17] for the Jalalabad city region looked to strengthen the connection between Jalalabad City and its rural hinterland. This ambition aimed to enhance urban-rural value chains, improve basic service delivery, address environmental decline, and redirect urban expansion away from risky areas and in more sustainable ways.

Located in Nangarhar Province, Jalalabad is nestled along the Kabul River between a landscape of valleys and ridges and strategically located along an important trading route between Kabul and Peshawar in Pakistan making it an important economic hub [FIG. 2–3]. Like Kabul, the city has been strongly influenced by large-scale planning and nation-building efforts that had been supported by the Soviet Union. Roads, bridges, dams, and networks of canals, as part of an agricultural improvement scheme, were the Soviet's counterpoint to the American-sponsored Helmand Valley project. However, waves of conflict since the Soviet-Afghan War left much of the infrastructure in tatters. After

FIG. 2 Jalalabad Strategic Development Framework. Ministry of Urban Development and Land-MuDL

FIG. 3 OPPOSITE PAGE Nestled along the Kabul River between a landscape of valleys and ridges, the city of Jalalabad in eastern Afghanistan is an important city region, strategically located along the important trading route between Kabul and Peshawar in Pakistan. The Ministry of Urban Development and Land (MUDL), prepared by Sasaki

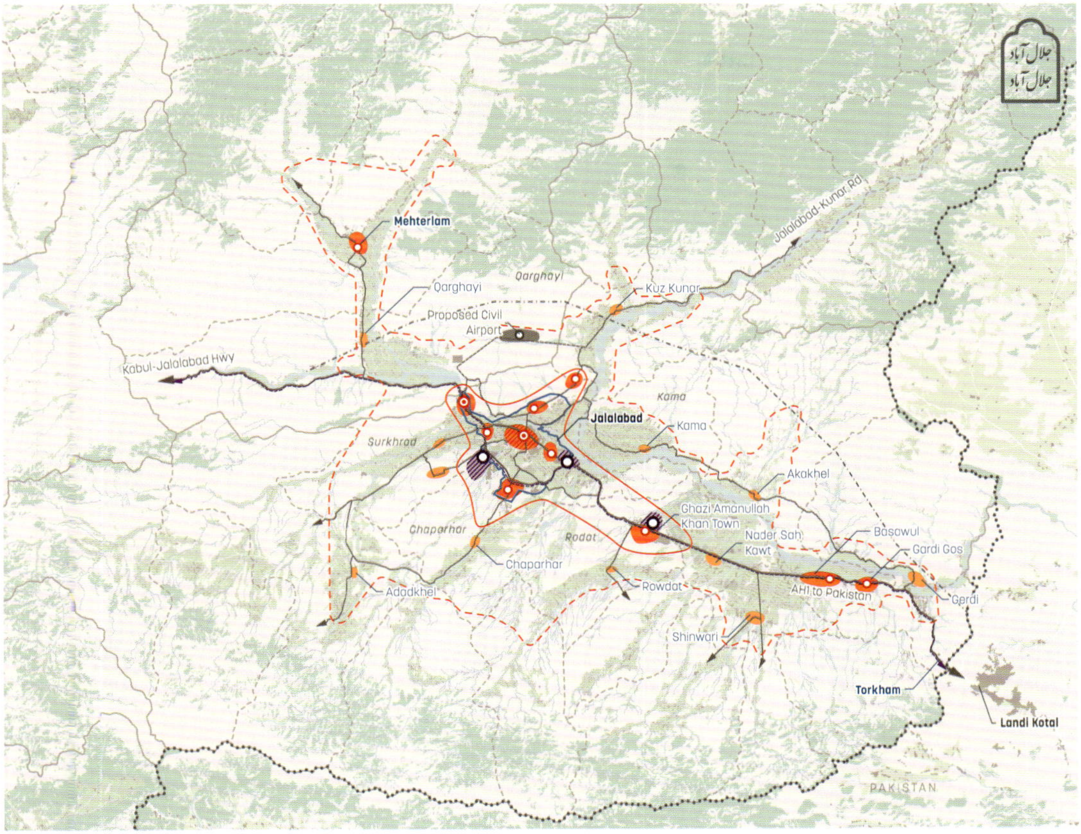

2001, Jalalabad saw massive urban-to-rural migration resulting in land grabbing, deforestation, and degradation of valley hydrology. Informal urban expansion placed a strain on service provision with many people lacking access to waste services, education, training, jobs, and healthcare. Likewise, residents have also been exposed to environmental hazards due to development on steep hillsides or in flood prone areas along river embankments. Thus, the focus on the city region requires us to foreground the socio-ecological links between Afghan livelihoods and their landscape. In other words, past planning approaches that specified problems in narrowly technical ways should be replaced with flexible strategies that provide concrete social and environmental benefits to communities.

After establishing a holistic baseline assessment which included an extensive outreach and stakeholder workshopping, a rapid landscape assessment[18] was conducted to contextualize the SDF within its regional systems and ecologies. This allowed for a better understanding of the upstream or downstream impacts of proposed policies and intervention strategies. This assessment was developed using geodesign techniques of overlaying available land cover data to identify areas of risk mitigation,

National Boundary (Durand Line)
District Boundary
Municipal Boundary
Major Roads
Primary Roads
Provisional Alignment for Future Rail Corridor
CASA 1000 Alignment
Agricultural Areas
Urban Areas
Water (Floodplain)

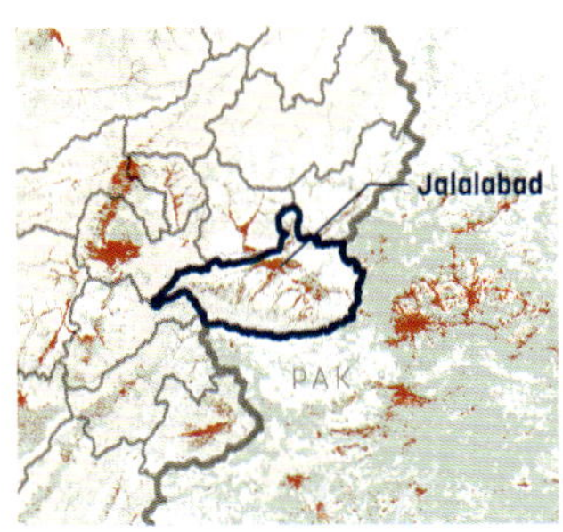

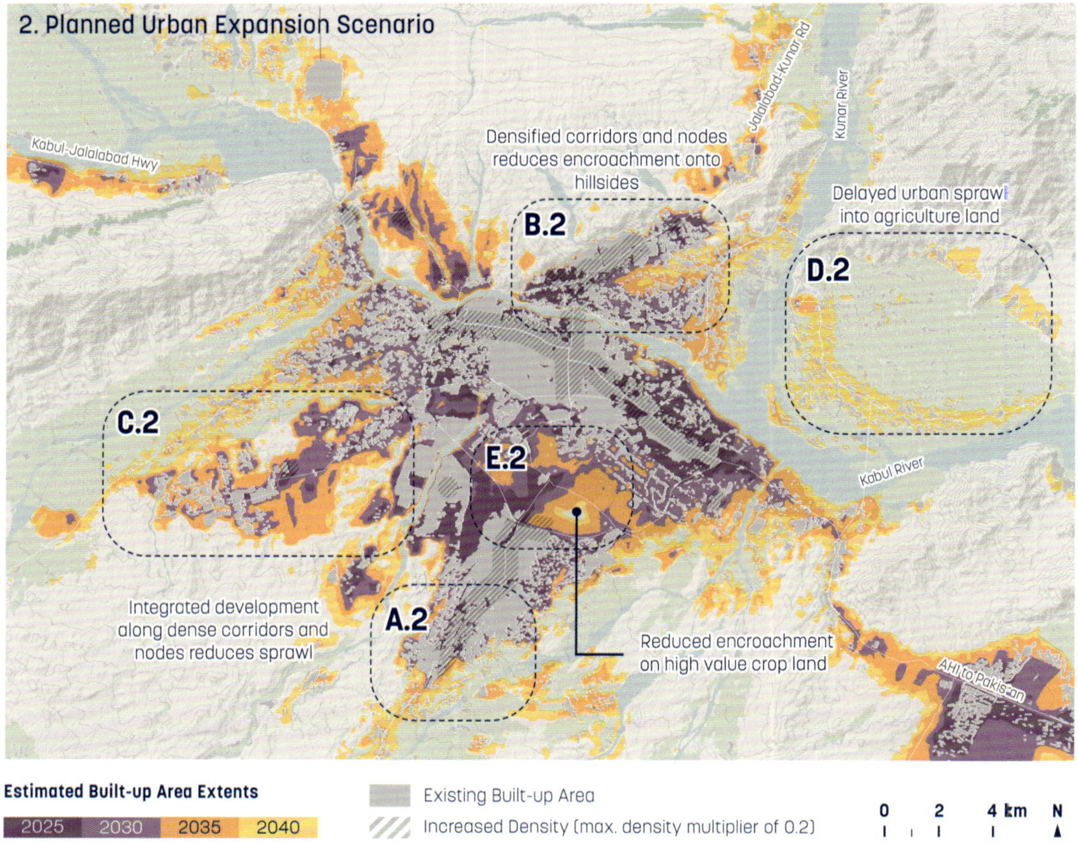

FIG.4 Rapid Landscape Assessment and Probabilistic Urban Expansion Scenario. The Ministry of Urban Development and Land (MUDL), prepared by Sasaki

protection of natural resources, and other ecologically sensitive areas. Additionally, a probabilistic urban expansion model[19] was developed to project visual scenarios for how urban areas may expand based on projected population growth both with and without intervening strategies [FIG. 4]. An additional overlay of the rapid land assessment and expansion model produced a loose zone-based spatial framework meant to guide the municipal decision-making process in a much more visually accessible manner. This framework serves as a guide for policies and intervention strategies which align with the overall goals of addressing existing risks and vulnerabilities and curbing future urban expansion away from risk-prone or otherwise vulnerable areas.

To address the multiple contingent factors involved in the implementation process such as political preference, uncertainty of funding, or shifting priorities due to a change in leadership, open-ended planning and design toolkits were developed. These toolkits translate the broader vision goals and objectives into implementable steps—covering topics of urban development, economy, culture, landscape, and ecology.[20] Each tool was tailored to address existing urban-rural conditions and included *catalytic* strategies that linked amenities, infrastructure, housing, and transit to economic and social development opportunities. The toolkits are meant to provide implementation guidance through engagement with local stakeholders and contractors that may help bridge the uncertainty of political change by promoting continuity through local buy-in and ownership.

While the foundational aim of the SDF was to provide for basic needs, such as water and wastewater services, it also had a more holistic aim. Strategies were selected to improve urban resilience by addressing a range of social, economic, and environmental systems with the objective of identifying projects of a catalytic nature. For example, an underserviced, peri-urban neighborhood located between the steep hills and agricultural fields of District 8 faces a number of challenges such as seasonal flooding, a lack of economic opportunities, and a shortage of open spaces. To reposition the district as an emerging gateway between Jalalabad's city center and a new airport in the north, targeted public investment along a key corridor exemplifies the catalytic potential of the collective strategies. Social facilities, markets, and training centers anchor future private investment at important nodes of the corridor and link to the provision of basic needs. The proposal to turn a flood prone drainage corridor into a multifunctional open space that improves the neighborhood's resilience to flooding, but can also catalyze further investment, unlocking social and economic opportunities such as markets and shops along the park [FIG. 5]. Such amenities and economic opportunities can be supported by women's training programs that put the social development of Afghan women front and center.

Ultimately, in navigating the socio-ecological context, aligning international best practices with local specificities of implementation will continue to be difficult. While the SDF provides both guidance based on sustainability and environmental protection within an open ended, anticipatory investment framework, it will still be up to municipal officials and policymakers to seek social understanding, choose which strategies to employ, and react to emerging challenges. This process will require cooperation between the local and central government alongside community engagement to align and translate the overarching goals and objectives of the SDF into local expertise and equitable practices. This means it will be imperative that intervention strategies are chosen transparently with an eye towards the public good, and that community engagement is prioritized in their implementation.

Toward a Reflexive, Landscape-Based Approach

The scale of the "city region" places processes of urbanization and development within a broader territorial context of landscape change crossing multiple jurisdictional boundaries creating spatial uncertainty in terms of

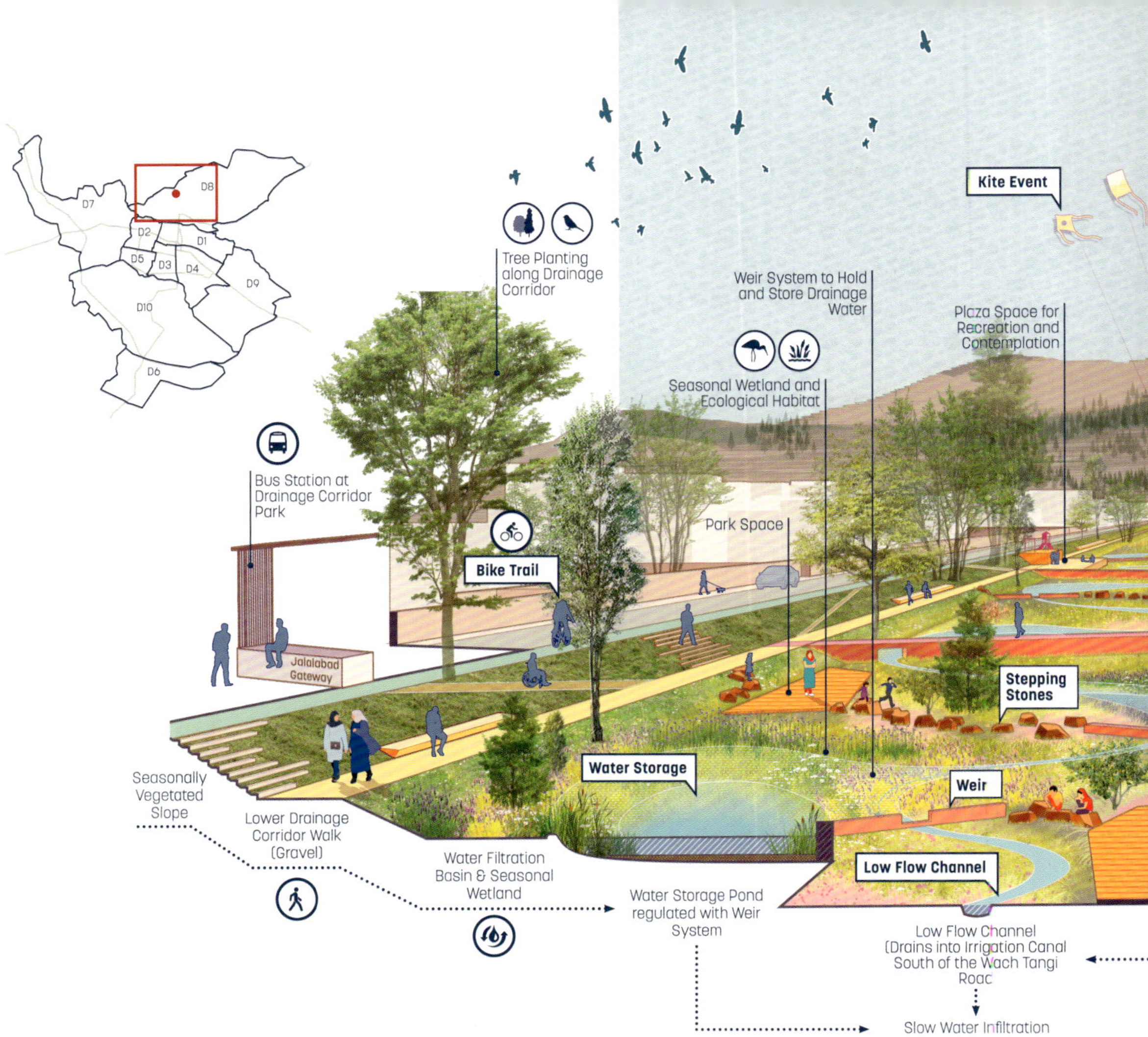

FIG.5 This project in District 8 proposes to redevelop a linear drainage corridor into a multifunctional open space that would provide residents with recreational opportunities during the dry season and reduce their vulnerability to flooding during heavy spring rains. The Ministry of Urban Development and Land (MUDL), prepared by Sasaki

what, where, and how interventions will impact others. This also means that interventions are multi-sectoral: implemented by various actors with distinct disciplinary perspectives and possibly narrow, competing interests that are subject to political change—all of which can bring new forms of temporal uncertainty. Issues of transparency, lack of data, sharing of information, and the presence of powerful speculative interests further adds to levels of uncertainty in managing complex projects. In view of these challenges, the landscape-based approach allows us to contextualize planning at the intersection of humans and the environment, while taking a reflexive approach allows us to contextualize the relationship between our own "expert" proposals and the people who will be impacted by them. In service of this aim, there are several key threads that summarize this approach.

Think with systems and ecologies. Do not force rigid technical solutions onto problems where systems and ecological processes create uncertainty and change. Look for broader contextual factors that influence risks

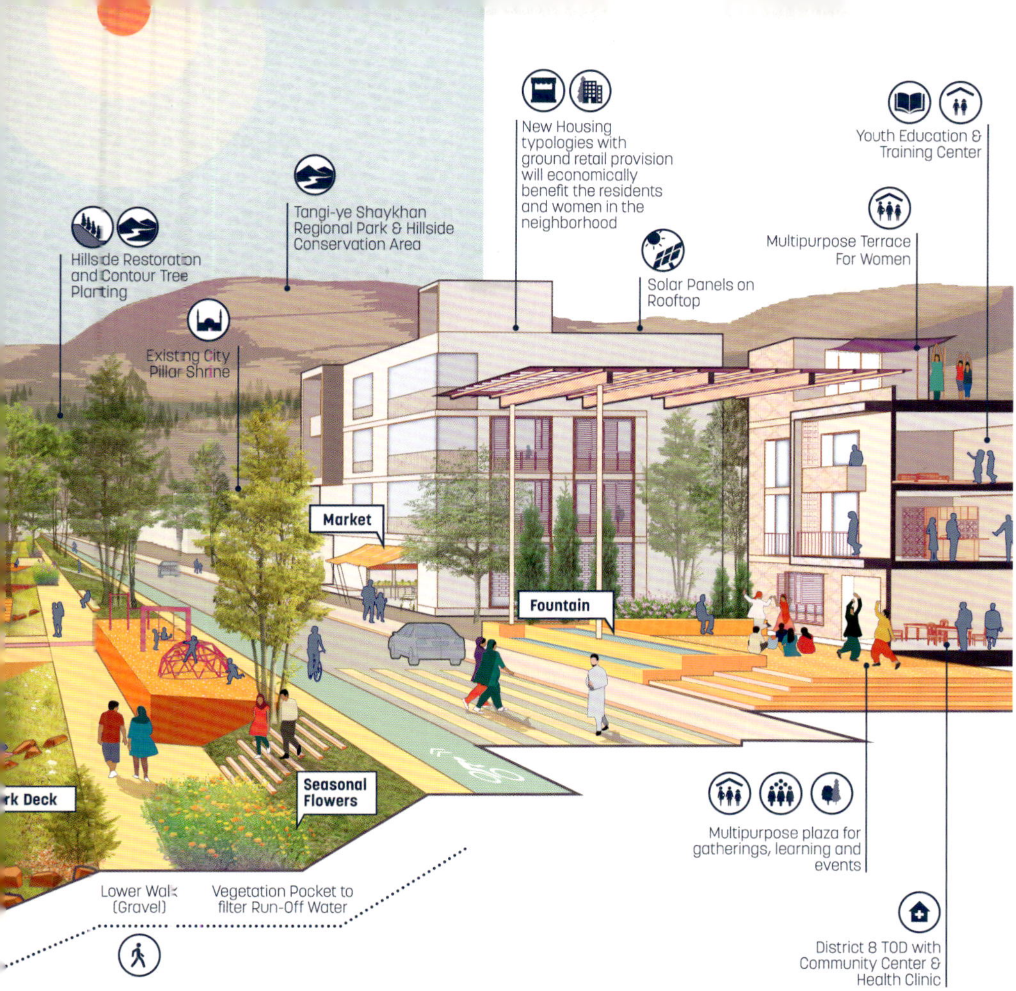

and vulnerabilities in the landscape and social dynamics. Incorporate methodologies and models that can adapt in real time and examine multiple scenarios. The solutions may thus be multiple, variable, and cross-sectoral.

Embrace contingency. Change happens, expect it to. Look at where funding is allocated for a project intervention, where it is not, and which interests (political or financial) are driving certain kinds of interventions over others. Look for indirect ways to address path dependencies and institutions where technocratic ideologies prevail. Emphasize positive social, environmental, economic, and political goals linked to globally important goals like sustainability and resilience. Where there may be lower government capacity (i.e. personnel and resources), the question of what should be done versus how it will be implemented is critical.

Aim for impact. Entrenched cultures and economic conditions don't transform overnight. Identify areas where change can be meaningful and

ACKNOWLEDGEMENTS

The authors would like to genuinely thank Sasaki and the Afghan Ministry for Urban Development and Land (MUDL) for their perspectives, reflections and critical thinking.

yet possible. Addressing basic needs may reveal opportunities for catalyzing change that can scale up to achieve broader city or national goals. Support local capacities for planning, implementing, and measuring to ensure plans will have more success of being supported and implemented in the long term. This must start by translating "best practices" to the context by incorporating local knowledge and meeting the needs of traditionally marginalized groups such as women, minorities, and migrants.

Embrace fiduciary responsibility and accountability. It is incumbent upon all actors involved to cultivate a working culture of fiduciary responsibility. We must strive to break free of business and political constraints that often shirk accountability. Each position of power, be it managerial, political, or technical, comes with a different set of responsibilities for maintaining openness and transparency in evaluating where time and resources should be spent to ensure the greatest benefit to the communities we seek to provide for and empower.

Seek social understanding and relinquish control. Don't impose. Develop a shared vision that is open to change by local communities. Integrate the needs and values of local stakeholders like community organizations and developers, but also farmers, construction firms, teachers, and others that can build a broader sense of ownership over the plan and its implementation. Ensure transparency in the decision-making process by making data open and available. Most importantly, invest in people—look to transfer knowledge through institutional partnerships and collaboration. Direct resources transparently to address local issues as defined by established community-based processes (such as through the local Wakil-e-Gozar and community development councils in Afghanistan) that can foster continued engagement and recognition.

The expansion of interdisciplinary scopes of work presents a range of challenges for how problems are defined and which solutions are appropriate. As alluded to in our reflections on our role vis-a-vis the history of planning in Afghanistan, we argue that we must first confront the lingering perspective of the technical expert. Drawing on an interdisciplinary framework, we should instead seek a more reflexive, landscape-based approach toward planning with uncertainty. We do not claim that the points above are necessarily the only way forward, nor do we argue that past techniques should be abandoned. Instead, what is required is greater dialogue between practitioners, city leaders, local community organizations, and residents that negotiates between local practices and global expertise, contextualizes old techniques, explores new strategies, and acknowledges the inevitable uncertainties in the implementation of any plan. As history shows us, governments may come and go—as with their plans—but people and places will remain to bear the legacy.

Endnotes

1. James Reed, Liz Deakin, and Terry Sunderland. "What Are 'Integrated Landscape Approaches' and How Effectively Have They Been Implemented in the Tropics: A Systematic Map Protocol." *Environmental Evidence* 4, no. 1 (January 7, 2015): 2551. Also see: Bas Arts, Marleen Buizer, Lumina Horlings, Verina Ingram, Cora van Oosten, and Paul Opdam. "Landscape Approaches: A State-of-the-Art Review." *Annual Review of Environment and Resources* 42, no. 1 (October 17, 2017): 439–63.
2. The SDF project was completed in 2020 by MUDL and a consultant team led by Sasaki. See: MUDL, *Jalalabad Strategic Development Framework,* (2020). Available at: https://issuu.com/sasakiassociates/docs/_jalalabad_strategic_development_framework_full_sm.
3. Government of the Islamic Republic of Afghanistan, National Urban Policy (NUP), 2019-2021, (Kabul, 2019).
4. For compelling work on the landscape as both a medium and aesthetic, see William J. T. Mitchell. *Landscape and Power.* University of Chicago Press, 2002. James Scott's work in state legibility projects is also relevant, see Scott, James. *Seeing Like a State: How Certain Schemes to Improve the Human Condition Have Failed.* New Haven: Yale University Press, 1998.
5. See Cynthia Clapp-Wincek and Emily Baldwin, "The Helmand Valley Project in Afghanistan" (Report, U.S. Agency for International Development, 1983); Richard Tapper "Nomadism in Modern Afghanistan," in *Afghanistan in the 1970s,* Louis Dupree and Linette Albert (eds.) (Praeger, 1974), 126–43. For a similar strategy of settling Pashtun nomads, see James W. Spain, *The Way of the Pathans* (London: Robert Hale Ltd., 1962), 126.
6. Clapp-Wincek and Baldwin, "The Helmand Valley Project in Afghanistan," viii, 7, 10, 29.
7. Baron, "Sector Analysis," 52.
8. Proposals described in Baron, "Sector Analysis," 50; Quote from Clapp-Wincek and Baldwin, "The Helmand Valley Project in Afghanistan," 5.
9. A mixed view as to the success of the venture can be found across a range of reports and other literature: Clapp-Wincek and Baldwin, "The Helmand Valley Project in Afghanistan"; Baron, "Sector Analysis"; Also see Nick Cullather, "Damming Afghanistan: Modernization in a Buffer State," *The Journal of American History* 89, no. 2 (2002), 512–37.
10. Tim Weiner, "With Taliban Gone, Opium Farmers Return to Their Only Cash Crop," New York Times, Nov. 26, 2001, B1. In 2000 it was estimated that the Helmand Valley produced 39 percent of the world's opium: United Nations Drug Control Programme, Afghanistan Programme, Afghanistan: Annual Opium Poppy Survey 2000 (Islamabad, 2000).
11. Elke Beyer, "Competitive Coexistence: Soviet Town Planning and Housing Projects in Kabul in the 1960s," *Journal of Architecture* 17, no. 3 (June 1, 2012).
12. May Schinasi. Kabul *1773–1984: Birth and Growth of a Royal Capital* [Kaboul 1773–1984: Naissance et Croissance d'une Capitale Royale] (University of Naples, Department of Asian Studies, 2009): 132.
13. Elke Beyer, "Competitive Coexistence": 309–32. Also see: Jean-Baptiste Michel, "Paris: What Le Corbusier Dreamed of for the Right Bank" [Paris : ce dont rêvait Le Corbusier pour la rive droite], GEO (2016).
14. Mohammad Nasir Ghorghost, Kabul Guide [رهنمای کابل] (Kabul: Government printing house, 1966): 130.
15. For more on this, see: JICA, The study for the development of the master plan for the Kabul metropolitan area in the Islamic republic of Afghanistan: Final Report, September, 2009.
16. The Kabul Urban Design Framework (KUDF) was developed as a loose framework between 2017–2019 that began to address some of the previous issues of the master planning process. It referred to the earlier vision of Babur and identified strategic areas for investment. However, it has been approved as a master plan, reflecting the problem of institutional path dependency and entrenched expectations for technical comprehensiveness. This is also illustrated by the top-down approach to the plan development which lacked extensive engagement.
17. SDFs for all five provincial capital cities including Herat, Jalalabad, Kandahar, Khost and Mazar-e-Sharif can be found online at: https://issuu.com/sasakiassociates.
18. Some of the key data used included: ecological sensitivity (food and agriculture, ecosystem services, groundwater sensitivity, and surface water) environmental risk (landslide, flash flood, floodplains, and water bodies), existing built-up areas, composite (geology) urban expansion scenario, risk mitigation, development limitation, landscape preservation, preliminary spatial framework zones.
19. The used scenario modeling method "evaluates the potential of urban growth without planning controls (or a "business as usual" case) based on a set of assumptions about probability and desirability of development. For the SDF the model compares a scenario for unplanned growth with a scenario of planned growth. These models provide more intuitive projections of how and where informal growth may occur based on a set of transparent and parametric assumptions like nearness to existing and proposed employment zones, transit, or amenities.
20. MUDL, *Jalalabad Strategic Development Framework,* 310-471.

1.4

Ecological Infrastructure as a Systematic Approach to Water Issues

Guangzhou's Sponge City Planning

Hexing Chang, Dong Wang

Origin and Development of the Sponge City Theory

China today is facing multiple water problems such as water scarcity,[1] drought, urban flooding,[2] water pollution,[3] and loss of biological habitats.[4] These water crises stem from a series of systematic, interrelated problems. The Sponge City theory is a comprehensive and systematic solution based on the characteristics of China's water issues.

The concept of Sponge City originated in an academic context where the term "sponge" originated as a metaphor for a certain adsorption function of cities. Trevor Budge, an Australian population researcher, likened this metaphor to the phenomenon of cities' adsorption of population.[5] As early as 2003, the Chinese landscape architect Kongjian Yu used the term "sponge" to describe flood mitigation abilities in natural systems, stating that "natural wetlands on both sides of rivers act as sponges, regulating the abundance of river water and alleviating droughts and floods."[6] Yu proposed an ecological infrastructure approach to solve water problems which has been continuously applied in planning projects across Chinese cities,[7,8] including Taizhou,[9] Weihai,[10] and Beijing.[11]

After Beijing suffered devastating floods in 2012, Yu wrote to the top leaders of the Beijing Municipal Government as well as the Chinese Central Government, suggesting that "the establishment of a 'green sponge' could mitigate the flood disaster."[12] Meanwhile, the 2012 ASLA excellence award was presented to Yu for his Qunli Stormwater Park that defined the concept of a "green sponge" for a water-resilient city.[13] The news of the award was widely broadcasted and reached hundreds of millions of Chinese, specifically through a 2012 China Central Television report during the evening's primetime with a long interview on Yu's initiative.[14] The reports about this novel design approach in the context of Chinese cities also gained the attention of the central government and it started to be discussed among scholars and the public.[15] Between 2012 and 2014, Yu was invited as an expert to participate in the drafting of the

OPPOSITE PAGE View of Daguan Sponge Wetland Park: With the "Sponge City" theory, the former low-lying land was transformed into an urban rainwater wetland corridor to provide comprehensive ecosystem services. Turenscape, 2018

central government's urbanization report organized by the Ministry of Housing and Urban-Rural Development (MOHURD).[16]

Through the promotion of this planning approach by Yu and several other experts, "green sponge" started to be adopted by decision makers on different levels of governance. In December 2013, President Xi Jinping officially endorsed the Sponge City concept at the central government's urbanization conference. In 2014, the MOHURD issued a set of technical guidelines[17] which provided instructions to improve urban drainage and flood prevention, implement low impact development (LID) construction, and accelerate research on the construction of sponge cities.[18] In 2015 and 2016, the central government launched 30 pilot cities to test the feasibility of the concept.[19,20]

Since the Sponge City concept was introduced in China, it has been influential among both academia and practice. However, most of the relevant research in China is focused on LID technology, urban drainage systems, and stormwater management which still heavily rely on engineering measures. Yu believes that the Sponge City concept is more capable than conventional modes of gray infrastructure for water management as it opens new ways to solve the water problems and related ecological problems which Chinese urban and rural regions are facing across different scales. Yu proposes to make the whole country a "green sponge system" to store and recycle rainwater, introducing the notion of "sponge lands."[21] According to him, cohesive, hydro-ecological infrastructure systems should interact with the network of parks and wetlands throughout built environments. Yu advised different cities on the implementation of such large-scale projects of ecological infrastructures,[22] as well as the leaders of the State Council. Yu argues that "the most effective and holistic solution to climate change is the construction of sponge lands."[23]

To tackle water issues across scales and regions, the research objective must be extended from the individual water body to the entire watershed ecosystem. The structure and function of the water system should be restored through ecological approaches that enhance the ecosystem services: *supporting, provisioning, regulating,* and *cultural services*.[24] The core of the Sponge City theory lies in the construction of hydro-ecological infrastructures,[25] the combination of specific ecological technologies, and inspiration from traditional water-adaptive landscapes which can inform contemporary concepts of water management.

Problems and Challenges: Guangzhou's Severe Water Problem Syndromes

Guangzhou is located in the transitional zone between the hills of the central Guangdong Province and the Pearl River Delta (PRD). With strong peaks in precipitation and a high groundwater level, Guangzhou is experiencing frequent floods, water pollution, destruction of the water ecosystem, seasonal droughts, and water shortages.[26] This leads to severe water problems, especially with an increasing intensity and frequency of storm surges due to climate change.[27] The destruction of natural rainwater storage systems, and rapid urban growth with an expansion of impermeable surfaces led to a sharp increase in storm water runoff in urban areas and an increased risk of flooding. The coastal city of Guangzhou thus faces threats from both storm water and rising tides.

With multiple sources of pollution, including surface water runoff, domestic and industrial sewage, the pollution in water bodies has reached serious levels. Some of the domestic and industrial sewage gets discharged directly into rivers, resulting in the pollution of certain river sections. The growing number of impermeable surfaces leads to an increasing surface runoff of contaminated water. Additionally, the destruction of the traditional water-adaptive, rural landscape and the excessive use of fertilizers caused agricultural pollution.

Due to large-scale land reclamation, the amount of rivers and natural wetlands has been reduced and the stability of the ecosystem has been disturbed. Many rivers in Guangzhou were channelized, covered, cut off, or even filled due to urban expansion. Single-purpose engineering measures have broken the material and energy cycles between water, soil, and aquatic organisms, which led to the loss of the self-purification ability of the water system and made diverse waterfront habitats disappear.

Learning from Traditional Water-Adaptive Landscapes

With the increasing scale of urbanization, more than half of the original agricultural landscapes in the PRD have been destroyed. To solve the region's water problems, pipe networks, pumping stations and other engineering measures were introduced, causing a repeated failure in the current water management regime. Ancient communities, which had been living in the PRD for centuries, learned to adapt their modes of production to the local natural environment. Over time, they had created a series of unique water-adaptive landscapes. These traditional approaches to water and landscape management can provide valuable models to inform resilient contemporary planning practices.

Water-Adaptive Landscape for Agricultural Production

Despite the constant threat of droughts and floods, the PRD has been used as a region for agricultural production throughout history. Over time, local peasants gradually developed an agricultural water-adaptive landscape pattern consisting of flat fields with ponds, high fields with weirs, and low fields with polders. This landscape formation addresses the whole watershed, from upstream retention to midstream deceleration to downstream adaptation.

At the water source, agricultural fields, woodlands, and rainwater retention ponds are scattered across the landscape and create a vital ecosystem for water catchment and flood mitigation. During the rainy season, this field-pond system located in the upper watershed acts as a series of natural sponges that store rainwater and provide freshwater for irrigation during dry periods via canals. It also serves as a retention system that chemically and mechanically cleans out pollutants and nutrients. In addition, woodlands that grow around the ponds effectively retain water and reduce soil erosion.

To lead water through this field-pond system, a series of weirs is used to delay flood peaks and divert water into designated ponds. At the low end of the watershed where water is discharged from the field-pond system, a series of polders with banks and ponds has been created to protect the fields from floods. As early as the Ming Dynasty (1368-1644),

FIG. 1 Fish ponds after modern agricultural transformation in Shunde, Guangdong Province. Kongjian Yu, 2005

the people dug ponds and built dikes in low-lying areas with poor conditions for agricultural production. The ponds were used to store water for fish, while fruits and vegetables were planted on the dikes, forming fruit-dike fish-ponds. By the early Qing Dynasty (1636-1912), the fruit trees planted on the dikes were replaced with mulberry trees for the cultivation of silkworms, forming mulberry-dike fish-ponds [FIG. 1].

Water-Adaptive Landscape as a Form of Habitation

Throughout history, people who settled in the PRD accumulated deep ecological knowledge, resulting in a specific form of living that is strongly connected to the natural environment. These traditional settlements are characterized by the flow of water: First, an upstream water catchment system, second, a midstream water-storage and drainage system, and third, a downstream adaptation system to protect the settlements from floods. Across villages, a network of wells and ponds is distributed and connected to the individual building courtyards to collect rainwater on site. The sloping roofs and the natural terrain were used to store and purify rainwater effectively, ensuring the infiltration of rainwater into the ground for natural water circulations.

The canals in traditional villages and towns act as systematic storage and drainage networks. They were used to drain rainwater into ponds, and further distribute water across the village. Such canals served as the main artery of the flood control system in ancient Guangzhou.

Since ancient times, the city of Guangzhou has experienced frequent storm surges and flooding. In the process of coping with floods and tides, residents have built water barriers and storage systems which have shaped unique urban forms. Ancient Guangzhou was built on an elevated plateau next to the Pearl River. The contours of the city walls were circular, reducing frontal pressure of floods. Large storage systems such as ponds and lakes both inside and outside the city provided storage space, achieving resilient adaptation to floods and tides.

The benefits from these traditional, water-adaptive landscape models have not received sufficient attention and were gradually destroyed in the process of modern urbanization. Instead, single-purpose engineering measures have changed the way people perceive and respond to their water environment. Contemporary forms of habitation often disregard the principles of traditional water-adaptive landscapes—from deceleration to fast discharge, from adaptation to confrontation.

Construction of a Sponge System at a Regional Scale

In contrast to conventional modes of water engineering, Sponge City planning embraces the ancient wisdom of traditional, water-adaptive landscapes in the PRD. The planning applies three key strategies of "retention at the source, deceleration during the process, and resilient adaptation at the end."[28] This holistic approach combines contemporary ecological water management with local landscape wisdom and systematically solves flooding, pollution, and wetland habitat problems. These principles are applied at a regional scale creating a landscape-driven ecological security pattern which prioritizes different areas according to their flood vulnerability [FIG. 2].

Retention at the Source: Water Conservation Forest and Paddy Fields

The planning scheme first identifies traditional water-adaptive landscapes such as the woodlands and pond systems in rural areas, to store upstream rainwater. Landscape elements that have the potential for water storage include water conservation forests (upstream woodlands) and paddy fields.

Through a comprehensive analysis of the land-use type, rainfall, hydrology, soil, and topography, important water conservation forests are identified. They provide essential services by protecting water sources and regulating the hydrological processes of the watershed. They are located in the north of Guangzhou's urban region, in Zengcheng, Conghua, and Huadu, and add up to about 2,430 km2.

The hydrology and soil composition of the existing paddy fields are similar to those of natural wetlands and serve as areas for rainwater retention and storage. Paddy fields have been identified in low-lying areas across Zengcheng, Conghua, Huadu, and Nansha Districts, adding up to 544 km2.

Deceleration During the Process: System of Ponds and Streams

Sponge City planning aims to restore wetlands and ecological river banks. It uses weirs and ponds to slow down the water, allowing rivers to purify, nourish surrounding habitats and provide humans with freshwater, rather than being discharged quickly. Ponds that are located along rivers can additionally help to slow down and purify water runoff. Such existing ponds could be identified inside the project perimeter across an area of about 2,033 km2. The river network, finally, is the key element in this process of deceleration as it collects most of the runoff water. By combining the current water system with the historical one, a water network with a total length of 1,205 km is created. Continuous vegetation buffer zones are planned along the rivers to restore the natural form and diverse habitats.

Resilient Adaptation at the End: Flood Storage Wetlands

The concept of resilient adaptation is implemented at the bottom of the watershed in the low-lying coastal areas of Guangzhou, aiming to overcome rigidity with flexibility. The planning concept proposes to restore the traditional pond system in the PRD in the context of climate change. This will improve the flood resiliency and recreate a landscape pattern where people live in harmony with water.

Wetlands that are located in the lower reaches of the PRD have the

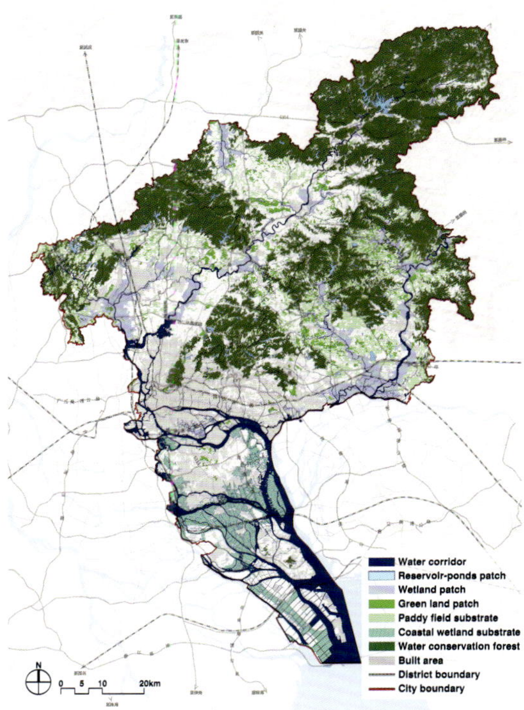

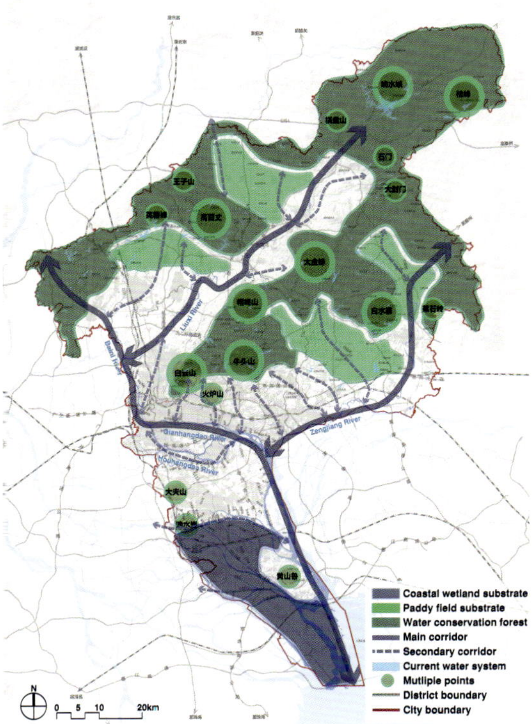

FIG.2 TOP LEFT Comprehensive landscape-driven ecological security pattern: A comprehensive assessment of the Pearl River Delta's water ecosystems in the municipality of Guangzhou. Turenscape, 2016

FIG.3 TOP RIGHT Patterns of Hydro Ecological Infrastructure: The Area of Hydro Ecological Infrastructure in Guangzhou is 4,883.8 km2, accounting for 65.7 percent of the total area of Guangzhou. Turenscape, 2016

FIG.4 Ecological spatial structure of the Sponge City: The basic structure follows the pattern of "Two Zones, Three Axes, Four Patches, Eighteen Corridors, and Multiple Points." Turenscape, 2016

biggest potential for resilient adaptation. Through GIS spatial analysis, 2,218 km2 of wetlands could be identified that have the potential for water storage.

Urban Scale Sponge System

The key landscape patterns described above are integrated into a proposed regional hydro-ecological infrastructure which constitutes the spatial structure and ecological pattern of Guangzhou's Sponge City planning [FIG. 3]. Its basic structure follows the pattern of "Two Zones, Three Axes, Four Patches, Eighteen Corridors, and Multiple Points" [FIG. 4].

Two Zones: includes the northern ecological conservation forest zone and the southern coastal wetland zone. The forest zone serves the conservation, dispersion, and storage of water upstream; the wetland zone is the main area for the adaptation to floods and tides in lower reaches.

Three Axes: The major rivers form three axes, carrying most of the city's runoff, and providing drainage and flood prevention services.

Four Patches: Four major ponds create a system of paddy fields that are the main carriers of dispersed retention at the source.

Eighteen Corridors: A system of corridors is formed by eighteen major streams and green belts that connect ecological patches and ponds, together creating a sponge network. Corridors are the main element to slow down the water flow.

Multiple Points: A series of small-scale ponds and parks collects rainwater runoff from communities.

Policies and Guidelines: Defining Design Principles Across Scales

Guangzhou's Municipal Government acts as the main body responsible for the implementation of the Sponge City concept. Members from different departments of the government—including planning, housing, water, transportation, forestry, urban management, environmental protection, agriculture, meteorology, and finance, among others—have set up a leading group called Sponge City Construction Office. This group is responsible for all issues related to the Sponge City initiative and jointly promotes the construction of Sponge City projects while ensuring the training of personnel, education, financial support, etc.[29]

Drainage zoning and evaluation systems serve as management tools to guide design processes across scales and to achieve large ecological infrastructure patterns. Based on the underlying hydrological structure,

the city is structured into three levels: eight watersheds, 35 districts, and 176 units. A set of indexes is defined to assess the performance of planning and construction processes, including binding indicators, such as the ratio of total annual runoff catchment or water quality requirements, as well as guiding indicators, such as ratios of green roofs and permeable pavements.

At the urban region level, the main indicators and assessments of the Sponge City framework will be incorporated into the city's master planning guidelines. At the district regulatory plan level, new projects are supposed to incorporate Sponge-City-related indicators and requirements, aiming to achieve both the binding and guiding indicators.

FIG.5 Aerial view of Daguan Sponge Wetland Park, Guangzhou, China. Turenscape, 2016

ACKNOWLEDGEMENTS

Guangzhou's Sponge City Planning has been done by Turenscape, a landscape design and planning firm based in Beijing, China, commissioned by Guangzhou Municipal Planning and Natural Resources Bureau in 2016. The authors thank the project and design lead Kongjian Yu and the project team Min He, Baiqiang Ren and Yue Liu for their contributions in this project.

Since 2010, the landscape architecture and planning firm Turenscape has been part of Guangzhou's Sponge City planning across scales. A detailed planning for the Tianhe Intelligence Business District (TIBD) at a district scale as well as a wetland park inside the TIBD at the scale of a city block have been realized [FIG. 5]. Together with the overall urban region planning schemes, these two planning projects showcase the complete range of what it means to build a Sponge City ecological infrastructure as a systematic landscape approach across multiple scales. Daguan Wetland Park in the TIBD serves as a prototype for the implementation of Sponge City guidelines, built as an important water storage corridor, relieving flood pressure, improving water quality, and providing attractive open spaces for the local residents.

Conclusion

The massive constructions of gray infrastructure and impervious surfaces in times of rapid urbanization have significantly altered the natural water cycle in metropolitan areas such as Guangzhou. Solutions of complex water problems through single-purpose engineering measures are often counterproductive. Throughout history, the PRD's ancestors have accumulated a deep understanding for the local conditions, the management of water and adaptation to floods through the cultivation and maintenance of land over centuries. In contemporary urban and landscape planning, it is important to learn from this ancient wisdom and promote these "arts of survival"[30] from agriculture, settlement, and water conservation projects. They provide the tools to build resilient, hydro-ecological infrastructure to protect crucial ecological services and inform the spatial structure of Sponge Cities.

Endnotes

1. Hao Wang, *Research on Chinese Water Resource Problem and Sustainable Development Strategy* (Beijing: China Electric Power Press, 2010).
2. Chunmiao Zheng, Jie Liu, Guoliang Cao, Eloise Kendy, Hao Wang and Yangwen Jia, "Can China Cope with Its Water Crisis? - Perspectives from the North China Plain," *Groundwater* 48, no. 3 (2010): 350-54.
3. Y. Hou, S. P. Li and W. W. Zhou, "The Analysis of Current Urban Storm Water Problem and the Discussion of Countermeasures," in *China Water Wastewater the 9th Annual Conference Publication*, 2012.
4. Liwei Xing and Zhenguo Niu, "Mapping and Analyzing China's Wetlands Using MODIS Time Series Data," *Wetlands Ecology and Management* 27, no. 5-6 (2019): 693-710.
5. Trevor Budge, "Sponge Cities and Small Towns: A New Economic Partnership," in *The Changing Nature of Australia's Country Towns*, ed. David Jones and Maureen Rogers, (VURRN Press, 2006), 281-290.
6. Kongjian Yu and Dihua Li, *The Way to Urban Landscape: Communicating with Mayors*, (Beijing: China Architecture & Building Press, 2003), 149-153.
7. Kongjian Yu, Zhang Yuan and Liu Yunqian, "Ecological Infrastructure Priority: Wuhan Wulijie Ecological City Case," *Planners* 28, no. 10 (2012): 26-29.
8. Lin Mo and Kongjian Yu, "Structure the Urban Green Sponge: Study on Planning an Ecological Stormwater Regulation System," *Urban Studies* 5 (2012): 130-34.
9. Kongjian Yu, Dihua Li and Xili Han, "On the 'Negative Planning'" *City Planning Review* 9 (2005): 64-69.

10. Kongjian Yu, Xuesong Xi and Sisi Wang, "Townscape Planning Based on Ecological Infrastructure: A Case Study of Weihai, Shandong," *City Planning Review* 32, no. 3 (2008): 87–92.
11. Kongjian Yu, Shifang Wang, Dihua Li and Qiao Qing, "Ecological Baseline for Beijing's Urban Sprawl: Basic Ecosystem Services and Their Security Patterns," *City Planning Review* 34, no. 2 (2010): 19–24.
12. Kongjian Yu, "Rang Yu Hong Bu Shi Zai Hai, Er Cheng Fu Yin" [Making Storm Water as a Gift but Not Hazard], *Bihui Online*, 2012, http://www.whb.cn/zhuzhan/bihui/20190814/283106.html.
13. American Society of Landscape Architects, "AWARD OF EXCELLENCE: A Green Sponge for a Water-Resilient City: Qunli Stormwater Park," 2012, https://www.asla.org/2012awards/026.html.
14. China Central Television (CCTV), "Hui Hu Xi de He Dao" [News Probe: The Breathing River], China: China Network Television, August 25, 2012, https://tv.cctv.com/2012/08/25/VIDE1355099970633231.shtml.
15. Shuqiu Dong and Zhigang Han, "Study on Planning an 'Eco-Sponge City' for Rainwater Utilization," *Urban Studies* 18, no. 12 (2011): 37–41.
16. Kongjian Yu, "Based on Nature, Conform to Nature and Utilize Nature: 'Sponge City' and Urban Ecological Resilience," *Architectural Practice* 01 (2021): 58–65.
17. Ministry of Housing and Urban-Rural Development of China, "Di Ying Xiang Kai Fa Yu Shui Xi Tong Gou Jian (Shi Xing)" [Notice of the Ministry of Housing and Urban-Rural Development on Issuing Technical Guidelines for Sponge City Construction-Low-Impact Development Rainwater System Construction (Trial)], 2014, http://www.mohurd.gov.cn/wjfb/201411/t20141102_219465.html.
18. Ministry of Housing and Urban-Rural Development of China, "Zhu Fang He Cheng Xiang Jian She Bu Cheng Shi Jian She Si 2014 Nian Gong Zuo Yao Dian" [Work Highlights of the Urban Construction Department of the Ministry of Housing and Urban-Rural Development in 2014], 2014, http://www.mohurd.gov.cn/wjfb/201402/t20140214_217084.html.
19. State Council Information Office Website, "16 Chinese Cities to Carry out Sponge City Construction Pilot This Year," 2015, http://www.scio.gov.cn/video/qwjd/34146/Document/1616546/1616546.htm.
20. Ministry of Finance of China, "Wo Guo 16 Ge Cheng Shi Jin Nian Kai Zhan Hai Mian Cheng Shi Jian She Shi Dian" [Announcement of the List of Pilot Cities Supporting the Construction of Sponge Cities by the Central Government in 2016], 2016, http://jjs.mof.gov.cn/zxzyzf/csgwzxzj/201604/t20160425_1964216.htm.
21. Kongjian Yu, "Key Technologies for Construction of Water Ecological Infrastructures," *China Water Conservancy*, 22 (2015): 1-4.
22. Yue Lu, "Lü se hai mian wei cheng shi jie ke" [Yu Kongjian, the Dean of the College of Architecture and Landscape Architecture of Peking University: The Green Sponge for Urban Thirst]," The Xiamen Website, 2013, http://zt.xmnn.cn/a/mlxmgtdz/zjft/201308/t20130816_3452835.htm.
23. "Envisioning Climate Resilience: Experts from the Lincoln Institute Network Weigh in on Promising Land and Water Policy Solutions," Lincoln Institute of Land Policy, January 12, 2021, https://www.lincolninst.edu/publications/articles/2021-01-envisioning-climate-resilience-experts-from-lincoln-institute-network-weigh-in-on-promising-land-and-water-policy-solutions.
24. Millennium Ecosystem Assessment, MEA, *Ecosystems and Human Well-Being,* Vol. 5, (Washington, D.C.: Island Press, 2005).
25. Kongjian Yu, "Gou jian mei li zhong guo de shui sheng tai ji chu she shi" [Hydro-Ecological Infrastructure: The Way to Beautiful China], Modern Water Conservancy Weekly of China Water Resources News, January 15, 2015, https://www.turenscape.com/news/detail/1659.html.
26. Qiang Zhang, Wei Zhang, Yongqin David Chen, and Tao Jiang, "Flood, Drought and Typhoon Disasters during the Last Half-Century in the Guangdong Province, China," *Natural Hazards* 57, no. 2 (2011): 267–78.
27. Han Zhang, Chuanhao Wu, Wenjie Chen, and Guoru Huang, "Assessing the Impact of Climate Change on the Waterlogging Risk in Coastal Cities: A Case Study of Guangzhou, South China," *Journal of Hydrometeorology* 18, no. 6 (2017): 1549–62.
28. Kongjian Yu, "Three Key Strategies to Achieve a Sponge City: Retention, Slow Down and Adaptation," *South Architecture*, (2015), 4–7.
29. Guangzhou Municipal Planning and Natural Resources Bureau, "Guang Zhou Shi Hai Mian Cheng Shi Zhuan Xiang Gui Hua" [Sponge City Planning of Guangzhou], 2017, http://ghzyj.gz.gov.cn/gzlpc/ywpd_cxgh_tzgg/201707/43c933ee3aed4b42b2b3a422752dcdfd/files/f5381be7638e466f93bc429e9adcd6e7.pdf.
30. Kongjian Yu, *Art of Survival: Positioning Contemporary Landscape Architecture*, (Beijing: China Building Industry Press, 1991).

1.5

Anchoring Our Cities in Ecological Identity

Jennifer A. Dowdell, Keith Bowers

Occurring at the confluence of physical, biological, and social sciences, urban ecology frameworks recognize the importance of our socio-ecological decisions in addressing legacies of inequity and ecological devastation in our communities, planning for a more resilient, equitable, and just future. Nature is frequently an after-thought or an added bonus in many comprehensive city plans. Traditionally urban planning efforts are guided by economic or social priorities and employ a variety of experts providing input in a siloed approach. However, this approach centers squarely on the ecological and geological underpinnings of the landscape and the human relationship to these systems. In this essay we share two specific case studies that reflect an innovative urban ecology framework planning process weaving ecosystem function and benefits with community input, identity, and connection to place.

Biohabitats is a U.S.-based mission-driven consultancy focused on regenerative design, conservation planning, integrated water strategies, and ecological restoration. We are an interdisciplinary group of natural resource scientists, landscape ecologists, landscape architects, environmental engineers, soil scientists, arborists, geomorphologists, and hydrologists. We have worked with our clients to engage a plurality of expertise and stakeholders, using nature's model of organisms and systems to guide our approach to the interrelatedness of all things. Additional disciplines who are engaged from the earliest stages in the planning process include transportation engineers, economists, historians, and engineers, as well as urban designers and community engagement specialists.

Nature as Part of Identity

Due to its significant mature tree canopy, the city of Atlanta, Georgia is known lovingly by many residents as the "City in the Forest." Surveys in 2008 and 2014 revealed a staggering 42 percent canopy coverage—the highest amongst any major metropolitan area in the U.S.—and a goal for many U.S. cities today.[1] Concurrently, though, Atlantans were witnessing pressures from new development resulting in increasing tree loss. In 2015, the Atlanta Regional Council released growth projections that concluded by 2050 the Metro region would see an increase of 2.9 million people, with 1.3 million of those expected in the city proper.[2]

Wishing to plan for this growth in a sustainable and holistic way, the City set out on a landmark comprehensive planning process called Atlanta City Design, which envisioned a future reflecting Martin Luther King Jr's notion of the Beloved Community.[3] His was a vision of an inclusive society where all individuals share in the wealth of the earth's resources—where there is no poverty, hunger, or racism and where conflicts are resolved peacefully.[4] The basic tenets of Atlanta City Design are Equity, Progress, Ambition, Access, and Nature. As part of this overarching plan a "Nature Strategy" was envisioned to preserve the forested character of the city. It would focus on preserving and celebrating

OPPOSITE PAGE Team site visit for Atlanta City Design: Nature Project. Jennifer Dowdell

FIG.1 Community members tell their "nature stories" during the Atlanta City Design: Nature project launch. Jennifer Dowdell

FIG.2 OPPOSITE PAGE Stakeholder Needs and Opportunities. City of Atlanta Department of City Planning

the unique identity of nature in the community and a renewed connection to the city's rivers, streams, forests, and greenways. The idea was to create an urban ecology framework that promoted Design for People, Design for Nature, and Design for People in Nature. Important components of the Nature Strategy would be the protection of urban habitat and biodiversity, increased and equitable access to open space, environmentally sensitive design guidance for new development, and an update to the City's tree protection ordinance.

In the spring of 2018, Biohabitats' interdisciplinary consultant team initiated a collaborative community planning process to develop this ecological framework with the Atlanta Department of City Planning. Our planning team included landscape ecologists, natural resource scientists, local landscape architects, environmental engineers, transportation planners, community engagement specialists, arborists, and an environmental nonprofit focused on land conservation.

Biohabitats began the effort in the community with a listening and learning workshop [FIG. 1] to reveal how nature is experienced by residents, in their own words. The power of storytelling is inextricably linked to the development of an urban ecology framework, as it allows for an exploration of the interdependence of community and nature, finding the wonder in birdsong, the flurry of pollinators in a garden or meadow,

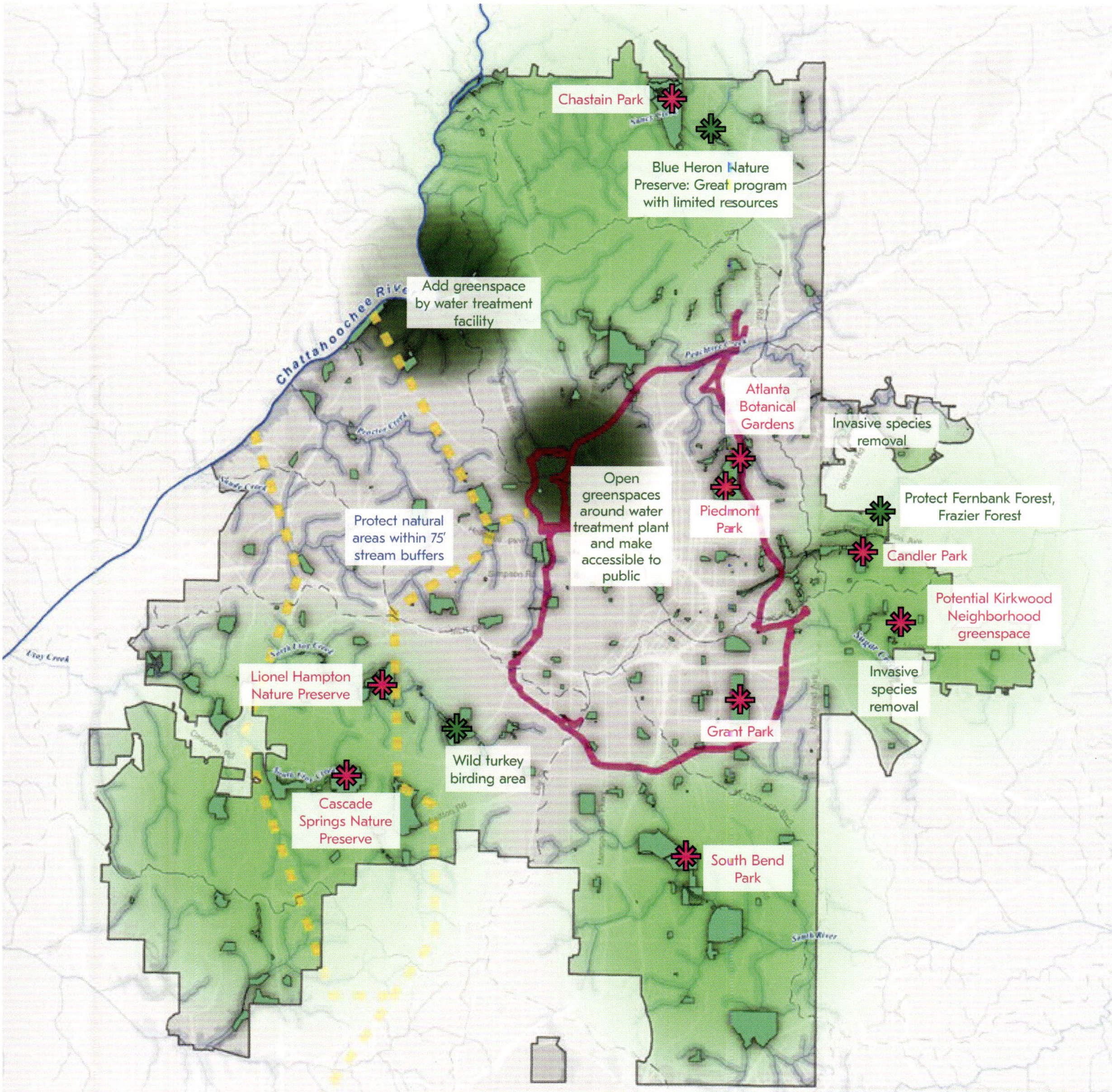

Stakeholder Interviews - Needs + Opportunities

Forest Preservation — Protection of tree canopy, removal of invasive species, and implementation of native tree replacement program.

- Implement ecological best practices
- High concentration of quality trees in private properties
- Acquire additional greenspace for access/protection

Rivers, Creeks, and Streams — Remove overgrown invasive vegetation, improve water access, protect riparian edges, and improve water quality.

- Rivers, creeks, and streams with adequate buffers that facilitate ecological improvements and connections.

Watershed Ridges and Creek/Stream Headwaters — Protect top of watersheds and stream headwaters to improve water quality and quantity downstream.

- Watershed areas

Parks and Linear Greenspaces — Implement ecological best practices

- Atlanta BeltLine
- Signature greenspaces with opportunities to implement ecological best practices
- Parks and open spaces with opportunities to implement ecological best practices
- Power line easements as opportunities to create connected food producing landscapes

0 1 2 miles

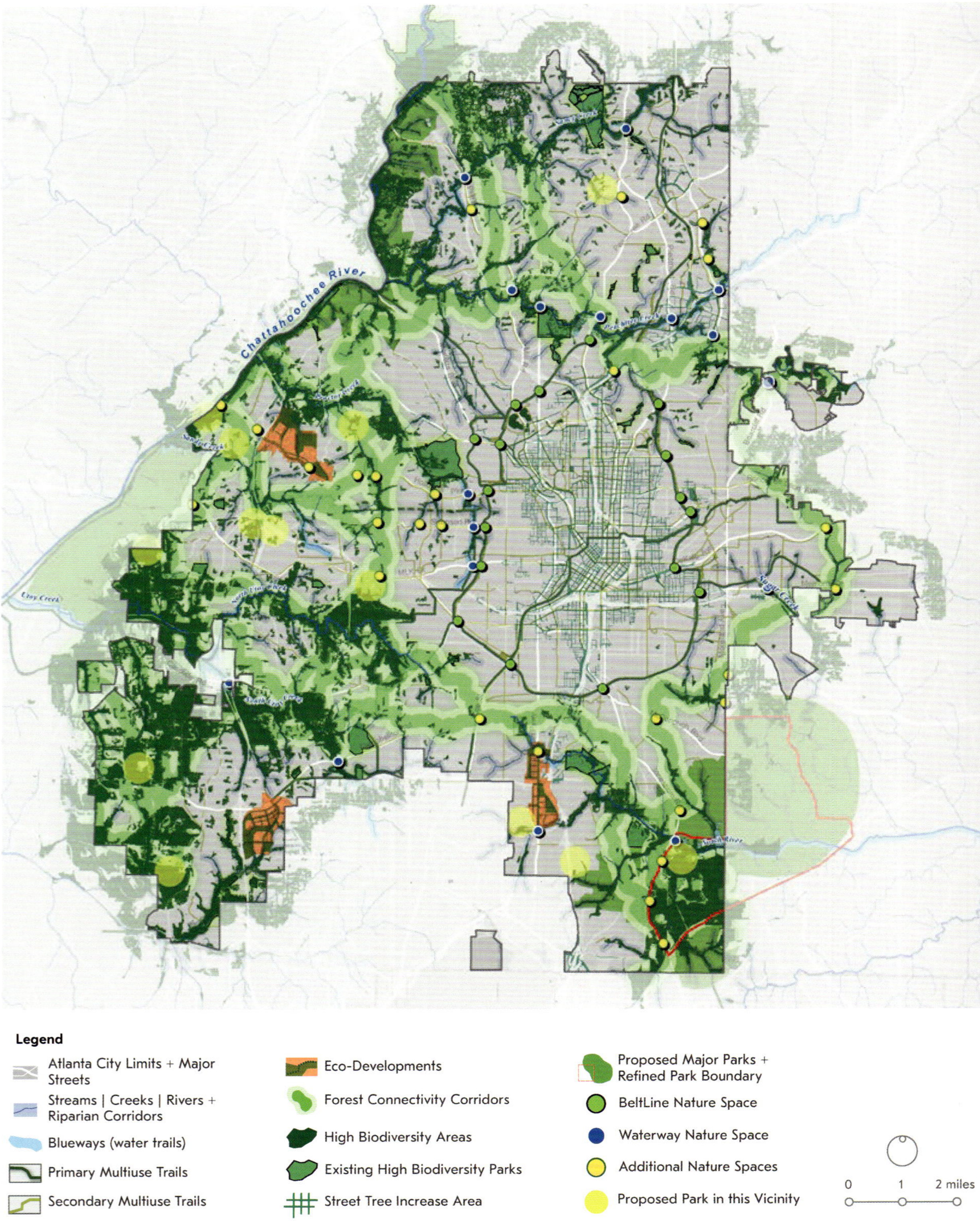
Chattahoochee River
Legend
Atlanta City Limits + Major Streets
Streams | Creeks | Rivers + Riparian Corridors
Blueways (water trails)
Primary Multiuse Trails
Secondary Multiuse Trails
Eco-Developments
Forest Connectivity Corridors
High Biodiversity Areas
Existing High Biodiversity Parks
Street Tree Increase Area
Proposed Major Parks + Refined Park Boundary
BeltLine Nature Space
Waterway Nature Space
Additional Nature Spaces
Proposed Park in this Vicinity
0
1
2 miles

the sounds of a stream gurgling along a wooded corridor just steps away from a neighborhood school, worship house, or community center.

The participants' words say it all: "smelling the damp soil at the edge of a creek, feeling the dirt between my toes, seeing majestic trees as I opened my front door, hearing the calls of owls at night and birds at daybreak." Atlanta residents described feelings of freedom, peace of mind, calm, soothing, healing, connection, bliss, happiness, birth, breathing, refreshing, joy, and tranquility. Nature was seen as a place for meditation, a safe space for losing one's self, an opportunity to feel a connection to something much larger—a communion with humanity throughout the world. For many it was also a space of play and wonder, harkening back to childhood and family.

It is the knowing and the naming of nature by the community that infused this planning effort with a deeper knowledge of relationships and experiences. Their stories from that initial launch day stayed with our team for the next two years [FIG. 2] as we worked to develop an urban ecology framework that was responsive to the community and reflective of the unique ecological character, history, and potential of the City. The planning process involved months of iterative data analysis and community feedback focused on habitat and biodiversity, ecosystem services, parks, and open space, and environmental justice and climate justice. Using geospatial analysis tools, historic ecological patterns were layered at the city scale, along with current conditions associated with hydrology, geology, soils, landcover, habitat and biodiversity species, floodplain, riparian corridor buffers, and historical streams. Existing data and studies of social vulnerability (including health indicators, race, and economic status), tree canopy change, food, and park deserts were also examined and overlaid with historical patterns of nature that settlement may have disrupted.

The final plan, *Atlanta City Design: Nature* [FIG. 3] detailed five layers of socio-ecological guidance to accommodate significant population growth:[5]

1. Designing for wildness at two large urban parks that bookend the city,
2. Designing for ecological function through the preservation of significant biodiversity hot spots and habitat corridors across the city,
3. Designing for retreat and adventure through increased connectivity and access to greenways, blueways, parks, and open space,
4. Designing for heightened awareness and interactivity with green space and increased tree canopy in the urban center,
5. Promoting green infrastructure and ecological design for new development in population growth zones.

Atlanta had effectively embraced the opportunity to look at city planning through the lens of ecology: aligning natural corridors with

FIG.3 Atlanta City Design: Nature - the final urban ecological framework. City of Atlanta Department of City Planning

benefits to community health and wellbeing, securing equitable and safe access to nature, considering climate change resilience, and preserving and enhancing habitat and biodiversity.

Biodiversity as a Seed for Ecological Planning

An ecological approach to planning reinforces the notion that urban communities have a reciprocal relationship with nature. If we steward our natural resources, restore ecological function, and preserve the remnants of once-dominant ecosystems, all members of our community benefit. This approach focuses on the fact that *biodiversity,* in particular, serves as a strong surrogate for many of the benefits that we take for granted in our relationship to nature and to our long-term resilience as a global society. As E.O. Wilson has noted, "The loss of a keystone species is like a drill accidentally striking a power line. It causes lights to go out all over."[6]

Prioritizing biodiversity in our urban communities is one way to stem the sixth great extinction while healing the habitats that define our metropolitan and peri-urban landscapes. If we design for biodiversity then we increase the potential for a variety of plant communities and wildlife to thrive in their native habitat, providing resilience in response to climate change impacts or pests that might threaten to eradicate a species and impact an entire community (i.e., chestnuts, hemlocks, and ash trees most recently in the U.S.). We are creating the conditions for trophic cascades and expansive food webs that connect back to a community's ability to access food and resources. With an urban ecological framework grounded in promoting biodiversity, we are creating the potential for a world of possibility and a dynamism to respond to an unknown future.

Furthermore, access to nature has been proven time and time again to increase life expectancy, decrease recovery times from major surgeries, increase test scores, improve concentration, increase health metrics, and lead to greater happiness.[7,8] Unfortunately, access to green space is inequitably distributed in many of today's cities and the integration of open and natural spaces into underserved communities often leads to gentrification and, ultimately, displacement of those most vulnerable. Our challenge in each of these efforts is to address this head-on, asking the question of client and stakeholder alike, how do we think creatively to serve the needs and desires of the existing community.

Our planning process is both iterative and interdisciplinary. It is iterative in the sense that we seek out and respond to feedback from community members throughout the planning process. And interdisciplinary in that we assemble teams to include public engagement specialists, funders, urban designers, landscape architects, arborists, and economic development experts. We attempt to break down traditional walls between expertise. We promote the same process with our clients so that Parks is speaking to Transportation is speaking to Public Works is speaking to Planning.

This approach is grounded in the tradition of landscape architecture and landscape ecology pioneers like Ian McHarg, Richard Forman, and Joan Nassauer and informed by the latest science on habitat function, climate change, and social vulnerability. We begin by setting the context, examining, and cataloging existing ecological conditions. We examine the site through the experience and understanding of community members. And then with the input of the community, we attempt to forecast future change and long-term viability through a socio-ecological lens. The end-product is a flexible and adaptive plan tested against both community input and client goals.

Filling the Gaps: Vacancy as the Foundation for Enhanced Corridors and Patches

Inherent in our work is the necessity to examine the city at multiple scales. Since nature does not end at a political or property boundary, we look beyond the edges of the neighborhood to the city, and beyond the city to regional and continental relationships. A view through the lens of ecology reinforces the cascading effects of every decision and the potential for greater function, healing, and connection. Such a view also permits solutions that satisfy differing community needs and drivers.

Prior to our work in Atlanta, Biohabitats supported a green network planning process in collaboration with the City of Baltimore's Planning Department and Office of Sustainability. Baltimore, Maryland's largest city, lies midway between our nation's capital in Washington, D.C. and the historic colonial capital in Philadelphia, PA. It serves as a pivotal port of entry for the U.S. economy and is home to literary and historical giants including poet, Edgar Allen Poe, and the first black Supreme Court Justice, Thurgood Marshall. Baltimore is infamous in the public imagination thanks to popular television dramas like *Homicide: Life on the Streets* and the *Wire*.

In direct contrast to the issues facing Atlanta, Baltimore is experiencing a diminishing population, down from 900,000 residents in the 1950s to around 609,000 today.[9] In the aftermath of the financial crisis of 2007-2009, the city recorded 16,800 vacant buildings and approximately 16,000 vacant parcels where structures once stood.[10] The Jacob France Institute has noted that this widespread vacancy impacts communities of color at much higher rates than more affluent, predominantly white, neighborhoods. And the patterns of vacancy seen in Baltimore have resulted in a term coined by Morgan State University professor Lawrence Brown: the "black butterfly." This refers to the shape of an area across the city in plan-view that reflects patterns of historic and systemic racism policies like redlining, segregation, and historic disinvestment in communities of color.[11]

FIG.4 TOP Baltimore Green Network neighborhood pilot project concept. City of Baltimore Department of Planning, Office of Sustainability

FIG.5 OPPOSITE PAGE Baltimore Green Network Map. Baltimore Department of Planning, Office of Sustainability

Former Baltimore Mayor, Stephanie Rawlings Blake, created a series of programs in the early 2010s to provide incentives for redevelopment and vacant land adoption but it did not have the desired effect at a scale to serve community needs. These communities, fragmented by vacancy, were underserved in access to open space and affordable goods and services. The City's Office of Sustainability within the Department of Planning saw an opportunity to plan in parallel for community revitalization and a citywide green network that met multiple goals associated with biodiversity and ecosystem services. The end result would provide a playbook for reinvestment with pilot projects in neighborhoods across the city.[12]

Like Atlanta, the Baltimore Green Network Plan views the city through a lens of ecology and community input. Baltimore has its own unique ecological story to tell, one that many residents know as deeply as their family roots. It sits at the northern end of the Chesapeake Bay, our nation's largest tidal estuary. The region provides important habitat stops among wetlands, marshes, fields, and forests for birds traveling their annual routes between the Arctic Circle and warmer wintering spots southward along the Atlantic Flyway. The Bay is also home to over 3,700 native species of plants and animals and serves as the economic and ecological heart of the region—known for its crab cakes, oysters, and other seafood delicacies and its variety of water sports and recreation.[13] Baltimore's landscape is defined by a series of rivers and streams that course through the city, emptying into the Inner Harbor at the Middle Branch of the Patapsco River and then eventually into the Bay.

To develop the Green Network Plan, the Biohabitats team worked with Baltimore's City Planning department to develop a method to categorize vacant lots for ecological function, open space access, economic redevelopment potential, pedestrian safety, livability, and connections to historic resources. The city planning staff met regularly with residents to build a deeper understanding of specific community needs and desires for economic opportunities, increased safety mechanisms, and equitable access. While looking outward to the habitat corridors and patches that extended beyond the city boundaries, our team also looked inward to see

Baltimore Green Network Vision Plan

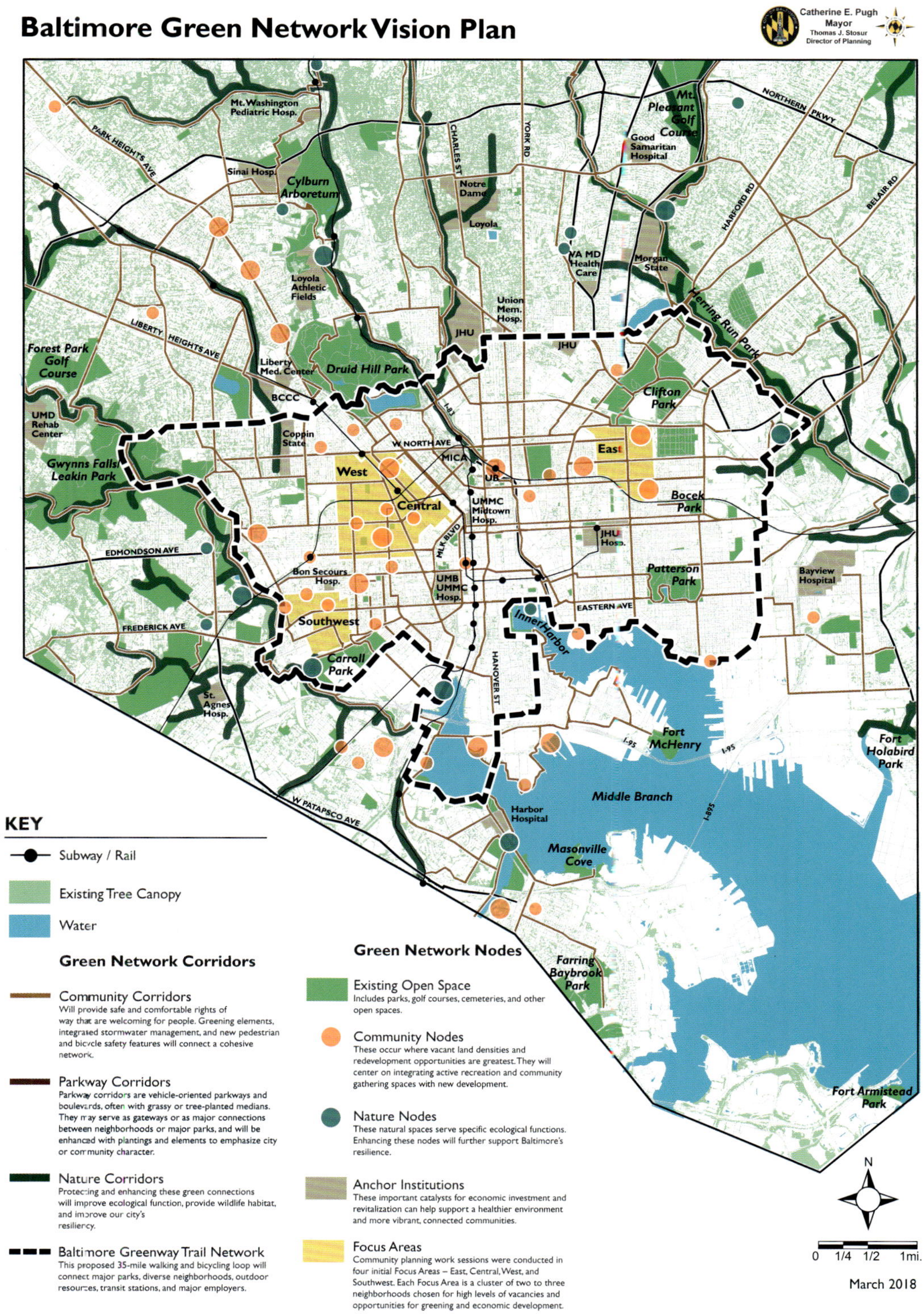

ACKNOWLEDGEMENTS

Baltimore Green Network Plan: Client: City of Baltimore Department of Planning, Baltimore, MD
Team: Biohabitats Inc., with Floura Teeter Landscape Architects, Toole Design Group, Living Design Lab; Partners include Civic Works, Rails to Trails, Blue Water Baltimore

Atlanta City Design Nature: Client: City of Atlanta Department of City Planning, Atlanta, GA
Team: Biohabitats Inc., with Perez Planning & Design, Planners for Environmental Quality, Alta Planning and Design, American Forests, the Conservation Fund, Cooper Carry, & Neil Norton

the flows for wildlife habitat in the forest and stream corridors. After determining a series of focus areas for vacant utilization, more detailed design discussions were held with community members to explore how green infrastructure could be integrated in parcels in their neighborhoods.

Each participating neighborhood had specific priorities to integrate with green space; securing ecological function from small actions that create novel habitat. In one community, residents converted closed streets to a central park space with plantings that doubled as gateway features [FIG. 4]. Pollinator gardens were added along with upgrades for stormwater management and a water play feature. Flexible social spaces connected nearby residential streets. Another neighborhood designed a playground in a pocket park surrounded by new native woodland and pollinator gardens. A third neighborhood developed a plan for a park with a memorial for a fallen female firefighter alongside a playground designed specifically for small children and their elderly caregivers. A local institution agreed to support the maintenance and community programs associated with the park space as the concept gained momentum with a local community organization that provided pro-bono design and construction support. These plans were a step beyond the typical urban planning result: a promise to the community that the City had real intentions to implement the projects.

The final Baltimore Green Network plan [FIG. 5] provides a framework of nodes and corridors serving the community and nature. It targets resources in areas of underinvestment with funding strategies and partnership opportunities and provides a framework for connecting the City's residents, especially those in underserved communities, to nature. New parks and natural areas provide opportunities to create enhanced ecological features, increased tree canopy, and integrated green infrastructure practices.

Conclusion

In Atlanta and Baltimore, an urban ecological framework approach centers city planning efforts in a deeper understanding of socio-ecological conditions at nested scales. From the micro-scale pocket park integrating play and habitat features, to neighborhood open spaces with enhanced forest and stream corridors, the importance of storytelling and community engagement is critical to the success of each. Economic development, water quality, and wildlife all benefit. Unforeseen circumstances allow plans to evolve as communities take ownership and express their needs. This approach embraces the organic and dynamic nature of living systems as foundational to planning for a resilient city. It assumes that the community's basic needs are being met already. If not, those will likely be the primary concern at the neighborhood scale. An urban ecological framework may have to wait until housing, education, food equity, transit access, etc. are addressed, if these cannot truly be addressed in parallel with long-term planning work. In polarizing times, we have seen seeds of doubt sown with regard to climate change, science- and data-based work, and the importance of biodiversity to long-term resilience. There is a strength to starting in the community, uncovering and sharing personal relationships and experiences with nature that speak to an individual's identity and health; creating a unique connection to the science and the implications of inaction. This ecological planning approach, taking a holistic view of urban ecology, seeks to revitalize the urban fabric by capitalizing on the unique landscape typologies that define a city's identity, increasing citizen involvement and becoming a springboard to improved policies.

Endnotes

1. Georgia Tech GIS Research Team at the Georgia Tech Center for Spatial Planning Analytics and Visualization Team, "Urban Tree Canopy in the City of Atlanta," *Trends in Atlanta's Tree Canopy Coverage from 2008 to 2014,* accessed March 13, 2021, https://www.arcgis.com/apps/Cascade/index.html?appid=2bd29ac86b5546078d84b6c7faeca066.
2. Atlanta Regional Council, "Atlanta Regional Council Forecasts Show Metro Atlanta Population to Grow by 2.9 Million and Reach 8.6 Million by 2050," *Press Release*, October 10, 2019, https://atlantaregional.org/news/press-releases/metro-atlanta-population-to-grow-by-2-9-million-and-reach-8-6-million-by-2050-atlanta-regional-commission-forecasts-show/.
3. City of Atlanta Department of City Planning, "Atlanta City Design: Aspiring to the Beloved Community," *Atlanta City Design,* accessed March 13, 2021, https://online.flowpaper.com/72b006f2/ACDSecondPrintFINAL180820/#page=10 and https://www.atlcitydesign.com/.
4. The King Center, "The Beloved Community," *The King Philosophy - Nonviolence 365,* accessed March 13, 2021, https://thekingcenter.org/about-tkc/the-king-philosophy/.
5. City of Atlanta Department of City Planning, "Atlanta City Design: Nature." *Atlanta City Design,* accessed March 13, 2021, https://www.atlantaga.gov/home/showdocument?id=48625.
6. E.O. Wilson, "E.O. Wilson Biodiversity Foundation Website - Mission Statement," accessed March 13, 2021, https://eowilsonfoundation.org/mission-statement/.
7. Matthew P. White, Ian Alcock, James Grellier, Benedict W. Wheeler, Terry Hartig, Sara L. Warber, Andie Bone, Michael H. Depledge & Lora E. Fleming, "Spending at least 120 minutes a week in nature is associated with good health and wellbeing," *Nature.com Scientific Reports*, Volume 9, Article Number 7730, (June 13, 2019), https://www.nature.com/articles/s41598-019-44097-3.
8. Jill Suttie, "How Nature Can Make You Kinder, Happier, and More Creative," *Greater Good Magazine: Science-Based Insights for Meaningful Life,* (March 2, 2016), https://greatergood.berkeley.edu/article/item/how_nature_makes_you_kinder_happier_more_creative.
9. Colleen McHugh, "Cutting Through the Red Tape: How Baltimore's Vacant Lot Programs Have Made it Easier for Communities to Revitalize the Underutilized and Blighted Spaces in Their Neighborhoods," *web.mit.edu/nature/projects,* Fall 2021, accessed March 13, 2021, http://web.mit.edu/nature/projects_12/pdfs/McHughBaltimoreVacancy1SMALL.pdf.
10. Ian Duncan, "In 2010, Baltimore had 16,800 vacants. Eight years and millions of dollars later, the number is down to 16,500," *The Baltimore Sun,* April 26, 2018, https://www.baltimoresun.com/maryland/baltimore-city/bs-md-ci-vacant-demolition-blocks-20180227-story.html.
11. Brett Theodes, Eric Hangen, Brady Meixell, Christina Baird, Daniel Wood, Lionel Foster, Elizabeth Forney, and David Hinson, ""The Black Butterfly": Racial Segregation and Investment Patterns in Baltimore," *The Urban Institute,* February 5, 2019, https://apps.urban.org/features/baltimore-investment-flows/.
12. City of Baltimore Department of Planning, "Baltimore Green Network Plan," September 2018, accessed March 13, 2021, https://www.baltimoregreennetwork.com/.
13. Caitlyn Johnstone, "Train Your Eye To Watch for Winter Birds," *Chesapeake Bay Program,* December 23, 2020, https://www.chesapeakebay.net/news/blog/train_your_eye_for_winter_birds.

2 BUILDING ECOLOGICAL INFRASTRUCTURES

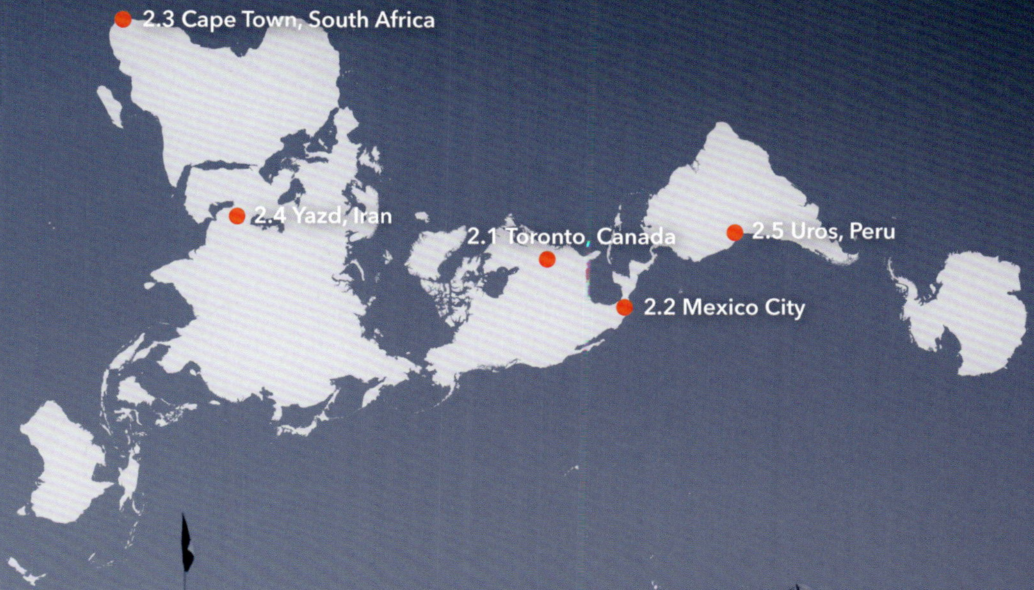

Building Ecological Infrastructures demonstrates the potential of designed or natural landscape systems to serve as performative urban infrastructures by cleansing water, regulating floods, and restoring culture through a transdisciplinary landscape approach offering ecologically rich environments that mitigate environmental degradation while sparking new socio-economic processes that strengthen metropolitan resilience. The chapters highlight built projects and programs that can improve livability in urban environments using hybrid, nature-based solutions facilitated by innovative technologies that seek a balance of local ecology with complex engineering.

2.1

Port Lands Flood Protection

A Landscape Infrastructural Approach

Shannon Baker, Sonja Vangjeli

The Don River drains one of Canada's most urbanized watersheds, its headwaters originating from the glacial aquifers of the Oak Ridges Moraine stretching about 38 km to Toronto's Lake Ontario shoreline. The Port Lands Flood Protection Project (PLFP), one of the largest river revitalization projects currently underway in North America, will recreate a kilometer-long naturalized outlet for the flood-prone channelized river by moving 1.4 million cubic meters of soil on underused post-industrial brownfield lands, resulting in a 30-hectacre park system of diverse landscapes and riverine habitats. A unique example of a landscape infrastructural approach on a massive scale, the $1.25 billion project will provide flood protection to 250 hectacres of surrounding postindustrial lands only two km away from the central business district, preparing the area for redevelopment and unlocking billions of dollars of investment on Toronto's waterfront. The project reimagines the connection between land and water, river and lake, as well as the connection between people and place. To realize this vision on a complex post-industrial lakefill site, a significant multi-disciplinary effort is underway to design and construct creative landscape and infrastructural solutions to mitigate risk while restoring ecology and public uses to the site. The project is the outcome of a decades-long planning and design process, spearheaded by community advocacy in the 1980s–1990s to reintegrate the river valley with the city and revitalize its ecology after a long history of industrial degradation and urban transformation over the past two centuries.

Historical Evolution

The Don River has been co-evolving with the city of Toronto since its founding in 1793. Perceptions of the river, and the series of plans and major transformations it has undergone over the past two centuries have reflected the aspirations of the city and its shifting attitudes toward nature during each period of its growth.[1] In the span of a century the river valley and marshland at its outlet were transformed from a biodiverse ecosystem that supported Indigenous peoples pre-colonization, to a central productive landscape that supplied timber and energy for the establishment of the new town of York, to a marginal industrial wasteland and liability

OPPOSITE PAGE Port Lands Flood Protection and Don River mouth under construction showing excavation, cutoff walls, and river channel meander, in close proximity to Toronto's downtown core. Stephanie Braconnier, Waterfront Toronto

FIG.1 Channelized river and industrial polluting land uses in the Port Lands, circa 1930. City of Toronto Archives.

FIG.2 Hurricane Hazel flooding in 1954. City of Toronto Archives.

that needed "improvement." Over the course of the 19th century the river became a cheap sink for the wastes of industrial production and urban expansion, making it a sacrificial landscape for the city's growth and prosperity.[2] The heavy pollution, foul odors, and fears of water-borne diseases, coupled with the desire to eliminate unpredictable flood impacts, led to a series of major engineering works to "tame the river" and its marsh into a predictable infrastructural landscape for industry and transportation.[3] The Don Improvement Project of 1880 and the Harbor Commissioners Plan of 1912, transformed the natural meander of the river and vast Ashbridges Bay Marsh at its outlet into a series of concrete channels, docks, and filled port industrial areas, seeking to "improve nature" into a controlled system for economic development [FIG.1].[4] In the 20th century the river valley continued to play a key infrastructural role with the construction of the Don Valley Parkway, as a transportation corridor that facilitated suburban expansion, but severed the Lower Don from its surrounding communities. The outward growth of the city also continued to increase sewer discharges into the river further polluting its lower reaches, to the point that in 1969 an environmental group called Pollution Probe held a symbolic funeral announcing the death of the Don River.[5]

The catastrophic flood impacts of Hurricane Hazel in 1954 [FIG.2] brought to light the river's vital ecological function as a stormwater management corridor for the city's most urbanized watershed, marking a turning point in attitudes towards the value and need for conservation of the river valley and its system of ravines. Growing community activism over the following decades led to the formation of the Task Force to Bring Back the Don, a grassroots organization formalized by Toronto City Council in 1990 to begin the renewal of the most degraded lower part of the river. Its 1991 report featured a restoration strategy by environmental design firm Hough Stansbury Woodland which included the re-creation of minor meanders within the existing channel and gradual re-creation of a delta and marsh where the river meets the lake.[6] The strategy was based on the understanding of the valley as an interconnected "natural" and "human" system that would require interventions over many years to "return the river to a state of health" and recreate a sense of place.[7] This vision established the idea of "a naturalized river mouth bordered by parks" as part of larger plans to redevelop the waterfront in the 2001 Central Waterfront Secondary Plan.[8] After a series of environmental assessments led by public agencies Waterfront Toronto and the Toronto and Region Conservation Authority, an international competition was held in 2007 and won by the landscape architecture firm Michael Van Valkenburgh Associates (MVVA) with the Port Lands Estuary Proposal. The proposal was the basis of design for the PLFP project, which, after another decade of efforts to secure funding, began construction in 2018. The Don River has gone full circle from the center of York, relegated to the industrial periphery, and now to be revitalized as the center of the City's future waterfront development in the Port Lands. Like its predecessors, this vision for the river mouth reflects the values of its time, balancing the desire for naturalization with engineered flood control to enable waterfront redevelopment on a post-industrial landscape.

FIG.3 Construction workers anchoring logs and boulders to build bioengineered river bank.
Vid Ingelvicks & Ryan Walker

Building Ecological Infrastructure

The PLFP project is being designed and engineered with nature; referencing natural systems and analogue sites in its design evolution, and mimicking natural forms with bioengineering elements. The work of designing and reconstructing the river necessitates work across disciplines. Led by landscape architects, a team of environmental, geotechnical, civil, structural, water resource, marines and coastal and electrical engineers, soils scientists, aquatic and terrestrial biologists have worked inter-disciplinarily in order to create a highly complex system of ecological infrastructure. This collaborative and iterative interdisciplinary design process created a constant feedback loop, wherein complex site conditions were responded to with innovative solutions, driving changes to the design ranging from the form of the river, to the shape of the landforms on site, constructing nature in a post-industrial landscape. The design process differed from what can traditionally be a more siloed one, wherein each discipline provides input in isolation in a more linear workflow. Working in a collaborative and iterative way fostered design innovation, with team members challenging and inspiring one another to find creative and resilient solutions to design problems. This approach could serve as a model for future landscape infrastructure projects, wherein landscape architects take a lead role in integrating other disciplines into a larger design vision.

The aim of PLFP is to recreate an ecologically functional river mouth, protect at-risk lands from flooding, and thus spur the revitalization of a large portion of Toronto's waterfront. Once lifted out of the floodplain, the new neighborhood envisioned on Villiers Island will establish new connections between downtown Toronto, the river, and the lake with an approach that is defined by sustainability, resiliency and innovation. The re-creation of the mouth of the river achieves these aims through a series of highly engineered systems that will ultimately perform with high ecological integrity [FIG.3]. A key component of this restoration is the return of the river to a more natural meandering form through the fill material placed in the early 1900s, when the marshlands were filled and the river was channelized. Preliminary work done through the environmental assessment stage extended the river south and then west in a gentle arch to the inner harbor and Lake Ontario. In the detailed design stage, the path of the river was reviewed by landscape architects, hydrologists, and ecologists, and more sinuosity was incorporated into the meander belt of the river. Through careful study of analogous sites along the Lake Ontario shoreline such as the Humber Bay marshes

FIG.4 Don River's new naturalized outlet into the Toronto Harbor in baseflow and regulatory flood conditions. Michael Van Valkenburgh Associates

and Duffins Creek, the geometry of the meanders bends was adjusted to reflect a more natural form, elevations were more finely resolved, and features such as natural levees and valley frames were incorporated into the design. A hydrodynamic model was used throughout the design process to establish critical design parameters for flood conveyance, and to calibrate floodplain stabilization features.[9] Riverbank and lowland valley features were designed to accommodate fluctuating water levels, and to convey flood waters during a regional storm. The incorporation of a more sinuous channel created larger and more contiguous riparian habitat zones, creating ecological as well as experiential complexity [FIG. 4].

The lake level has significant influence over the ecological habitat created along the length of the mouth and has also been a significant factor

in the excavation and construction of the river valley. The fill material used to create the Port Lands in the early 1900s is of low geotechnical quality, and is also underlain by compressible peats, given the historical presence of the Ashbridges Marsh. These soils are now also heavily contaminated because of years of industrial use. The shallow groundwater elevation resulting from the proximity of the lake, combined with environmental contamination and low geotechnical quality soils necessitated the creation of an engineered river valley system constrained on either side by cutoff walls and a horizontal risk-management measure barrier which effectively isolates the river valley from surrounding soils and groundwater. Thus, although the river will be reconnected to the lake in a much more natural form, not all ecological functions can be fully restored. The hydraulic cycle of the river will never be reconnected via groundwater given the presence of contaminants in the surrounding area soils and groundwater, and the fluvial geomorphological processes will be arrested with bioengineered elements such as rootwads and crib walls, constraining the river within its protective barrier [FIG.5]. Although it is an isolated system, this isolation protects the river from the underlying contaminants, and protects against those contaminants also reaching the lake.

The industrial heritage and invisible remnant infrastructures of the Port Lands have also been integrated into the design of the river valley and parks, influencing the landforms and construction techniques in ways that are not readily apparent. The constraint of treating and retaining most of the soil on site due to contamination and balancing cut and fill, despite the large-scale excavation of the river valley, resulted in a design opportunity to create a striking promontory park overlooking the outlet of the river where an industrial dock and Marine Terminal once stood.

FIG.5 Don River mouth under construction, showing installation of bioengineered crib wall (anchored logs and boulders) and fabric encapsulated soil (FES). Sonja Vangjeli

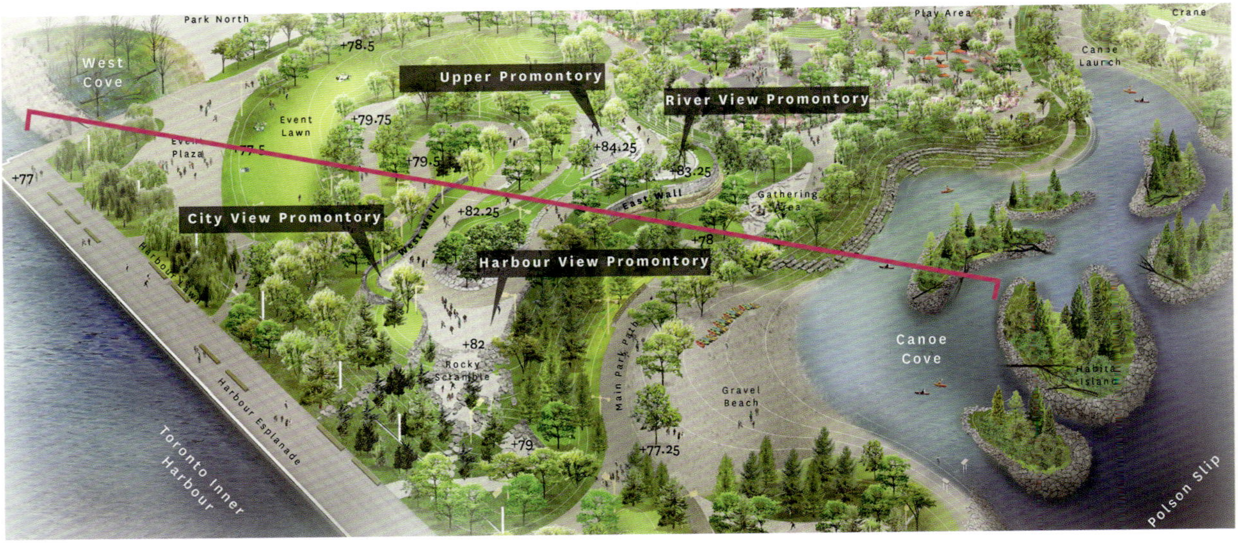

In 2017, Marine Terminal 35 was fully engulfed in fire, and was later assessed to be structurally unsound. In the master planning stages of the project, the building, a listed heritage resource, was to be incorporated into the plans for Promontory Park south [FIG. 6], a regional destination park envisioned for the site. The demolition of the building changed the vision for the site, and the plans shifted to accommodate more excess fill from the river valley excavation into a large landform. The site, a quay bounded by two slips, is retained on three sides by dockwalls that are tied back across the site, and diagonally to one another in some instances. The constraints of the dockwall system had to be carefully considered and balanced against the desire to store as much excess fill on site as possible. In order to balance these two somewhat opposing project objectives, a system of lightweight fill and mechanically stabilized earth retaining walls have been designed in order to minimize load on the dockwall tiebacks and maximize fill where possible. Ultimately, the promontory landscape will appear as a natural rock outcrop, taking inspiration from the shale-lined Don Valley further upriver, affording park visitors dynamic views back to the skyline of Toronto, and creating varied habitat for wildlife [FIG. 7].

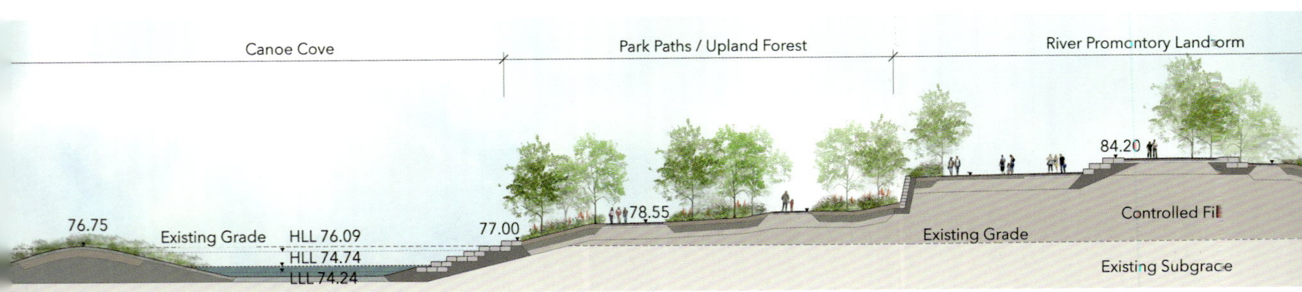

In addition to the large promontory, the design for the park also imagines a canoe cove, created along the northern boundary of what is now Polson Slip. This undulating landscape will create a more diverse aquatic habitat, as well as afford park users with more opportunity to interact with the mouth of the river. The habitat to the south will build on what has been created at the West Cove in Promontory Park North [FIG. 8] as part of the advanced work through the Cherry Street Lakefilling project, which created the aquatic habitat at the mouth of the Keating Channel. The creation of the Promontory Park South landscape requires careful consideration of the geotechnical conditions underpinning the landscape, the marine engineering considerations of the dockwall limitations, as well as environmental considerations regarding contamination. The historic Atlas Crane, one of the last on the Great Lakes, will also be preserved in situ, adding complexity to the geotechnical considerations for soil movement and settlement, as well as dockwall loading. Construction sequencing of this area is complex, involving soil storage, dockwall modifications to create the cove, and careful soil management related to the requirements of the environmental regulations.

FIG.6 OPPOSITE PAGE Promontory Park and Canoe Cove rendered axonometric showing the diversity of park experiences created along the new river bank. Michael Van Valkenburgh Associates

FIG.7 BOTTOM Sections through Promontory Park and Canoe Cove showing the topography created with excavated soil. Michael Van Valkenburgh Associate

FIG.8 ABOVE West Cove showing habitat creation techniques to be used along the river valley. Vid Inglevics & Ryan Walker

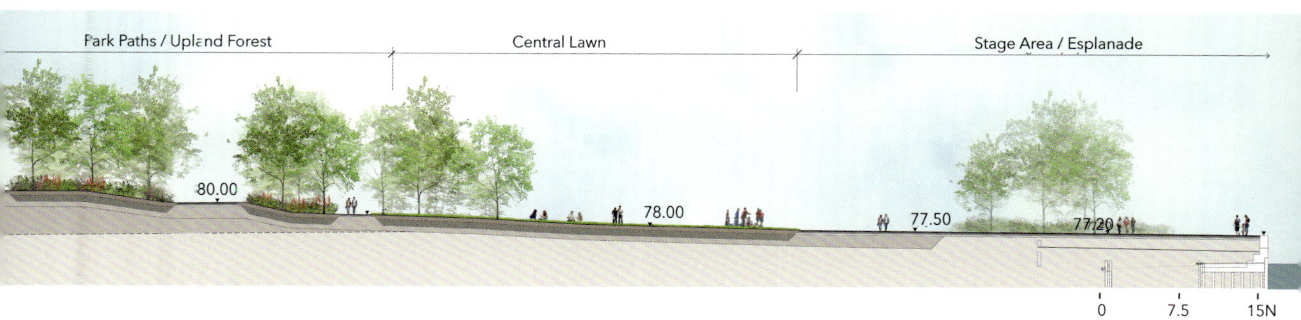

Leading With Landscape

The river valley is part of a larger system of parks and enabling infrastructure that will connect adjacent urban fabric and facilitate future development on Villiers Island. Once fully developed, Villiers Island will be home to between 8,000–10,000 people, and nearly 3,000 jobs in a neighborhood that will be a ten-minute walk from end to end. Creating streets that integrate within larger systems of the city necessitated taking a low impact design approach to the streets, using natural systems, or mimicking them in order to retain water on the landscape instead of letting it run off into the lake. Enhanced grass swales, bioswales, and open planters with structural soil cells have been incorporated into the streetscapes in order to capture water, create soil volume, and encourage a healthy soil microbiome The proximity to the lake, and the influence of lake levels on groundwater also impacted the design approach for the urban forest. Understanding that many of these tree pits will be partially inundated for periods of time seasonally influences their placement, as well as the species selected. The streets of the Port Lands were designed to be read as part of the parkland and riverine systems to which they are adjacent; in some instances the native planting design is somewhat irregular, referencing a hedgerow typology to create mid and upper canopy, as well as groundcover, thus varying the habitat provided.

The landscape architectural approach to the design of the parklands of PLFP acknowledges what is by now well understood; there are innumerable benefits for humans to spend time in nature and to form and strengthen connection with it. The design for the park system creates a place for people to reconnect with nature within walking distance of Downtown Toronto [FIG. 9]. The landscape approach emphasized

FIG. 9 Rendered view of the Don Greenway habitats and opportunities for viewing wildlife. Michael Van Valkenburgh Associates

programming and activation that capitalizes on improved access to the lake and creating strong connections to the public realm and regional trail system to ensure the site is widely accessible.[10] Given its size and situation, the design of River Park North also incorporates nature play on a scale not present elsewhere in Toronto.

Building ecological infrastructure on heavily degraded post-industrial sites requires a unique balance of engineering and ecological principles to control risks and provide enough certainty and safety for human habitation, while establishing living ecological systems and habitat for other species. The collaborative efforts of a team of highly specialized technical disciplines led by landscape architects with a systems-based approach has created design opportunities out of site constraints and constructability challenges. The unique site design is a physical manifestation of the collaborative design process. The integration of multiple site histories in the design will make for a rich layered landscape that will reveal glimpses of the story of the Don River's shifting identity and its reciprocal relationship with the city. The PLFP project will restore the central role of the Don River as part of Toronto's image and aspirations, inspiring further river revitalization efforts in the Don Narrows and its upper reaches and ravines, as well as work toward improving the health of the whole watershed. The territory of PLFP is bound to a system of interconnected infrastructural, cultural, and ecological field conditions. The planning and design of the Port Lands acknowledges this complexity and has been approached from a system-based perspective, which may serve as a model for future landscape infrastructural projects of this scale. Conceptualized as part of a larger whole, the reconstructed infrastructure weaves together the built with the natural. The design of those elements typically conceptualized as apart from nature, part of the human fabric of the city, have been knit with intention into the ecological framework within which they sit.

Endnotes

1. For an in-depth history of the many transformations the Don River and its surrounding landscapes have undergone, as well as the changes in perceptions and attitudes toward the river in relation to the growth of the city, please refer to Jennifer Bonnell's *Reclaiming the Don*.
2. Jennifer Bonnell, "Making an Industrial Margin," *Reclaiming the Don*. (Toronto: University of Toronto Press, Scholarly Publishing Division, 2014), 29–43.
3. Paul S. B. Jackson, "From Liability to Profitability: How Disease, Fear, and Medical Science Cleaned Up the Marshes of Ashbridges Bay," in *Reshaping Toronto's Waterfront*, eds. Gene Desfor and Jennefer Laidley (Toronto: University of Toronto Press, 2011), 75–96, 88.
4. Bonnell, "Taming a 'Monster of Ingratitude,'" *Reclaiming the Don*, 44–74.
5. Ray Ford, "Death and rebirth on the Don River," Canadian Geographic, June 1, 2011. https://www.canadiangeographic.ca/article/death-and-rebirth-don-river.
6. The Task Force to Bring Back the Don, *Bringing Back the Don*, (Toronto: 1991).
7. Michael Hough, Cities and Natural Process (Florence: Taylor & Francis Group, 2004), 39–56, 40.
8. Bonnell, "Remembering the Don," *Reclaiming the Don*, 177–187.
9. Michael Van Valkenburgh Associates, *Waterfront Toronto Design Review Panel Presentation*, January 24, 2018.
10. Michael Van Valkenburgh Associates, *Parks, Public Realm and River Projects, Basis of Design Report*, May 21, 2020.

2.2

Urban Water as a Resource, Not as Waste

The Case for Medium-Scale Hydric Districts in Mexico City

Adriana Chávez, Elena Tudela, Víctor Rico

The Hydric Districts is an alternative, medium-scale vision to address the water crisis in Mexico City while enhancing livability and urban biodiversity. Unlike large-scale, conventional gray infrastructure or small-scale green infrastructure projects, the medium-scale Hydric District expands the conventional notion of water resources through the principal premise that urban waters—rain, gray and black water—are a valuable resource and not waste.

The Ongoing Water Crisis in Mexico City

Water shortages are part of everyday life in Mexico City. According to SACMEX, Mexico City's Water Authority, 18 percent of the population does not receive water daily. At the same time, 32 percent cannot satisfy their most basic water needs and have to buy water from additional water trucks, known as *pipas*.[1] According to SACMEX, Mexico City residents use on average 320 liters of water daily, yet 77 percent of the inhabitants consume less than 150 liters per day.[2] Iztapalapa, an eastern low-income borough of two million inhabitants, cannot provide tap water to every household[3] due to a lack of water. The Iztapalapa water consumption rate is 235 liters per inhabitant per day. In contrast, the western, generally high-income borough of Miguel Hidalgo, with approximately 355,000 inhabitants, has a water consumption of 506 liters per inhabitant per day.[4] The contrast between Miguel Hidalgo and Iztapalapa exemplifies the vast inequalities in the water distribution of Mexico City, where wealthier areas use and receive more water than marginal areas across the city.

The current water management is extractive and relies on massive gray infrastructures such as the Lerma-Cutzamala system and an array of wells that deplete the city's aquifers.[5] The Lerma-Cutzamala system extends for more than 127 kilometers to deliver 22 percent of Mexico City's water. This water management system transcends Mexico City's administrative boundaries to operate. It is located in the State of Mexico, at a distance of 120 kilometers to the west of Mexico City. The complex system transports water from 1,600 meters above sea level, traversing the Mexico City Valley up to 2,702 meters. The remaining 68 percent of the water demand comes from the city's aquifers, three percent from springs

OPPOSITE PAGE Mexico City's grey infrastructure with surrounding built form. Oficina de Resiliencia Urbana (ORU)

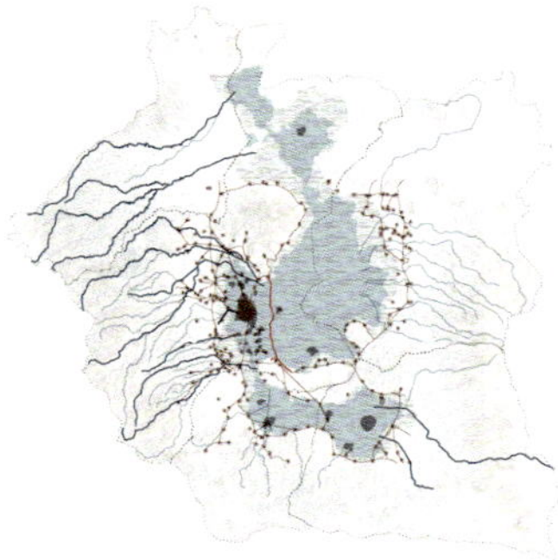

1325 - 1521

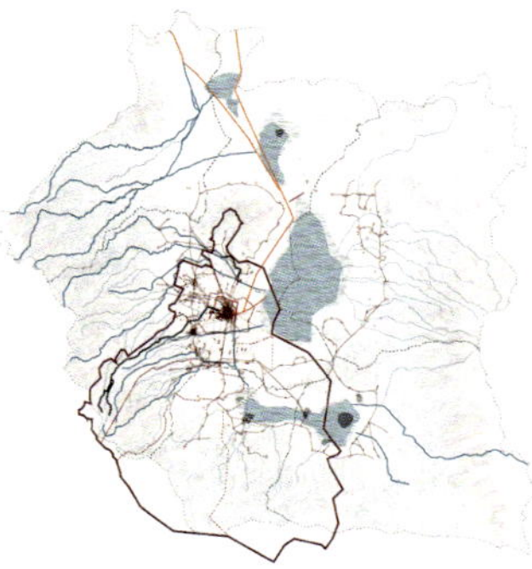

1824-1902

1950-1970

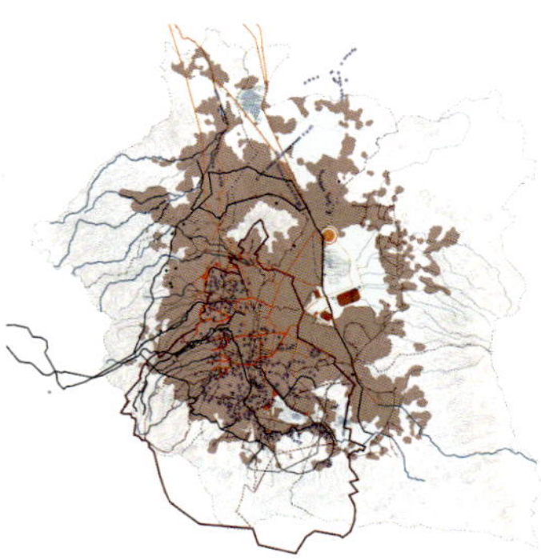

2000-2019

and seven percent from treated water.[6] Once it is used, water is expelled outside of the city's basin through a massive sewage system. The system is extractive and inefficient, while demanding enormous amounts of energy to operate. The linear water management is based solely on water import, aquifer depletion and sewage [FIG. 1].

Mexico City's water balance is uneven: the amount of the water extracted from the aquifer almost doubles the water volume currently infiltrated.[7] This water is extracted by 454 wells[8] that dehydrate Mexico City's underground at a rate of 14.6 cubic meters of water per second.[9] Exacerbating the drainage of the aquifer is the lack of green open spaces and permeable surfaces throughout the city that allow for water to naturally recharge the aquifer below. Mexico City has been built as an impermeable surface. Streets and open spaces are covered by asphalt and concrete, lacking natural water infiltration and creating a vicious cycle aligned to its intense water extraction model. This extraction model has associated collateral damages such as land subsidence, causing soil instability which compounds earthquake risks [FIG. 2].

Mexico City faces a paradoxical water challenge: while the city faces water shortages, it also faces periodic floods. Each year, during the summer rainy season, Mexico City confronts floods that can severely damage critical infrastructure. For example, in 2011, a flood event caused the evacuation of more than 2,000 homes, closed the subway system, affecting livelihoods and exposing the population to health risks due to polluted water and sewage overflows on the city's streets.[10] Despite significant investment in gray infrastructure to keep expanding the drainage system at larger scales, no gray infrastructural project has been successful in preventing floods during the rainy season. Floods are a recurring event related to the basin's wet ecology. Continuing to ignore ecological methods related to passive systems of this geography (e.g., capture or infiltration) will exacerbate the lack of access to needed water.

Mexico City's sewage system combines rainwater coming from the streets together with water consumed primarily by households, services, and industries, rendering gray water, black water, and rainwater (*residual* water). At a household level, water is used for the main hygiene activities of washing (i.e., clothes, dishes, showers) and sanitation (i.e., toilets).[11] The polluted water from these hygiene activities, whether in homes or public buildings, is at a rate of 71,000 liters of wastewater per second.[12] Of this, 85 percent is gray water, while 15 percent is black water.[13] The total amount of *residual* water that is treated in the city's 49 treatment plants[14] is only 15 percent,[15] including the new treatment plant in Atotonilco.[16] At the end of the linear cycle, the water is discharged into the Mezquital Valley, to the north in the State of Hidalgo, and into the Gulf of Mexico.[17] In a city that is currently experiencing a water crisis, due to water scarcity, amid floods and an abundance of rain, water cannot be regarded as a disposable resource. Ultimately, the city relies on a linear system of water import or extraction, usage, pollution, and drainage, while dismissing one of the city's most valuable assets: gray water, black water, and rainwater.

The Hydric District proposes to stop dehydrating the basins, a shift from a linear system of water extraction and expulsion to a circular model that is cyclical and keeps water in the basins as much as possible using decentralized circular water systems. This Hydric District proposal entails a paradigm shift in thinking from the prevalent notion of water as waste in Mexico City to wastewater as a valuable resource. In parallel, the broader urban fabric throughout Mexico City needs to undertake surface and gray infrastructure that favors absorption of greater amounts of rainwater for storage, infiltration, recharge, treatment, and reuse, by way of combining eco systems of gray infrastructure and nature-based solutions.

The Historic Evolution of the Water Crisis

Mexico City is the embodiment of a dramatic geographic transformation that started before 1520. Indigenous settlements inhabited a valley that accommodated five large wetlands during the dry season or a single water body—known as the Texcoco Lake—during the rainy season. The system was fed by 48 perennial and intermittent rivers and ravines, which dispersed into the mountains' fertile soil. Indigenous urban configurations attempted to adapt to the cyclical hydrological regimes of the valley's landscape, which varied from the rain and dry seasons. They built systems such as *albarradones* (dykes) and *chinampas* (agricultural parcels surrounded by water) to inhabit a seasonal and amphibious territory, using canals and agricultural floating islands as a mode of living with water.

In contrast, the Spanish conquerors saw water and seasonal floods as a significant threat to their urban expansion plans due to the difficulties implied through their methods of building in floodable wetlands. The decision to establish a new colonial settlement and the political center of the Spanish crown on the very epicenter of the Aztec Empire drove Spanish decision-makers to deploy a series of engineering strategies, in contrast to the Indigenous methods that worked with the cyclical hydronic systems. By lengthening the use of the water each season, they drained the basin progressively by eliminating the water from Mexico City's valley.[18] These infrastructural solutions started an irreversible process that has shaped the city, moving it from a managed waterscape to drained land.

Colonial city planning continued to neglect the hydrological structure, the water bodies, and the ecological structure of the land.[19] More recently, during the early 1900s, the construction of the first aqueducts, which conducted potable water to the city, recorded a point of no return for the aquifer's overexploitation. Towards the middle of the 20th century, draining the aquifer completely became an imminent endeavor that was viewed as a way to avoid floods and support the urban expansion that paralleled population growth.[20] Today, the valley's natural landscape system, formed

Symbology

- Lake
- Perennial river
- Intermittent rivers
- Topography
- Mexico City watershed
- Roads
- Settlements
- Water supply
- Dam
- Drainage
- Buried rivers
- Wells
- Mexico City political boundary
- Boroughs
- Urban sprawl
- Regulatory basins

FIG. 1 Mexico City's political boundaries evolution, urban expansion patterns and water supply and drainage infrastructure from 1325 to 2019. ORU - Oficina de Resiliencia Urbana, Anita Berrizbeitia and Arzoz

by rivers and wetlands, has been erased and neglected by the city's massive urban expansion; runoff water now flows on impervious surfaces. The water that flows downstream and the remnants of a once-robust ravine system are directly channeled to a series of dams and tunnels. Instead of water bodies that drain and fill cyclically with the seasons, we see on the lower lands a flooded urban fabric, including severe damage to livelihoods and public infrastructure such as hospitals, schools, and the transport system.

Between the Large-Scale Grey Infrastructure and the Small-Scale Green Infrastructure

The city's historical approach to address the water crisis has been either at the large scale of gray infrastructure[21] or, more recently, at the small scale, through piecemeal, green infrastructure projects. Large-scale gray infrastructure has proven insufficient, although the implementation of green infrastructure is incipient, disjointed, and currently lacks an operational framework to ensure its adequate long-term performance.

In recent years, Mexico City's government, including SACMEX and SEDEMA (Secretary of the Environment), has been implementing green infrastructure pilot projects with a goal to create multifunctional green spaces to support the city's sustainability.[22] Recent green infrastructure projects undertaken by the city include Towards a Water-Sensitive Mexico City (2016), Plan Hídrico de la Delegación Miguel Hidalgo (2016), Parque Lineal La Viga (2016), Quebradora Water Park (2017), Eco-ducto (2018), Parque la Mexicana (2018), Parque Lineal Ferrocarril de Cuernavaca (2019), Parque Cuitláhuac (2020), and Parque Cerro de la Estrella (2020). The efforts to build a new network of public spaces are part of Mexico City's Green Infrastructure Plan (2020). Although this vision and accompanying built projects represent a significant effort by the city to expand green infrastructure, they lack the large-scale investment of the gray infrastructure projects, which have opposite methods and goals.

FIG.2 Section through Mexico City's water basin showing the complexities of the territorial water regime. ORU - Oficina de Resiliencia Urbana, Anita Berrizbeitia and Arzoz

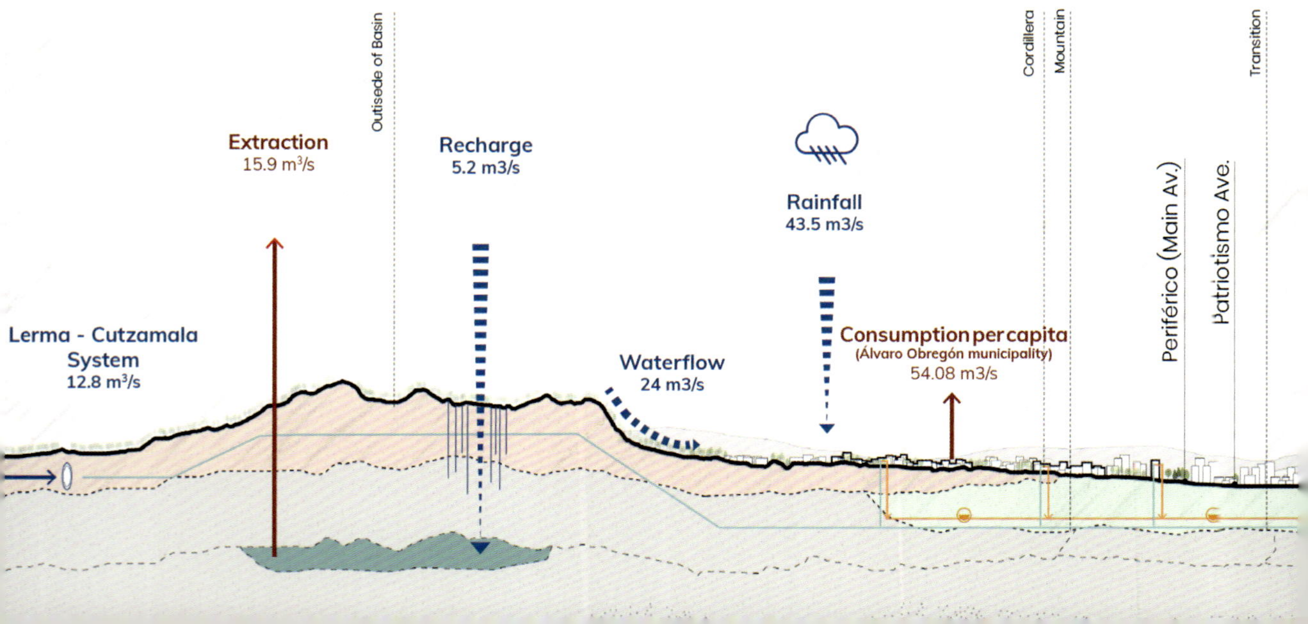

These small-scale green infrastructure projects serve as demonstrational and educational projects with broad social and environmental benefits, but are piecemeal, segregated, and built in the absence of a systemic, coordinated vision. The projects do not sufficiently address the necessary infrastructural functions of water harvesting, storage, treatment, and reuse; and their lack of an operative framework fails to respond, at the required scale, to the challenges of the water crisis.

In the face of the 21st century's growing challenges, water supply and drainage challenges will increase. With more frequent floods over an impermeable, asphalted, sinking mega-city, the water supply and associated drainage system will become even more inequitable. Communities will have less water; at the same time, they will also experience more floods. In response, the Hydric District advances a scalar approach and a shift from an extractive strategy to a more circular water management model. This idea represents the untapped potential of a new landscape approach to tackling one of Mexico City's most significant crises.

Landscape Approach to Transform the Water Paradigm Through Medium-Scale Solutions

The current water crisis is an opportunity to rethink water infrastructure with an innovative landscape approach, one that integrates green infrastructure into the city fabric with an interconnected ecosystem approach using public and private spaces, such as roads, parks, buildings, and water treatment plants inside of Mexico City's dense urban fabric. Mexico City is too large and complex to implement a water-sensitive urban model at the scale of the entire city. On the other hand, green infrastructure has failed to address the scale of the water crisis. Therefore, a medium-scale intervention that can tackle both the large-scale infrastructural issues and the more local-scale aspects of water, and one that is sensitive to the urban

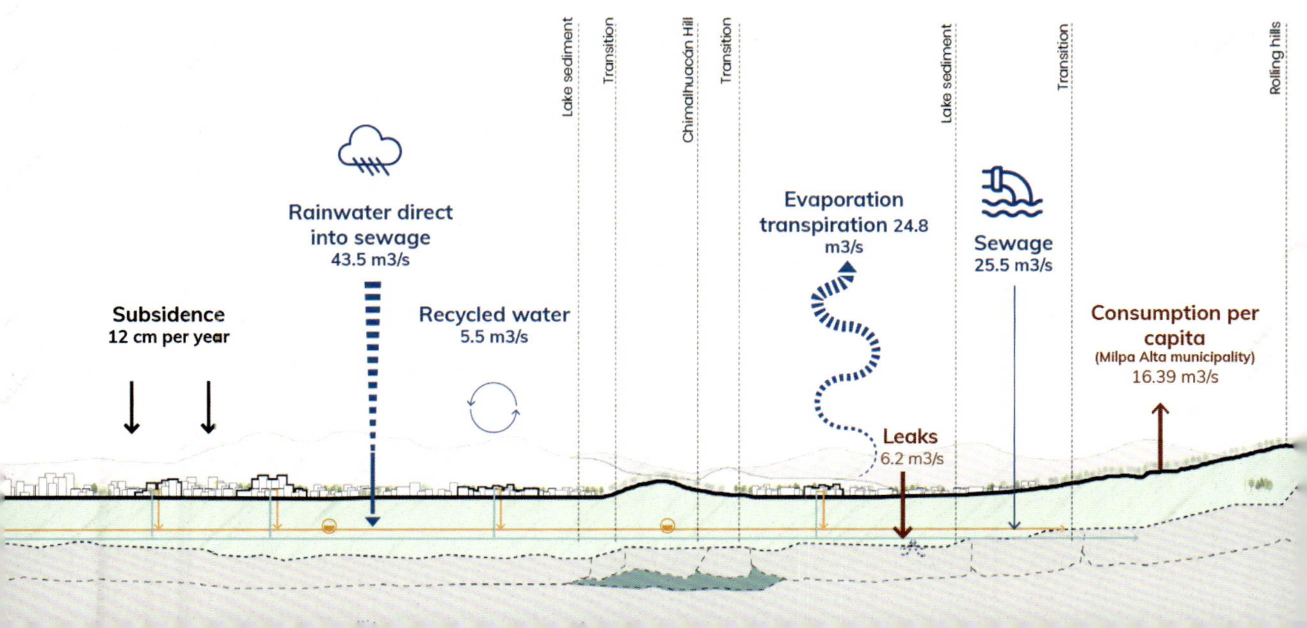

context, would have a positive impact on the city's water crisis. The medium-scale Hydric District will allow the implementation of integrated infrastructure solutions for capturing, storing, treating, and reusing the *residual* water currently channeled into the sewage system. A landscape approach can potentially help the city transition from the linear paradigm of water extraction and drainage to a circular water management model that can be replicated and escalated across the city.

The Medium-Scale Hydric District Framework and the Case of Tacubaya

The medium-scale Hydric District case study is set in Tacubaya, a historic neighborhood in Mexico City. At its core, the medium-scale Hydric District is a tool for urban planning and landscape design that uses water as a resource and not as waste. The model presents a design framework to integrate green and gray infrastructures for alternative decentralized urban water management by capturing, retaining, storing, treating, reusing, and infiltrating water. While this model aims to improve quality of life, urban identity, habitability, and perception of security, it will most importantly expand the current water availability in Tacubaya [FIG. 3].

Implementing the first medium-scale Hydric District in Tacubaya is politically, and spatially, feasible because:

There is a political will to invest in the neighborhood. In 2016, the city established the System of Action by Cooperation, or Sistema de Actuación por Cooperación (SAC) Tacubaya, an urban planning instrument to redevelop and densify the historic neighborhood of Tacubaya.[23]

Local authorities have shown willingness to revitalize the neighborhood's parks, streets, schools, and transport nodes, especially in areas where more underserved communities live. Yet, the series of public projects in this area lack an integrative framework for sustainable water management.

Tacubaya is a strategic neighborhood connected to Mexico City's economic center that has a strong relationship with water. A remnant of Tacubaya's historic hydric legacy still exists in the neighborhood's urban form within its historic parks, gardens and streets and is an ideal area for testing new collaborative schemes for water governance. The management model is no longer sufficient for providing the most basic water services for new development and is becoming increasingly central to the negotiation between urban development and water sustainability in the city, especially between government, NGOs, citizens, and private developers.

The conceptual design framework for the Tacubaya Hydric District proposes three main strategies:

Reveal the History

Using the historical understanding of a city as a point of departure, Mexico City, like many other cities, developed gradually, in layers and fragments. The strategy identifies an opportunity to portray the historical hydrological regimes in these layers as an important contributor to the city's urban structure.

Consolidate and Expand the Open Space System

Expand open spaces and incorporate multiple green infrastructure solutions to minimize the amount of impervious surfaces, so that the territory will function more like a sponge that allows water to infiltrate and replenish the aquifer, and less like a giant sewer that expels all types of water.

Urban Water, as a Resource, Not a Waste

Transcend the traditional extraction, import, contaminate, and drain cycle of water to create a system that integrates gray water, black water, and rainwater as an asset, and not as waste. Implementation of various strategies includes: capturing and storing water pouring from the sky, and treating and reusing gray and black waters while retaining and infiltrating water into the aquifer.

The three strategies are interrelated guidelines from Tacubaya's urban-environmental history. The introduction of water treatment facilities and green infrastructure in the Hydric District approach leverages the city's roads,

FIG.3 Tacubaya as a pilot project to test the Hydric District framework. ORU Oficina de Resilienca Urbana, Anita Berrizbeitia and Arzoz

FIG.4 Water-related interventions derived from the Hydric Districts: A Model for Sustainable Water Management Framework, Mexico City. ORU - Oficina de Resiliencia Urbana, Anita Berrizbeitia and Arzoz

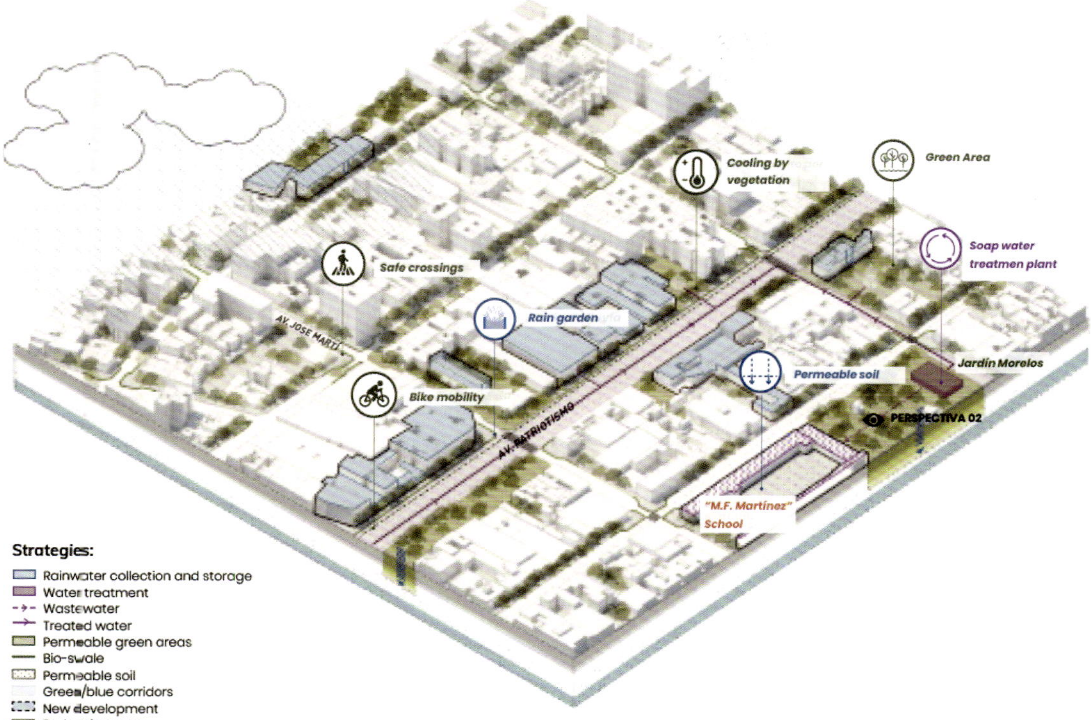
Cooling by vegetation
Green Area
Soap water treatmen plant
Safe crossings
Rain garden
AV. JOSE MARTÍ
Permeable soil
Jardín Morelos
Bike mobility
PERSPECTIVA 02
AV. PATRIOTISMO
"M.F. Martínez" School
Strategies:
Rainwater collection and storage
Water treatment
Wastewater
Treated water
Permeable green areas
Bio-swale
Permeable soil
Green/blue corridors
New development
Pedestrian area
Bikeway

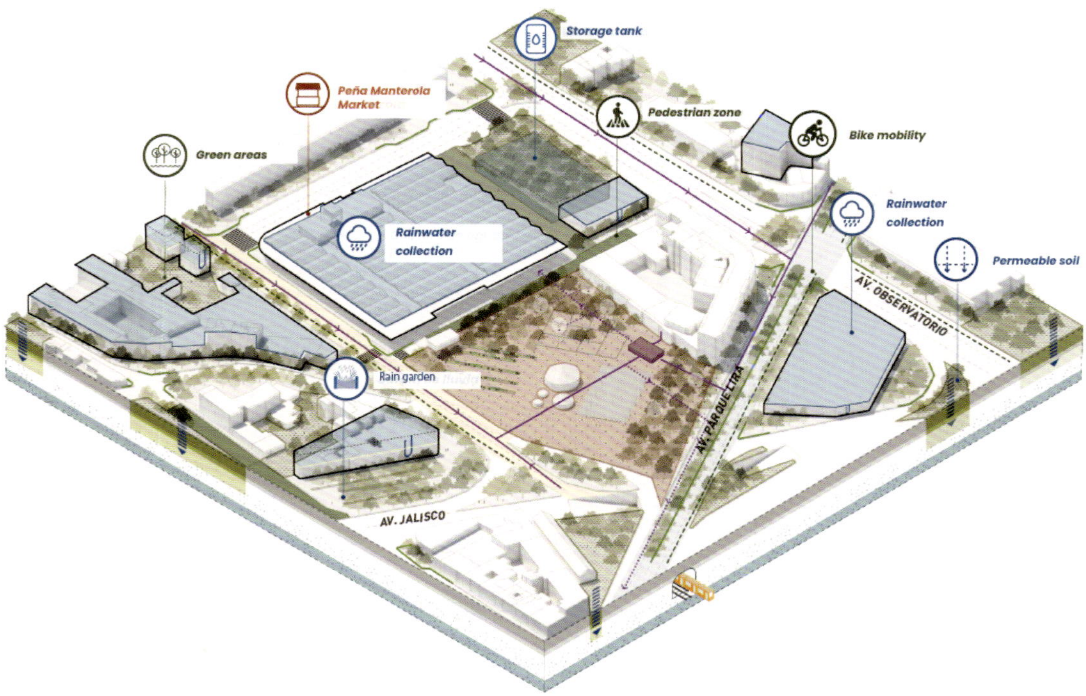
Storage tank
Peña Manterola Market
Pedestrian zone
Bike mobility
Green areas
Rainwater collection
Rainwater collection
Permeable soil
AV. OBSERVATORIO
Rain garden
AV. PARQUE LIRA
AV. JALISCO

open spaces, and buildings as infrastructural layers that expand water access for all and mitigate floods in Tacubaya.

The medium-scale Tacubaya Hydric District incorporates retrofitted open spaces such as parks, squares, streets, urban facilities, and new urban developments so that the whole district becomes a circular water management unit. Water from buildings is treated and reused in secondary activities that don't need potable water (e.g., toilets, car washes, street cleaning, etc.). Sustainable Urban Drainage Systems manages urban rainwater and runoff.

The proposal presents two design solutions for the Tacubaya Hydric District: (1) collecting and storing rainwater, in public buildings, streets, and public spaces; and (2) treating and reusing gray water and black water to envision public facilities as producers of gray water and black water and recipients of treated water for secondary activities [FIG. 4]. The solutions transform the current residual water into an additional source of water to city residents that desperately need it.

The vision includes 10 strategic interventions such as: (1) Tacubaya River Linear Park that recuperates the old river bed to mitigate floods and provide public space for leisure; (2) Water and connection corridors, as a street network with SUDS; (3) Interventions in the surroundings of historic buildings like Casa de la Bola or Edificio Ermita; (4) Recuperating historic gardens and plazas; (5) Connection between Tacubaya north and south; (6) Transformation of the Lira Park into the Lira Forest; (7) Construction of four local water treatment plants; (8) Revitalization of a network of markets; (9) Public amenities as water producers and receivers; and (10) Network of developments that treat and reuse water. Each of these interventions will integrate the three lenses of the framework previously mentioned to foster new models and alternative ways of inhabiting cities, guided by the universal principles of equity and sensitivity to the environment.

Conclusion

In the next 50 years, we foresee a more water-sensitive and decentralized model for Mexico City. The medium-scale Hydric District is a replicable and scalable framework, functional for other city areas. Scaling up medium-scale Hydric Districts across the city creates a path to achieve the vision of seeing wastewater as a valuable resource in cities that suffer from water shortages, and as a means to minimize the depletion of the world's aquifers. As a fundamental life resource, water is also evidence of the vulnerability of a population, whether abundant or lacking. One Hydric District can fulfill the essential need for water to residents, promote aquifer recharge and expand livable neighborhoods in cities.

ACKNOWLEDGMENTS

The project was completed under the guidance of Anita Berrizbeitia, Professor of Landscape Architecture and Chair of the Department of Landscape Architecture, Harvard Graduate School of Design, and with the support of the David Rockefeller Center for Latin American Studies, Mexico Innovation Fund Grants.

PROJECT TEAM

ORU team: Adriana Chávez Sánchez, Bernal Pérez Gálvez, Carolina Crespo Uribe, Elena Tudela Rivadeneyra, Iván Guzmán Estrada, Lauréline Lhuilier, Néstor Rangel Hernández and Victor Rico Espínola.

Collaborators: Mónica Arzoz Canalizo and Andrea Olavarrieta De La Torre.

Harvard Graduate School of Design: Anita Berrizbeitia

Client team: Mexico Innovation Fund Grants at the David Rockefeller Center for Latin American Studies

Endnotes

1. "Proyecto Final De Ley De Agua y Sustentabilidad Hídrica," Ciudad de México: Sistema de Aguas de la Ciudad de México, (2018).
2. Secretaría de Educación, Ciencia, Tecnología e Innovación. Gobierno de la Ciudad de México. ¿Cuánta agua residual se produce en la Ciudad de México? Ficha 2, 2019.
3. Michael Kimmelman, "Mexico City, Parched and Sinking, Faces a Water Crisis," The *New York Times*, February 17, 2017. https://www.nytimes.com/interactive/2017/02/17/world/americas/mexico-city-sinking.html.
4. Secretaría del Medio Ambiente de la Ciudad de México, «Delegación x delegación, habitante x habitante», accessed May 18, 2021, http://www.cuidarelagua.cdmx.gob.mx/delegacion.html.
5. *Sistema de Aguas de la Ciudad de México* (Ciudad de México: Infodf), accessed July 10, 2021, http://www.infodf.org.mx/pdfs/resoluciones/recur11/RR.1048-2011.pdf.
6. World Bank, "Agua urbana en el Valle de México: ¿Un camino verde para mañana?", *Comisión Nacional del Agua, Asociación Nacional de Empresas de Agua y Saneamiento, México* (2013).
7. Cecilia Lartigue, Sobreexplotación de mantos acuíferos en la CDMX, causa de fractura de tuberías y fugas de agua, Boletín UNAM-DGCS-212 (March 26, 2017). https://www.dgcs.unam.mx/boletin/bdboletin/2017_212.html.
8. Instituto de Acceso a la Información Pública del Distrito Federal *Expediente RR.1048/2011* (Ciudad de México, 2011).
9. Secretaría del Medio Ambiente de la Ciudad de México, «¿De cuánta agua disponemos?», accessed May 18, 2021, http://www.cuidarelagua.cdmx.gob.mx/consumo.html.
10. "Residents evacuated after floods in Mexico City," *BBC*, creado el 7 de septiembre de 2011, consultado el 16 de diciembre de 2019, https://www.bbc.com/news/av/world-latin-america-14823749/residents-evacuated-after-floods-in-mexico-city.
11. Secretaría de Educación, Ciencia, Tecnología e Innovación, Gobierno de la Ciudad de México. ¿Cuánta agua residual se produce en la Ciudad De México? Ficha 2, 2019.
12. Secretaría del Medio Ambiente de la Ciudad de México, «Pabellón Hídrico», http://www.data.sedema.cdmx.gob.mx/cambioclimaticocdmx/images/biblioteca_cc/pabellon-hidrico.pdf.
13. Secretaría de Educación, Ciencia, Tecnología e Innovación, Gobierno de la Ciudad de México, ¿Cuánta agua residual se produce en la Ciudad De México? Ficha 2, 2019.
14. Secretaría del Medio Ambiente de la Ciudad de México, «Pabellón Hídrico», http://www.data.sedema.cdmx.gob.mx/cambioclimaticocdmx/images/biblioteca_cc/pabellon-hidrico.pdf.
15. Secretaría de Educación, Ciencia, Tecnología e Innovación, Gobierno de la Ciudad de México, ¿Cuánta agua residual se produce en la Ciudad de México? Ficha 2, 2019.
16. Lorena Torres Bernardino, *La gestión del agua potable en la Ciudad De México: Los Retos hídricos De La CDMX: Gobernanza y Sustentabilidad* (Ciudad de México, CDMX: Instituto Nacional de Administración Pública, A.C., 2017).
17. Water drainage has created a productive territory which uses Mexico City's untreated water to irrigate agricultural fields to grow food that goes back to Mexico City.
18. For example, transformations of the Churubusco River in 1904 and the concretization of the La Piedad River in 1942 transformed the city's waterways into roads. Large-scale infrastructure started as a trend. Such is the case of the Great Canal, constructed in 1900 under President Porfirio Diaz, which, despite its extensive efforts to control water, did not stop floods.
19. Jorge Legorreta Gutiérrez, *El Agua y La Ciudad De México: De Tenochtitlán a La Megalópolis Del Siglo XXI* (Ciudad de México, CDMX: Universidad Autónoma Metropolitana, Unidad Azcapotzalco, División de Ciencias y Artes para el Diseño, Departamento de Evaluación del Diseño en el Tiempo, 2006).
20. From 1967 to 1975, a profound drainage system was built. The project consisted of a 68-kilometer system of concrete tunnels. However, overexploitation of underground water led to subsidence, which reversed the slope with which that system drained the water out of the city, resulting in an inefficient infrastructure. On the other hand, as the city demanded more water, in 1952, the supply system expanded outside of the basin, bringing water from the Lerma system that grew into the Lerma-Cutzamala system in 1978.
21. Sistema de Aguas de la Ciudad de México, ed. *El Gran Reto Del Agua En La Ciudad De México. Pasado, Presente Perspectivas De Solución Para Una De Las Ciudades Más Complejas Del Mundo* (Ciudad de México, CDMX: SACMEX, 2012).
22. "Infraestructura Verde CDMX," *Infraestructura Verde CDMX* (México, CDMX: SEDEMA, Gobierno de la Ciudad de México, 2018).
23. SEDUVI, "SAC TACUBAYA," SAC TACUBAYA, accessed July 10, 2021, http://seduvi.proyectosurbanos.cdmx.gob.mx/cetram/sac_tacubaya.html.

2.3

Livable Waterways for a Water-Sensitive Transition for Cape Town

Tamsin Faragher

"Camissa," as Cape Town is known to the Cape's Indigenous Khoisan people, refers to a "place of sweet waters." Located halfway between Europe and the East, the Cape became a critical fresh water stop for sailors and traders halfway *en route* to India in the 1500s. Over time, the area was settled and Cape Town, the Mother City, now occupies this freshwater landscape [FIG. 1]. The city's relationship with water, however, extends beyond its origins and has become central to its history and contemporary identity.

Most recently, the city captured global attention with an unprecedented 1:590-year drought that faced Capetonians with a potential "day zero."[1] Even though the drought ended in 2019, the focus on water remains critical with action directed through *Cape Town's Water Strategy*.[2] Aimed at transitioning the city to water sensitivity by 2040, key strategic actions include crafting a new relationship between Capetonians and water through livable waterways.

Today's waterways are, however, a far cry from the sweet waters of the past. In fact, if the health of waterways were a measure of a city's health, then Cape Town's would require life support.[3] The main conspirator in this "water health pandemic" is the "anti-nature" effect from the European-engineered stormwater infrastructure found throughout the city.[4] Masterminded to drain large parts of Cape Town's wetlands, it enabled development and resulted in the proliferation of segregated communities during the apartheid years [FIG. 2].

This chapter considers the transformative impact that the most recent drought has had on the City of Cape Town's strategic approach to water and the public's relationship with water. It investigates the effects that urban development and infrastructure have had on urban water resources and, more specifically, waterways. Thereafter it proposes and motivates for a landscape approach for the revitalization of waterways, before concluding with an overview of the implementation policy and early outcomes of the Livable Waterways Program. The task ahead is significant, as are the potential rewards. Healthy waterways are critical for resilience and livability. They are also important for connecting and integrating divided communities to nature resulting in a healthier, water-sensitive city.

OPPOSITE PAGE Winter flooding in Du Noon, north of Cape Town in winter 2021. Large portions of Cape Town are located in floodplains and wetlands positioned above aquifers that make them vulnerable to flooding in the rainy winter season. Bruce Sutherland, City of Cape Town

FIG.1 Confluence of the Liesbeek and Black Rivers and the Raapenberg Wetland where the battle of D'Almeida is believed to have occurred in 1510 (sahistory.org.za), Observatory, Cape Town. Bruce Sutherland, City of Cape Town

Water Scarcity in Cape Town

South Africa is one of the world's most unequal countries.[5] The staggeringly high unemployment rate and income disparities are experienced nation wide and the consequences exert extreme pressures on the natural and urban environments. Home to approximately four million Capetonians, rapid urbanization and the associated urban sprawl characterize this city, which in the year 2000, was thirty times its size than at the turn of the century. The sprawl located predominantly to the southeast started as a result of the Group Areas Act of 1950[6] and has negatively impacted the Cape Fynbos Biome.[7] The impacted ecologies include endemic aquatic ecosystems located in a small number of perennial and seasonal rivers and wetlands that are unique to the Cape.

The highly engineered concrete canals and culverts that obstruct the historic ebbs and flows of seasonal flooding further compound the urban impacts on the ecological integrity of the natural systems and their functions.[8] Drainage channels, located across the Cape Flats that overlie the Cape Flats Aquifer, are a prime example of this. Supplied with stormwater in the wet winter season and all-year with treated sewage flows, they have established a system of artificial "rivers" and canals that flow throughout the year.

The natural seasonal fluctuations of the water table, though partially managed, are still a significant hazard to families relocated to the Cape Flats during the Apartheid years. While the Apartheid laws have been

repealed, limited housing opportunities for low-income households, in-migration, population growth, and smaller, but greater numbers of households have forced informal settlement to occur throughout Cape Town's floodplains and wetlands. Despite the planning regulations that are in place to combat this, these "less valuable" landscapes have also attracted the attention of developers looking for "cheap" land. Given the significant impact of existing urbanization on the natural environment, the future thirst for land will escalate the loss of biodiversity and critically endangered areas and further expose families to flooding [FIG. 3].

These escalating urban development issues cannot be treated in isolation from the urgency of rainfall patterns and temperature increases caused by climate change. Expectations of greater unpredictability and fewer, shorter rainfall events with greater volumes will further increase water scarcity. Impervious surfaces created by paving and hardened grounds compacted by high temperature exposure,[9] will exacerbate these effects by concentrating runoff. This will heighten the risk of flooding and simultaneously limit groundwater infiltration [FIG. 4].

FIG. 2 Drainage canal in the Philippi Horticulture Area, above the Cape Flats Aquifer, Cape Town. Masixolo Feni, https://www.groundup.org.za/article/water_2541/

While rainwater is desirable for groundwater recharge and waterway flow, surface water is often polluted from road surfaces, agriculture, sewage from leaking infrastructure and discharge, and spills from wastewater treatment works, which makes it unsuitable. This combination of pollutants significantly impacts water quality across the city. In addition to the pollutants from formal systems, there are also those generated by informal sanitation. Because informal settlements and backyard communities develop spontaneously, they are sometimes established in advance of municipal services. In these instances, waterways are sometimes used for solid waste, graywater and sewage disposal, in addition to illegal dumping that further pollutes and sometimes damages the infrastructure. Recent monitoring of public health and recreation, ecological health, and physio-chemical properties, shows a progressive deterioration over all monitoring areas across watersheds.[10] This could be attributed in part to the lack of sanitation in informal settlements, but the significant impact of ageing infrastructure and leaking and overflowing sewers, cannot be understated. The threat of pollution impacts ecological connectivity and viability with the concomitant risk to human health, property values, security, amenities, flooding, water supply potential, ecosystem resilience, livability, and resilience.

The failure to manage these threats and waterways can be attributed to the treatment of waterways as stormwater infrastructure. This function was up until recently undertaken by engineers in the Roads Department, a profession that has traditionally regarded stormwater as a "common enemy."[11] In mitigation of this criticism, the national government is responsible for water resource management and raw water provision, which technically includes waterways. Waterways within municipal areas are consequently treated as stormwater infrastructure which falls under municipal responsibilities. This "infrastructure" treats stormwater as waste and disposes of it into wetlands, retention ponds and the sea in the name of flood management. While the stormwater management mandate now lies within the Water and Sanitation Department, the institutional legacy endures, as does the inability of the governance to enable complex, integrated water management across government spheres and within the municipality.

This complexity increased when the growing city's water demand exceeded the available supply from local watersheds and reliance was moved to the Western Cape Water Supply System (WCWSS) watersheds towards the north. Through this process, water became a "dammed" and "piped," invisible resource supplied by the national government and treated and engineered into and throughout the city by the municipality.

Counterintuitively, water resources from far afield were thus prioritized over the Cape Flats Aquifer and the Table Mountain Group Aquifer that lie beneath the city. These resources were used in the recent past by private individuals for garden irrigation. During the drought,

some extended their use to include household supply and, in addition, the variety of users also increased to include non-household users.[12] The municipality has for the first time begun to operationalize groundwater for supply and by 2040, it will represent seven percent of the city's water supply. Until now, there has been limited incentive (and no mandate) for the municipality to manage waterways and groundwater. This will need to change given the shifts in supply to sources within their management area.

And Cape Town's urban water cycle is changing in a number of ways. These include the introduction of treated effluent for groundwater recharge that creates circularity and reduces wastewater outflows. Re-establishing the ecological functioning of waterways will potentially improve water quality and, where practical, they will reconnect to aquifers for recharge, while also providing flood management.[13] Together, these interventions are establishing a hybrid urban water system comprising the natural and urban water systems and centralized and decentralized sources at various scales, which is important for water resilience.

FIG.3 Wetland in Noordhoek divides affluent, Lake Michelle and informal settlement, Masiphumelele, Cape Town. Bruce Sutherland, City of Cape Town

Even though the bulk of Cape Town's water will continue to be surface water from the WCWSS, the rehabilitation and restoration of local watersheds and waterways will improve the ecological "infrastructure-like"

functioning, over and above increasing water supply.[14] Additional services include storage in aquifers and wetlands, filtration in wetlands, conveyance and transportation by rivers, flood management by floodplains and wetlands' inundation,[15] and water collection.[16] Associated social services include building community resilience and sustainability by improving community health and livability, providing attractive amenities and opportunities for community integration.

The poor state of the Cape Flats could be seen as a metaphor for the pain and damage caused in the Apartheid years, and prior. Waterway remediation and rehabilitation will be enormously challenging, but this work, because of the history, has powerful symbolic potential.[17]

Why a Landscape Approach?

FIG.4 Flooding in the north of Cape Town. Bruce Sutherland, City of Cape Town

Given the scale of the issues and their location at the nexus between urban and natural systems, a "combination approach"[18] has been adopted for waterways intervention. Referred to as a "landscape approach," it incorporates an ecosystem approach using nature-based solutions, a water-sensitive city concept, and resilience. Where an ecosystem approach is overarching, a nature-based solution approach is applicable directly to watersheds and, thereby, waterways. It promotes desirable landscape functions using concepts such as connectivity and a systems-thinking framework[19] that is integrative.[20]

The European Commission frames nature-based solutions as an opportunity for transdisciplinary research into the design and implementation of solutions based on nature that overcome the bias towards development alternatives based on narrow economic perspectives focused on short-term gains.[21] Cohen-Shacham et al.[22] build on this framing and define nature-based solutions as "actions to protect, sustainably manage, and restore natural or modified ecosystems that address societal challenges effectively and adaptively, simultaneously providing human well-being and biodiversity benefits." The approach looks for ways to work with ecosystems rather than imposing conventional engineering solutions to achieve outcomes.

The water-sensitive cities concept narrows the focus of nature-based solutions to water in cities and encompasses natural and urban water systems. It seeks to create a resilient urban water-supply system that is underpinned by the principle of diverse water-supply sources utilizing centralized and decentralized infrastructure. The desire to provide ecosystem services for the built and natural environment, as well as to nurture socio-political capital for sustainability and water-sensitive behaviors[23] is a principle that is common to nature-based solutions. These principles intersect with the reliance principles of flexibility, redundancy, and adaptability. Resilience is defined as "the capacity of individuals, communities, institutions, businesses and systems in a city to survive, adapt, and thrive no matter what kind of chronic stresses and acute shocks they experience."[24]

As previously discussed, improving watersheds and waterways will have multiple benefits referred to as the "resilience dividend." This concept expresses the sum of the benefits that derive from project investments that are based on resilience principles, compared to investments that ignore these principles.[25] Interventions that offer multiple benefits are desirable, especially to fiscally constrained municipalities. The adoption of alien-invasive-plant removal from watersheds, a non-engineered solution, is an example of a nature-based solution that represents a recognizable shift in water-management thinking. The project will increase water availability in the watersheds, improve ecological functioning and provide low-skilled jobs. The City of Cape Town Water Strategy (2019) estimates that desalination will cost R9/ℓ[26] and alien-vegetation clearing R1-2/ℓ. This comparison illustrates the significant cost-effectiveness of nature-based solutions compared to highly engineered augmentation options.

Making the Case for Livable Waterways

Cape Town's waterways are the veins and arteries of the city. They connect across boundaries and have the potential, through restoration, rehabilitation, and development to regenerate and heal communities previously divided by apartheid planning. These communities are nowadays divided by crime, poverty, and the associated social alienation and trauma.

Waterways across the city are the connector of water-cycle elements. Interventions can improve livability and urban environments by providing attractive recreation amenities; ecological infrastructure corridors using a hybrid of nature-based solutions and "gray" infrastructure to build biodiversity, structure faunal and floral movement, providing eco-services (flooding, cooling, improved air quality); and increase decentralized supply options to build water resilience. By creating livability and recreational value, a new relationship can be nurtured assisting behavior change and a new appreciation for nature and the eco-services waterways. This will increase access to much-needed green spaces that have the potential to improve mental health, one of Cape Town's most acute chronic health problems. Since waterways are the most visible part of the water system, they play a strong communication and educational role that is key for the transition to a water-sensitive city.

Implementation Through Policy, Strategy, Approach and Early Outcomes

The City of Cape Town has recognized the important role that waterways play and have therefore launched the Livable Urban Waterways (LUW) program. It was first rooted in the Water Resilience Profile[27] and permeated into other policies, including the Resilience and Water Strategies, where it is framed as an important component of the water-sensitive city transition.

Against this policy framework, it was possible to create an Implementation Framework that sets out broad principles, criteria, and monitoring and evaluation metrics, amongst others. A multi-disciplinary team drawn from officials working across departments prepared the framework and have been driving the process of project identification and preparation. Because the approach uses a framework, implementation is not limited to "water" projects. Though nascent, the program has already impacted several projects that range from water-sensitive planning to canal "softening."

While the LUW program is initially directed towards "pilots" to "prove" concepts, it is worth noting that conceptually aligned projects have been underway across the city for decades. Scoped as "landscape" or "public space projects," they were nevertheless largely based on LUW-aligned principles. The Liesbeek River has seen a number of LUW-type projects implemented over the last 30 years. These include

municipality-led projects (Liesbeek River Trail and Two Rivers Urban Park), community-led projects (Upper Liesbeek River Park), NGO-led projects (Friends of the Liesbeek), and university-led projects (University of Cape Town, Living Lab). Design and implementation have been varied by landscape architects, environmentalists, and others [FIG. 5].

Landscape architects are skilled at designing nature to create amenities in urban and natural contexts and would be expected to have a leadership role in implementing LUW projects. But this is not always the case. In South Africa, landscape architects' roles are not widely understood in relation to waterway development, rehabilitation, and restoration. While this is the dominant narrative, there is a tentative, but growing recognition indicating that the status quo may be changing, not only within the built environment, but also within the municipality.

Over and above, technically skilled individuals who work transversally have been an important part of integrating LUW. Professionals who work across departments and projects have been most able to fulfill this role. The genesis of the Resilience Department and the multidisciplinary nature of their work has been an essential enabler of this change. Much has been achieved through influence, rather than policy compliance.

FIG.5 Liesbeek Upper River Park, Newlands/Bishopscourt, Cape Town. Tamsin Faragher

Oversight of project charters by a landscape architect is however proving to be key to ensure that a landscape approach is realized at a project level. The need for this became apparent through project preparation phases where the broad nomenclature and lenses used by professionals appeared to cause misalignment that had the potential to limit project impact. Rehabilitation and restoration are critical components of livable waterway-making, but these approaches are not always possible due to location. A green-grey hybrid infrastructure has however shown potential, in relation to water treatment and storage for use. By interrogating interventions from this perspective, it has been possible to identify opportunities for a landscape approach that builds water resilience.

Consideration must be given to the significant risk of ongoing water pollution. Given that ageing and failing infrastructure, high levels of informality and increased urbanization on waterways are likely to remain for the foreseeable future and will most likely increase, a central part of successful implementation is finding ways to manage and mitigate their impacts. Lastly, while project implementation is an important part of a transition to a water-sensitive city, management and maintenance that are not mainstream will ultimately determine success.

Conclusion

A return to *Camissa*, the "place of sweet waters," is achievable. But for progress to be made towards water sensitivity by 2040, the very real challenges that have been identified will need to be tackled. The drought has already started to craft a new relationship between Capetonians and their waterways. We can only speculate how different Cape Town's waterways would be if they had followed a landscape approach, rather than European engineering practices that were used at the outset of Cape Town's development. Nevertheless, livable waterways are important for creating water sensitivity, resilience, and addressing past injustices towards a healthy water sensitive city.

Endnotes

1. *"Day Zero"* refers to the time in 2018 when the water supply system would be turned off in areas and supply would be limited to designated water points from where 21ℓ per person per day would be distributed.
2. "City of Cape Town, "Our Shared Water Future - Cape Town's Water Strategy," Cape Town, 2019.
3. "Kevin Winter, "Liesbeek Living Lab," interview by Tamsin Faragher, Cape Town, March, 2021.
4. "Neil Armitage, personal email to author, June 2021.
5. "Statistics South Africa, Poverty and Inequality Report, "How Unequal is South Africa?," Statistics South Africa, accessed June 23, 2021, http://www.statssa.gov.za/?p=12930.
6. "The Group Areas Act of 1950 created the legal framework to establish particular neighborhoods as "group areas" where only people of a particular race were able to reside. It displaced hundreds of thousands of people and broke up families, friends, and communities.
7. "In The Fynbos Biome, "biome" refers to the two key vegetation groups (Fynbos and Renosterveld).
8. "Liz Day, Dean Ollis, Tumisho Ngobela, and Nick Rivers-Moore, "Water Quality of Rivers and Open Water Bodies in the City of Cape Town: Status and Historical Trends, With a Focus on the Period April 2015 to March 2020," City of Cape Town, Cape Town, August 2020, https://resource.capetown.gov.za/documentcentre/Documents/City%20research%20reports%20and%20review/Inland_Water_Quality_Report_FULL.pdf.
9. "International Association of Hydrogeologists (IAH), "Climate Change Adaption and Groundwater," IAH, 2019, https://iah.org/wp-content/uploads/2019/07/IAH_Climate-ChangeAdaptationGdwtr.pdf.
10. "Liz Day, Dean Ollis, Nick Rivers-Moore, and Tumisho Ngubela, "Cape Town Inland Water Quality Report," City of Cape Town 2019.
11. "CSIR Building and Construction Technology, "*Guidelines for Human Settlement Planning and Design, Volume 2,*" CSIR, 2000, http://www.dhs.gov.za/sites/default/files/documents/publications/HS_Volume_2_B.pdf.
12. "During the drought, Capetonians changed behavior and used alternative water sources to reduce their municipal water usage. The municipality used water management interventions including very effective water pressure management. Together, an almost 50 percent reduction in water usage was achieved.
13. "The high-water table across the Cape Flats breaches the aquifer during winter. Aquifer recharge must therefore be managed in a manner that does not exacerbate flooding.
14. "Suzanne Ozment, Kara DiFrancesco, and Todd Gartner, "The Role of Natural Infrastructure in the Water, Energy and Food Nexus," in *Nexus Dialogue Synthesis Papers* (Gland, Switzerland: IUCN, 2015).
15. "Karin M. Krchnak, D. Mark Smith, and Andrew Deutz, "Putting Nature in the Nexus: Investing in Natural Infrastructure to Advance Water-Energy Food Security," in *The Water, Energy and Food Security Nexus - Solutions for the Green Economy. Background Papers for the Stakeholder Engagement Process* in *The Role of Ecosystems in Disaster Risk Reduction* (Bonn, Germany: IUCN, The Nature Conservancy, 2011).
16. "J. Dalton and R. Murti, *Utilizing Integrated Water Resource Management Approaches to Support Disaster Risk Reduction*, ed. K. Sudmeier-Rieux and M. Estrella (Bonn, Germany: United Nations University Press, 2013).
17. "National Department of Water and Sanitation, "Cape Flats Aquifer Management Strategy," City of Cape Town, 2016.
18. "E. Cohen-Shacham et al., "Nature-Based Solutions to Address Global Societal Challenges," IUCN, 2016, https://portals.iucn.org/library/node/46191.
19. "Saskia Keesstra et al., "The Superior Effect of Nature Based Solutions in Land Management for Enhancing Ecosystem Services," *Science of The Total Environment* 610–611 (January 1, 2018): 997–1009.
20. "Carsten Nesshöver et al., "The Science, Policy and Practice of Nature-Based Solutions: An Interdisciplinary Perspective," *Science of The Total Environment* 579 (February 1, 2017): 1215–27.
21. "Nesshöver et al., "The Science, Policy and Practice of Nature-Based Solutions."
22. "Cohen-Shacham et al., "Nature-Based Solutions."
23. "T. H. F. Wong and R. R. Brown, "The Water Sensitive City: Principles for Practice," *Water Science and Technology* 60, no. 3 (July 1, 2009): 673–82.
24. ""100 Resilient Cities," The Rockefeller Foundation, accessed June 23, 2021, https://www.rockefellerfoundation.org/100-resilient-cities/.
25. "City of Cape Town, "Cape Town: *Resilience Strategy,*" City of Cape Town, 2019, https://resource.capetown.gov.za/documentcentre/Documents/City%20strategies%2C%20plans%20and%20frameworks/Resilience_Strategy.pdf.
26. "R9 is '9' South African Rands. The current equivalent value for R9 is around 0.63 USD (1R equals around 0.07 USD).
27. "City Water Resilience Assessment Cape Town, "Water Resilience Profile," City of Cape Town, 2019, https://www.resilienceshift.org/publication/cape-town-water-resilience-profile-cwra/.

2.4

Qanatscape

Revealing the Historic Water Landscape of the Qanat to Inform Future Green Infrastructure in Cities of Arid Iran

Malihe Chamani

As a way of conducting water to the dry lands of ancient Persia, a system of underground water channels was developed as a "natural reaction" of inhabitants adapting to changing climates[1] and the harsh conditions of the arid environment. Around 2,400 years ago, when climatic conditions in central Iran changed, leading to decreasing surface water flows and increasingly difficult access to fresh water, local experts, based on a "collective wisdom," began to excavate tunnels. Starting from dried-up fountains, they dug in a horizontal direction, aiming to reach the groundwater table and find an access to water again.[2] In this way, they invented a new technique called *qanat* (meaning "to dig" in Persian) which is basically a horizontal underground tunnel with shaft wells in periodic intervals for ventilation. This system enabled the conveyance of groundwater to the earth's surface for the irrigation of agricultural land,[3] which then enabled the development of human settlements.

The locations of underground water sources were detected along the foot of mountains by qanat practitioners examining natural indicators.[4] Once an access point to the aquifer could be found, a flat plane suitable for agriculture and trading was chosen for the establishment of a settlement. Precise land engineering determined the course of the underground canal, which was then dug and dredged over generations by diggers (*moqani*). Every 25 to 50 meters, shaft wells were excavated as a means to remove soil during the initial phase of construction, to provide air to the diggers who were working underground and, later, for regular maintenance while the system was in use.[5]

In Iran, almost 20,000 qanats provided 75 percent of all the country's water for irrigation and household consumption until the 1970s.[6] Today, qanats are rarely used for agriculture and industry. Instead of distributing potable water as in the past, the qanat water has either become contaminated or the system has been partially destroyed and is no longer functioning, especially in urban areas such as Tehran. Today, underground water is predominantly distributed by pumps and individual wells instead of the previous, collaborative water sharing regime of qanats. Across the vast Iranian dryland, with its very low precipitation and high evaporation rates, the traditional knowledge of water management has largely been abandoned. Today's modern water

OPPOSITE PAGE A Persian garden landscape outside of Mahan city with the typical central water axis revealing the first layer of the Qanatscape. In the background are up to 4,000-meter high mountains which are the source of water supplying the qanat system. Bagh-e Shahzadeh in Mahan, Iran, 2014. Photograph by S. H. Rashed. Courtesy of UNESCO WorldHeritage Center, S. H. Rashed

system is far detached from ancient Iranian culture, especially in the urban context of cities.

One of the traditional cities developed based on a qanat system is Yazd, in central Iran, which was registered as a UNESCO World Heritage site in 2017.[7] Currently, 2,330 qanat branches still exist across the state of Yazd while only 10 qanat branches are still active and working in the main city.[8]

Qanatscape: The Archetype Landscape in Arid Regions of Iran

Absent the existence of qanats, the Iranian landscape would be dominated by vast drylands, surrounded by high mountains in the north and west, as well as sandy deserts in the center and east. The oasis landscape that has been created by qanats is characterized by a common pattern: Located far away from natural rivers, the "hidden water"[9] of the qanat infrastructure dictates a regional order and structure to the settlements [FIG. 1]. It establishes a system of landscape hierarchy through water cycles and, in addition, a social organization, collaboration, responsibility, cohesion, identity, and sense of belonging to a place.

By looking at arid Iranian landscapes from a holistic view, we can start to understand how they have been fundamentally shaped by the qanat system. We see that qanats enable the habitation and cultivation of

FIG. 1 Aerial view of a typical Persian qanat. Outside of Jupar City, Kerman, Iran, 2014. Photograph by S. H. Rashed. Courtesy of UNESCO World Heritage Center, S. H. Rashed

Qanatscape	Landscape Architecture Principles	
Macro Landscape Hidden water Green infrastructure Oasis model	- Requires regular maintenance of underground canals, especially after floods. - Development based on ecological capacity of water resource. - Conservation according to legal and landscape boundaries *(Harim)* of qanats. - Integration of mountains, city (or village), and desert. (Land management) - Protection of the natural course of green infrastructures created by qanats. - Preservation of iconic landscape views. - Implementation of traditional ecological knowledge (TEK) practices.	**Protect**
Middle Landscape Visible water Cultural landscape Water network	- Interconnection of fresh air corridors, underground and surface water with the urban landscape form. - Rehabilitation of the qanat water network as a heritage blue infrastructure. - Reuse of water and minimizing evaporation based on TEK. - Zero-energy vision for the landscape urbanism architecture. - Enhance thermal convenience (qanat-microclimate-base design). - Building resiliency of blue and green landscape systems. - Optimization of agricultural irrigation systems. - Consider principles of cultural landscape protection based on UNESCO convention. - Honor collective memories and rehabilitate traditional events and customs.	**Restore & Enhance**
Micro Landscape Touchable water Sense of identity	- Using and recycling vernacular materials. - Attention to traditional climatic principles of urbanism and architecture. - Following the quadrilateral garden form *(Charbagh).* - Re-design and empowerment of water storages systems (*Ab-anbar* and *Payab*) as both productive landscape and social places. - Enhancement of local, social hubs. - Keep linear form of water in the main urban spaces. - Construction on site based on principles for maximal shading and cooling.	**Enhance & Construct**

FIG.2 A systematic hierarchy of Qanatscapes with focal points across three different scales. Malihe Chamani

the land, and that the widespread pattern of such integrated landscapes follows a unique pattern and inner logic which serves as a tool for assessment, planning, decision-making, and design. This leads me to refer to these landscapes collectively as a *Qanatscape*. Taking all the natural conditions, building techniques, and spatial effects of both agricultural land and settlements into account, the Qanatscape can be explained across three scales: the regional, geographic scale (Macro Landscape), the scale of cultural landscapes (Middle Landscape), and the scale of sites (Micro Landscape) [FIG. 2].

Macro Landscape: Hidden Water and the Qanatscape Territory

Across central Iran, several territories of qanats are distinguishable by the sharp contrast of green and dry lands between the high *Elborz* and *Zagross* mountain ranges and the two large deserts called *Dasht-e-Kavir* and *Dasht-e-Lut*. The Qanatscape territory is divided into four main parts: First, "high mountains whose stones are mixed with mud [and] are likely to contain groundwater," as the ancient scholar Karaji indicated;[10] second, some lines of "spaced spoil craters [areas surrounding an opening] that snake along the surface"[11] in an alluvial fan, representing the "hidden water" tunnels which appear in arid environments, kilometers away from cultivated land; third, a qanat-structured settlement; and fourth, rectangular fields of irrigated farmland which extend to the point where no more water is available [FIG. 3].

Erich Schmidt, a German scholar, published a fascinating study combining aerial photos, drawings, sketches, a description of architectural elements, and archeological objects. This allowed him to trace the relationship between topography, roads, water infrastructures, agricultural land use, and settlements. His book *Flights over Ancient Cities of Iran* (1940) constantly "shifts between scales and between history, geography and anthropology."[12] It relies on important geographical histories of the medieval Islamic period[13] "to render the multiplicity and interconnection of settlements with their immediate landscape and large region." For example, his aerial photograph of Turut village (or Torud), a typical Qanatscape settlement, "captures a clear border between inhabited territory and the desert that absorbs the hidden underground water from the heart of the mountains."[14] Together, these images visualized the Qanatscape territory as an iconic landscape pattern across barren drylands, characterized by black dots that are surrounded by donut-shaped mounds, tracing lines across the land that terminate in oasis-like cities or villages.

As mentioned, one of the best-preserved qanat-based cities in Iran is Yazd, located on the edge of a desert and 1,216 meters above sea level.[15] The territory of Yazd's Qanatscape is bordered by the western *Shir-Kooh* mountains, which rise up to 4,100 meters. The core city was established 40 kilometers away from *Shir-Kooh*, and is surrounded by green qanat-based districts (originally, they were isolated villages). Approximately 300 qanat fountains across the *Shir-Kooh* aquifer[16] irrigate and bring prosperity (*Abadani*, literally "turning a place to green by water" in old Persian) to many villages and cities along the edge of the central desert, not just to Yazd. Prior to the construction of modern, fossil-fuel-powered deep wells for industry and agriculture, the Yazd landscape served as a sustainable and environmentally harmonic model that utilized renewable resources, such as groundwater and wind, to accomplish essentially the same task but with far fewer negative environmental impacts.

FIG.3 Section of a typical qanat system connecting groundwater from the mountainous region to the arid city and irrigated farmlands. Malihe Chamani

FIG.4 Qanatscape landscape containing different units as satellite villages around the historical core of Yazd. The footprint of the modern city is visible in the background, partially covered by the green landscape structures of the original Qanatscape. Map composed by Malihe Chamani, 2021. The original old map (1956) released under permission of the Cultural Heritage and Handicraft Organization of Yazd in 2013. The new map of Yazd is available on the Yazd Municipality website.

Middle Landscape: Exposing Water in the Cultural Landscape Along Qanats

Greenery and culture arise from the point where fresh water from the qanat emerges on the earth's surface, becomes accessible, and provides prosperity. This critical point is called *farhang* in Persian, meaning "culture." The etymological roots of both *farhang* and "culture" relate to cultivation, the working of land for the growing of plants.[17] The root of the word in *Avestan,* a language spoken in the second millennium BCE in Eastern Iran,[18]

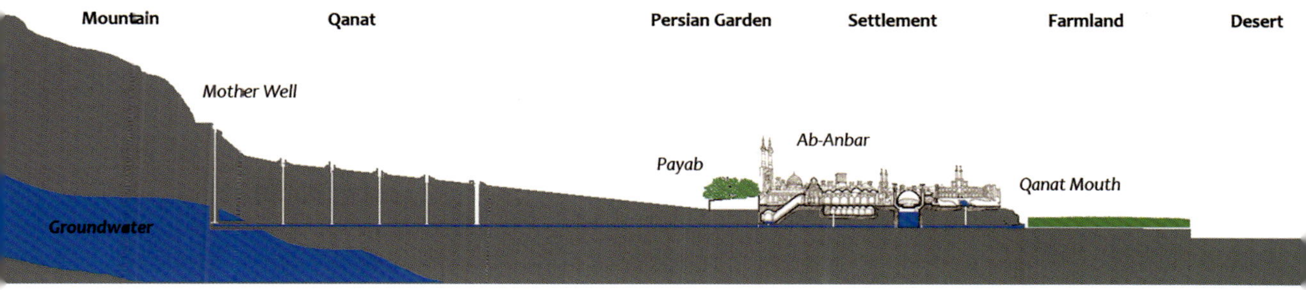
Mountain
Qanat
Persian Garden
Settlement
Farmland
Desert
Mother Well
Ab-Anbar
Payab
Qanat Mouth
Groundwater

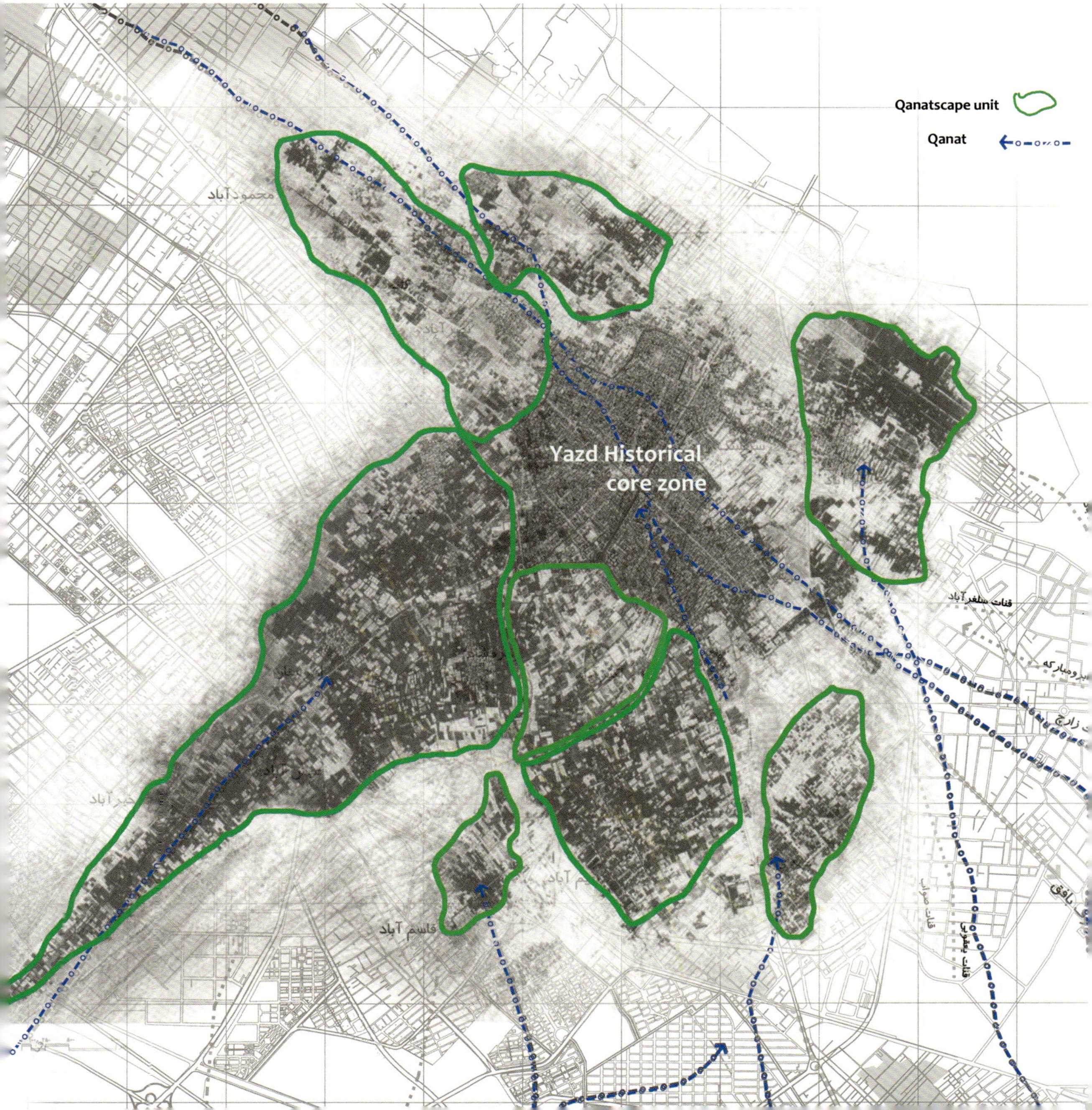
Qanatscape unit
Qanat
Yazd Historical core zone
محمود آباد
قاسم آباد

refers to dragging, training and education, as well as the mouth of water.[19] Therefore, *farhang* (culture) literally originates from the first place in which people touch the water, begin to organize in a collective manner, create public spaces, and restructure the landscape.

Qanat-based cities are "the product of the interrelationship between their cultural and physical environments." In 1979, Heinz Gaube studied the spatial pattern and physical morphology of the Iranian cities of Herat, Isfahan, and Bam.[20] The spatial pattern and landscape form of these three cities have been developed based on qanats to respond to the cultural needs of inhabitants and, at the same time, to adapt to their surrounding environment.[21] The characteristic pattern is an expression of the "cultural landscape" as the evolution of a human society over time, shaped by the physical constraints and opportunities of its natural environment.[22]

The structure of a Qanatscape's unit (a city or village) is essentially the result of a conscious spatial ordering through the hierarchical distribution of water. This process creates organic lines across the territory, guiding the view to man-made structures, making the water visible, and, consequently, developing a culture, identity, and sense of belonging. This hierarchical order is imprinted into the landscape around the main watercourse of the qanat (*Shahjub*) and subordinate channels (*Jub*) which lead water outward from the distribution pond (*Maqsam*) into water storage basins (*Ab-anbar*) in each neighborhood.[23] These historical landscape elements (*Shahjub, Maqsam, Jub and Ab-anbar*) together create one unit of the green Qanatscape landscape infrastructure network.

The Qanatscape pattern at the middle scale is based on the green, vegetated parts of the landscape. To sustain the landscape character, a water-based, cultural landscape approach is required that constantly distributes water across the system.

The Yazd's Qanatscape is like a puzzle where each unit has been arranged around the core city as a satellite village. The role of these satellite villages was to moderate the hot and dry weather by creating microclimates to preserve food and fresh agricultural products, to protect the soil and water for agriculture, and to act as an energy-food-water nexus.[24] The form and location of these green patches of the satellite villages is shown in an old map of Yazd from 1956.[25] The map reveals how the natural landscape structure was enriched by the Qanatscape units before modern urban development had started [FIG. 4].

Micro Landscape: Feeling Water Along Architectural Axes

A closer examination at the neighborhood scale of the Qanatscape reveals the dominant quadrilateral landscape form of historic Persian gardens, central courtyards, and squares (*Meydan*). All these parts are based on the central qanat water axis, which generally is a channel leading from the main qanat canal into the settlement, organizing open spaces, in terms of defining their function according to different seasons and in terms of optimal water distribution. The symmetry around the water axis of the *Shahzadeh* Persian Garden, for instance, is an outstanding example of how the Qanatscape defined architectural form. It provided comfortable, cool air in contrast to the hot and dry climate outside. The same pattern can be seen in traditional Iranian houses, mosques, schools, and other building typologies.

A Qanatscape unit consists of a hierarchical water network: The first place of water access (*payab*) was usually located at a public cistern, where drinking water was available to the entire community and which also served as an important place for social interaction. The next crucial component of a Qanatscape unit was the *Maqsam*, where water was distributed at different times of the day by a *Mirab* (guard and water-distribution supervisor) who was elected and paid by the neighborhood community.[26] In the past, each Qanatscape community had its own leader and social organization to manage and count "every cup of water,"[27] overseeing and regulating the water distribution. These organizations were important parts of the community, providing identity and a sense of belonging, as they also facilitated cultural events such as fire ceremonies, nature and spring celebrations, and religious and sacred rituals [FIG. 5]. They even cultivated distinct modes of written and spoken language that were slightly different in each Qanatscape community. Such peculiar cultural characteristics highlight the potential of Qanatscapes to rehabilitate social qualities that could enhance the daily life of people living in climatically challenging cities and villages.

The impact of social cohesion, as part of the sustainable practices of Qanatscapes, could help to bring prosperity back to the region. Planning principles could be developed based on environmental characteristics, traditional cultural knowledge, the integration of the landscape into a broader context, and the appreciation of qanats as a socio-cultural heritage that is deeply embedded in the natural environment, creating an effective, landscape-informed infrastructure that has been collectively crafted and operated over hundreds of years.

Future Sustainable Prosperity (Abadani)

"On the Iranian Plateau, reliance on qanats have promoted high levels of social and ecological adaptation."[28] Today, without the vital, multi-functional landscape infrastructure of the Qanatscape, places that are far away from permanent sources of surface water are either limited to low-yielding agriculture or have been completely abandoned. Modern urban and rural development and the introduction of gray infrastructures detached the city from the context of its natural environment. Aerial photos since 2002 indicate that green structures across Yazd have nearly vanished. As local residents have reported, this has resulted in the city becoming climatically less comfortable, especially in times of global warming. Today, all urban and rural households of Yazd are supplied with drinkable water by conventional water pipes. However, the construction of dams has completely ignored the qualities of the Qanatscape, cutting through the original flow and inner logic of the qanat system.

With its holistic understanding, encompassing the landscape, natural environment, as well as social factors, the Qanatscape forms a remarkable landscape typology. From its infrastructural qualities to its social sensitivity, it is an under-investigated field of research. It provides a rich body of knowledge for both landscape research and practice. It has the potential to not only rehabilitate an expansive and effective heritage infrastructure but also to inspire new investigations and landscape systems through design and planning principles.

Qanatscape serves as a kind of "land strategy" that has been able to adapt to environmental change over time while balancing societal demands and climatic conditions.[29] The qanat as a unique landscape infrastructure of central Iran represents a specific pattern that could be rethought and remodeled in future landscape planning and design. As a sustainable model that makes use of the natural water cycle and ensures the renewability of natural resources, it not only plays a formative and vital role in the landscape structure of central Iran, but also comprises an important cultural heritage. The study of such socio-environmental systems that have been crafted by practices arising out of traditional ecological knowledge can serve as a landscape approach to rethinking the management of regional landscapes and informing the built environment.

FIG.5 Social activities around the qanat system with exposed bodies of water. Malihe Chamani, 2018 & 2019

Endnotes

1. Majid Labbaf Khaneiki, "Qanat and Ecology," interview by Malihe Chamani, ICQHS Yazd, Iran, August 12, 2020.
2. Ali Asghar Semsar Yazdi and Majid Labbaf Khaneiki, *Qanat Knowledge, Construction and Maintenance* (The Netherlands: Springer, 2017).
3. Abdolkarim Behnia, *Qanat Construction and Qanat Maintenance* (Iran: UNESCO Publication, 1989).
4. Yazdi and Khaneiki, *Qanat Knowledge, Construction and Maintenance*.
5. Ibid.
6. Hans E. Wulff, "The Aqueducts of Iran," *Issue of the Scientific American,* Bd. CAIS (Circle of Ancient Iranian Studies) venue, (1968): 94-105.
7. "World Heritage List UNESCO," UNESCO, 2017, https://whc.unesco.org/en/list/1544/.
8. "Yazd Jihad-e-Keshavarzi," qanat.jky, accessed June 2019, http://qanat.jky.ir/#/search/map.
9. Abu Bakr ibn Muhammad ibn al Hassan Al-Karaji, *The Excavation of Hidden Water* [*Estekhraj-e Ab-ha-ye Penhan*] (Tehran: Iranian National Commission for UNESCO PRESS, 1994 [1010]).
10. Ibid. Abu Bakr ibn Muhammad ibn al Hassan (Husayn) Karaji (953-1029 AD) was a Persian mathematician and engineer. He is considered one of the founders of Algebra in the Islamic world. See also Yazdi and Khaneiki, *Qanat Knowledge, Construction and Maintenance*.
11. Julia Watson, *Lo-TEK Design by Radical Indigenism* (New York: TASCHEN, 2019): 235.
12. Negar Sanaan Bensi, "The Qanat System: A Reflection on the Heritage of the Extraction of Hidden Waters," in *Adaptive Strategies for Water Heritage, Past, Present and Future*, ed. Carola Hein (The Netherlands: Springer, 2020): 41- 56.
13. Manu Sobti und Seyed Ali Hosseini, "Re-Examining 'Persianate Civitas': Networked Urbanities and Suburban Hinterlands in Erich Schmidt's Flights," in *The Historiography of Persian Architecture* (New York: Routledge, 2016).
14. Erich Schmidt, *Flights Over Ancient Cities of Iran*, (Chicago: University of Chicago Press, 1940).
15. "Yazd," Wikipedia, last modified June 6, 2021, https://en.wikipedia.org/wiki/Yazd.
16. Ann K. S. Lambton, "The Qanāts of Yazd," *Journal of the Royal Asiatic Society* 2, no.1 (April 1992): 21 - 35.
17. "Culture," LEXICO, Oxford Dictionary, accessed, June 16, 2021, https://www.lexico.com/definition/culture.
18. "Avestan," Wikipedia, last modified June 17, 2021, https://en.wikipedia.org/wiki/Avestan.
19. "Aliakbar Dehkhoda," [Dehkhoda Encyclopedia] Tehran University, accessed, June 16, 2021, https://dehkhoda.ut.ac.ir/.
20. Henry Gaube, *Iranian Cities* (New York: New York University Press, 1979).
21. Masoud Kheirabadi, *Iranian Cities: Formation and Development* (Syracuse, NY: Syracuse University Press, 2000).
22. UNESCO, *Operational Guidelines for the Implementation of the World Heritage Convention* (Paris: UNESCO World Heritage Center, 2008).
23. Michael E. Bonine, "From Qanātto Kort: Traditional Irrigation Terminology and Practices in Central Iran," *IRAN* 20, no. 1 (January 1, 1982): 145-59.
24. Khaneiki, "Qanat and Ecology."
25. Mohammad Mehreyar, Farhad Fakhari, Bahram Ghadiri und Shamil Fathollah Yuf, *Pictorial Documents of Iranian Cities in the Qajar Period*, (Tehran: Shahid Beheshti University and The National Cultural Heritage Organization, 1999).
26. Mohammad Moin, *Moin Farsi Encyclopedia* (Iran: Amirkabir Publication, 2009).
27. Yazdi and Khaneiki, *Qanat Knowledge, Construction and Maintenance*.
28. Ibid.
29. Khaneiki, "Qanat and Ecology."

A·LA

2.5

Eternal Ephemera

Soft Infrastructures in the Floating City of Uros, Peru

Alberto De Salvatierra

> "Uros in Lake Titicaca, Peru is a civilization that predates the Incas. However, they possess no solid monuments, built no stone cities, and are semi-nomadic. It would seem that the secret to their civilizational longevity arises from their unique relationship with a single material: reeds."
>
> — Alberto de Salvatierra[1]

The research and documentation presented in this essay were conducted by the author from May to August 2016, with additional drawing production occurring from September 2020 to February 2021 in collaboration with Anagha Patil.

It could be easily said that the history of human civilization is one of grass. Wheat, rice, maize and sugarcane—which account for over 60% of the world's caloric intake[2]—are only but a few of the species of grass that were pivotal in the development of large urban centers, and that are still important today. But in addition to providing food, drink, paper, fuel, and clothing, these graminoids have also been directly used as building materials. Because of their overall tensile strength and lightweight nature, they can be buoyant in water and have been used to make rafts and boats.[3] Uros in Lake Titicaca, Peru thus becomes of unique interest as it is a floating city made almost *entirely* out of "grass": specifically, Totora reeds (*Schoenoplectus californicus ssp. tatora*).[4] Little literature has been dedicated to this water civilization beyond superficial and picturesque treatments aimed at foreign tourists. However, growing environmental pressures and economic forces are precipitating a slow exodus from these settlements to nearby cities like Puno or Juliaca. In a few decades, the soft infrastructures used for the buoyant nature of this city might be slowly abandoned and eroded. Their ability to inform landscape epistemologies will be lost.

Operating outside traditional understandings for a city and its "urban fabric," vernacular constructions like Uros often resist fixed, normative frameworks or spatial conditions in relation to human habitation. Yet, this project, perhaps paradoxically, aims to record and index the shifting nature of the *indeterminate* boundaries—both physical and abstract—that exist across, arguably, artificial territories. Taking a material as the point of departure (totora reeds), one can explore existing phenomena and relationships in a perennial wet gradient between the aqueous and the buoyant. When "dry land" is as fluid as the water that sustains it, preserving a simple set of guidelines allows for a critical examination when the only constant is "grass."

OPPOSITE PAGE Photograph revealing the section and construction of a floating island in Uros, built almost entirely out of "grass." Alberto de Salvatierra, 2016

FIG.1 View of Uros Khantati Island from a boat. Alberto de Salvatierra, 2016

The Uru (People) and (the City of) Uros

The Uru—or "children of the sun"—are so ancient, so the legend goes, that they existed *before* the first humans settled the Andes[5] because—supposedly—Lake Titicaca was the site where the maker of the universe first created heaven and earth and the people that inhabit it.[6,7] Genetic studies partially support this narrative: the Uru people share HLA alleles with Easter and Pacific Islanders, and could have begun the Tiwanaku civilization of Bolivia, placing their potential origin around 110 CE or earlier—predating the emergence of the Incas by more than one thousand years.[8] However, when the Uru actually transitioned into a water-based, semi-nomadic lifestyle is a matter of debate. Residents of the islands often say they were spurred to build their floating islands to escape the successive conquests of the altiplano by the Tiwanaku, Inca, and Spanish empires.[9] This would place the founding of Uros sometime between the 6th and 16th centuries. More recent, Western anthropologists affirm this transition to the water did not occur until the 1800s.[10] However, the origin of Uros is hard to ascertain as many oral traditions and cultural histories have degraded over time as Indigenous languages and religions were replaced through assimilation.[11] Yet, regardless of when the present iteration of Uros arose, a remarkable attribute remains: this floating city, woven entirely out of plants, existing in a state of permanent decay that must be constantly replenished and built anew, has lasted centuries. Uros is, anachronistically, a city where past is present and ephemera, *eternal* [FIG. 1].

But the longevity of Uros is not due to solid-stone monuments or structures like those of the Andean civilizations that rose after it and fell before it. Neither is it due to any "modern" material with which cities are built today. Instead, Uros relies exclusively upon a curious rhizomatic

plant that has no leaves, and carries out photosynthesis through its water-repellent stems: totora reeds—a subspecies of the giant bulrush sedge found primarily in Lake Titicaca.[12] A keystone species of the lake's ecology, totora reeds single-handedly sustain fish species that swim above their roots, water fowl that nest in clusters of their stems, and the Uru that use all parts of the plant for the construction of their city.[13] The reeds even behave like a living map of the lake bottom, "since they indicate the zones that are between two and five meters deep."[14] In short, totora reeds are a uniquely versatile plant that has facilitated their use as a mono-infrastructural material that can be used to create the island foundations, building plinths, walls, roofs, and boats of the Uru [FIG. 2].[15]

Building the Floating Islands

> "Living in Uros requires sea legs to handle the moving and swaying of the islands, mountain lungs to breathe the thin and oxygen-poor air at 14,000 feet (Lake Titicaca is the highest navigable lake in the world), and black blood to handle the freezing winter temperatures."
>
> — Cristina Suana[16]

Uros is comprised of around 125 floating islands.[17] However, this number varies from year to year as satellite imagery going back to 1969 reveals [FIG. 3].

FIG. 2 Detailed view inside Uros Khantati Island. Alberto de Salvatierra, 2016

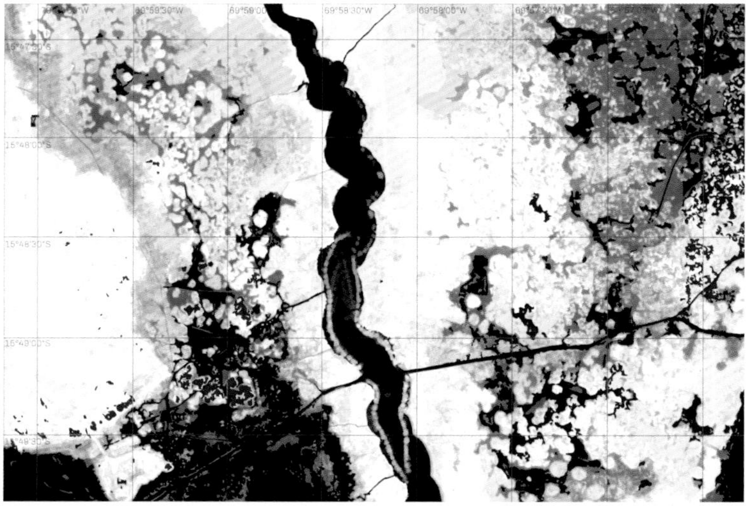

As recently as 2002, there were only around 33 islands.[18] Curiously, prevailing narratives by residents describe their numbers as declining because younger generations are less likely to stay on the islands and adhere to the agrarian lifestyle of their parents—choosing instead to make a living in Puno, a growing city of around 128,000 thousand inhabitants located on the western shores of Lake Titicaca just five kilometers away from Uros. Yet, this reality, that of an increasingly depopulated Uros, might not be at odds with the explosive growth in islands it has experienced in the last two decades. Tourism in Lake Titicaca is relatively recent, and only in the last fifteen years have residents of Uros begun a concerted effort to expand their islands to accommodate bed-and-breakfast-style lodging for visitors. The author stayed at one such island, Uros Khantati, that despite hosting two community dining halls, one kitchen, three half-bathrooms, one

FIG.3 Composite temporal aerial plan (18 satellite images from May 2002 to August 2020) showing growth and displacement of Uros' islands over time. Alberto de Salvatierra, with Anagha Patil, 2021

FIG.4 Uros Khantati Island Section. Alberto de Salvatierra, with Anagha Patil, 2021

shower and sixteen bedrooms ranging in size from one to four occupants, distributed across 29,000 sq ft,[19] only four permanent residents live on the island. But how are the islands built? The exact science has been poorly and imprecisely defined, and therefore became a central interest of this project.

Upon marriage, a new couple—with the help of friends and relatives—will set out to begin building an island of their own.[20] Much like a house (but spread out in a deconstructed fashion with rooms free-standing and separated from one another), each family clan will establish their own little island, which will grow or contract depending on how many children or family generations are living on them [FIG. 4]. Uros Khantati, the island most closely studied and measured for this project, was already 16 years old in July 2016.[21]

To begin the process of construction, viable totora reed root blocks, or *khili*, must be found. These are scouted at the edges of the totora reed fields and must already be partially unmoored from the lake floor—often occurring only after heavy rains. An initial island requires about four to six starter blocks. Typical "starter blocks" measure five meters wide, five meters long, and 1.5 meters deep and take about one day for three to five men to move one to two meters across the lake.[22] They are dragged *very* slowly in the front by motorized boats since they are very heavy. In the back, they are pushed by men swimming in the water. Moving these blocks to their final location can take up to a year. According to residents, up until a few years ago, starter blocks of 20 meters by 20 meters were common, but changing lake morphologies as a result of changing climate patterns have reduced this building resource, and now only smaller blocks remain.[23]

An initial island requires about four to six of these five-meter by five-meter blocks that, once assembled, are tied together with nylon [FIG 5: Step 2]. Before nylon, blocks were tied together with ropes woven from totora reeds. Each block is also individually anchored to the lake floor. Once this initial setup is complete, several tons of totora reeds are harvested and layered in alternating directions to a thickness of 1.5 meters. Similar to stacking pancakes on top of one another, the layers of totora reeds remain in place through gravity. The island is now three meters deep.[24]

In areas of the island that will contain a structure (e.g. a bedroom), an additional reed foundation or "plinth" of one to 1.5 meters is layered upward to compensate for the sinking of the heavier structure relative to the rest of the island that only receives/supports foot traffic. Once these bases are complete, free-standing rooms, built as independent buildings, are placed on top.[25,26] This makes each island function similar to a deconstructed multi-generational house, requiring one to go outdoors to move between different programmatic areas (e.g. going from the kitchen to the dining hall or from the bedroom to a bathroom). Hallways do not exist. This deconstructed layout however is not accidental. It permits for targeted maintenance and reconstruction of different rooms as they naturally decay from weathering and use.[27] Although much

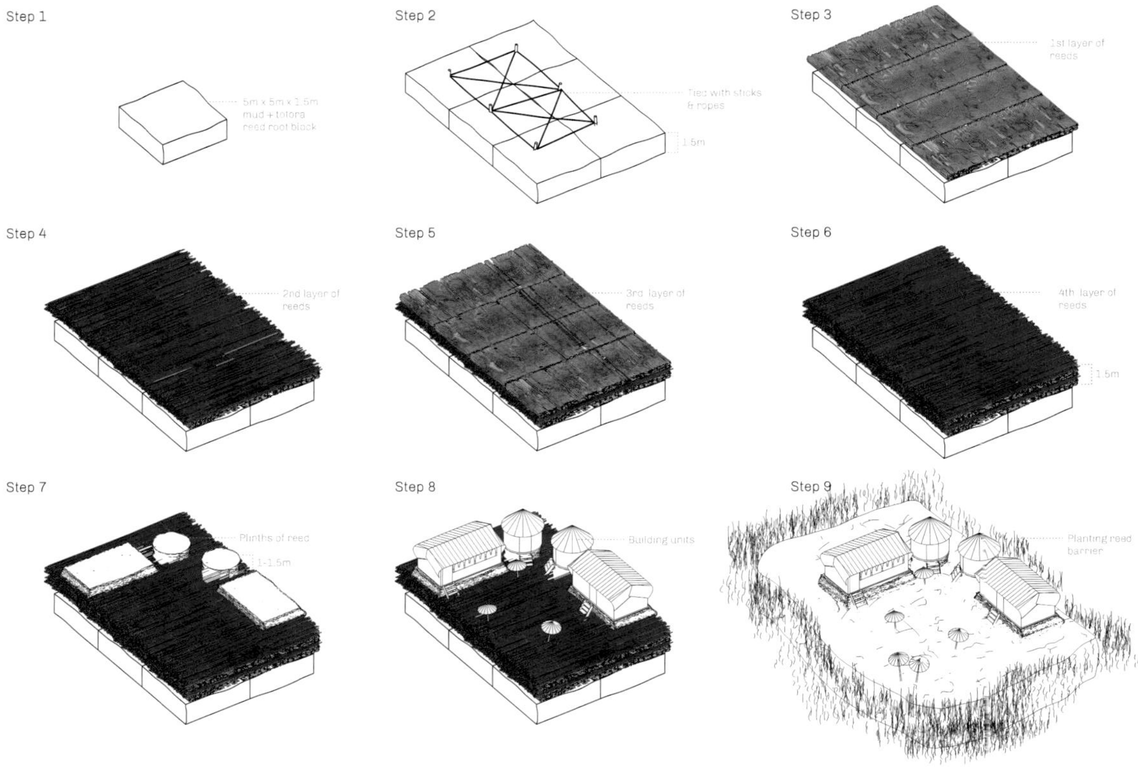

Step 1
5m x 5m x 1.5m
mud + totora
reed root block
Step 2
Tied with sticks
& ropes
1.5m
Step 3
1st layer of
reeds
Step 4
2nd layer of
reeds
Step 5
3rd layer of
reeds
Step 6
4th layer of
reeds
1.5m
Step 7
Plinths of reed
1-1.5m
Step 8
Building units
Step 9
Planting reed
barrier

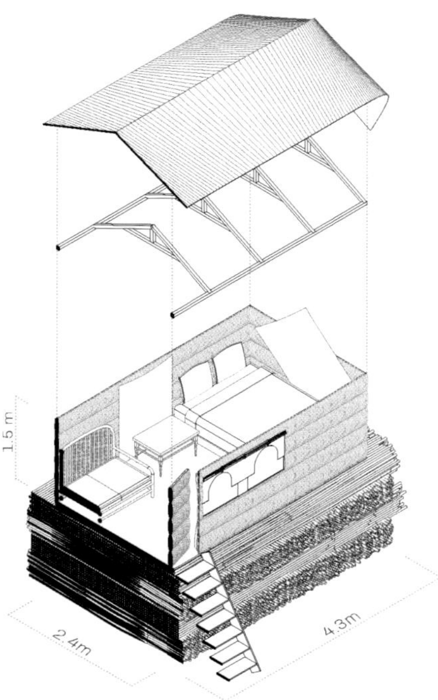

1.5 m
2.4m
4.3m

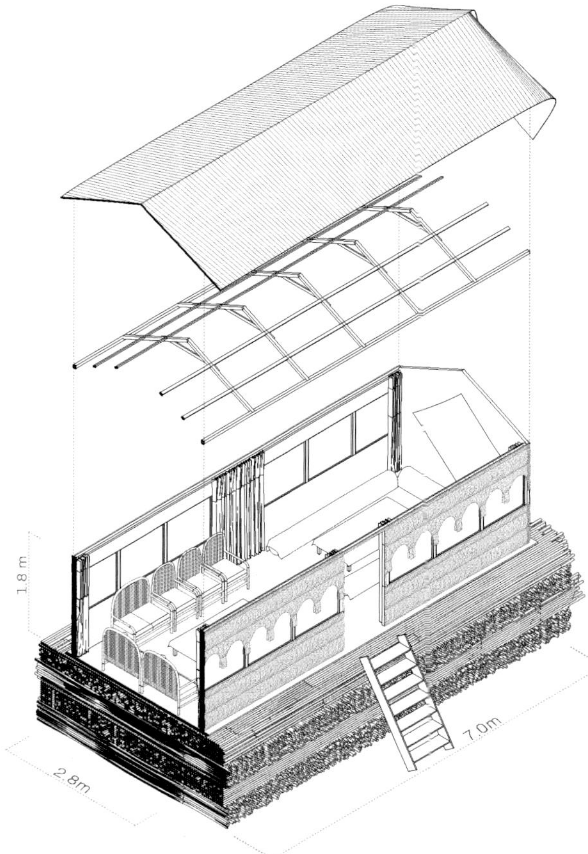

1.8 m
2.8m
7.0m

labor is required to build a new island, island maintenance is even more time intensive. The ground must be completely "refreshed" with added layers of totora reeds every two weeks in the rainy season and every three weeks in the dry season.[28] Building foundations only last about 1.5 years, and buildings have to be similarly replaced every two years. Ornamental decorations, such as parasols and welcome arches, last about one to 1.5 years, respectively. Fishing boats will also last about one year and the island's anchors for two.[29] An island's root-block foundation will last between 25 to 30 years,[30] as their submersion in water prevents the temperature changes and extreme weathering that occur above the water. But, how do the islands actually float? The totora-reed layers, which sit on top of the root blocks, are naturally buoyant due to their aerenchyma—soft plant tissue that contains air spaces.[31] However, the root blocks themselves remain afloat due to both the underwater anaerobic decomposition that traps gases in their root mass and the air trapped inside the totora roots inside the mud blocks.[32]

At the conclusion of the construction of the island, totora reeds are planted around the island—providing both privacy and a windbreak for the island structure and its inhabitants. These planted totora reeds also attract fish and water fowl, which provide a source of food for the Uru. However, this planting will only happen once the family of that island has decided they like the location of their island as sometimes islands are moved via motorized boat if a location proves unfavorable. Adding all these elements together, every island simultaneously becomes "...a floating village, an aquaculture farm, and an artificial wetland synthesized into a single living infrastructure."[33] Julia Watson, in her book, *Lo—TEK, Design by Radical Indigenism,* succinctly elaborates on the ecosystem services these islands provide, particularly water-quality regulation and filtration:

> The Uros floating islands improve the water quality of the lake... The islands actively filter water by reducing suspended solids and dissolving organic carbon, while also breaking down nutrients and other water-borne pollutants. Nutrients circulating in the water coming into contact with the rooted undersides of the islands are consumed by microbes, while a smaller fraction is taken up by the porous stems of the reed, called the *chullu*. Suspended solids additionally slough off into the benthic zone below the island, while organic solids stick to the microbial layer and become the base of the freshwater food web, offering a more bio-diverse habitat for fish.[34]

Beyond the scale of single islands, the dynamics of Uros as a whole are more complex and are undergoing a shift towards centralization. In the past, most islands were self-sufficient. Each containing all the resources needed for its inhabitants to survive. More collective activities, like that of trade, were conducted by traveling to specific islands. And other

FIG.5 Section of bedroom and community dining hall. Alberto de Salvatierra, with Anagha Patil, 2021

ACKNOWLEDGMENTS

This research was generously supported by the Cornell University Robert James Eidlitz Travel Fellowship, the Harvard University Graduate School of Design Penny White Prize, the Center for Civilization, and Panono–a Berlin-based, 360° x 360° full-spherical, 108 megapixel Panoramic ball camera company. Special thanks to Cristina and Victor who hosted the author on their island–Uros Khantati–and for providing unrestricted access for photographic and drawn documentation. Special thanks to their son Eddy who walked the author through the stages of construction of a "typical" island.

programs, such as education, were performed individually by each family. Yet, as modernization has reached Uros, the construction of specialized non-residential islands (or portions of islands) has emerged—a primary school is now situated in the family island of one of Uros' residents.[35] For other, more technology-dependent programs, like healthcare or banking, the Uru travel to Puno. In some ways, the observed relationship between Uros and Puno is that of a suburb and a "downtown." Yet, this is an oversimplification and further study of the macro-urbanistic patterns of Lake Titicaca is needed. It is only when the entire ecology—human and otherwise—of the Altiplano basin is understood that a territorial-scale distillation of its (water) urbanism can take place.

Towards a "Soft" Urbanism

Lake Titicaca exists in a constant state of flux—changing both seasonally and across decades. Even Uros itself, resisting boundaries, is never still. The islands which constitute it, shift and oscillate—evolve and cycle—in response to seasonal and other forces. In addition to the variable gradient of the water's edge and the position of the islands on the lake, population changes and building patterns throughout the years also reveal an urbanistic condition that pulsates—as different reed beds become obsolete or are built anew—the layout and organization of Uros changes along with it. Documentation, whether drawn or photographic, aimed towards recording a catalogue of its urban conditions can only ever be relational (i.e. between the floating landforms and their watery context) rather than absolute. Cities, like Uros, situated in ever-changing mediums resist mapping. And Uros is not alone. Mapping the transformation of Uros presents similar difficulties to other urban patterns, such as informal urbanism, requiring tools beyond traditional morphological analysis to include building typology and permanence as introduced by McCartney and Krishnamurthy's scaled analytical morphological patterns.[36]

When material, environmental, and socio-cultural conditions are in a state of flux—evolving in a state of palpable indeterminacy—how might prevailing assumptions about cities and their spatial manifestations be re-thought? How might one address questions of resilience in the built environment in the contemporary but uncertain context of globalizing forces, economic pressures, sea level rise and climate change? Landscape and architecture explorations of the indeterminate and ephemeral are not new, yet these concerns are both timely and acutely necessary to be critically addressed.

This essay belongs to a broader research agenda by the author to document historical, vernacular, and contemporary manifestations of soft urbanism[37]—articulating a potential for soft infrastructures to become more prevalent in the discourse of urbanism theory, urban morphology, and urban-design praxis. Landscape and its geographies are an inherently hybrid medium, and research insights might question how notions of solidity and permanence entrench biases of consumption. Does the soft and ephemeral introduce new ways to encode sustainability and resilience in an increasingly uncertain climate future? Soft cities—of which floating cities could be considered a subset of—often suggest a delicate temporality. Yet, Uros contradicts this due to its long history—having already outlived cities of stone and steel. Intersections and overlaps between amphibious architecture, hydrological landscapes, and natural ecologies, tempered by adaptive practices, integrate multiple spatial scales at which these soft infrastructures operate. These dynamics make Uros and its islands fertile territory for further exploration and syncretism.

Endnotes

1. Alberto de Salvatierra, "Reed Urbanism: Soft Infrastructures in the Floating City of Uros" (Lecture at 6th Biennial Design Science Symposium, Inclusive Narratives from Nature, Rhode Island School of Design, Providence, RI, 2019).
2. FAO (Food and Agriculture Organization), *Dimensions of need: an atlas of food and agriculture*. (Rome, Italy: Food and Agriculture Organization of the United Nations, 1995), 21.
3. Alexei Vranich, "Reed Boats and Experimental Archaeology on lake Titicaca," *Expedition*, 47(2), 2005, https://www.penn.museum/documents/publications/expedition/pdfs/47-2/reed%20boats.pdf.
4. Ben Orlove, *Lines in the Water* (Berkeley: University of California Press, 2002), 174.
5. Antonio Arnaiz-Villena, Jose Palacio-Grüber, Ignacio Juarez, Adrian Lopez-Nares, Jorge Nieto, Cristina Campos, and Jose Manuel Martin-Villa, "HLA in Uros from Peru Titicaca Lake: Tiwanaku, Easter and Pacific Islanders," *Human Immunology*, 80(2): 91-92.
6. Verónica Salles-Reese, *From Viracocha to the Virgin of Copacabana* (Austin: University of Texas Press, 1997).
7. Joseph Bastien, *People of the Water* (Salt Lake City: University of Utah Press, 2014).
8. Arnaiz-Villena, Palacio-Grüber, Juarez, Lopez-Nares, Nieto, Campos, Martin-Villa, "HLA in Uros"
9. Ben Orlove, *Lines in the Water*, 182.
10. Ibid, 182.
11. Ibid, 121-122.
12. Ibid, 174.
13. Ibid, 180.
14. Ibid, 174.
15. Xanic J. Rondón, Sandra Anne Banack, and Wilfredo Diaz-Huamanchumo, "Ethnobotanical Investigation of Caballitos (Schoenoplectus Californicus: Cyperaceae) in Huanchaco, Peru," *Economic Botany* 57, no. 1 (Spring 2003): 35-47.
16. Cristina Suana, "Conversations on Uros." Interview by Alberto de Salvatierra, July 29, 2016.
17. Alberto De Salvatierra, and Anagha Patil, *Composite Temporal Aerial Plan of Uros, Peru*, 2021, Map, Center for Civilization, Calgary, AB.
18. Ibid.
19. Alberto De Salvatierra, and Anagha Patil, *Island Section, Uros Khantati*, 2021, Drawing, Center for Civilization, Calgary, AB.
20. Cristina Suana, "Conversations on Uros."
21. Ibid.
22. Eddy Suana, "Construction Methods of the Uros Islands." Interview by Alberto de Salvatierra, August 2, 2016.
23. Ibid.
24. Ibid.
25. Ibid.
26. Alberto De Salvatierra, and Anagha Patil, *Building Unit Sections, Uros Khantati*, 2021, Drawing, Center for Civilization, Calgary, AB.
27. Cristina Suana, "Conversations on Uros."
28. Ibid.
29. Ibid.
30. Ibid.
31. Julia Watson, *Lo–TEK, Design by Radical Indigenism* (Cologne: Taschen, 2019), 278.
32. Ibid.
33. Ibid, 277.
34. Ibid.
35. Al Jazeera English, "Peru's Floating Classroom," YouTube Video, 2012, https://www.youtube.com/watch?v=s9q1X0ZSBVo.
36. Shelagh McCartney, and Sukanya Krishnamurthy, "Neglected? Strengthening the Morphological Study of Informal Settlements," *SAGE Open: SAGE Journals* (2018): 1-11.
37. Alberto de Salvatierra, and Dan Hapton, "Soft City, Soft Haus," *Ground Up Journal* Issue 10, (2021).

3 READING SOCIO-POLITICAL LANDSCAPES

Reading Socio-Political Landscapes identifies institutional, political, social, and economic actors in different geographies and describes in each case how these actors shape and co-produce physical environments. Instead of looking at isolated, contemporary sites, the chapters aim to discuss cohesive studies of large, territorial contexts and their inherent histories of social-environmental co-production. These landscape-informed readings allow us to identify multiple stakeholders, establish a mutual dialogue to engage with them, negotiate between different interests, and intervene effectively in these systems across multiple scales and time frames.

3.1

Forest Plantations as Spatiotemporal Reclamation Strategy

Julia Smachylo

Scattered throughout southern Ontario are traces of provincial plantation programs that have established a spatial and temporal system of landscape responses to environmental crises. At the end of the nineteenth century, much of southern Ontario's forests had been cleared, resulting in large areas becoming wastelands due to destructive forestry practices. Extensive deforestation had upset the biotic structures that had previously maintained the water table and prevented soil erosion. In response, provincial planting programs of this era established a legacy of forest management through the use of plantations as a spatiotemporal design strategy that can still be seen in their early stages in the landscape today.

Walking through the woods one might come across these stands: linear rows of evenly spaced pine that sit within lands managed by conservation authorities, land trusts, municipalities, and private landowners. Some have been meticulously managed, following prescribed thinning to maintain the health of the forest and to allow for understory regeneration into a mixed-wood stand, others have been left to their own devices. In reflecting on the legacy of these programs in response to the desertification of large areas of the region, this research brings attention to the role of plantations and their management as both an immediate and long-term designed response—with direct consequence to the environmental health of the region. The dynamics of these plantings continue to play-out across the landscape, where plantations—reforested/afforested, cultivated ecosystems—dominated by a single or a limited species selection have, and are still, mobilized as a living medium and territorial strategy.[1,2]

There are different kinds of tree plantations and recent literature highlights the potential benefits and shortcomings of a dominant-species approach. For instance, monocultures have proven useful in ecological restoration, wood production, and in providing ecosystem services, but also have been criticized for their connection to broader urban and industrial forces, adverse soil and biodiversity impacts, and exclusionary practices.[3] In addition, large-scale tree planting programs can potentially lead to adverse impacts in addressing climate change among other goals,[4] and as a tool to counter desertification, might not provide the contextual sensitivity required to support healthy ecosystems.[5]

OPPOSITE PAGE A sixty-year-old red pine plantation in Southern Ontario that has undergone thinning in 1995 and then again in late 2015/early 2016 through a selective marking strategy. Julia Smachylo

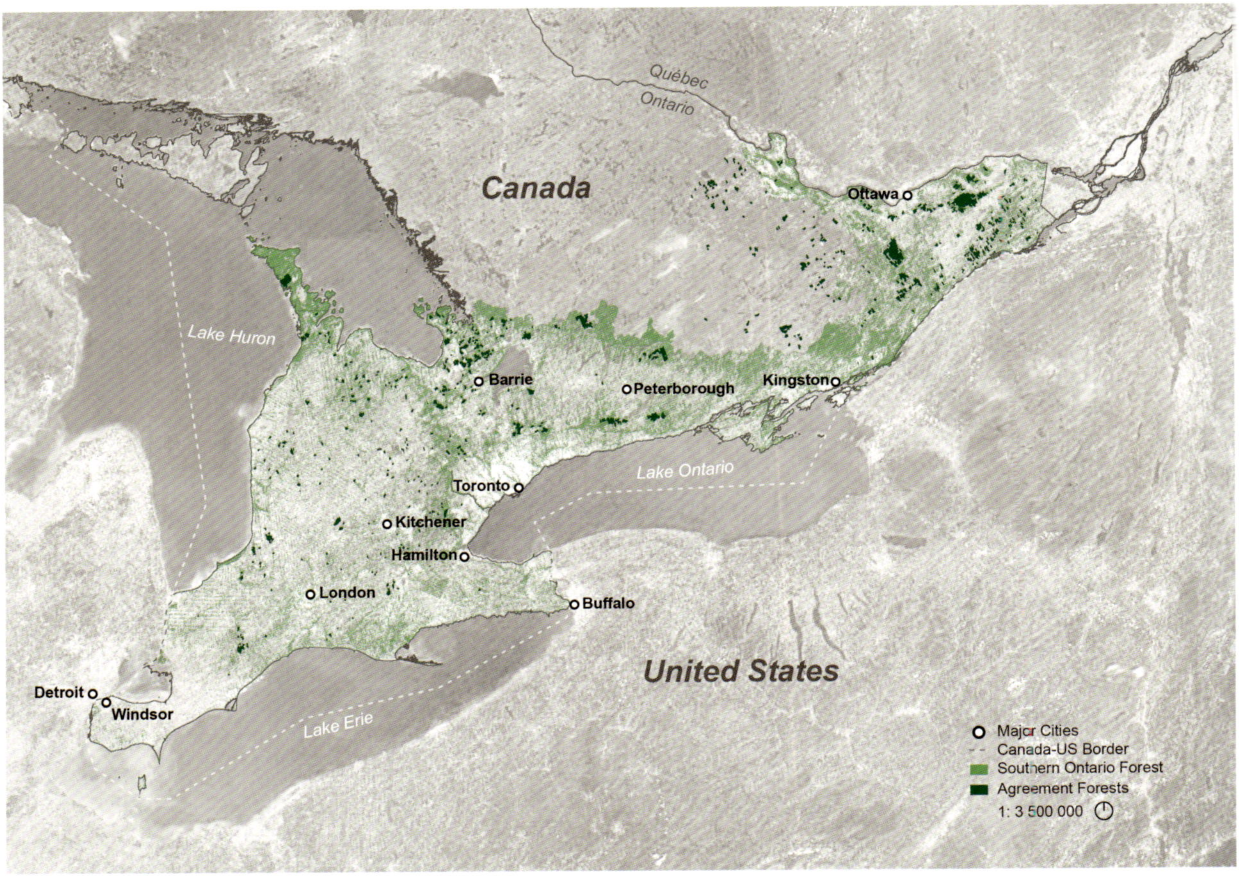

FIG. 1 Map showing forest cover and major cities in Southern Ontario. Prepared by Julia Smachylo (Data obtained from: DMTI CanMap Route Logistics, 2019; Ontario Ministry of Natural Resources, Southern Ontario Land Resource Information System (SOLRIS) 2008; Ministry of Natural Resources and Forestry, Agreement Forest Area, 1997)

Within Canada, the region of southern Ontario—the area south of the French River and Algonquin Park—hosts a diverse range of tree species, while also containing high levels of urban growth[6] [FIG. 1]. Within this region forested land is shrinking due to pressures from development and agriculture, with a total forest loss of 3,786 hectares recorded in 2006–2011.[7] At the same time, the Canadian government sees the potential for forested landscapes to play a key role in meeting climate change goals and maintaining ecological, economic, and social health.[8] In contributing to the debates referenced above, the following pages outline the use of softwood plantations as a landscape approach to soil and forest reclamation by the province of Ontario in the early to late twentieth century, and their legacy, which brings attention to the ongoing role of state spatial strategies to counter ecological crises.[9] In tracing the use of managed plantations by the province, their historic deployment as both an immediate and latent design response is highlighted, along with their current integration into nature-based climate strategies.

State Responses to Environmental Crises

Forests in southern Ontario have undergone dramatic change. By the beginning of the twentieth century, the dense white pine and hardwood forests that were once bountiful in the region had been depleted as a result of clearing for agriculture and trade. Human impact on the land had resulted in large areas becoming wastelands, and widespread soil degradation as a result of deforestation led to the abandonment of farms[10] [FIG. 2]. At the peak of the wasteland issue, due to drifting sand dunes, roads needed to be continuously ploughed of sand.[11] At the same time, the region was experiencing a timber scarcity, especially in hardwoods—the most economically valuable species. A provincial report in 1909 by forester Edmund Zavitz, *Waste Lands of Southern Ontario,* highlighted these issues and estimated that approximately 150,000 hectares of land were in need of immediate action to address degradation.[12] Along with the establishment of tree nurseries, flagship reforestation projects, and a commitment to further education and outreach, plans to address desertification set in motion the deployment of wasteland plantations[13] [FIG. 3-4]. Red pine (*Pinus resinosa*) was the most common seedling used due its tolerance to drought conditions, which made it an ideal species to anchor sandy soils. Jack pine (*Pinus banksiana*) and white pine (*Pinus strobus*) were used in eroding areas and finer sandy conditions respectively.[14] The use of this strategy also had an important temporal dimension, as it was able to address the conditions of abandoned agricultural areas within a generation (70–80 years) that would have otherwise taken centuries to re-seed without intervention.

The reclamation strategy of the early 20th century that mobilized pine plantations to address desertification set in motion a particular landscape approach that has informed subsequent policy and practice in southern Ontario. In countering the wasteland issue, from 1911 until the mid-'90s, the provincial government entered into a series of agreements with counties, setting in motion a large-scale tree planting program across the region.[15] Here, bought-up abandoned wastelands were planted with Agreement Forests, comprised of predominantly

FIG.2 TOP LEFT Soil erosion resulting in a wasteland condition, just after WWII. Supplied by Fraser Smith RPF from personal archives

FIGS.3–4 TOP RIGHT Abandoned farmland prepared for planting and early planting of seedlings, just after WWII. Supplied by Fraser Smith RPF from personal archives

government-managed softwood plantations.[16] During the program's lifespan, over 128,000 hectares of plantations and natural woodlands became part of this management strategy.[17] Arising from the success of Agreement Forests, the Woodlands Improvement Act was passed in 1966, which allowed for Woodland Improvement Agreements,[18] a program that provided provincial afforestation and forest-management services to private landowners that resulted in approximately 213 million seedlings planted on over 137,000 hectares.[19] As a result, "(i)t was largely through the reforestation taking place on these Agreement Forests, the plantations established with landowners under the Woodlands Improvement Act, and the smaller areas reforested by other landowners that the forested area of southern Ontario was increased to its present extent"[20] Here, the use of forest plantations as a territorial reclamation strategy produced a certain kind of forest, where provincial policy along with human and non-human dynamics shaped the configuration, species composition, and maintenance of these lands.[21]

Plantations as a Spatiotemporal Design Strategy

The plantations of the Agreement Forest and the Woodland Improvement Agreements were in fact designed systems—spatial and temporal management strategies—controlled to facilitate the emergence of a different forest type. They functioned as both an *immediate* infrastructural response and *long-term* landscape strategy, tied to the latent programming of future ecological systems combined with stewardship practices that came together over time to cultivate the regeneration of these stands in their development from softwood to hardwood forests.[22] Using plantations as a spatial and management framework initially rested heavily with the choice of species, their arrangement and maintenance as a primer for future growth. This set the stage for processes of forest succession that over time have slowly transitioned from earlier monocultures in both form—the arrangement of trees in neat and consistently spaced rows—and species composition. Years later, these landscapes have increasingly diversified through the adaptation of these living organisms to their environment in response to strategic human intervention.[23]

As an immediate response, pines are an excellent initial species to plant on sandy soils as these young trees do well in exposed conditions.[24] Over the next 30-plus years, their debris adds humus, their roots anchor, and water returns. The quick growth and shade of the pines provides the perfect conditions for less drought-tolerant hardwoods, which are native to the region, to return.[25] In addition to species selection, forest management practices through the selective thinning of trees removes sections of the forest canopy, letting light down to the understory, which aids in the transformation to hardwood stands.[26] This maintenance, which was provided by provincial foresters, adds another layer to this story, where the deployment of a single species was partnered with a multi-decade management strategy throughout the 20th century. Thus, as a design strategy, the deployment of pine, their arrangement in the land and their management over time has fast-forwarded the timescale of forest regeneration in this region [FIG. 5–6].

Presently, afforestation and reforestation through a plantation approach is still taking place. For example, the 50 Million Trees Program run by Forests Ontario provides a financial incentive and also the initial labor required to plant 10,000 trees a day—enough to cover an entire property with seedlings.[27] Here, trees are planted in rows, with attention given to landowner preference but also, importantly, to what will thrive in local conditions. In setting the stage for forest growth, once again softwood saplings are more heavily relied upon to ensure initial conditions that in 30-plus years will provide the shaded canopy to prompt the next wave of forest succession [FIG. 7].

FIG.5 A former cattle pasture, this plantation was established in 1979, likely through the WIA. The planted areas consist mainly of red and white pine, but also include white spruce, silver maple and red oak with an average height of 17 meters. The current landowners manage this stand through periodic thinning. Julia Smachylo

FIG.6 Previously open agricultural land, this stand was reforested 65 years ago. Succession has taken place within the spaces between trees aided by thinning which involved the removal of one of every three to four rows of trees combined with light selection cutting in the retained rows to open up the forest canopy. Julia Smachylo

Learning From Past Practices

The account outlined above highlights the continuing role that forest plantations have played in southern Ontario over the 20th century in addressing anthropogenic impacts. Learning from these past approaches foregrounds a more nuanced spatial and temporal scale, where plantations paired with management highlights the need to carefully consider our current planting responses and how they will develop over silvic lifecycles. In particular, the large-scale planting of trees is part of current government initiatives in addressing climate change in Canada, where the federal government has committed to nature-based climate approaches that include the conservation of 25 percent of land and oceans by 2050, and the planting of two billion trees on public and private land over the next 10 years. This is part of a broader ambition of surpassing the 2030 Paris Agreement targets and achieving a net-zero-emissions economy by 2050.[28]

In reaching this goal, how might former provincial government-initiated plantation responses to forest regeneration in southern Ontario inform this nature-based climate approach? Forests have been championed as a carbon sequestration strategy due to their carbon capture and soil reclamation potential, and in their regulation and maintenance of hydrological cycles.[29] At the same time, climate change raises questions of how we can ensure the health of our forests as these changes play out across the landscape over time. In meeting the challenge of planting two billion trees, this will rely on anticipating these climatic changes, while

FIG.7 Landowners have recently afforested this formerly agricultural property through Forest Ontario's 50 Million Trees Program. Approximately 8,700 seedlings have been planted with a diverse species mix. This particular area contains white pine, white spruce, Norway spruce, back walnut and hackberry. Julia Smachylo

also ensuring a planting strategy that is sensitive to local contexts and is able to absorb carbon quickly.

One particular challenge that has been raised in meeting these ambitious planting targets is the logistics of accessing native and genetically diverse seeds at such a large scale.[30] In learning from the plantation programs of the mid-20th century, the establishment of seed stations and educational outreach points to the potential of past approaches that are once again relevant.[31] Along with accessing and planting seedlings, their management over time was a key aspect of these previous planting strategies. With the wasteland plantings, Agreement Forests and WIA programs, forest management was predominantly the domain of provincial forestry professionals who ensured plantation thinning to maintain forest health and who helped to direct the trajectory of future growth. However, in the mid-1990s, due to changes in governance, the prevalence of provincial foresters dramatically declined due to political shifts, which has reduced the role of government, and instead brought an increasing diversity of people through extension forestry programs into the management of these lands. While previously ministry employees were performing these services, now these practices have become the domain of professional foresters and private consultants, aided by the stewardship of private landowners.[32] This raises important questions of *who* is involved in forest management and *how* a diversified stewardship model will impact these efforts.

In reflecting on the past century of forest management in southern Ontario, plantations have, and continue to be, mobilized as a living medium and territorial strategy in response to large-scale environmental pressures. Their legacy offers a lens through which to critically inform contemporary forest management, regional planning, and nature-based climate strategies. By focusing on the history of provincial planting programs, what is revealed are the intricacies of this spatiotemporal reclamation strategy that encompassed both an immediate and long-term response. In particular when following the legacy of these plantations as designed systems, what surfaces is the consideration given to multiple interacting human and non-human agents over time as part of a coordinated approach, one whose logics can be leveraged to inform contemporary environmental responses. For instance, what is revealed is the importance of an initial seeding strategy, species selection, and spatial configuration alongside the development of provincial nurseries that were able to respond to the magnitude of seedlings required, which in 30–50 years, would facilitate the next wave of mixed hardwood trees. But this is only half the story. Along with attention given to plant species was the careful maintenance of these stands over time. This changing constellation of species, biophysical conditions, and management practices have thus set in motion a landscape strategy with the ability to critically inform contemporary climate-based approaches.

ACKNOWLEDGMENTS

Support for this research was provided by the Canadian Social Sciences and Humanities Research Council Doctoral Fellowship and the Canada Program at the Weatherhead Center for International Affairs at Harvard University. I would like to extend a special thank you to the landowners and forest consultants who shared their insight.

Endnotes

1 For information on Ontario plantations see: OMNRF, *Afforestation Guide for Southern Ontario*, Toronto: Queen's Printer for Ontario, 2018. For additional resources on plantations and a review of plantation forestry trends in general, refer to: Corsa Lok Ching Liu, Oleksandra Kuchma, and Konstantin V. Krutovsky, "Mixed-Species Versus Monocultures in Plantation Forestry: Development, Benefits, Ecosystem Services and Perspectives for the Future," *Global Ecology and Conservation* 15 (2018): e00419.

2 The use of forest plantations is situated within provincial territorial strategies tied to forest management. Here, Elden's conceptualization of territory which integrates: economic, strategic, legal and technical considerations within a particular geographic and historical context is used. See: Stuart Elden, "Land, Terrain, Territory," *Progress in Human Geography* 34, no. 6 (2010): 799–817.

3 Milica Topalovic, "Plantation Landscapes of Palm Oil and Ethics of Visibility," in *Into the Woods*, edited by Jennifer Sigler, *Harvard Design Magazine*, 2018, no. 45, 118–127; Liu, Kuchma and Krutovsky, "Mixed-Species Versus Monocultures in Plantation Forestry."

4 For instance, a recent article published by the Yale School of Environment points to the potential of projects such as China's Great Green Wall and Pakistan's Billion Tree Tsunami to negatively affect natural ecosystems, impacting water availability while also taking resources from other projects that might have greater ecological benefit. They also point to potential displacement and conflict between competing land uses. See: Adam Welz, "Are Huge Tree Planting Projects More Hype than Solution?", *Yale Environment 360*, April 8, 2021, https://e360.yale.edu/features/are-huge-tree-planting-projects-more-hype-than-solution.

5 Rosetta Elkin, "Planting the Desert: Cultivating Green Wall Infrastructure," in *Revising Green Infrastructure: Concepts Between Nature and Design*, edited by Daniel Czechowski, Thomas Hauck and Georg Hausladen (CRC Press, 2014), 301–322.

6 Natural Resources Canada, The State of Canada's Forests: Annual Report, Cat. No. Fo1-6E (Print) ISSN 1196-1589, 2020, https://www.nrcan.gc.ca/our-natural-resources/forests-forestry/state-canadas-forests-report/16496.

7 Government of Ontario, "Forestry | Deforestation," December 10, 2019, https://www.ontario.ca/page/deforestation.

8 PMO (Office of the Prime Minister), *Minister of Environment and Climate Change Mandate Letter*, Rt. Hon. Justin Trudeau, 2019, https://pm.gc.ca/en/mandate-letters/2019/12/13/minister-environment-and-climate-change-mandate-letter; Environment and Climate Change Canada, *A Healthy Environment and A Healthy Economy*, 2020, https://www.canada.ca/content/dam/eccc/documents/pdf/climate-change/climate-plan/healthy_environment_healthy_economy_plan.pdf; PMO (Office of the Prime Minister), *Minister of Environment and Climate Change Supplementary Mandate Letter*, Rt. Hon. Justin Trudeau, 2021, https://pm.gc.ca/en/mandate-letters/2021/01/15/minister-environment-and-climate-change-supplementary-mandate-letter.

9 For more on state spatial strategies see Neil Brenner, *New State Spaces: Urban Governance and the Rescaling of Statehood* (Oxford University Press, 2004).

10 Ontario Department of Agriculture (ODA), *Reforestation of Waste Lands in Southern Ontario 1908*, Toronto: Printed by The Legislative Assembly of Ontario, 1909; R. S. Carman, "The Glacial Pot Hole Area, Durham County, Ontario," *The Forestry Chronicle* 17, no. 3 (1941): 110–120; Scott T. McPherson and V. R. Timmer, "Amelioration of Degraded Soils Under Red Pine Plantations on the Oak Ridges Moraine, Ontario," *Canadian Journal of Soil Science* 82, no. 3 (2002): 375–388.

11 Ontario Department of Agriculture (ODA), *Reforestation of Waste Lands in Southern Ontario 1908*.

12 Ibid.

13 Ibid.; OMNRF, *Afforestation Guide for Southern Ontario*, Afforestation Guide.

14 Kenneth A. Armson, *Ontario Forests: A Historical Perspective* (Fitzhenry and Whiteside Limited and Ontario Forestry Association, 2001).

15 In response to the wasteland issue, the 1911 Counties Reforestation Act instigated the Counties Forest Program which enabled counties to pass by-laws to purchase or lease degraded lands for reforestation purposes. See: Armson, *Ontario Forests: A Historical Perspective*. Building on the small-scale success of early reclamation experiments, in 1921 the provincial government replaced the Counties Reforestation Act with the Reforestation Act of 1921, which remained active until the mid-90s. This Act made the program more financially beneficial and allowed the government to enter into agreements with counties to reforest and manage municipal land at the province's expense. For additional resources see: Richard S. Lambert and Paul Pross, *Renewing Natures Wealth A Centennial History*, The Hunter Rose Company, 1967; Ministry of Natural Resources, *Evergreen Challenge: The Agreement Forest Story*, Ontario, Canada: Queen's Printer for Ontario, 1986; Ed Borczon, "Agreement Forests – The Challenge and the Accomplishment," *Forestory*, 10, no.1, (Spring 2019): 5-17. In 1927, the Reforestation Act was replaced by the Forestry Act (1927) which expanded the program and brought the ministry in direct relation to the selling and disposing of timber. See: Ministry of Natural Resources, *Evergreen Challenge: The Agreement Forest Story*.

16 Ministry of Natural Resources, *Evergreen Challenge: The Agreement Forest Story*.

17 Today, the majority of restored lands under the Agreement Forest program reside under the management of Conservation Authorities and municipalities as highlighted by: Ed Borczon, "Agreement Forests - The Challenge and the Accomplishment," 5–17; OMNRF, *Afforestation Guide for Southern Ontario.*

18 Paul L. Aird, *Forest Legislation a Digest of the Statutes of Ontario* (Richmond Hill Ontario: Published by the Ontario Professional Foresters Association with Assistance from the Ministry of Natural Resources, 1996).

19 Ontario Ministry of Natural Resources, *Critical Review of Historical and Current Tree Planting Programs on Private Lands in Ontario*, 2001. In addition, the Woodland Improvement Agreements was the first landowner program in southern Ontario where the government entered into a 15-year agreement with private landowners to manage these lands, see: OMNRF, *Afforestation Guide for Southern Ontario.*

20 Armson, *Ontario Forests: A Historical Perspective*, 167.

21 Program outcomes from this time pointed to the necessity of making investments in both seeding stock and maintenance that included cutting back competing species, as well as fire, disease and invasive species management, see Armson, *Ontario Forests: A Historical Perspective.*

22 For more on landscape infrastructure see Pierre Bélanger, "Landscape as Infrastructure," *Landscape Journal* 28, no. 1 (2009): 79–95; Pierre Bélanger, *Landscape as Infrastructure: A Base Primer* (New York, NY: Routledge, 2016).

23 For more on soil restoration see T. S. McPherson and V. R. Timmer. "Amelioration of Degraded Soils Under Red Pine Plantations on the Oak Ridges Moraine, Ontario," 375–388. For more information see: OMNRF, *Afforestation Guide for Southern Ontario.*

24 The choice of pine also has an economic dimension as this species provides a financial incentive through harvesting. Personal correspondence with Fraser Smith RPF 2371, 2021.

25 Armson argues that though once seen as sterile environments, single species plantations have over time gained biodiversity and cultural value. Armson, *Ontario Forests: A Historical Perspective.*

26 OMNRF, *Afforestation Guide for Southern Ontario*; Ed Borczon, "Agreement Forests - The Challenge and the Accomplishment," 5–17.

27 "50 Million Tree Program | Forests Ontario," https://forestsontario.ca/en/program/50-million-tree-program.

28 PMO, *Minister of Environment and Climate Change Mandate Letter*, 2019; GOC (Government of Canada), *Moving Forward Together: Speech from the Throne to Open the First Session of the Forty-third Parliament of Canada*, Governor General, 2019, https://www.canada.ca/en/privy-council/campaigns/speech-throne/moving-forward-together.html; Environment and Climate Change Canada, *A Healthy Environment and A Healthy Economy*; PMO, *Minister of Environment and Climate Change Supplementary Mandate Letter*, 2021.

29 Forest plantations in particular have been highlighted as part of an integrated solution as per Alain Paquette and Christian Messier, "The Role of Plantations in Managing the World's Forests in the Anthropocene," 2010. In Ontario, forest plantations are also being used as part of climate mitigation responses. See: OMNRF, *Afforestation Guide for Southern Ontario*, 2018; PMO, *Minister of Environment and Climate Change Mandate Letter*, 2019; GOC (Government of Canada), *Moving Forward Together: Speech from the Throne to Open the First Session of the Forty-Third Parliament of Canada*; Environment and Climate Change Canada, *A Healthy Environment and A Healthy Economy*; PMO, *Minister of Environment and Climate Change Supplementary Mandate Letter*, 2021.

30 Personal Correspondence with Fraser Smith RPF 2371, 2021.

31 As part of the province's initial wasteland reclamation strategy, nurseries were set up to provide local seed. For more information see, Ontario Department of Agriculture (ODA), *Reforestation of Waste Lands in Southern Ontario 1908.*

32 This shift in management is tied to political shifts in the mid-90s due to the Harris Conservative Government's *Common Sense Revolution* platform that significantly reduced the budget for environmental programs. During this time, environmental governance at the provincial level was restructured and its primary responsibilities transferred to municipalities, albeit within the retained policy structure and power of the province. See: Shannon Logan and Gerda R. Wekerle, "Neoliberalizing Environmental Governance? Land Trusts, Private Conservation and Nature on the Oak Ridges Moraine," *Geoforum* 39, no. 6 (2008): 2097–2108; Mark Winfield, *Blue-Green Province: The Environment and the Political Economy of Ontario.* UBC Press, 2012.

3.2

Earth Moves

Singapore's Land Reclamation Projects and the Construction of Territory

Hans Hortig

Arriving on a barge to Singapore, a load of sand transforms from a cheap, generic material into an exorbitantly priced piece of land or property: Cambodian river sediments are transformed into public-housing complexes, Indonesian islands into industrial estates, and Vietnamese sand into beaches along the Singapore Strait. How does the metabolic transformation of sand unfold and who are the actors facilitating, guiding, and profiting from the process of making new land? Can a landscape approach help to conceptualize the production of land to rethink its design?

This essay is based on the chapter "Sand Hinterland–The Construction of Territory" that will be published in the book *Hinterland–Singapore Beyond the Border* by Milica Topalovic and Hans Hortig, Chair of Architecture and Territorial Planning, ETH Zurich.

This essay explores the unprecedented scale of land reclamation in Singapore, how sand trade figures in official narratives and how soil is recast to justify Singapore's ongoing project of territorial extension. By tracing the process of land reclamation, the metabolic relations between the city and its hinterland are highlighted and the urbanism of sand accumulation is framed as a project of urban and territorial design.

Different Types of Sand

During the 1990s, the increasing global demand for construction material made sand and gravel aggregates the world's "most extracted" material by volume, before harvested biomass and all fossil energy sources, including oil and gas.[1] Used for land reclamation and by the construction industry, two specific types of sand are in high demand: sea sand and riverbed sand. Land reclamation projects use enormous quantities of coarse sea sand and gravel aggregates as fill material. When used for reinforced concrete, the salt mixed in with the sea sand is likely to cause corrosion of reinforcing steel rods, which threatens structural stability. Although salt can be washed out of sea sand, the costly process of washing currently favors the use of river sand in concrete and sea sand for coastal reclamation. Therefore, non-salty sand, either extracted directly for the riverbed or from the surrounding deposits, is essential for the building industry. Desert sand, the most common type of sand on earth, is not used as a resource for construction of any kind because it lacks the internal coherence and bearing capacity necessary to be used as an aggregate for both concrete and land reclamation.[2]

The compositional specificities of each sand type can explain why certain sands are in high demand, so much so that they have become

OPPOSITE PAGE Land reclamation is a practice of inverting land and sea–a sign of urban civilization's preference for the terrestrial over the marine realm. At Tekong Island, Singapore explores new terrain. The perimeter bond defines the first polder project of the island state. The new land will be drained and thus lies below sea level allowing for reduced use of sand in the reclamation. Tekong Reclamation, Singapore; Hans Hortig, 2019

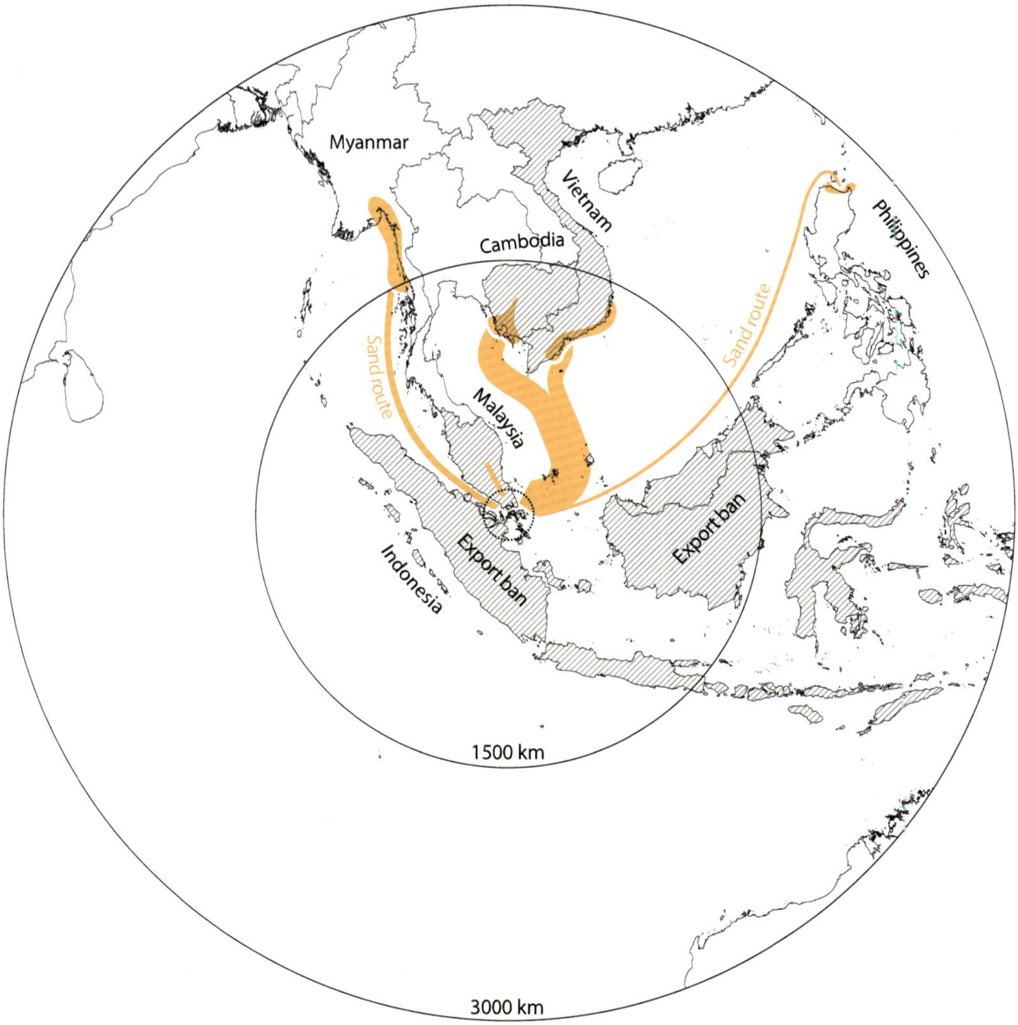

TRADING AGAINST THE BANS:
Discrepancies in the UN Comtrade report in 2014

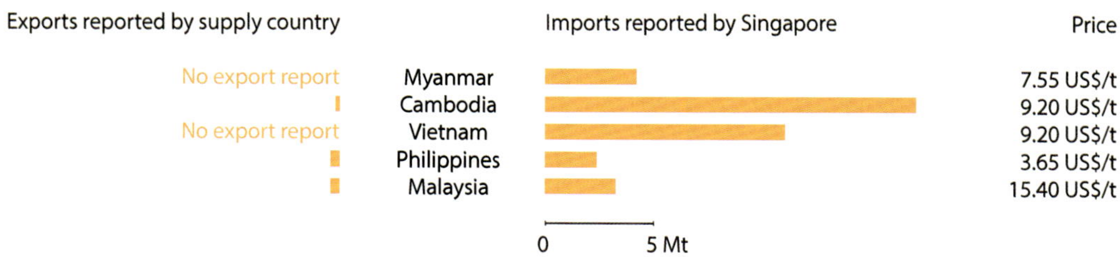

limited resources. Sand is mined at beaches and coastal quarries, dredged in riverbeds and from the ocean floor to be sold as raw material for construction. The river estuaries and shallow seawaters of Southeast Asia have become Singapore's most resourceful sand hinterlands.

From Local Mining to Sand Wars

Singapore is not the only country using land reclamation to expand on its existing territory, but the speed and extent at which the country's land area has changed is breath-taking. Approximately one quarter, or 145 square kilometers, of the island-state's land area has been artificially added.[3] While Singapore's early reclamation efforts relied on the locally organized cut-and-fill technique, large-scale reclamation works required sand imports from neighboring countries from the 1980s onwards.[4] By the early 1990s, most of the sand available within the domestic territory had been put into use and the lion share of material used for land reclamation as well as sand for the construction of buildings and infrastructures had to be imported.[5] Regional sand trade peaked in 2002, when 77 percent of the world's dredging vessels were recorded as being in operation in and around the Singapore Strait[6] [FIG. 1].

The concomitant island-wide redevelopment process—also portrayed as tabula rasa[7]—together with the pursuit for territorial expansion through land reclamation has propelled Singapore to the number one spot in the planetary ranking of natural sand imports since 2008.[8] Citing a wide range of reasons—from supply shortage to a nationalistic rhetoric on the loss of territory—regional suppliers exposed export bans (Malaysia 1997, Indonesia 2007, Cambodia and Vietnam 2009) forcing the island-state to enlarge its sourcing hinterland.[9] Today, Singapore's sand hinterland comprises trading routes extending all over Southeast Asia's archipelagic geography. Although importers are required to document the origin and verify the legality of sand, the possibilities to forge documents within the supply chain are high and reports on dubious deals are frequent. Investigative reports on extraction sites and practices carried out by NGOs and local journalists uncovered sand smuggling networks from nations under embargoes, yet the records remain fragmentary.[10]

The profits generated by the sand trading industry are vast as Singapore imported around US$360 million of sand in 2018 alone.[11] This figure reflects only official trade, excluding any form of illegal transactions. In 2008 for example, it was estimated that sand worth SG$35 million was smuggled from a single site on the Johor River despite Malaysia's trade ban.[12] Repeatedly, countries in the region have accused Singapore of consuming their territories while, at the same time, local decision makers—legally and illegally—continued to issue extraction permits. Even as concerns over the loss of an important material resource and ecological devastation were well founded, in the public discourse, sand

FIG. 1 At its origin, sand is fluid, carried by water, and accumulates in layers along riverbanks and beaches. Constantly moving and slowly settling, sand is commonly in suspension with water or mixed with other materials. Here, at the frontier of sand extraction, industrial technologies–suction pipes, dredging pumps and auger suckers–function as both material sieving machinery and apparatuses of disambiguation, separating and sorting ambiguous states of physical matter into established material categories–mud, dirt, or dust becoming gravel, sand, or other predefined types of aggregates. Architecture of Territory, ETH Zürich, 2017

trade was mainly portrayed as a threat to national identity and territorial sovereignty. The increasing interstate power plays accompanying the serial bans and concessions over sand trade became veritable battles and treaties of Southeast Asia's "sand wars."[13]

Outsourcing and Brokerage

While information on the countries of origin and the quantities of traded sand are generally available, the sites of extraction, social-environmental conditions under which sands are mined, and details of trading agreements surface in academic research only recently,[14] and remain largely unknown to the public. The only official data available are provided by the United Nations Commodity Trade Statistics Database (UNCOM), who cites general figures of trade among nations, but does not reveal any details pertaining to sites of extraction or the nature of trading contracts. Although questions of transparency have been raised often, pointing to the lack of regulations on sand extraction and trade at transnational levels,[15] and to the obscure behaviors of state institutions and companies involved in the sand trade across the region,[16] Singapore's government has defended this information vacuum by arguing that matters of sourcing sand are "national security matters" and are thereby subject to "strict confidentiality."[17] Since Singapore's Building and Construction Authority categorized sand as "sensitive goods" and "essential construction materials" in 2011, importation has been subjected to control by governmental agencies and requires importation licenses.[18] Through this regulatory framework, Singapore's government has been able to secure sand imports from various foreign sources without being actively involved in any trade. Formally, government agencies only buy sand from authorized private contractors[19] and therefore are not linked to the full supply chain, trade contracts, or the circumstances and consequences of extraction and trade. This type of hinterland—hands-off, barely regulated and opaque—offers a more flexible, and thus more secure mode of supply than fixed and transparent contracts at the national or international level, which would be exposed to various forms of scrutiny and resistance [FIG. 2].

In a vague, weakly regulated stratum between sub-state and supranational levels, the sand business is negotiated among middlemen, from local mining tycoons and politicians to ship owners and globally operating dredging companies. In this setting, Singapore's government does not exert full control over the process of sand importation, leading detractors to conclude "that prosperity has come at the cost of its neighbors' corruption and environmental destruction."[20] The choice to procure sand through a network of agents, and in part from the informal market, has been useful in also allowing the government to relegate the responsibility for the social and environmental consequences of unregulated sand extraction to the corresponding authority or to third-party actors.

FIG. 2 In the archipelagic geography of Southeast Asia, Singapore and any other sand buyer have access to myriad coastal sites and river estuaries for extraction, making it easy to "diversify sources" and ensure a "flexible supply." It is precisely this provisional and changeable supply chain spanning thousands of kilometers that has been the crucial feature of Singapore's sand hinterland. Google Maps, 2018

Terrapolitics and Sand Urbanism

Sand has not only shaped the island state's urban form, but nearly every segment of its development. Used as the essential material component of concrete, the sand supplied by the transnational sand-trading industry has effectively fueled the country's public housing program, in which over 80

1819—1965

Shaping the colonial port

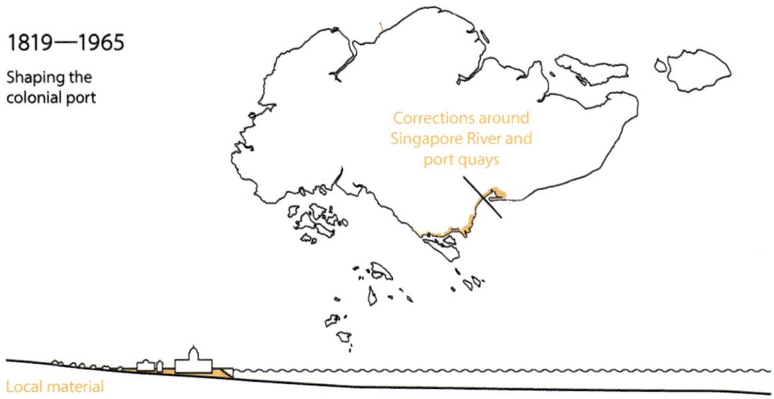

1965—1975

Tabula rasa and nation buidling

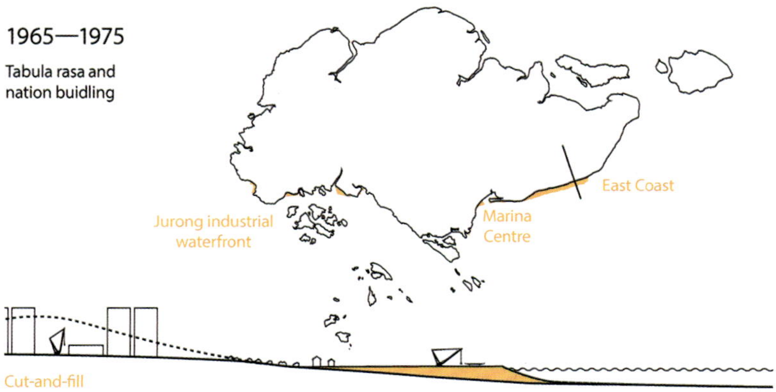

1975—PRESENT

Global city on foreign land

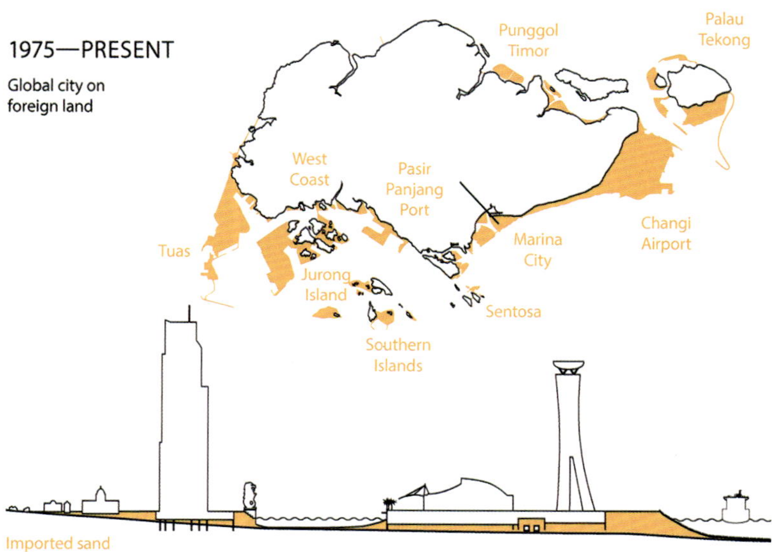

percent of Singaporean residents now live.[21] Newly reclaimed land has also enabled the expansion of infrastructures and industries serving Singapore's global economic ambitions.[22] The steady flow of sand across national borders has been central to the development of a repertoire of political and regulatory strategies that shaped Singapore's urban and national identity. In governmental rhetoric, land reclamation is often portrayed as the island state's right to development, a necessity to ensure economic growth and social progress.[23] "Land-scarcity" serves as a useful mantra that justifies unregulated trade, environmental havoc, and various forms of illegal extraction in the hinterland. It has operated as a parallel philosophy, applied to (sand) resource governance, which has no intersection with and no bearing on the conception and practice of sustainability.

Although Singapore is positioned as a world leader in urban sustainability, it has not addressed the issue of sand extraction in its sustainable development strategy;[24] its government diffuses responsibility for sand extraction through its internal regulations and lax control on international trade. The island state's government ratified two UN conventions, demonstrating the country's responsibility in avoiding ecological degradation and protecting coastal and marine ecosystems,[25] inside and outside its national territory, yet its approach on sustainable urban development is limited to its national boundaries. Strategies of sand sourcing and of land reclamation are entirely found on spectacular techno-solutionism,[26] on land marketing and boosting revenues, profoundly ignoring social, political, and ecological dimensions of land production in the hinterland and in the city.

Average estimates show that revenues from leasing reclaimed land in Singapore are 25 times higher than land production costs.[27] Therefore, making land from the sea has been comparable to a form of alchemy in which the government has created prime sites and high returns "out of nothing."[28] Once released into the urban economy, most of Singapore's reclaimed land is being used by water-dependent industries, port facilities, or national security installations [FIG. 3]. Singapore's specific coastal arrangement—the bundling of infrastructure, industry, and military facilities along the island's edges functions as part of the country's wider border zone. In effect, a series of inaccessible parcels have cordoned off the city from the sea—less than ten percent of Singapore's coastline is publicly accessible.[29]

Land as Project

Hinterland by no means involves only physical extraction of raw materials but includes a wide array of expansionary systems of extraction, trade, accumulation, and regulation.[30] In the case of Singapore's sand hinterland, informal trade, strong internal regulatory systems, local resource efficiency, political rhetoric, as well as access to water-dependent infrastructures and

FIG. 3 Surrounding almost the entire island, reclaimed land facilitates some of the city-state's most important urban functions—the airport, the central business district and several industrial estates—and continues to enlarge Singapore's terrestrial boundaries by extending into the sea. Architecture of Territory, ETH Zürich, 2017

the shipping industry assemble, creating particular interplays that enable the physical expansion of the island state.

The critical analysis of Singapore's sand consumption, trade, and reclamation stresses the need to reconceptualize the practice of building land. If Singapore continues its ambitious program of physical growth, sourcing methods need to be improved to include transparent contracts and trading agreements. The "Singapore model"—which has been replicated in the region[31]—should be based on thoughtful practices of sourcing sand, instead of taking advantage of uneven regional geographies. Alternative strategies of sand sourcing and of land reclamation should move away from an insistence on spectacular techno-solutionism, on land marketing and boosting revenues. Additionally, they need to address social, political, and ecological dimensions of land production in the hinterland as well as in the city [FIG. 4].

FIG.4 At the end of the flow, sand becomes omnipresent in the city, naturalized, inevitable, yet detached from any apparent connection to other places or geographies. Any connotation of land as "culture" or as "nature," is stripped off to reduce the new land to property. On demand, additional "ecologies" might be added retrospectively in the form of lawns, palm trees or artificial reefs. Inhabitants of the frontiers of extraction are largely excluded from the geographies of accumulation. Forest City, Johor, Malaysia; Hans Hortig, 2019

The process of land reclamation needs to be part of the public discourse—the use of actual sites of reclamation should be open to public debates. The publicly impenetrable, mono-functional coastline, occupied by industry and logistics, urgently needs to be revised through mixing with other programs to create meaningful open spaces along the coast. This possible public rediscovery of the sea could evoke a new form of engagement and reflection on the maritime history of the island-state foregrounding the shared regional culture and heritage.

A landscape approach highlights the relation between territories of extraction, trade, and accumulation of sand. It foregrounds the role of critical research to question the current practice of planning and land production. Designers and planners could play an important role in proposing integrative practices of building land which include environmental, social, and political systems within and outside of Singapore.

Endnotes

1 Friedolin Krausmann, Simone Gingrich and Nina Eisenmenger, "Growth in Global Materials Use, GDP and Population During the 20th Century," *Ecological Economics* 68 (2009): 2696–2705.

2 Michael Welland, *Sand: The Never-Ending Story* (Berkeley, LA: University of California Press, 2010), 14.

3 "Total Land Area of Singapore", Open Government Products --A Division of GovTech. Accessed February 2, 2021, https://data.gov.sg/dataset/total-land-area-of-singapore.

4 Kog Yue-Choong, "Environmental Management and Conflict in Southeast Asia: Land Reclamation and its Political Impact" (working paper, The Institute of Defense and Strategic Studies IDSS, Singapore, 2006).

5 S. K. Pui, "100 Years of Foreshore Reclamation in Singapore," (paper presented at the Proceedings of 20th Conference on Coastal Engineering ASCE, November 9-14, 1986).

6 Bill Guerin, "The Shifting Sands of Time - and Singapore," *Asia Times*, July 31, 2003, http://www.atimes.com/atimes/Southeast_Asia/EG31Ae01.html.

7 Rem Koolhaas and Bruce Mau, "Singapore Songlines: Portrait of a Potemkin Metropolis... or Thirty Years of Tabula Rasa," in *S, M, L, XL* (New York: Monacelli Press, 1995), 1008–89.

8 "All Countries Import of All Natural Sands." United Nations, United Nations Statistics Division Commodity Trade Statistics Database (UN Comtrade), http://comtrade.un.org/data/.

9 The Economist, "Such Quantities of Sand," *The Economist*, February 28, 2015, 28.

10 See for example: Elan Perumal and Stuart Michael,

"Sand Pirates: Millions Floated out of the Country via Sungai Johor," *The Star*, June 2010, https://www.asiaone.com/News/AsiaOne%2BNews/Malaysia/Story/A1Story20100624-223708.html; "Shifting Sand: How Singapore's Demand for Cambodian Sand Threatens Ecosystems and Undermines Good Governance," *Global Witness Limited*, May 2010, 2021, https://www.globalwitness.org/en/archive/shifting-sand-how-singapores-demand-cambodian-sand-threatens-ecosystems-and-undermines-good/; Chris Milton, "The Sand Smugglers," *Foreign Policy*, August 4, 2010; Fazlin Abdullah and Goh Ann Tat, "The Dirty Business of Sand: Sand Dredging in Cambodia," Lee Kuan Yew School of Public Policy and National University of Singapore, 2012.

11 "All Import of All Natural Sands by Singapore," UN Comtrade, http://comtrade.un.org/data/.

12 Elan Perumal and Stuart Michael, "Sand Pirates: Millions Floated out of the Country via Sungai Johor," *The Star*, June 2010, https://www.asiaone.com/News/AsiaOne%2BNews/Malaysia/Story/A1Story20100624-223708.html.

13 Barney Henderson "Singapore Accused of Launching 'Sand Wars,'" *The Telegraph*, February 12, 2010, Accessed April 4, 2021, https://www.telegraph.co.uk/news/worldnews/asia/singapore/7221987/Singapore-accused-of-launching-Sand-Wars.

14 See for example Robert John and William Jamieson, "Singapore's Scentless Growth is Built on the Brutal Extraction of Cambodian Sand and Imported Labour," *Failed Architecture*, March 3, 2020, https://failedarchitecture.com/singapores-scentless-growth-is-built-on-the-brutal-extraction-of-cambodian-sand-and-imported-labour/.

15 Pascal Peduzzi, "Sand, Rarer Than One Thinks – Why Is This Issue Important," *Global Environmental Alert Service. United Nations Environmental Programme (UNEP)*, March, 2014.

16 "Shifting Sand: How Singapore's Demand for Cambodian Sand Threatens Ecosystems and Undermines Good Governance," *Global Witness Limited*, May 2010, 15.

17 Joshua Comaroff, "Built on Sand: Singapore and the New State of Risk," *Harvard Design Magazine* 39 (2014): 140-143.

18 Singapore Government, Building and Construction Authority, *Importers' Licence Scheme* (18 February 2016), available from https://www.bca.gov.sg/ImportersLicensing/importerslicensing.html; Parliament of Singapore, Building and Construction Authority (Amendment), *Bill 2009* (18 February 2016), available from https://www.parliament.gov.sg/sites/default/files/090002.pdf.

19 "Shifting Sand: How Singapore's Demand for Cambodian Sand Threatens Ecosystems and Undermines Good Governance," *Global Witness Limited*, May 2010, 2021, 30–33.

20 Chris Milton, "The Sand Smugglers," *Foreign Policy*, August 4, 2010.

21 "Annual Report: Key Statistics FY 2019/2020 (2020)," Housing and Development Board, https://services2.hdb.gov.sg/ebook/AR2020-keystats/html5/index.html?&locale=ENG&pn=1.

22 Milica Topalovic, "Constructed Land: Singapore in the Century of Flattening," in *Constructed Land: Singapore 1924-2012,* ed. Hassler and Topalovic (Singapore: ETH Zurich, 2014), 51-63.

23 As early as 1964, Lee Kuan Yew, then Prime Minister of Singapore, defined the rhetoric of land scarcity promoting the Foreshore (Amendment) Bill that enabled state reclamation projects without compensation for the loss of sea frontage. See "Speech by the Prime Minister, Mr. Lee Kuan Yew, in Moving the Second Reading of the Foreshores (Amendment) Bill at the Legislative Assembly on 10th June, 1964," *National Archives of Singapore, Singapore Government Press Statement*, http://www.nas.gov.sg/archivesonline/data/pdfdoc/lky19640610c.pdf.

24 See for example: "The Sustainable Cities Index 2018," ARCADIS, https://www.arcadis.com/media/1/D/Sustainable_Cities_Index_2018_Arcadis.pdf.

25 The Convention on Biological Diversity in 1996 and the UN Convention on the Law of the Seas in 1994.

26 Singapore's government has been exploring innovative technologies that would enable the extraction of new types of infill materials, available on the domestic territory. Additionally, it has funded strategic research projects focused on reducing waste and increasing resource efficiency in construction processes, where new uses are being sought for excavated soils and recycled building materials. Built examples are the Jurong Rock Caverns, a massive underground crude oil storage that frees up above-ground space or the Semakau Landfill, an island mainly constructed with ash produced in Singapore's four incineration plants.

27 Milica Topalovic, "Constructed Land: Singapore in the Century of Flattening," in *Constructed Land: Singapore 1924–2012,* ed. Hassler and Topalovic (Singapore: ETH Zurich, 2014), 56.

28 Topalovic, *Constructed Land*, 56.

29 Topalovic, *Constructed Land*, 57.

30 Neil Brenner and Nikos Katsikis, "Operational Landscapes: Hinterlands of the Capitalocene," *Architectural Design* 90 (1), (January/February 2020), 22–31; Milica Topalovic et al, ed. *Hinterland: Singapore, Johor, Riau*, (Singapore: ETH Zurich, 2013).

31 Simultaneously, Singapore's *fait accompli*—the destruction of the coastline for industry and infrastructure and the simultaneous flattening of the terrain—spread across the border to the Indonesian Batam Island, and the Malaysian side of the Johor Strait where long coastal stretches have been reclaimed during the last thirty years.

3.3

"Hic et Nunc"Palimpsests

Reconstructing Historical Natures through the Malm Territory of Extraction

Berta Flaquer

"How did things get to be this way?" is the question William Cronon learnt from his father at an early age as the most basic question to keep always in mind when moving through the world.[1] It is a question that would help him to keep wondering about a specific place's history and to avoid any alienation to the past.

Part of this essay includes research conducted along the PhD thesis preliminarily entitled "Territories of Extraction: urbanization as socionatures reproduction" previously appearing in the Cogitatio *Urban Planning* journal, and the U&U PhD seminar proceedings.

Today, we are living in a climate emergency where the desire of "a green new world" appears to be the norm and the way to go in many different contexts and disciplines. Such "green" imaginaries and the associated capital reinvestments have also begun to completely reshape urbanization processes at various scales and temporalities in and through territories of extraction, such as the Malm territory. "Green" fossil-free steel, data centers, wind-power parks, and battery factories are rapidly emerging and expanding at an unprecedented pace across the Malmfälten region in today's northernmost Sweden. Historical investments by the Swedish state as well as private enterprises are underway in order to expand extraction and produce more wealth. These financial investments will require more labor. Local newspapers have forecasted that it will possibly lead to a rapid increase of about 20 percent of the region's population in the next 15 years.[2]

These transformations altogether re-articulate the *problematique*—revolving around the multiple complex relations in the appropriation and exploitation dialectics of extraction—of the Malm territory. "Malm," meaning "ore" in the Swedish colonial language, signifies the minerals from which surplus value can be extracted. Mining activities across the Malmfälten region are closely linked to large-scale forestry and the hydropower industries and appear at first sight as the most visible forms of value extraction across Sápmi [FIG. 1]. Yet, they are just additional forms of the commodification of nature which were socially-produced over time, and join the list of what Jason Moore calls "historical natures,"[3] such as taxed lands, large-scale reindeer herds, dried fish, leather, etc.

Sápmi is a colonized nation without national borders that stretches across a geographical area between today's countries of Sweden, Norway, Finland, and Russia. Colonial extraction industries in the Malm territory have historically expanded beyond Sápmi and even the Swedish state, engaging in mining enterprises, among others, in Liberia, Algeria,

OPPPOSITE PAGE Facebook data center in Luleå. The third phase of expansion is currently under construction and occupying former nature reserve grounds. Berta Flaquer, 2020

Greenland, or Canada. Since its formation in the mid-1500s, the Swedish state has pursued a project of empire-building. It mobilized its powers of science and technology to recurrently establish new strategic ways of mapping, categorizing, and surveying the world "outside," in order to systematically enable forms of appropriating both human and extra-human "Cheap Natures."[4]

Probing beneath the surface of this present "green everything,"[5] moving through multiple scales of time and space and cutting across different processes of urbanization, a whole set of appropriation relations are still masked and rendered invisible in territories of extraction such as the Malm territory. These invisible forms of appropriation are embodied by all the "constitutive outsides"[6]—of different nature(s), Indigenous, and particularly women; through complex interlinkages between the First World and Third World, struggles of socially deprived and dispossessed, artisans and peasants, exploited lands, watercourses, and forests. These are all different historic dimensions of a systematic appropriation of nature that are rendered indispensable for the process of continuing capital accumulation to proceed.

FIG. 1 Landscape patterns of the appropriation of nature in the Malmfälten region in Sápmi: (top left to right) 1. The so-called *Kaptensgropen* ("The Captain's Pit") in the sinking mining town of Malmberget; 2. The exploitation of Julevädno's waters for hydropower production in Harsprånget (the largest hydropower plant in Sweden); 3. The ongoing "forest genocide" in Sápmi of the Swedish logging industry (marketed itself nationally and internationally as "green" and one of the most "sustainable" in the world). Berta Flaquer, 2020

"Hic et Nunc" Palimpsests

Questioning how things got to be the way they are—but now taking into account the invisibilized relations of appropriation—this essay argues that *hic et nunc* (here and now) historical reconstructions across multiple scales are urgently needed. Here and now palimpsests aim to depict how different relations of appropriation processes have been continuously co-producing historical natures in each wave of capital accumulation alongside relations of exploitation. As this text argues, it is these invisibilized relations that have enabled the expansion of the extraction industries and its continuous reproduction. Processes of exploitation and appropriation form dialectic relations under a capitalist system that underpin an uneven asymmetrical tendency towards different forms of increasing exploitation.[7] Asking how

things got to be the way they are, thus, implies to revisit past exploitation and appropriation relations, to study how they are brought back to the present, and to speculate how they could project into the future.

Many possible palimpsests of extraction can be traced. Here, some diachronic reconstructions are sketched throughout the long-term history of the specific Malm territory across six different scales: planetary, national, region, settlement, household, and body.

FIG. 2 Video still showing Clive Sinclair-Poulton, then-Chairman of UK-registered Beowulf Mining Plc. (Jokkmokk Iron Mines AB) at an international mining conference in Stockholm in 2013. He is rhetorically asking "what local people?" when questioned about what local (Indigenous) communities might think about a new mining exploitation in Gállok, while showing a slide of a seemingly uninhabited landscape and referring to Northern Sweden's very low population density compared to London's. Video still, Youtube, 00:45, 2014 https://www.youtube.com/watch?v=XIvmbifyQ80

Planetary

What drove the expansion of extraction in the Malm territory at the planetary scale has been the continuous appropriation of the non-commodified "outside," such as large-scale forestry and logging for energy production, to allow the chasing of cheap iron and its capitalization elsewhere.

The iron-ore frontier first moved from its centers in Germany and Hungary to expand into (southern) Sweden,[8] where, by the mid-18th century, the Bergslagen region accounted for as much as 35–40 percent of the world's entire iron-ore needs.[9] At that moment in time, Sweden played a key role in the main problem of early capitalism: the delivery of cheap inputs into the factories in Europe to fuel the industrial revolution.[10] Yet, simultaneously, the newly formed Swedish state also moved on to define its political boundaries, making territorial claims "outside," especially towards the northern areas of Sápmi which the maps of the time left undescribed as *tenebrosum* (dark), or, even worse, as *ignotum* (unknown).[11] At that time, cartography was improved in representation and accuracy. In the context of Sápmi, as in the case of many other regions that were subject to colonial endeavors, cartography became an essential political technology for the appropriation of land and the expansions of the Swedish extraction frontier.

In response to accumulation crises, following patterns of colonialism, the frontier was each time expanded more deeply into Indigenous lands of Sápmi [FIG. 2.], several Third World countries, and planetary scales. At the core of this scalar expansion of Swedish extraction lies the concept

Nu har malmströmmen från Svappavaara kommit i gång

Nya LKAB-gruvan effektivast i världen

Svappavaara blir en kvinnogruva

Trea i landet

of the "constitutive outsides."[12] In this context, Sámi, plus activist groups beyond Sápmi and the Swedish state, have recently found common ground in their historical land-right struggles and organized resistance at a regional and even planetary scale. As well-established, formal democratic processes of the Swedish state have proven to be ineffective to guarantee minorities' fundamental rights, international bodies like the UN International Labor Organization (ILO) had to intervene. Such international pressure has helped to overcome a culture of near-sightedness at the local level as well as in terms of time.

National

Following a paradigm of incremental growth as an intrinsic part of processes of expanded reproduction of extraction, and since Swedish industrial colonization has effectively taken off after the building of the *Malmbanan* railway and the formation of the industrial region of Malmfälten in Sápmi,[13] both ore and energy outputs began to steadily rise subsequent to each appropriation crisis and new wave of capital accumulation. Today, more than 75,000 tons of ore are produced every day in the Kiruna mine alone. While Sweden as a whole makes up 92 percent of Europe's production,[14] this accounts to just around three percent of the world's total.[15]

To revise how the strategic foundations at the national scale were actually laid out, it is necessary to go back to the period of early capitalism and state formation in the mid-16th century and scrutinize the processes that led to the delineation of the state's borders in the north—in other words, the colonization of Sápmi.[16] At the center of these processes lies the conception of the private property system as we know it today. To implement this system, Sweden mobilized a state apparatus based on a triad of: (a) the Swedish taxation system, (b) the Swedish church, and (c) the Swedish judiciary.

(a) The taxation of leather became the first form of extraction in Sápmi,[17] only to be shortly after followed by the attempt to build a northern empire based on large-scale reindeer herding, which, from the early 17th century on forced the Sámi to transition from a hunter-gatherer society into nomadism.[18] Towards the latter part of the 19th century, land taxation was expanded to Lappmarken and the Swedish state systematically dispossessed Sámi from their lands and waters through the introduction of a private property system.[19] In this process, taxation became the mechanism to mediate appropriation between scales: Traditionally, taxation in Sweden occurred at the unit of the village. When this practice was applied to the context of Sápmi, it meant that *siida* (family-based herding communities) were taxed as villages and Sápmi became thus directly assimilated into the national legal apparatus.

(b) Early on, and in cooperation with the Swedish state, the church sought to take territorial control over the northernmost areas that were inhabited by Sámi. In a process of Christianization, the church aimed to assimilate Sámi into the Christian state following several strategies, including the eradication of the Sámi language and religion, as well as the provision of schools and education. By the end of the 19th century, this had led to the common perception of all Sámi and Tornedal Finns as being primitive people.[20]

(c) Established in Lappmarken during the first decades of the 17th century and adopted to the village as the basic unit of Sweden's countryside, the Swedish judiciary meant, in the context of Sápmi, the split between two courts: One under Sámi customary law (at the settlement and regional scale) and another one under the state's law (at the national scale).[21] This judiciary split and scalar distinction became very important for the implementation of the private property system and the appropriation of land.

Until today, private property relations are at the core of the ongoing *problematique* of extraction and the colonization of Sápmi. They mask historical struggle relations between Sámi and the Swedish state in a context of capitalist extraction.

Regional

Starting from the Bergslagen region, to the formation of the Malmfälten region, and later moving on to directly or indirectly shaping other regions beyond the Swedish state, the regional scale of the Malm territory has been continuously co-producing historical natures in close interlinkages with the state and the national scale.

Once British capital had first flown into Sápmi to be invested in the opening of mines, a process of spatial transformation started and began to form the Malmfälten region, such as through the construction of railway lines connecting areas of extraction with harbors along the coast. Later on, after the first British investment company went bankrupt in 1889, the Swedish state began to steadily increase its influence and interventions over time.[22] However, at the time when the state had become the sole owner of the mines, the capital that had been accumulated and redeemed by the state moved on to circulate beyond the Swedish state and engage in mining undertakings in various Third World countries. As the owner in control of the extraction market, the state could introduce financial incentives and abolish mining and export restrictions in order to sustain a continuous market expansion. Over time, the Swedish state adopted an approach of market liberalization, distanced itself from local affairs in the Malmfälten region, and delegated responsibilities to the local municipalities while simultaneously keeping its political control.[23] At the same time, Sweden sought to attract outside investments and began to market itself as one of the most attractive places for mining enterprises in the world. This was achieved, for instance, by lowering the mineral tax to 0.05 percent as of 2005.[24]

Historically, in order for capital accumulation to proceed, the

FIG.3 TOP TO BOTTOM 1. Vattenfall's large drawing rooms in Stockholm from where 2,200 drawings were produced for Harsprånget, a temporary town for migrant workers involved in the construction of a large-scale hydropower plant, around 1945; 2. Marianne Ekman portrayed at Porsi site around 1960, representing the "new" female professional cartographer in the male-dominated hydropower world; 3. Newspaper *Aftonbladet* in 1965, announcing the new LKAB mine in Svappavaara to become "the most efficient in the world" as well as "a women's mine;" 4. Sámi homes and trees flooded after the newly built water reservoir in Áhkájávrre had been filled in 1941, which then violently forced the dispossessed Sámi to move elsewhere. 1. Nils Forsgren, in Harsprånget. Storverket som aldrig höll på att bli av [Harsprånget. The great work that was never gotten rid of], 1995; 2. Börje Rönnberg, image archive Municipality of Kiruna; 3. newspaper clipping from Aftonbladet, September 6, 1965, Photo: Andrea Luciani, ArkDes Collections; 4. Nordiska Museet, "Suorva," https://www.nordiskamuseet.se/artiklar/suorva

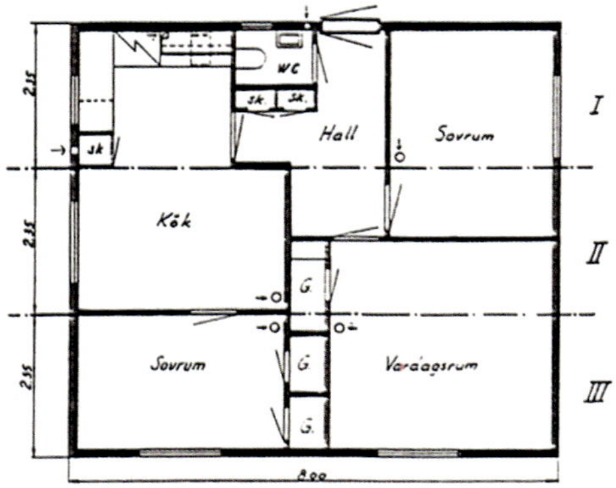

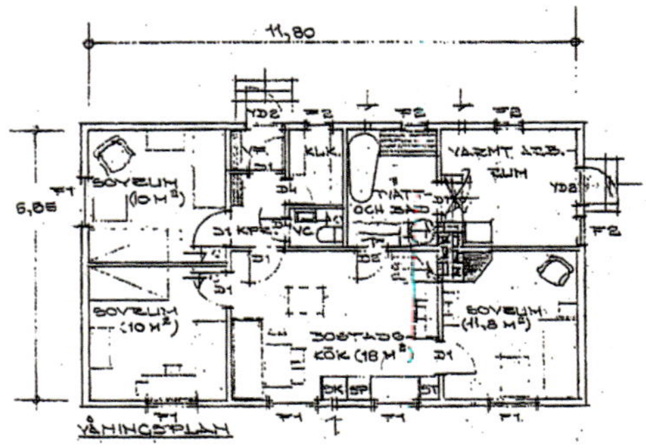

necessary constitutive outsides had to be produced by identifying non-capitalized natures along the frontier in the regional scale. Several borders, spatial limitations, and national legislations were therefore put in place, such as: The limitation of land for cultivation through which the forestry industry was able to expand, while the space for traditionally cultivated forests and mountain reindeer husbandry was decimated; the Reindeer Grazing Act from 1919 that favored industrial colonization over large-scale reindeer husbandry (which had become a burden and was no longer profitable), limited cross-border relations of Indigenous communities, and started the most violent episode in Sámi history with forced relocations throughout the 1920s and early 1930s; the Water Act in 1918, the Reindeer Grazing Act in 1928, and the National Park legislation in the same year which all introduced regulations of the watercourses, restrictions for fishing, and led to a loss of important pastures as well as bad ice conditions during winter which threatened the safe movements of reindeer herds across water bodies.

Settlement

Sinking mining towns, temporary labor towns, coastal processing and shipping towns, military towns, reconverted towns to accommodate migrants and refugees, as well as Indigenous market towns are all specific settlement types that have historically been put in place in order to expand the different forms of extraction across the Malm territory. They were reorganized over time in relation to the various forms of co-producing historical natures [FIG. 3.1, 3.4].

One key strategy can be traced at the settlement scale and across the Malmfälten region from the early periods of colonization until today: Already back in 1670, the governor from Västerbotten county Johan Graan proposed to "encourage Swedish people to move into Lappmarken and help increase its population."[25] The focus back then was to solve the mining transportation issue and, therefore, the Lappmark Proclamation of 1673 was put in place. Today, this strategy of attracting Swedes into the region has been brought back and projected into the future as part of ambitions of a new "industrial boom" and the "green transition." Local and national newspapers are calling for the need to attract more labor to Malmfälten and for "more people to move up north."[26] Practices of "fly-in fly-out" and other forms of temporary employment have long become a reality. In future, more specialized, intellectual labor is needed in more capital-intensive and technologically advanced mines, but also temporary construction workers in specific industries, such as data centers, wind parks, or for the construction of the new town of Kiruna.

However, these specialized settlements mask a more complex reality that had to be put in place in advance. The state first had to create a constitutive outside from the Sámi settlements. It did so through a set of strategies including the denying of the right to build houses and the establishment of a particular Sámi school system.

Household

Most significantly, it is at the scale of the individual home that the metabolic relations to nature have been co-produced throughout history. However, the formation processes of such metabolic relations at the scale of a household across the Malm territory have followed conflicting, and sometimes contradictory logics of separation and subordination of nature and women, both within Sweden as well as in industrial colonies. At their core are the violent and dialectic relationships of "progress" and "retrogression." If the latter are now taken into account, the reconstruction of historical natures at the household scale has to articulate the exploitative patterns brought about by the international as well as the sexual division of labor which both form the basis of capitalist processes of accumulation.

[FIG. 4] present two selected "artifacts" that can illustrate some of such historical relations. They show two "housing solutions" which were built right after the period of the most pronounced exploitation of Sámi around 1928, when the Swedish industrial colonization of Sápmi was most rapidly accelerated. On the side of progression was the *Skivhus* [FIG. 4.1–4.2] which served the housing of the *vattenrallare* (itinerant construction workers of the hydropower industry). They were particularly

FIG.4 *Skivhus* and *Samebostäder*: 1. (top left) Prefabricated Skivhus modules (2,35×8,00 meters) were transported from the factory by rail and then by car. Pictured is a module that is being unloaded in the temporary hydropower labor town of Harsprånget, around mid-1940s. 2. (top right) A *Skivhus* plan layout composed of three modules. The majority of family houses were built out of two or three and in some cases four elements, bachelor houses consisted of up to 14 elements. 3. (bottom left): A *Samebostäder* house in Lappstan. The house in the image has been renovated and transformed with a complete new distribution. 4. (bottom right): 1954 floorplan of the *Samebostäder* house which reflects an astonishing racist idea of Sámi lifestyle by the state at the time. Sámi families were supposed to live in houses of just 58 square meters which was below Swedish standards at the time. The smallest housing type was less than 15 square meters, intended for unmarried reindeer herders.
1. Nils Forsgren, in Harsprånget. Storverket som aldrig höll på att bli av [Harsprånget. The great work that was never gotten rid of]; 2. Archive Porjus Arkivkommitté; 3. Berta Flaquer, 2021; 4. Susanne Spik, in Lappstan, Jokkmokks samhälle [Jokkmokk's community], 2000

dependent on the state for the provision of dwelling and had to endure weak housing rights, which applied only to industry employees (largely male who were discouraged to move with their family or to permanently settle in the area). The houses were constructed as light wooden modules that could easily be transported in a trailer to a new location once the construction of a hydropower plant was finished, to then be rearranged, forming a new, temporary labor town.

On the side of retrogression, the *Samebostäder* (special houses for the Sámi) [FIG. 4.3–4.4] were introduced for Sámi who had long been dispossessed from their land, denied further access and the right to build houses, and were forced to live in tents (*Sámi goahte*). Therefore, an architect from Stockholm was commissioned to design "appropriate" houses. Yet, the houses were much smaller than the Swedish standards at the time. The floor-plan layouts reveal astonishingly racist ideologies of industrial colonization, as well as patriarchal ideals of women as domestic housewives. Such perceptions, which must have been typical at the time, can still be traced, for example, in the case of the entrance and rooms which were arranged in a certain sequence that would serve the Sámi men entering the home after the herding work in the forest to first "get clean."[27]

Body

At the very core of the Malm territory *problematique*, we can identify the invisibilized forces and discrimination at the body scale, which affected particularly women. They were, along with nature(s), increasingly externalized and forced outside, to be subordinated to the colonial, capitalist-patriarchal civilized society [FIG. 3.2.–3.3].[28] Across time, several such invisibilized relationships can be traced, linking the violent processes towards women, all the way from mines in Sweden to Swedish corporations engaging in mining industries in colonial localities, far beyond the Swedish state boundaries [FIG. 5].

One example for this subordination of women across planetary scales is the case of Swedish bourgeois women who moved to the town of Yekepa[29] in American-colonized Liberia in the 1960s together with their husbands to start a family and produce white children, seeing it as their duty to spread the virtues of civilization and European culture among the colonized local population. Thus, similar to the First World housewives back in Sweden, the Swedish women in Africa rose to become proper housewives based on the subordination and subjection of the Third World women in Yekepa, who served them as subsistence producers. These women constituted the hidden, non-waged foundation to the extended reproduction of extraction of a Western "civilized society" [FIG. 5.4].[30]

Today, under the paradigm of the new International Division of Labor (IDL), such patterns of extended reproduction of extraction have even deepened, and of course not only across territories of extraction. The invisibilized relations make it difficult to grasp the ways in which Indigenous communities, logistic spaces, and processes of manufacturing and consumption elsewhere in the world are all interrelated and linked to the spatial shaping of specific localities. The concept of the Planetary Mine[31] is thereby helpful to elucidate and explain such complex interlinkages across scales. It is crucial to making visible—*hic et nunc*—how the historical social mediation relations have been continuously reproduced.[32]

FIG.5 CLOCKWISE 1. Household electrification completely transformed domestic labor for First World housewives in 1960s Sweden; 2. Wives of Lamco workers engage in a charity activity in Yekepa, a mining town in colonized Liberia, run by the American-Swedish mining company LAMCO; 3. A newspaper article highlights how the Sámi in Lappstan in Jokkmokk are still nomads despite the fact that they now live in their own homes; 4. A woman fishing in the swamps close to LAMCO facilities in Yekepa Liberia, illustrating the social and economic disconnect between the colonial enclave and the local population. 1. "koka electrisk!" [cook electric!], cover of FERA's magazine "ERA", 1933; 2. Newspaper Lamco News, 1967, http://www.thejll.com; 3. Susanne Spik, in Lappstan, Jokkmokks samhälle [Jokkmokk's community], 2000; 4. Råvarugruppen, Plundring eller Planhushållning, 1980

Alternatives, Beyond the Expanded Reproduction of Extraction

When thinking about real alternatives to capitalist urbanization, it is productive to raise the question of how things got to be the way they are. Looking at this *problematique* through the lens of extraction, it is crucial to recognize that all parts across different dimensions and scales are essentially part of the same process. A process of extended urbanization that is exploitative and increasingly deepening, that has been historically co-produced, and is characterized by contradictions of invisibilized forms of appropriation under a colonial, capitalist patriarchy.

Through the case of the Malm territory, this chapter has illustrated how different relations that enabled the expanded reproduction of extraction have constantly reconfigured processes of urbanization throughout time and across scales—from the planetary to the individual body. It is at the scales of the household and body where mechanisms of subordination have appeared most violently, and have particularly affected women. The dialectics of exploitation and appropriation can help to identify and explain contradictory connections between different localities within the complex web of urbanization processes; between the First and Third World, across colonies and various forms of nature(s). All the different actors that are part of the process of extended extraction essentially share the same common struggle against exploitation. In this process, hegemonic mental conceptions such as "green" and "sustainable" need to be urgently questioned in relation to capitalism's historical re-articulations which have continuously masked a whole set of invisibilized relations of appropriation. Alternatives to capitalist modes of expanded urbanization and reproduction of extraction thus need to be examined well beneath their "green" appearing surface. It needs to be uncovered how they are actually being articulated within the context of historic extractivism, to then search for more nuanced futures that relate to the past without noncritical narratives of productivism, and, most importantly, futures that truly aim to eliminate the social relations of exploitation that sustain the system of capitalist modes of the expanded reproduction of extraction.

Endnotes

1 William Cronon, *Changes in the Land. Indians, Colonists, and the Ecology of New England* (New York: Hill and Wang, 1983).

2 "Historisk satsning i norr på fossilfri industri – kräver 100 000 inflyttare" [Historic Investment in the North in Fossil-Free Industry – Requires 100,000 Immigrants], *svt*, May 26, 2021, https://www.svt.se/nyheter/lokalt/norrbotten/historisk-satsning-i-norr-kraver-100-000-inflyttare.

3 Jason W. Moore, *Capitalism in the Web of Life: Ecology and the Accumulation of Capital* (New York: Verso, 2015), 11–12.

4 Moore, *Capitalism in the Web of Life,* 189–192.

5 Protect the Forest and Greenpeace Nordic, "More of Everything. The Swedish Forestry Model," January 17, 2021, Youtube video, 59:08, https://www.youtube.com/watch?v=q51FMbTOn_Q.

6 Sue Ruddick, Linda Peake, Gökbörü S. Tanyildiz, Patrick Darren, "Planetary Urbanization: An Urban Theory for Our Time?," *Environment and Planning D: Society and Space,* vol. 36, no. 3 (2018) 387–404.

7 Moore, *Capitalism in the Web of Life,* 102.

8 Jason W. Moore, "Amsterdam is Standing on Norway Part

II: The Global North Atlantic in the Ecological Revolution of the Long Seventeenth Century," *Journal of Agrarian Change*, vol. 10, no. 2 (April 2010), 188–227.

9 Bert I Högbom, *Grängesbergkoncernens malmfält: vägledning för besökande* [Grängesberg Group Ore Field: Guide for Visitors] (Stockholm: Esselte AB, 1950), 7–11.

10 Moore, "Amsterdam is Standing on Norway Part II."

11 William R. Mead, "Scandinavian Renaissance Cartography," in *The History of Cartography,* vol. 3, Part 2: Cartography in the European Renaissance, ed. David Woodward, 1781–1805.

12 Silvia Federici, *Caliban and the Witch: Women, the Body and Primitive Accumulation* (New York: Autonomedia, 2004), 68–75; Achille Mbembe, "In Conversation: Achille Mbembe and David Theo Goldberg on 'Critique of Black Reason,'"Interview by David Theo Goldberg, *Theory Culture & Society*, Global Public Life, March 7, 2018, https://www.theoryculturesociety.org/blog/interviews-achille-mbembe-david-theo-goldberg-critique-black-reason.

13 Åsa Össbo, *Nya vatten, dunkla speflingar: industriell kolonialism genom svensk vattenkrafturbyggnad i renskötselområdet 1910–1968* [New Waters, Dark Reflections: Industrial Colonialism Through Swedish Hydropower Building in the Reindeer Husbandry Area 1910-1968] (Umeå Umeå University, 2014), 52–86.

14 SGU Sverige Geologiska Undersökning [Swedish Geological Survey], "Ore Production and Trends," last modified October 13, 2020, https://www.sgu.se/en/mineral-resources/mineral-statistics/ore-production-and-trends/.

15 U.S. Geological Survey, "Iron Ore," Mineral Commodity Summaries, January 2021, accessed June 30, 2021, https://pubs.usgs.gov/periodicals/mcs2021/mcs2021-iron-ore.pdf.

16 Lennart Lundmark, *Stulet Land: svensk makt på samisk mark* [Stolen Land: Swedish Power on Sámi Land] (Stockholm: Ordfront, 2008).

17 Lundmark, *Stulet Land*, 21–26.

18 Lennart Lundmark, *Uppbörd, Utarmning, Utveckling: Det Samiska Fångstsamhällets Övergång till Rennomadism i Lule Lappmark* [Collection, Impoverishment, Development: The Sámi Fishing Society's Transition to Nomadism in Lule Lappmark] (Lund: Arkiv för studier i arbetarrörelsens historia, 1982); Lennart Lundmark, *Så länge vi Har Marker: Samerna Och Staten under Sexhundra År* [As Long as We Have Land: The Sámi and the State for Six Hundred Years] (Stockholm: Rabén Prisma 1998) 33–42.

19 Åsa Össbo, *Nya vatten, dunkla speflingar: industriell kolonialism genom svensk vattenkrafturbyggnad i renskötselområdet 1910–1968* [New Waters, Dark Reflections: Industrial Colonialism Through Swedish Hydropower Building in the Reindeer Husbandry Area 1910-1968] (Umeå: Umeå University, 2014), 240–244.

20 Lundmark, *Stulet Land*, 70.

21 Lundmark, *Stulet Land*, 34–39.

22 Karin Myhr Jansson et al., *The Book of LKAB 1890–2015* (Luleå: LKAB; Centrum för näringslivshistoria [Centre for Business History], 2015).

23 Simon Haikola and Jonas Anshelm, "State Regulation of Mining in a Post-Fordist Economy: Local Vulnerability in the Shadow of Hierarchy," *Political Geography*, 62, 68–78.

24 Simon Haikola and Jonas Anshelm, "Mineral Policy at a Crossroads? Critical Reflections on the Challenges with Expanding Sweden's Mining Sector," *Extractive Industries and Society*, vol. 3, no. 2, 508–516.

25 Gudrun Norstedt, *Lappskattelanden på Geddas karta: Umeå lappmark från 1671 till 1900-talets början* [Lapp Tax Lands on Gedda's Map: Umeå Lapland from 1671 to the Beginning of the 20th Century] (Umeå: Thalassa, 2011).

26 svt Nyhetter, "Historisk satsning i norr på fossilfri industri – kräver 100 000 inflyttare" [Historic Investment in the North in Fossil-Free Industry --Requires 100,000 Immigrants], *svt*, updated June 30, 2021, https://www.svt.se/nyheter/lokalt/norrbotten/historisk-satsning-i-norr-kraver-100-000-inflyttare.

27 Susanne Spik, *Lappstan, Jokkmokks samhälle: Jokkmokks socken, Jokkmokks kommun, Lappland, Norrbottens län: dokumentation* [Lap Housing, Jokkmokk's Community: Jokkmokk Parish, Jokkmokk Municipality, Lapland, Norrbotten County: Documentation] (Jokkmokk: Ájtte, 2000).

28 Maria Mies, *Patriarchy and Accumulation on a World Scale: Women in the International Division of Labour* (London: Zed Books, 1986), 145–174.

29 Yekepa was a mining town that was established by the former American-Swedish mining enterprise LAMCO in 1963 after the company had started to explore ore reserves in Liberia in 1953. It was destroyed and abandoned during the First Liberian Civil War in the 1990s. See also "The Yekepa Memory Project," accessed June 30, 2021, http://www.thejll.com/yekepa/home.shtml.

30 Mies, *Patriarchy and Accumulation on a World Scale*, 74–111; Maria Mies, "Maria Mies: Author and Activist. On Women and their Role in Revolutionary Struggles," interview by Jeanny Gering, recorded in Cologne, Germany, December 2013, Vimeo video, 44:40, accessed, June 30, 2021, https://vimeo.com/88111566?fbclid=IwAR2cHsTkZGP_L5lvIDBljK_ieZpctDcxQV7wizRfrjQ2Jq2AuL5Xhnq48tA.

31 Martín Arboleda, *Planetary Mine: Territories of Extraction under Late Capitalism* (New York: Verso, 2020).

32 Martin Arboleda, "*De la fábrica global a la mina planetaria*" [From the Global Factory to the Planetary Mine], Interview by Nicolas Allen. *Jacobin América Latina,* no. 3 (otoño-invierno 2021), 64–74.

3.4

The Living and Breathing Map of Sámi Reindeer Herding

Kjerstin Uhre, Eli Ristin Skum

Sámi reindeer husbandry is based on ancestral customs and traditional knowledge—a close and complex relationship between nature, reindeer, and reindeer owner. The right to own reindeer is signified by a registered personal reindeer mark, a custom of the Sámi that is at the heart of these relationships. For the Sámi, "owning reindeer means the possibility of engaging in pastoralism, developing a herd, and prescribing different rights to land."[1] This chapter is an attempt to understand how the relationship between humans, animals, and landscape is materialized, mapped, and practiced through the custom of reindeer marks. This question is timely due to recent changes in the Norwegian Act of Reindeer Husbandry that makes electronic, individual labeling of all domesticated reindeer mandatory.[2] During the consultations on these changes, both the Sámi Parliament and the Norwegian Association of Sámi Reindeer Herders opposed the proposal.[3] Even though reindeer pastoralists have been open to the introduction of new technologies, such as snow mobiles, all terrain motorcycles, drones, computers, and geographic information systems, they reject the idea of individual electronic labelling. Based on field conversations and life experience in a semi-nomadic Sámi reindeer-herding community, this chapter calls for a landscape approach that acknowledges local and Indigenous documentation systems for socio-environmental relationships, spatial-temporal ecological knowledge, and their functioning in safeguarding animal welfare and the ecosystems that are necessary for multispecies survival.

The authors are a veterinarian and reindeer pastoralist researching reindeer health and an architect researching contested landscapes in the European Arctic. Together, in their long-lasting partnership, they are establishing critical cartography and landscape theory in conversation with literature on Sámi reindeer husbandry and animal welfare, as well as field observations in Northern Norway.

Migratory Landscapes

Seasonally migrating species on land, in the ocean, and in the air depend on coherent functional ecosystems to survive. It is vital to their welfare to be in the right place at the right time. Across the continents surrounding the Arctic Ocean, reindeer (*Rangifer tarandus*) inhabit the highly transformative zone between the snowline's annual thawing retreat and frosty expansion.

Reindeer pastoralists belonging to Indigenous Peoples across Northern Eurasia have adapted a style of herding and husbandry that agrees with the reindeers' affiliation to their seasonal pastures. Reindeer marks are documented from many regions of reindeer husbandry and

OPPOSITE PAGE Spring Migration, Giddajohtin, starts by the end of April. The reindeer, herders, and reindeer owners migrate through an increasingly fragmented landscape to the calving grounds in the coastal mountains. Kjerstin Uhre, Áisaroaivi 2015

are probably as old as reindeer pastoralism. Sápmi, the Sámi Nation that extends across Fennoscandia, is divided between four countries [FIG. 1] and is represented in three of them with Sámi Parliaments, namely in Norway, Sweden, and Finland, but not yet on the Kola Peninsula in the Russian Federation. During the 19th and 20th centuries, assimilation processes in Fennoscandia resulted in the loss of language, sustenance, and cultural identity in many coastal Sámi communities.[4] Sámi reindeer herders contributed to maintaining Sámi language and traditional knowledge despite the different assimilation policies in each of the four countries. Since the 1970s, Norwegian-Sámi communities have seen a turbulent, partial revitalization of Sámi culture in families, neighborhoods, and places with friction between and within communities.[5] For Sámi reindeer husbandry, however, the 1970s was the period when the fragmentation of pastoral reindeer landscapes began to accelerate.

The challenge of landscape planning and conservation in outfield areas concerns the many and often competing claims on land and natural resources. It is widely acknowledged that the loss of pastures, through either direct encroachments or disturbances, provokes avoidance behavior by reindeer and is *the* most serious threat to reindeer pastoralism.[6] Moreover, "administrative encroachment further erodes herders' freedom of action on the land remaining to them."[7] Reindeer graze approximately 40 percent of the Norwegian mainland, but 89 percent of these pastures lie within five kilometers of physical infrastructures and buildings.[8] Plans for increased mineral extraction, hydro- and wind-power generation, linear infrastructure, such as roads and overhead power lines, and leisure infrastructure are an expression of competing interests in the land, leading to a bit-by-bit depletion of the landscape.

The field accounts in this chapter are from the reindeer grazing district 22, Fiettar, that comprise 14 *siida* units belonging to a migration system of 200 kilometers, reaching from Ánarjohka close to the Finnish border to the Hammerfest area at the Northern Norwegian coast.[9] The district is subject to cumulative effects of multiple landscape encroachments, including the plans of a copper mine to deposit mine tailings in the sea, which is currently debated as one of the largest environmental controversies in Norway.

A Living Indigenous Protocol

Sámi reindeer marks, *bealjjemearka* (earmarks), confirm ownership; a person's reindeer mark is also a symbolic, iconographic expression of identity and belonging, as well as the right to practice reindeer husbandry.[10] The Reindeer Husbandry Act prescribes that each reindeer in the Sámi reindeer area is to be marked by its owner's registered earmark by October 31st of its birth year.[11] Displaying all the hallmarks necessary to be regarded as a legal documentation system, the reindeer marking tradition is an example

FIG.1 Sámi reindeer husbandry pasture areas in Sápmi / Northern Fennoscandia. Kjerstin Uhre, sources: Satelite image from Nasa, the borders between reindeer husbandry areas are compiled by Johanna Roto, Nordregio. From: Paliskuntain yhdis-tys 2014, Mustonen and Mustonen 2011, Landbruksdirektoratet 2014, Sametinget 2014

of Indigenous protocol that has been integrated in State protocol. When Sámi reindeer marks were first included in a Norwegian law in 1879, the Norwegian legislators' concern was to obtain proof of reindeer ownership and exercise control. The concern of the Reindeer-Sámi leaders, on the other hand, was to include rules for keeping family marks within families and to avoid re-marking.[12] Sámi historian Bård A. Berg notes that the rules on reindeer marking hold a special position in all husbandry laws, as they are always based on cultural customs and cannot be executed without careful knowledge of reindeer husbandry.

A good reindeer mark is distinguishable from other marks, open to further development for the next generation, and difficult to alter. The reindeer mark bureau of the County Governor approves new reindeer marks and updates the public register. Based on a family's basic mark, *vuođđomearka*, each successional family in the same lineage has an identifiable mark, *mearkaoalli*, as a specific combination of cuts and notches that form the starting point for new reindeer earmarks within the

FIG.2 Reindeer marks in reindeer grazing district 22, Fiettar, as registered in 2014. Kjerstin Uhre, Source: Landbruksdirektoratet, 2014

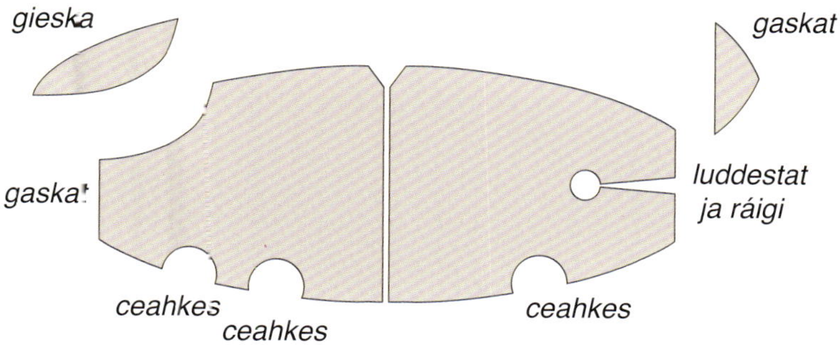

family.[13] Inherited marks with a history of previous owners who have been important to the pastoral community, *árbemearku*, are associated with reindeer luck.[14] The design of reindeer marks builds on an old system that combines main cuts (*váldu sánit*) and secondary cuts (*smávva sánit*) in the left and right ears of reindeer. Social anthropologists Ivar Bjørklund and Harald Eidheim note that "*váldu ja smava sánit*" means "big and small words." Knowing the words, one can "read" human and economic relations between reindeer owners by studying a herd's earmarks [FIG. 2].[15] Reindeer-mark literacy is a core competence of Sámi in reindeer husbandry.

The different cuts and notches of the individual earmarks make the ears fold in a certain way; the fur grows accordingly and shapes a recognizable sculptural form. Reindeer marks on living animals thus work as furry infographic devices, mobile documents, and maps in the terrain that can be read at a distance (with or without binoculars) or at close range, feeling it with the hands. In the public register of reindeer owners, the earmarks appear orderly as diagrams. There is a great diversity of individual characteristics within a group of reindeer carrying the same reindeer mark. Following cultural traditions during calf marking, Sámi reindeer owners keep the cut-off from a *váldu sátni* from each calf. In 2018, Per Jonny Aslaksen Skum, a professional reindeer herder, explained:

"My father, Aslak Aslaksen Skum, taught us to sew the *váldu sátni* on a string. *Áhčči* (father) kept his yield-strings for several decades. The string is both an account of the yield and an archive of the individual calves. I use it to memorize the calves and which females brought up the calf to be better able to recognize them in the pastures. During the autumn slaughter, I will remember which females have the best maternal qualities, *Sákku-nálli* (high-quality breeders), and keep her offspring in the herd." This account explains a common saying among reindeer herders: "If the earmarking fails, the reindeer husbandry fails" (fieldnotes, Fieddarvággi 2018).

This account conveys the underlying ethics and animal welfare systems integrated into the practice of earmarking calves in reindeer husbandry [FIG. 3-4]. The strings connect yield-accounting, animal welfare,

FIG. 3 The earmark system is a visual language, the oral description of this mark, belonging to Per Jonny Aslaksen Skum reads: *[Gurot bealjji* (left ear): *Gieškalahkki ja guokte ceahkes maŋil. Olgeš bealjji* (right ear): *Gaskat, gaskat sisa luddestat ja ráigi. Ceahkes maŋjil].* Kjerstin Uhre and Eli Ristin Skum

FIG. 4 Per Jonny Aslaksen Skum sew the *gieska* from the male calves' right ear and the *gaskkat* from the female calves' left ear into a string that becomes a material account of the calves in the summer pasture. Kjerstin Uhre 2015

and herd flourishing depending on different breeding decisions. Further, the material practices in calf marking inform the decision-making system in meat production to the professional Sámi reindeer herder in a detailed, individual-oriented, and contextual manner.

The *Siida* and the Reindeer Year

The *siida* is a family-based working community of Sámi reindeer owners.[16] The reindeer year contains intensive and extensive periods that are organized according to reindeer's needs and preferences. The whole *siida*, and all the *siidas* in a reindeer grazing district, are summoned to events such as spring migration, calf marking, autumn work, and separation of the summer herds into smaller winter herds [FIG. 5]. The reindeer year starts when the calves are born from late April to early June. May is called the reindeer calf month, *miessemannu*.

FIG.5 During autumn work, reindeer owners spend hours in the working pens to inspect the health and stature of their reindeer. The visible reindeer marks signify the personal relationship between a reindeer and its owner. Kjerstin Uhre, Áisaroaivi 2015

For children and young people growing up with reindeer husbandry, calf marking, taking place during the summer, is the main event for acquiring social skills in getting along with reindeer, people, and landscape.[17] "Childhood experiences of and in nature hold for a person's cosmology, especially for the concern felt for everything that is alive."[18]

The children and youngsters need to adapt practical marking skills and learn ethics and commitments connected to the sphere of ownership [FIG. 6].

Each reindeer's appearance, fur color, stamina, and antler quality, together with the earmark and the landscape in which it is observed, inform herding decisions. The reindeer roam freely in the summer pastures, fatten, and tend the calves until September when the herd is collected. During autumn work, reindeer owners spend hours in the working pens to inspect the health and stature of each individual and select animals for slaughter. In the skinning of reindeer that are slaughtered, the ears are kept attached to the hide as a token of ownership. When reindeer are sold and slaughtered at slaughterhouses, the ears are cut off the hide and clasped together with a note on the reindeer's age, sex, and weight. The bundles of ears and information sheets are then stored in a freezer for owners to check the settlement of the sale.

Next follows a grazing movement through the autumn lands, where the summer herd is divided into several winter herds. The agricultural authorities hire professional reindeer herders, who are well versed in reading earmarks, to assist them in conducting annual control of the number of reindeer in the winter herds of selected *siida* units. In the preparatory work for changes in the Reindeer Husbandry Act, the Norwegian Agriculture Agency communicated the intention to erase this cultural practice: "There is a need for a more efficient and precise public control of reindeer numbers than the current cumbersome system with counting corps in the field."[19]

Herds and herders advance to the winter pastures when the rivers are frozen. The herders manage the untrampled snow through close supervision of the reindeer throughout the winter to secure access to fresh snow that allows the reindeer to dig frozen plants, berries, and lichen. In

FIG.6 Seven-year-old Reindeer-Sámi girl Inga Ragnhild Isabel Persdatter Skum holds the white calf correctly when bringing it to her parents to be marked. The calf-marking session is one of the last arenas left to pass traditional knowledge on to the subsequent generation of reindeer owners. Kjerstin Uhre, Fieddarvaggi 2018

some cases the pastures are closed by icy crusts, making it potentially necessary to provide additional feed. By the end of April, *Giddajohtin* (spring migration) starts towards the calving grounds.

The Map in the Terrain

Maps derive power from being part of a governance system. Denis Wood believes that the contribution of Indigenous and critical mapping to cartographic criticism calls the authority of state maps into question.[20] For example, in 2020, an assessment conducted by the organization Protect Sápmi on behalf of the Sámi Parliament analyzed the impact on reindeer husbandry by planned copper mining in Nussir and Ulveryggen. A series of maps demonstrating knowledge and effects that are underrepresented in the public impact assessment, revealed that the mining operation would reduce the economy of reindeer husbandry in the area by 50 percent.[21] Sámi epistemology implies that "experience, knowledge, and a personal relation to the object is crucial if the documentation is to be regarded as truthful and reliable."[22] Geir Grenersen, Kjell Kemi, and Steinar Nilsen argue that, in a Sámi context, "the animal in the wild can be observed as a vital source for information connected to nearly all aspects of the herders' practice."[23] Bjørklund and Eidheim describe the Sámi reindeer mark as a culturally defined "map."[24] The ear-map has been hiding in plain sight for cartographers searching for Indigenous cartography, studying signs on artefacts rather than living animals. In this respect, the earmarked reindeer is a walking, breathing map that shows its own way of navigating the territory.[25] Perceiving the reindeer mark as an Indigenous map that is alive and in motion also includes the mental mapping of multiple inter-relationships of Sámi pastoral landscapes. The *boazu* (semi-domesticated reindeer) carries its own documentation on its entitlement to protection and access to pastures.

On Caring and Counting

The North Sámi term for a reindeer herd is *eallu*, derived from the word *eallin*, meaning "life course" or "life as it is lived."[26] Herders' fundamental task is to keep the herds socially well-functioning and flourishing, and to pass on how to care for life as it is lived. *Čappá-eallu,* meaning a beautiful herd, connotes a healthy herd that is well provided for and consists of diverse age groups.[27] Sámi ethics distinguish between completely free, semi-domesticated, and domesticated animals. The responsibilities towards them differ according to how well they can fend for themselves.[28] The agreement of voluntary companionship between reindeer and humans is embedded in the Sámi myth of the origin of reindeer herding. "The ancestor of reindeer herders, *Njávešeatni*, also recognizes the reindeer's perception and point of view." [29] Ole Henrik Magga, Mikkel Nils Sara, and Nils Oskal explain that all creatures—including predators—are entitled to their share of available resources necessary for their existence. Even insects have an ancestral mother, *Maddu*, that will punish people that harm her offspring.[30]

Informed by a mechanical worldview with human rationality at its center, Western ethics have historically not included non-human species in the moral discourse.[31] Elina Helander-Renvall notes that premises in the current environmental discourse place wild animals and extra-human nature outside the traditional perception of things in Sámi culture.[32] Martha Nussbaum's capabilities approach to justice for non-human species resonates with aspects of Sámi thinking on the dignity, will, and intention of animals.[33] She lists the destruction of habitats on a list of cruel acts that do wrong to animals. Nussbaum argues that the right of individual, "wild" animals to flourish includes the right to habitat.[34] In this context, the commitment to manage and protect land where the *siida* has the right to graze their reindeer is a demanding task when it comes to writing legal disputes over land uses. Therefore, many cases end in the court system.

The Norwegian Agriculture Agency emphasized in 2019, as part of their preparatory work to changes in the Act of Reindeer Husbandry, that traditional earmarking was not prohibited, but that individual electronic tagging of domestic reindeer would become mandatory.[35] While the requirement for individual labelling of fully domesticated animals—such as cows or sheep—is explained by requirements for the traceability and documentation of animal health concerning food safety, in the case of the labelling of reindeers, the authorities' justification is their need for more efficient and accurate control of reindeer numbers.

When a semiotic system is targeted and erased, we see a case of "semiocide:" the extinction of a semiotic system.[36] Weakening the use and relevance of the multimodal communication system of the Sámi reindeer mark is as a continuation of the destructive process of losing their languages, a trauma that Sámi communities experienced during the assimilation period. Furthermore, electronic labelling using ear-clips can potentially compromise the welfare of the reindeer.[37] However, the authorities' rationale of efficacy and control subvert and disregard the material practices that maintain animal welfare and landscape-relationships in Sámi reindeer husbandry.

The *boazu* live freely in natural habitats, which allows them to express their distinctive character and instincts. While reindeer in this regard live at the mercy of nature, the personal relationship between a reindeer and its owner, indicated by the reindeer mark, is integrated with the herding system within the *siida*. Sometimes, harsh weather, predator attacks, closed pastures, or human disturbance can cause reindeer to stray from their herd and *siida* grounds. In the case that stray animals are noticed, a herder will inform their owners and care for them until they are collected. Also, in the case of fatal events where reindeer get injured or ill, killed by cars or caught by predators, the reindeer mark is inspected to notify the respective owner. Such notifications require reindeer-mark literacy among the larger pastoral community. From the reindeer's perspective, the reindeer mark signifies its right to be cared for within the *siida*.

Wayfinding Maps to the Future Landscape

A visually recognizable *bealjjemearkka* (earmark) is necessary in securing the welfare of *boazu* during all potential events across the reindeer year. The cultural significance of the custom of reindeer marking to Sámi reindeer husbandry is undisputed, well described in literature, and integrated in legislation. Yet, the complex layers of relations, skills, and belonging that are materialized through reindeer marks cannot be reduced to simple digits. As this chapter argues, the traditional Sámi reindeer mark exists as a tangible connection between the pastoral community and the spatial environment via the reindeer's movement.

The Sámi reindeer mark practice materializes intangible landscape values that are physically present, mediated, and represented in the territory. Carrying its *bealjjemearkka* as a headpiece, the *boazu* pursues its course of life leaving traces in the landscape that intersect with the encroachments, prospects, and development plans that reconfigure future landscapes. In these present and future landscapes, the reindeer pastoralists' efforts to protect migratory routes and seasonal pastures benefit both endemic species and the multiple seasonally migrating species that journey over planetary distances. The reindeer mark thus brings the planetary scale of animals' right to habitat back into the landscapes of regional decision-making and spatial transformations in the European Arctic.

Endnotes

1 Kathrine Ivsett Johnsen, Svein D. Mathiesen, and Inger Marie Gaup Eira, "Sámi Reindeer Governance as Competing Knowledge Systems: A Participatory Study," *Ecology and Society* 22, no. 4 (2017): 13.

2 Landbruks og mat departementet [Norwegian Agriculture Agency], "Lov om endringer i reindriftsloven, LOV-2019-06-21-62" [Law on changes in the Reindeer Husbandry Act of 2019], (2021). https://lovdata.no/dokument/NL/lov/2019-06-21-62.

3 Landbruks og mat departementet [Norwegian Agriculture Agency], "Høringsnotat om endringer i reindriftsloven" [Consultancy Note on Changes in the Act of Reindeer Husbandry] 15th January 2019. https://www.regjeringen.no/contentassets/862275ff3c7947308a3635aae56fc942/horingsnotat-om-endringer-i-reindriftsloven.pdf.

4 For queries about the mandate for the Commission to Investigate the Norwegianisation Policy and Injustice Against the Sámi and Kven/Norwegian Finnish Peoples, see: https://uit.no/kommisjonen/mandat_en.

5 Britt Kramvig, "Landskap som hjem" [Landscape as Home], *Norsk Antropologisk Tidsskrift* 31, no. 1-2 (2020): 88-102. An English version of "Landscape as Home" is forthcoming.

6 Nicholas J. C. Tyler, Inger Hanssen-Bauer, Eirik J. Førland, and Christian Nelleman, "Shrinking Resource Base of

Pastoralism: Saami Reindeer Husbandry in a Climate of Change," *Frontiers in Sustainable Food Systems* 4, no. 585685 (February 2021): 1-46.

7 Tyler et al., "Shrinking Resource Base," 1-2.

8 Erik Engelien, Iulie Aslaksen, and Jørn Kristian Undelstvedt, "Utbygging får konsekvenser for reinbeiteområder" [Development Holds Consequences for Reindeer Husbandry], *Statistics Norway, SSB Analyse* no. 16 (2020): https://www.ssb.no/natur-og-miljo/artikler-og-publikasjoner/utbygging-far-konsekvenser-for-reinbeiteomrader.

9 Geographical information of reindeer husbandry in Norway is accessible at Nibio Kilden: https://kilden.nibio.no/?topic=reindrift.

10 Johnsen et al., "Sámi Reindeer Governance," 33.

11 Landbruks og mat departementet [Norwegian Agriculture Agency], "*Lov om reindrift, LOV-2007-06-15-40*" [Reindeer Husbandry Act of 2007] §33, (2021), https://lovdata.no/dokument/NL/lov/2007-06-15-40/KAPITTEL_1#KAPITTEL_1.

12 Bård A. Berg, "*Mot en korporativ reindrift*" [Towards Corporative Reindeer Husbandry], Doctor of Arts diss., (University of Tromsø, 2000), 187.

13 Landbruksdirektoratet, "Retningslinjer for reinmerker for Vest-Finnmark" [Guidelines for reindeer marks for Western Finnmark], accessed, June 10, 2021, https://www.landbruksdirektoratet.no/nb/styrer-rad-og-utvalg/klagenemnda-for-merkersaker/retningslinjer-for-reinmerker-for-vest-finnmark?resultId=2.0&searchQuery=reinmerker.

14 Nils Oskal, "On Nature and Reindeerluck," *Rangifer* 20, no. 2-3 (2000): 175-180.

15 Ivar Bjørklund and Harald Eidheim, "Om Reinmerker: Kulturelle sammenhenger og norsk jus i Sápmi" [On Reindeer Marks: Cultural Connections and Norwegian Jurisprudence in Sápmi], *Tidsskrift for samfunnsforskning* 4 (1997): 562-578.

16 Mikkel Nils Sara, "Siida and Traditional Sámi Reindeer Herding Knowledge," *The Northern Review* 30 (Spring 2009): 153-178, 158, https://thenorthernreview.ca/index.php/nr/article/view/9.

17. Oskal, "On Nature and Reindeer Luck," 178.

18. Arne Johan Vetlesen, *The Denial of Nature. Environmental philosophy in the era of global capitalism* (Oxon and New York: Routledge, 2015), 206.

19. Landbruks og mat departementet [Norwegian Agriculture Agency], "Reindrift. Lang tradisjon - unike muligheter" [Reindeer Husbandry. Long Traditions - Unique Possibilities] *Meld. St.* 32 (2017-2018), 9. https://www.regjeringen.no/contentassets/ffb8837d1f52425b962ceb23e5ccfc8e/no/pdfs/stm201620170032000dddpdfs.pdf.

20 Denis Wood, John Fels, and John Krygier, *The Power of Maps* (New York: The Guilford Press, 2010), 130.

21 Protect Sápmi, "Analyse av virkningen for reindriften vedplanlagt gruvedrift i Nussir og Ulveryggen i Kvalsund kommune" [Analysis of the impact on reindeer husbandry by planned mining in Nussir and Ulveryggen in Kvalsund municipality] (Report, August 2020), https://sametinget.no/_f/p1/i34eef697-e763-4735-8ab6-8390038be43b/analyse-av-virkningen-for-reindriften-ved-planlagt-gruvedrift-i-nussir-og-ulveryggen-i-kvalsund-kommune.pdf.

22 Geir Grenersen, Kjell Kemi, and Steinar Nilsen, "Landscapes as Documents - the Relationship Between Traditional Sámi Terminology and the Concepts of Document and Documentation," *Journal of Documentation* 72, no. 6 (2016): 1181-1196.

23 Grenersen, Kemi, and Nilsen, "Landscapes as Documents," 1188.

24 Bjørklund and Eidheim, "Om Reinmerker," 562-578, 571.

25 Kjerstin Uhre, "The Perforated Landscape: Contested Prospects in Sápmi," PhD diss., (The Oslo School of Architecture and Design, 2020), 328-335.

26 Mikkel Nils Sara, "Land Usage and Siida Autonomy," *Arctic Review on Law and Politics* 2, no. 2 (2011): 138-158, 150. https://arcticreview.no/index.php/arctic/article/view/25.

27 Oskal, "On Nature and Reindeer Luck," 176.

28 Ole Henrik Magga, Mikkel Nils Sara and Nils Oskal, "Dyrevelferd i Samisk Kultur" [Animal Welfare in Sámi Culture] *Landbruks og Matdepartementet*, Rapport, (2001): 1-21, https://www.regjeringen.no/globalassets/upload/kilde/ld/rap/2001/0017/ddd/pdfv/151133-utredning_dyrevelferd_samisk.pdf.

29 Sara, "*Siida* and Traditional," 171.

30 Britt Kramvig and Margrethe Pettersen, "Living Land - Below as Above," in eds: Mirna Belina *Living Earth, Fieldnotes from the Dark Ecology Project* (Amsterdam: Sonic Acts Press, 2016), 131-141, 138. See also Uhre, "The Perforated Landscape," 209-212.

31 Vetlesen, *The Denial of Nature,* 57.

32 Elina Helander-Renvall, "Relationships Between Sámi Reindeer Herders, Lands, and Reindeer" in *Routledge Handbook of Human-Animal Studies*, ed. Garry Marvin and Susan McHugh (London: Routledge, 2014), 246-258.

33 See Sara, "Siida and Traditional," 160-161 and Sara, "Land Usage," 148.

34 Martha C. Nussbaum, *Frontiers of Justice: Disability, Nationality, Species Membership* (Tanner Lecture of Human Values, 2006), (Cambridge, MA: Harvard University Press, 2007), Kindle Locations 4010-4011, 4189-4192, and 4489-4490.

35 *Meld. St.* 32 (2017-2018), 43.

36 Ivar Puura, "Nature in Our Memory," *Sign System Studies* 41, no. 1 (2013): 150-153. Ivar Puura's concept "semiocide" conveys a situation in which significant signs and stories are destroyed intentionally or unwittingly.

37 Some reindeer that are chipped with electronic ear-tags suffer from *gahččan bealji*, a condition where the ear breaks, collapses, or the cartilage changes due to infections or frostbite.

4 PLANNING FOR TERRITORIAL SYSTEMS

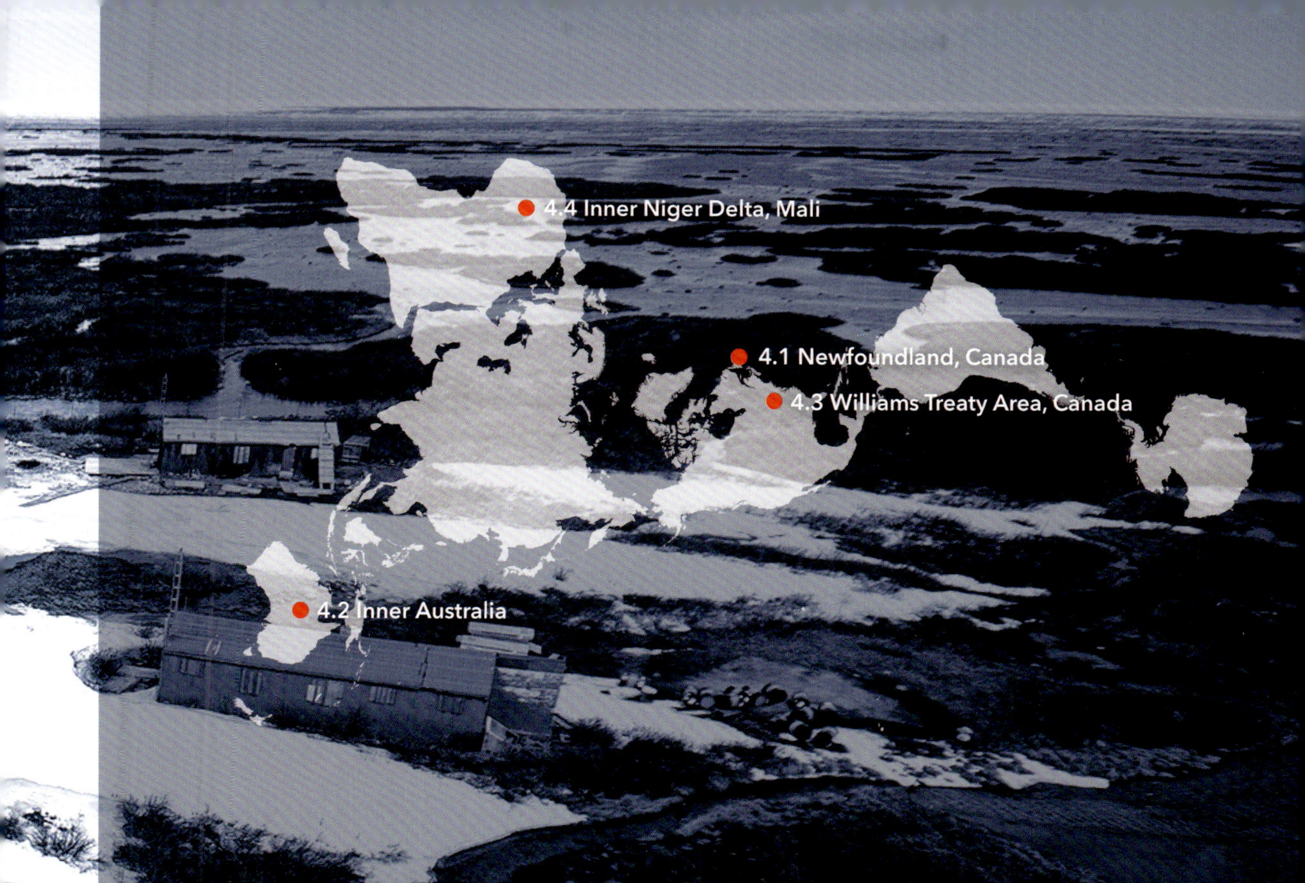

Planning for Territorial Systems discusses sites and regional contexts that are influenced by territorial resources, economies, infrastructures, livelihoods, and local and Indigenous knowledge systems. Through four very different but aligned lenses, the chapters present speculative visions of new territorial relationships to engage with the territory through cultural storytelling, mapping, policy shifts, and projective landscape projects. What emerges is an overall realignment of territorial actors—where the drivers of a landscape approach come from the people, the ground, and planning and design are secondary.

4.1

On the Edge

Re-Framing Our Understanding of a Nissological Territory

Matthew A. J. Brown, Sandra Cooke

Nissology | *the study of islands on their own terms.*

Islands have distinct identity and space formed through distance, creating unique societal development and culture that requires different approaches in both professional and academic pursuits.[1] With this recognition, Grant McCall coined the term "Nissology" in 1994.

Introduction

The island of Newfoundland is "on the edge." Geographically, it lies along the edge of the North Atlantic, it forms the eastern edge of Canada, and its settlements cling to the edge of its 9,656 kilometer-long coastline. Economically, it has been on the edge of decline since joining the Confederation, when the focus turned inward towards land-based territorial systems.

The condition along the coast of Newfoundland was the very reason for settlement on the island. The vital connection between land and sea was the source of livelihood for its inhabitants. Over the past 400 years, the people of Newfoundland have proudly established a way of life, a culture, and a deep and unwavering attachment to place, centered around their coastal existence. Thousands of outports (small coastal rural communities) scatter the rugged coastline, with an overall island population of half a million people [FIG. 1]. Since joining Canada in 1949, government pressures of industrialization, globalization, commodification, modernization, and urbanization have contributed to the decline, and in some cases loss, of rural outport communities.[2] The shift from rural, small-scaled economies, towards larger, centralized industries focused on resource extraction, has created a continuous boom-bust economic cycle, where the bust periods have resulted in massive waves of outmigration from the island.

While approximately half of the island's current population is now living in the urban center of St. John's,[3] there remain communities determined to stay in their rural settings. The viability of these communities hinges on creating new, diversified economic opportunities at the hyper-local scale, but also on re-framing our understanding of "territory" within the nissological context.

OPPOSITE PAGE Outport of Newtown, drone image. Dimana Kolarova

FIG. 1 Newfoundland patterns of settlement and population from 2011-2016. Nassim Sani & Zhengbang Wang | On the Edge Option Studio, University of Toronto

FIG. 2 Factors influencing the diversity of ecologies on the Island of Newfoundland. Camilla Campo-Herrera & Adeline Hu | On the Edge Option Studio, University of Toronto

An Island Territory – The Nissological

With an overall area of 108,860 square kilometers, the island of Newfoundland registers as the sixteenth largest in the world.[4] A long process of shifting tectonic plates and glacial movement has sculpted an incredibly varied landscape rich in geology and ecology. From the Long Range Mountains to fjords and low-lying river valleys to barrens, the dramatic and sublime landscapes are known around the world. This territory's sheer size, accompanied by the prevalent west winds, cold ocean currents, and varied coastline conditions, make for diverse island environments, characterized by six different climate typologies and a rich array of flora and fauna.[5] The thick boreal forests, sweeping barrens, undulating bogs and fens, and vast marshlands are rich in resources that were essential to initial rural settlement of the territory and continue to play a critical role in the health of the environment[6] [FIG. 2].

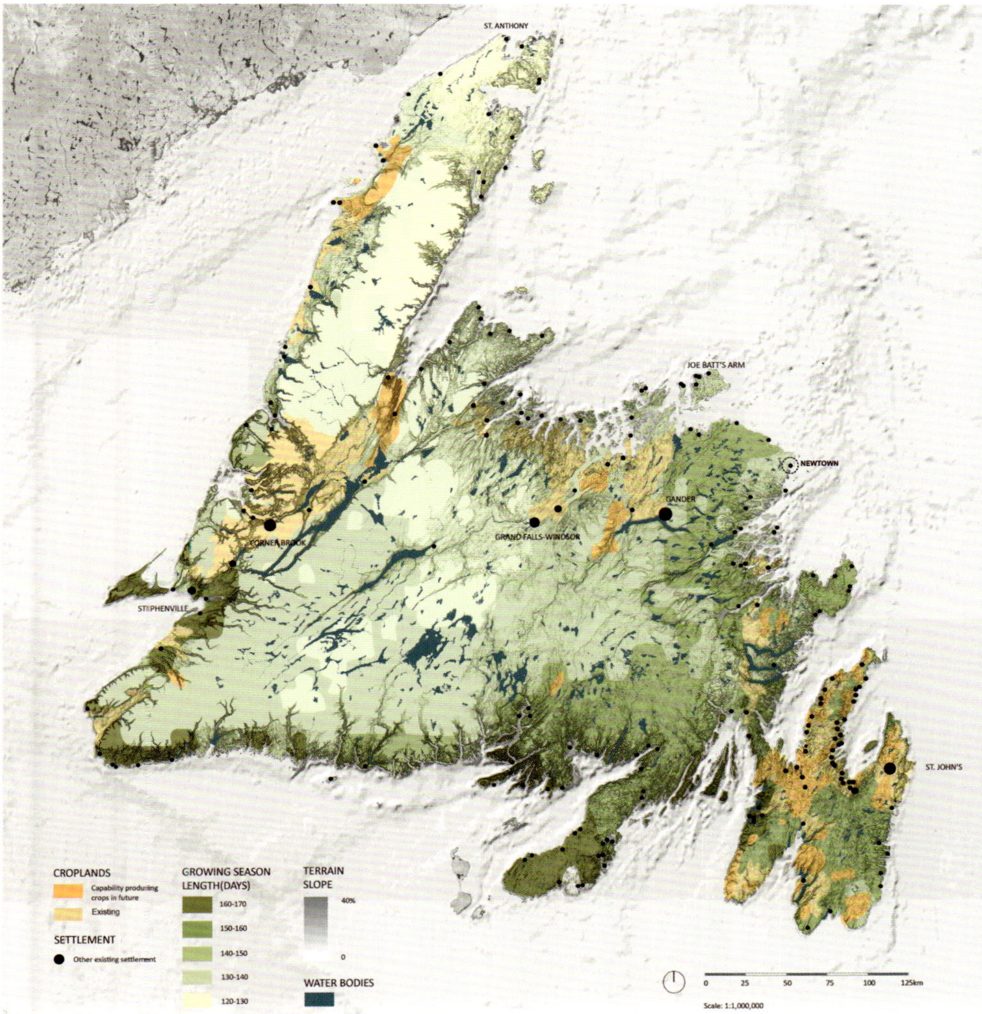

Settlement – The Outport

Since the first permanent settlements of the late eighteenth century, the people of Newfoundland have adapted to life at the interface between land and sea in the quiet bays, inlets, coves, tickles, and harbors. Historically, life was sustained by their surrounding resources, and each outport was autonomous, with its own independent economy. More than 1,500 tight-knit outport communities dotted the island's coastline, each functioning as an extension of family where the community worked together to pull through difficult times and celebrate periods of prosperity. Newfoundlanders' deep connection with the island is a product of this sense of community and dependency upon the landscape and seascape found throughout the rural outports. There is a strong sense of belonging within island communities, where even though many people were forced to leave, their ties to the rural condition remain.[7] As a marginal population, rural outport inhabitants were—and to some extent still are—out of sight and out of mind; self-sufficient, and outside of the awareness and influence of larger planning initiatives. [8] This, however, would change somewhat with Confederation.

Confederation – Territorial Systems

Joining Canada in 1949 was a turning point for the island, as the pressures to conform led to difficult times, as evidenced through the fishery and resettlement.[9] The fishery that had once respected natural limitations, suddenly became controlled by the Federal Government's promotion of fishing in deeper waters, with larger vessels and higher quotas, advanced technology, and new markets for frozen fish.[10] This shift could be appropriately described as the transition from quality to quantity for the sake of economic growth, but ultimately resulted in the collapse of the cod fishery, which had been the island's primary industry for more than 300 years.

The main promise that had secured the vote of outport Newfoundland to join Confederation was access to services such as electricity, health care, and education, but one unexpected outcome was "resettlement."[11] The government-sponsored "resettlement program" was an attempt to relocate people from isolated outports into growth centers, where new industries dominated and services like education and healthcare could be more easily provided.[12] Resettlement required an entire outport to agree, often tearing communities apart and pressuring many to leave behind their rural history, livelihood, and tradition. Although the majority resisted, over 30,000 inhabitants took a chance on this promise of opportunity.[13]

Joining Canada increased financial assistance from the Federal Government and new attempts to diversify the economy. During the initial years of Confederation, access to the interior of Newfoundland was expanded through the development of highways and road infrastructure, allowing further opportunities for industrialization, resource extraction, and manufacturing.[14] Within the first decade of Confederation, focus shifted to land-based territorial infrastructure as the answer to modernization. "Develop or Perish;" the signature slogan of Newfoundland's first premier, Joey Smallwood, summarizes the pressure felt by the province after joining Canada.[15] For years, Smallwood desperately tried to establish a strong economic foundation for the province on the basis of exploiting natural resources, which he touted as being easily accessible, extensive, and infinite.

To some extent, the myth of infinite natural resources persists today, as they continue to form the primary basis for the province's economy. After the collapse of the economy caused by the cod moratorium in 1992, the island scrambled to transition offshore oil production, which has provided the province with periods of economic prosperity over the past two decades. This economic gain has not, however, translated into a stable population, as the industry only leads in GDP and not employment.

Boom-Bust

The island economy's dependence on non-renewable resources has perpetuated the current boom-bust economic cycle. During the boom periods, wealth translates into investment through terrestrial infrastructural improvements, whereas the bust periods continue to prompt rural disinvestment, claiming the limited economic viability of rural communities. Following the collapse of the Cod Fishery in 1992, over 60,000 people left the island in search of work elsewhere.[16] Similarly, the turbulence of the offshore oil industry is directly tied to the island's migration patterns. With another projected population decrease of 7.6 percent over the proceeding 15 years,[17] a re-thinking of economic opportunity is required if rural communities are to persevere and remain in the places they hold so dear. The fact that so many communities have opted against financially attractive resettlement programs is evidence that urbanization is not generally viewed as a desirable alternative to the current situation. In Newfoundland, attachment to place and community remains unshakeable.

Re-Framing Our Understanding of a "Territory" for the Nissological Context

Our conventional understanding of territorial systems suggests large-scale, land-based areas, connected through ecological systems, infrastructural networks, and geo-political boundaries. While Newfoundland's rural outport communities are weakly tethered to one another via land-based systems, the relatively minuscule population, dispersed across the vast island, makes it difficult to justify large-scale infrastructural systems. Since Confederation, the focus on the development of rural roadways connected to the Trans-Canada highway has been problematic, as a continuous infrastructural investment is needed to sustain such an extensive network. Deteriorating roads, causeways, and bridges call into question the financial and ecological sustainability of this infrastructure at the full territorial scale. The island's current reliance on the automobile as the primary mode of transportation around the island will only become more difficult as sustainable solutions are required to counter the environmental challenges facing the world today. The opportunity for the nissological context lies in a re-examination of our understanding and definition of territory.

Ocean as Infrastructure – Re-Defining Territory

Key to the feasibility of speculative design strategies, and the communities that support them, is a re-reading of the ocean as a means to connect products with consumers, or to unlock the potential to expand production across a number of communities. In returning to a view of the ocean as a "territory" in itself, the ocean becomes not only a source of food, but also a primary means for connectivity, communication, and exchange (as it has been for centuries). The viability of communities "on the edge" is reinforced. Furthermore, this approach allows interior island territories to remain wild and rural, full of potential for the gathering of natural resources upon which these new industries would depend.

FIG.3 Community workshop. Thevishka Kanishkan

Community as Resource: The Hyper-Local Sustainable Economy

During a landscape-based research studio led by Brackish Design Studio at the University of Toronto's Daniels Faculty of Architecture, Landscape, and Design, site investigations and community workshops in rural outport communities identified opportunities and resources that hold the potential for sustainable local economies [FIG. 3]. Student's work tested provocations that explored the regenerative potential of design at this redefined territory at the hyper-local scale. The studio used the community of Newtown on the northern end of Bonavista Bay as their site for investigation. Through intensive community workshops, conversations, and field-based landscape explorations, students linked the human capital found within the community with the unique qualities and resources of the island landscape, to generate new ideas for communities to put into practice. The main goal of this studio was to create opportunities for new sources of livelihood in the rural coastal context. While the studio produced a variety of creative projects that vary in scale and program—from eco-tourism interventions to sustainable farming initiatives to adaptive re-use of heritage architecture—the following two projects are particularly innovative examples of how design thinking can bring together various untapped or overlooked natural resources, and combine them with locally-available skill, knowledge, and technology. The resultant proposals create new economic opportunities without requiring a shift in the locals' way of life. The mixing of local knowledge with fresh perspective becomes a platform for renewal.

Harvesting the Edible Coastal Landscape

Intrinsic to the culture and food of outport Newfoundland is the berry. The harsh northern coastal landscapes are prime habitats for native fruit-bearing shrubs like wild blueberries, partridgeberries, cloudberries, strawberries, crowberries, cranberries, and blackberries. The timing and availability of these fruits for locals create a more granular notion of seasons, beyond spring, summer, fall, etc. (i.e., "blueberry season"). The ubiquitous berries have forever been a staple ingredient in desserts and preserves [FIG. 4].

Through conversations, meals, and guided field investigations, Camilla Campos-Herrera identified the magnitude of the berry yield that is possible without the effort, energy, or resources typically required through industrial agricultural practices. While locals are aware of the berries proliferating in their midst, the short shelf life of this resource limits the opportunity for export beyond the local region and has not translated into any sort of business endeavor. Through research, Campos-Herrera

FIG. 4 The productive coastal landscape pertaining to berry habitat and seasonality. Camilla Campo-Herrera | On the Edge Option Studio, University of Toronto

explored opportunities for niche markets where berries could be used in the production of goods that could be suitable for export. The result of the studio project was a community-run small-batch distillery where berries could be foraged and used as the main ingredient in flavoring and fermenting specialty liqueurs to be exported to regional, national, and international markets. This type of small industry would become a generator for local employment in foraging, but also create new jobs within the distillery processing, packaging, and marketing, with key benefits to the tourism industry as well.

Kelp is on the Way

The wealth of resources that are drawn from the coastal landscapes of outport communities goes beyond the fishery. While learning about the variety of ocean products harvested by local fishermen, Chloe Lui noticed the abundance of kelp (*Laminaria digita*) growing within the tickle (a shallow waterway between rocky landforms) and along the coastline. While kelp and other seaweed have traditionally been used by communities as fertilizer for household gardens, the naturally occurring quantities of the aquatic plant prompted Lui to research other possibilities. Through the studio, Lui uncovered new processes that could transform kelp into a flexible, biodegradable textile. When combined with deep local traditions of crafts such as knitting and weaving, the potentials for a new sustainable fiber are immeasurable. Lui's project positioned kelp at the center of a new, local, closed-loop economy with opportunities from harvesting to processing to the creation of new products suited to local use as well as export. The material created from kelp fiber demonstrated promising potentials not only as wearable items but also as a sustainable construction material [FIG. 5].

The studio-based research was critical in debunking the premise that rural Newfoundland is no longer economically viable or profitable. Both Campos-Herrera and Lui's studio propositions demonstrate that our rural coastal environments, rich in untapped resources, can not only remain productive but also contain possibilities for sustainable economic development at a hyper-local scale. With hundreds of rural communities located throughout the diversified coastal landscapes of the island territory, there are certain to be other small-scale industries that could emerge from the synergies found between landscape-based resources and local knowledge. The studio work suggests this formula has the potential to create products and services with a much broader reach, beyond the island itself.

Taking Action

Through site-based studio investigations, it became evident that communities' knowledge of their environs extended far beyond the coastline, or any

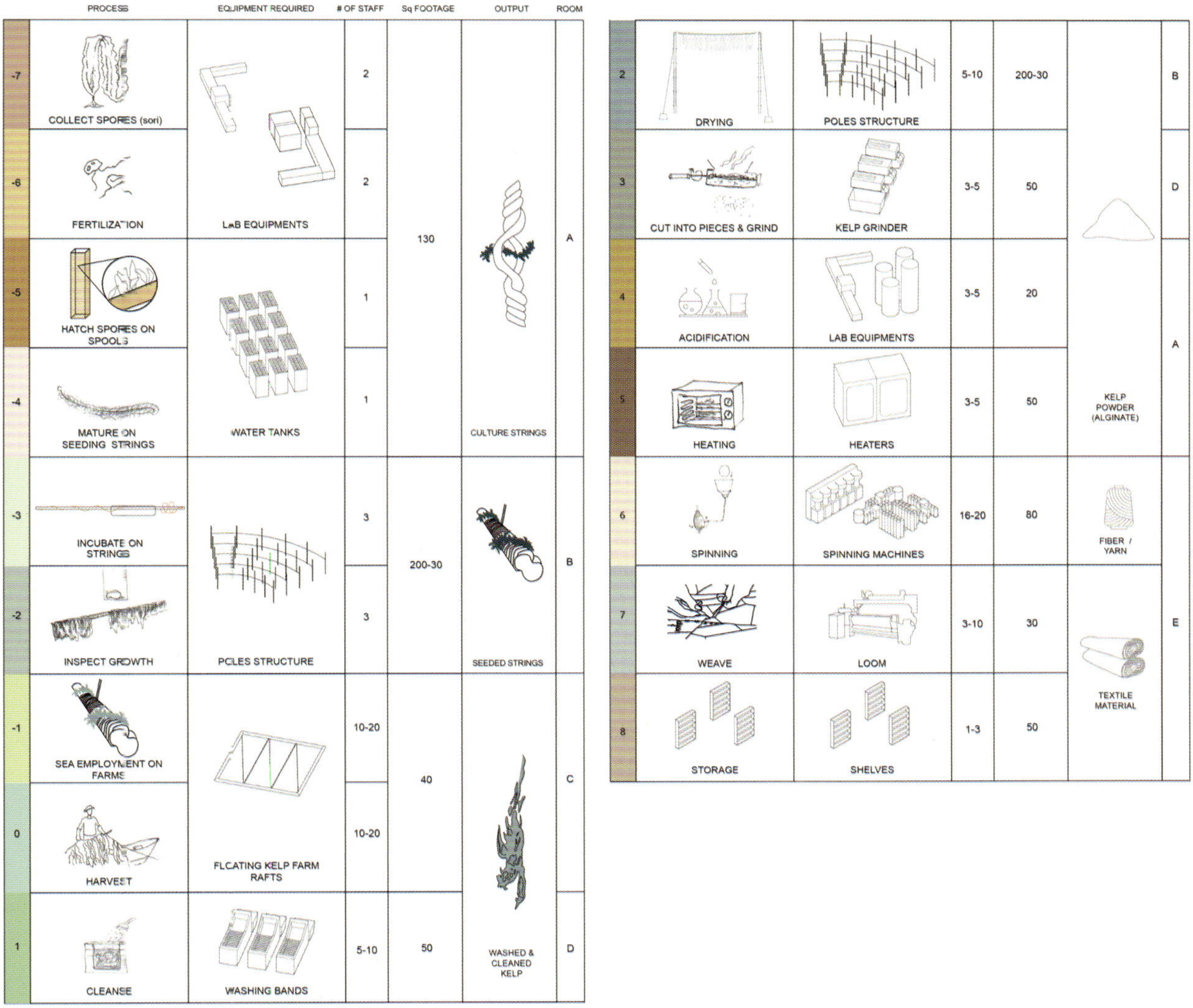

FIG.5 Employment opportunity from a local Kelp textile industry.
Chloe Lui | On the Edge Option Studio, University of Toronto

geopolitical boundary imposed through Confederation. "Territory" for a rural community can be understood as the extent of an area used in gathering essential resources, whether on land or water. In local maps, ocean environments are labeled with the same precision and accuracy as those on land. The advances in modern-day technology, increasing predictability of weather, and global positioning systems, provide the ability to further capitalize on the ocean as a connective infrastructure. Government agencies must rethink how to best connect rural communities of the island in order to strengthen a network of *local* resources.

Opportunities exist at the hyper-local scale, and it is time to consider what networks might best connect these rural outports with neighboring communities, with the rest of the island, and with global markets. This may mean re-allocation of financial resources away from unsustainable land-based infrastructures to where they have greater impact: the ocean and the *edge*.

The design community has a unique opportunity to insert themselves into research and decision-making at the infrastructural scale in Atlantic Canada, where the design disciplines' voices are typically underrepresented in favor of conventional engineering solutions. The studio research has reinforced the designer's ability to apply multi-scalar thinking and a landscape approach to develop solutions that marry a sustainable strategy toward natural resources, with community assets and human capital.

Endnotes

1. Grant McCall, "Nissology; A Proposal for Consideration," *Journal of the Pacific Society*, No. 63-64, Vol. 17, 1994.
2. Reginald Byron, *Retrenchment and Regeneration in Rural Newfoundland* (Toronto: University of Toronto Press, 2003), 1-15.
3. "Census Profile, 2016 Census," Newfoundland and Labrador, last modified August 9, 2019, https://www12.statcan.gc.ca/census-recensement/2016/.
4. Margaret Conrad and James Hiller, *Atlantic Canada A History 2nd Edition* (Toronto: Oxford University Press, 2010), 129.
5. "Landscape," Heritage Newfoundland & Labrador, last modified 2021, https://www.heritage.nf.ca/articles/environment/landscape.php.
6. Harry Thurston, *The Atlantic Coast: A Natural History* (Vancouver: Greystone Books, 2011).
7. Stephen Nolan, *Leaving Newfoundland. A History of Out-Migration* (St. John's: Flanker Press Limited, 2007), 93-109.
8. Godfrey Baldacchino, *A World of Islands* (Malta: Institute of Islands, 2007), 6.
9. Stephen Nolan, *Leaving Newfoundland. A History of Out-Migration* (St. John's: Flanker Press Limited, 2007), 93-109.
10. Gus Etchery, *Empty Nets. How Greed and Politics Wiped Out the World's Greatest Fishery* (Portugal Cove: Boulder, 2013), 117.
11. Margaret Conrad and James Hiller, *Atlantic Canada A History 2nd Edition* (Toronto: Oxford University Press, 2010), 129.
12. Sean Cadigan, *Newfoundland & Labrador, A History* (Toronto: University of Toronto Press. 2009), 241.
13. K. Hoggart, "Resettlement in Newfoundland," *Geographical Association Journal* Vol. 64. No. 3 (1979), 215-218.
14. Robert Mellin, *Newfoundland Modern. Architecture in the Smallwood Years* (Montreal: McGill-Queens University Press, 2011).
15. "Develop or Perish," Heritage Newfoundland & Labrador, last modified 2021, https://www.heritage.nf.ca/articles/politics/develop-or-perish.php.
16. Jennifer Bowering Delisle, *The Newfoundland Diaspora. Mapping the Literature of Outmigration* (Waterloo, Ontario: Wilfred Laurier Press, 2013), 9.
17. Rob Greenwood, "Demographics as Destiny: Regional Development, Population and Productivity," in *NL* (The Harris Center, Memorial University, June, 2019).

4.2 WaterLore for the Drylands

Strategies for Activating Cultural Waters in Regimes of Extraction

Antonia Besa, Gini Lee

On Mapping Cultural Waters in the Australian Drylands

Take a moment to imagine living in a drying world, where water in any form is the most precious commodity available. Imagine a place that has endured years of no rain, of rivers running dry where the little water that remains is bright green and the smell of dying fish precludes any idea of accessing the river. In the desert, water is a magnet for all living things, human and non-human, as long as it is sweet and accessible. The above imaginings describe the actuality of dryland areas of Australia during the all too familiar droughts, and they are the landscapes that we travel and research. In good times we experience water on the ground, flowing along the channels of contemporary landscapes, as much we also read the patterned traces from above of hydrological movement inscribed in rock and dune over eons. Occasionally, mineral-rich waters emerge from deep underground, bubbling up from springs or seeping from fissures in the rocky landscape. Water extracted from bores dug deep into the underground ancient aquifers primarily enable the industries that now populate the outback. Aboriginal people tell creation stories that help us to know why a water place exists and its importance in the life of the land and its beings, such as the ever-present Rainbow Serpent, the mythical dreaming creature that moves between the deep underground and above creating all the waters in all forms across the land. In recent times, of hotter seasons and infrequent rain, the spring and bore levels are dropping and remaining water is of barely usable quality.

Acknowledging the complexity of dryland water systems, the WaterLore project[1] devotes the agency of academic research to represent the multiple humanistic and scientific layers that contribute to existence in landscapes of sparse seasonal waters. The project's premise offers that in a warming, drying world it is necessary to review and adapt current unsustainable practices through reflection upon the water-driven records of places that are already dry—we can learn from people who already know how to work with less reliable water regimes. Over centuries of living with

OPPOSITE PAGE From the air we learned to interpret landscapes unfolding below us, navigating through the pilots' knowledge of the critical refugia water places, reading the formations and subtleties brought into visibility in flood times. Bridges and roads built as mining infrastructure often ignore the magnitude and temporality of the watercourse – here shown marooned and impassable as the waters take over. Gini Lee.

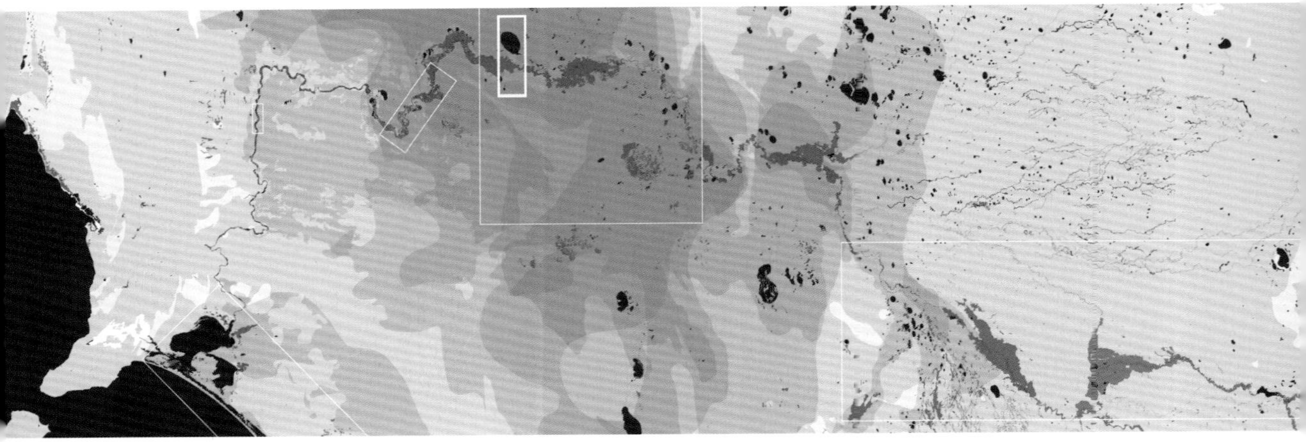

water absence and presence, in both regulated and unregulated systems of dryland water management, the successful and the questionable outcomes of designed water systems, places, and infrastructures are written over the territory. Critically, the messaging to communities and extraction-driven entities regarding water options for access and wise use is often framed by water trading economies as a functional resource, while ignoring the cultural mores of human, and associated non-human, attachments to water. While the above is a story of Australia, it is also pertinent to places that are equally subject to unsustainable economic and political agendas.

Water-focused mapping is an effective tool to explore the divergent and sometimes conflicting intersections between utilitarian and cultural water conceptions, revealing connections that are generally unnoticed. Assembling successful or questionable water-infrastructure designs through the medium of the layered map reveals the implications of water management and water significance over time. Palimpsest maps encourage critical speculation, highlighting positive results or prompting change through design. In *Undermining,* Lucy Lippard critically explores the potential in constructing artistic combinations of text and image to enable weaving parallel stories of environmental destruction and absent political will to conserve landscapes, in this case in mining operations.[2] The WaterLore maps achieve a similar result—albeit through different representative approaches—to bring to presence the beauty and distinctive qualities of water in our water-depleted landscapes, while simultaneously producing an active data-based record of what has been, is now, and potentially will be water availability in the future.

The essential framing upon which this project draws inspiration is in the definition of Lore with regard to ideas of cultural waters and cultural flows. Article 25 of the United Nations Declaration on the Rights of Indigenous Peoples confirms that:

Indigenous peoples have the right to maintain and strengthen their distinctive spiritual relationship with their traditionally owned or otherwise occupied and used lands, territories, waters, and coastal

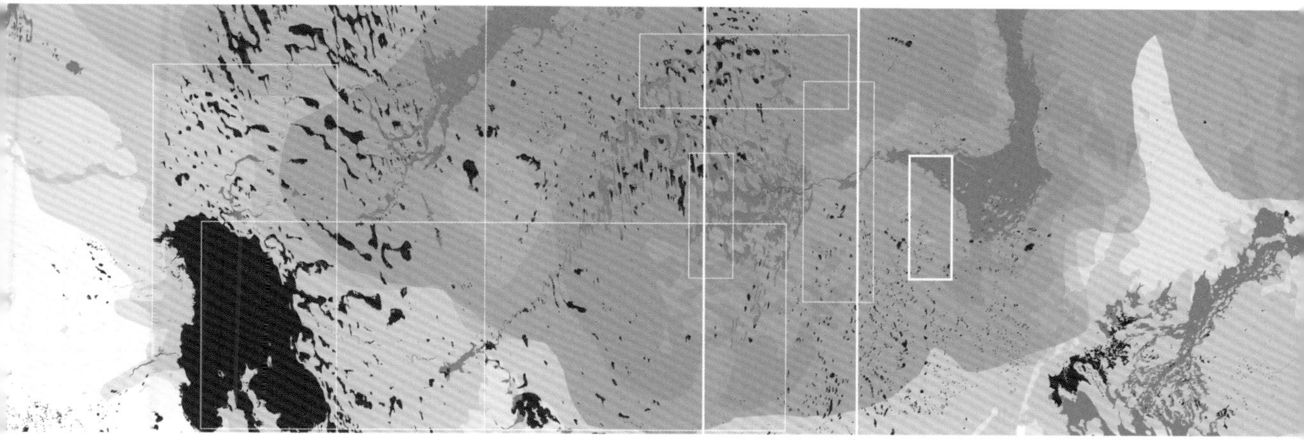

seas, and other resources and to uphold their responsibilities to future generations in this regard.[3]

Briefly, cultural water in Aboriginal terms means "water in the living cultural landscape is inseparable from land, people, ancestors, and social relations," supporting the concept of cultural water attached to place, networks, and customary practice as central to the cultural mapping of all landscapes.[4] Whereas cultural flows is defined as "the importance of sufficient-quality waters legally available to support and improve traditional, healthy, and economically beneficial lives," therefore confirming that the management of cultural flows needs ongoing custodianship and input of Aboriginal and local people in their country. Aboriginal and non-Aboriginal attitudes to water and its management in contemporary Australia vary widely, yet both groups "consider water as a spiritual, natural resource and a commodity essential to livelihood and of significant economic value."[5] For Aboriginal people, caring for water and water places is essential to the ongoing resilience and cultural integrity of the country under their custodianship. This infers a more conservationist practice in water management in terms of river and waterhole health, quality of life and wellbeing, and the ability to continue traditional practices such as fishing, medical- and water-based crafts, and spiritual practices.[6] Beyond purely cultural perspectives, the right to use and manage water is also essential to capacity building towards participating in decision making, ownership of water allocations, and collaboratively managing water resources, rights which are not currently enshrined in policy in the river systems described below.

FIG.1 Murrundi Millewa Murray Barka Darling River system and Kunari Cooper Creek system surface waters, floodplain and groundwater mapping as fundamental to the nature of territory. The rivers' Aboriginal names are included preceding the European names to aid in reconciling the erasure of First Nations language and sign posting after colonial settlement. Along the river these names will change according to the territorial boundaries of each tribal group. Antonia Besa and Gini Lee

Defining the Territory: The Fundamental Water Maps

Mapping cultural waters combines past, present, and future site forces unpacked from data collection and ground-truthing through the agency of fieldwork. Outback drylands fieldwork requires deep immersion, traveling solo and with others, focusing on where water appears. We sample

waters and the mud, sand, and stone caught up in the gathering, photograph, sketch, catalog qualities of the known and unknown found along the way, according to a planned water trail itinerary. Water stories are found in the historic record and through hearsay from encounters on site. Places of importance are detected and understood through incorporating visible and invisible systems, superficial and underground traces, precise conceptions, and subjective constructions into the landscape map. Superimposing spatial analysis tools, satellite images, and notions of practical, scientific, and historical knowledge, combined with in-situ observations, passing conversations, impressions from the air, and current news, confirms the water place's distinctiveness underwritten by found data and emerging narratives. Our premise is that the mapping project allows us to propose ideas for design-led installations according to circumstances that encourage novel speculation, or landscape curation and/or communication programs such as publication and exhibition [FIG. 1].

In *Water in a Dry Land,* Margaret Somerville employs an art-driven deep mapping methodology to examine the cultural waters of Australia's major Murray Darling River system. Her premise? To think about water differently requires considering how to create new, more abstract maps that combine Western and Aboriginal techniques and understandings embracing culturally specific languages as a form of storytelling.[7] Confirming this approach, the WaterLore base maps upend the typical approach to mapping landscape features. As the basis to survival in all landscapes begins with the availability of water, these maps eschew human-made territorial road and boundary markings in favor of the blurred boundaries of the overlapping and interconnected waters. Gleaned from layers of readily available hydrological geoscience data, surface and groundwater maps are superimposed to reveal the water landscapes that form and frame the distinct characteristics of the regulated Murrundi Millewa Murray Barka Darling River system and the unregulated Kunari Cooper Creek system. These maps reveal the extensive land prints of the continent's waters, absent of the fluctuations of slow, drying drought and

FIG. 2 Murrundi Millewa Murray Barka Darling River system and Kunari Cooper Creek system Hotspots of human water interface in time and place. Antonia Besa and Gini Lee

fast, wetting floods that typically shape life on the land. On the surface, the rivers are linear and permanent with a visible flow that varies over time. Unique in its context the often-ephemeral Kunari Cooper Creek's more irregular channel shape imperceptibly disappears to form a network of disconnected pools in the dunescapes during dry times.

Water Made X-Points: Hotspots as Nature Culture Interface

Mapping is presented as a method to interpret and represent critical issues and practices that collide in specific water places to provoke propositional thinking. As the artist William Kentridge defines through his writings and dynamic drawings, the representation of X points, as he calls these points of pressure, are "a membrane between the world that comes towards us and our projected understanding of the world, a negotiation between us and what is outside"[8] [FIG. 2].

Along the rivers and adjacent to the lakes and waterholes, certain places demonstrate the confluence of historical and contemporary water stories, inferred by typical cartography, written accounts, and various modes of production, and further confirmed when visited on-site through fieldwork journeys. The collected stories are not homogeneously located in the territory but rather converge in punctuated places, our nominated Hotspots, typically recurring at water X-points in the landscape. The twelve Hotspot maps presented in this research are, firstly, records of the site's morphology and natural ecology associated with water in its multiple forms. Then, a representation of human interventions and conceptions—infrastructures, memories, routes, symbolic meanings, practical actions, tourist attractions, administrative borders, nominations, and measures. Finally—as Kentridge puts it—the drawing is a vision, a desire, which blurs the boundaries of what exists, to speculate on what is possible. The latter makes the mapping a creative and imperfect piece distanced from cartographic accuracy and instead aiming to illustrate the disjunctions and dissimilar juxtapositions resulting from the events and

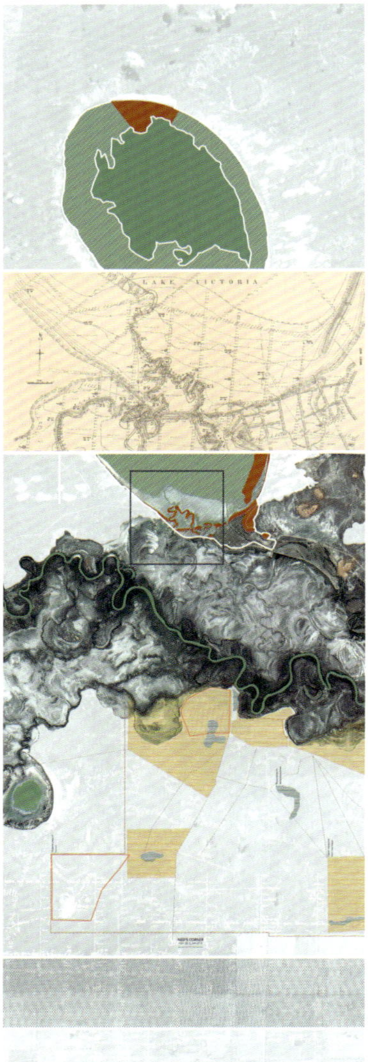

FIG.3–4 Hotspot 4 Ta-Ru Lake Victoria Rufus River and Counter Map proposing an interrupted walk around the Lake's margins crossing X-points of confluence beyond displacement. Antonia Besa and Gini Lee

forces present on site. The narrative extent determines the scope of each drawing, requiring gradual scalar approximations to deepen perspectives critical to understanding these pressure points. During the drawing out process, the mapping remains open to improvisation and unexpected turns, determined by understanding and negotiating the limitations of the sourced media against verification on site.

From each Hotspot map, a legible assemblage of tangible and intangible site conditions, the prospective agency of the deep map is revealed through developing counter maps rendered in greater detail. These counter maps enable alternative abstractions and superimpositions of more defined place knowledge to speculate upon possible working interventions bringing other knowledge or site operations to bear upon the landscape. Underpinning the prospective nature of counter maps is the ongoing intent that cultural waters and flows principles guide design explorations into what fundamentally has been observed. Namely, the economic and political nature of extraction and the spatial, material, and social outcomes that are impacted by water exploitation activities. The industries and organizations that support such overuse of both ground and surface water, also often lack good practice methods for environmental, cultural, and ethical resilience.[9]

Hotspot 4: A Rufus River Lake Victoria Confluence as Provocation for Traversing the Lake

The confluence of the Millewa Murray River with Ta-Ru Lake Victoria resonates with divergent story layers of deep and constant waters that

support many lives downstream—the sad history of the consequences of settler and First Peoples' interactions in the 1841 massacre recorded at the Rufus River mouth. The tragedy is remembered beside subsequent constructed embankments and flow regulators for waters entering the Lake, infrastructure that regulates Lake Victoria as an off-river storage dam since 1920. Yet, Ta-Ru has been home to the Barkindji Maruara people for tens of thousands of years and the Lake is of high cultural and spiritual significance including the presence of many ancient burial sites, flooded by damming the once ephemeral Lake. Ongoing archaeological research and management regimes of the Barkindji artifacts present around the Lake's margins reveal the intensity of multiple layers of conservation activities, both cultural and environmental.[10,11] It is a crossing point of lake and river, ancient and modern trading routes, road- and water-regulating infrastructure, farming and wetlands, and of a community-made outlook over the Lake. It's an experience to pause at the shelter to view the lake at high water and low, cattle grazing on the lakebed, rotting fence posts silhouetted against dead trees symbolic of the damming of the Lake to water city-folk downstream, and to marvel at the weir mechanism that lets measured water in and out. The counter map provokes a possible design method to effect traversing the floodplain. The design recognizes the ebbing and rising of water as critical natural and artificial events, enabling pauses to witness the landscape past and present and uncovering water stories to transcend the management regimes that exist today. The X-point is proposed as a line of travel with points of thickening at negotiated places—at interrupted ecologies, at points of measure, of infiltrat-

FIG.5-6 Hotspot 10 Tirrawarra Swamp dune landscape covered by pipes and drill holes as a result of industrial scale gas and petrol extraction. The Counter Map refutes current superficial rehabilitation works to recover and expose trace sites of abandonment for new water drawn occupations. Antonia Besa and Gini Lee

ing the margins—paying attention to the knowledge of the old ones and working with the new ones to renew memories of significance [FIG. 3–4].

Hotspot 10: Tirrawarra Swamp Reprised Sites of Extractive Tracing Along the Road

Underlying the Cooper Basin are the geological riches that designate this remote landscape as an industrial zone of intensity in an otherwise fragile wild place. Ancient forests have produced rich seams deep underground where oil and gas exploitation since the 1960s, has been facilitated by ready access to plentiful groundwater. Large scale infrastructure and permanent or mobile settlements are arranged over wide areas of plains and/or wetlands where old swamps are components of the landscape of mining exploration and extraction. Close examination of the mined Tirrawarra Swamp reveals a multi-layered place where the ecologies of the intermittent Kunari Cooper Creek, together with the presence of permanent waterholes and pastoral infrastructure, translates as a landscape dependent on surface and groundwater. Depletion of the groundwater due to industrial scale extraction is impacting upon the viability of other economies, while interruptions to the floodplain flow impacts the hydrological systems that support ecosystems downstream [FIG. 5–6].

The Tirrawarra Swamp/Gidgealpa Road is a site of extractive tracing of abandoned oil and gas mining/industrial sites where each trace is an X-point of water drawn from the ancient Great Artesian Basin beneath. Some of the sealed drill holes remain as ghostly marks weathered by wind, sun, and overland flow from rare floods. Mining-company-sponsored rehabilitation processes achieve a bare minimum predominantly concerned with visual management to disguise their presence alongside appropriate cultural clearances undertaken by the Dieri, Yandruwandha, and Yawarrawarrka First Peoples. Yet the industrial scale of these works in the fragile dune and swamplands means that many marks remain. The counter map celebrates the road and the various infrastructures that herald a working extraction site overlaying Tirrawarra's gridded swamp and dunescapes. Post abandonment, it is instructive to imagine a sequence of road markers along the road revealing the geological and water stories underneath and of working beneath the surface. The authors' proposition is to recover the water supply at these places along the road to make new landscape scale installations as new forms of rehabilitation to produce highly visible re-uses of these abandoned places. Yet to occur, our propositional maps are intended as prompts to engage local communities and policy-making collaborators to imagine that such projects could be realized. Recovering the landscape with a sequence of water infrastructures through judicious tapping of groundwater can promote air and land tourism through interpreting what lies beneath as sites of recovery.

On Activation and the Agency of the Map as Generator

The WaterLore exhibition project displays our analysis of contemporary aspects of critical water dryland landscapes and water management regimes, through the agency of the large-scale deep map. As a communication project this immersive exposition into the nature of cultural and ecological water systems over time, and the challenges arising from a warming planet, seeks to activate new thinking leading to landscape amelioration through the agency of discursive, open-ended mapping of territorial waters. The project acknowledges the importance of data as the basis for critical mapping as undeniable, yet it also confirms as equally pertinent, the ability for landscape architects and interdisciplinary designers to engage in fieldwork to ground truth mapped findings and assumptions. The Hotspots express current situations constructed to convey the critical issues at play to people familiar with these places but who are potentially unaware of the complexities and fragility of the interacting systems. Prompts drawn from the intersections of local dynamics are recorded above in two examples of how local maps may provoke proposals for design-led projects for sites—some speculative and some essentially pragmatic. Experiencing site qualities informed by community knowledge is facilitated by the scale and intensity of the human-scale WaterLore Exhibition maps and associated text and image water lexicons. Our ongoing intent is to offer the exhibition to local community halls, galleries, and meeting places associated with identified Hotpots where improved water futures may yet be realized through collaborative and design-focused action in and for place.

Endnotes

1. The WaterLore Project is an ongoing drylands water mapping research collaboration, first instigated at the University Melbourne and principally directed by Professor Gini Lee and landscape architect Antonia Besa. Involving a reference group of scientists, cultural landscape architects, and humanities academics the Project draws upon years of academic fieldwork and contemporary data collection to visualize and promote wise use of water and landscapes in the arid lands.
2. Lucy R. Lippard, *Undermining: A Wild Ride Through Land Use, Politics, and Art in the Changing West* (New York: The New Press, 2006).
3. "The United Nations Declaration on the Rights of Indigenous Peoples," United Nations, 2008, accessed March 15, 2021, https://www.un.org/esa/socdev/unpfii/documents/DRIPS_en.pdf.
4. Sue Jackson and Jon Altman, "Indigenous Rights and Water Policy: Perspectives from Tropical Northern Australia,' *Australian Indigenous Law Review*, 13 (1), (2009): 27–48
5. "Cultural Flows," Murray Lower Darling Rivers Indigenous Nations, 2007, accessed March 15, 2021, https://www.mldrin.org.au/what-we-do/cultural-flows/.
6. "Water for the Environment," Murray Darling Basin Authority, accessed March 15, 2021, https://www.mdba.gov.au/issues-murray-darling-basin/water-for-environment.
7. Margaret Somerville, *Water in a Dry Land: Place Learning through Art and Story* (New York: Routledge, 2013).
8. W. Kentridge, *Six Drawing Lessons* (Cambridge, MA: Harvard University Press, 2014).
9. Matthew Wiener, "Grounding Water," Scenario 05: Extraction, Fall (2015), accessed March 15, 2021, https://scenariojournal.com/journal/scenario-05-extraction/.
10. "Lake Victoria," Murray Darling Basin Authority, accessed March 15, 2021, https://www.mdba.gov.au/water-management/infrastructure/lake-victoria.
11. "The Rufus River Massacre, Lake Victoria South West NSW," Sovereign Union, 2019, accessed March 15, 2021, http://nationalunitygovernment.org/content/rufus-river-massacre-lake-victoria-south-west-nsw.

4.3

Conservation Through Indigenous Treaty Revival

Duffin's Creek, Williams Treaties Area

Sheila Boudreau, Gary Pritchard

In urbanizing areas, where significant stresses on flora and fauna are intensifying, improving landscape connectivity and integrating this effort with sustainable land management practices must become a priority.[1] As the World Wildlife Fund for Nature Canada states, the path forward is before us, "Indigenous knowledge systems and leadership are effective and just keys to successful conservation."[2] Recent research estimates that Indigenous Peoples are credited for preserving up to 80 percent of the world's biodiversity, through directly protecting land and water in their territories.[3] It is thus critical for governments and their agents to ask how they can work to acknowledge and work towards a system that respects this understanding. Co-created works that meaningfully engage Indigenous Peoples, such as the Government of Canada's 2018 report, One With Nature, lists a priority to "Promote Greater Recognition and Support for Existing Indigenous Rights, Responsibilities, and Priorities in Conservation."[4]

We offer the case of Duffins Creek, Williams Treaty area, in Canada, involving Indigenous-focused efforts to protect a threatened wetland complex from irreparable damage from development that only benefits as short-term economic gain. The intent is to prioritize Indigenous voices regarding conservation and First Nation rights, and to emphasize the need to act on non-Indigenous/settler communities' Treaty obligations. The chapter is organized into two distinct but connected parts to tell the whole story. The purpose of offering these complementary readings is to first provide a contextual framing and writing style that is typically used in Western culture to describe the policies and actors that have impacted conservation efforts in the Duffins Creek, Williams Treaty area, while the second reading offers a writing style from Indigenous perspectives, narrated rather than described, in keeping with Indigenous Traditional ways of teaching and learning. It is hoped that the reader will come away with an improved understanding and appreciation of First Nations and supportive efforts in conservation, and will in turn consider how they sit within this evolving space. Questions posed for the reader to consider throughout this chapter include:

OPPOSITE PAGE Duffins Creek Wetlands Water Lilies. Heather Pankhurst

What does it mean to be a land-based professional working in Ontario, Canada, when faced with unethical situations where duty to the public good and duty to the environment are ignored, and no substantive guidance to uphold Indigenous rights are given?

What issues arise when a failure to engage First Nations Treaty rights holders in the gathering of data, critical to fully understanding the land and waters, from those who have lived there for thousands of years?

What are helpful approaches that could be used, and changes in mindsets that are needed, for Indigenous/settler interactions to result in relationships based on respect, reciprocity, and responsibility?

Part I: Context, Treaties, and Policy

To frame the thoughts and experiences shared in this chapter, we begin, and end, with the land. The Duffins Creek headwaters comprises part of Ontario's Green Belt, located along the environmentally significant Oak Ridges Moraine, north of Toronto. Its watershed drains to Lake Ontario and connects two regional governments and five municipalities over 23,300 ha (57,575 acres) of land, with an approximate coverage of 10 percent urban and 70 percent rural. Assessed by Toronto and Region Conservation Authority (TRCA), responsible for watershed management under the Province of Ontario's Conservation Authorities Act (unique in Canada), it is also one of the healthiest streams in the Greater Toronto Area, with the highest proportion of natural cover in TRCA's jurisdiction. The ecological communities are categorized as forest (25 percent) meadow (11 percent), successional (three percent), and wetland (two percent). Redside Dace, a provincially and federally endangered fish species, also calls Duffins Creek home, and relies on clean, cool water for its survival. Increasing urbanization pressures threaten this colorful small fish, as it does for all flora and fauna present at Duffins Creek [FIG. 1].

The Province of Ontario's Municipal Zoning Orders (MZOs) was originally established under the Ontario Planning Act for emergencies and to advance pressing issues of provincial importance. This has now transformed into what is seen as an abuse of power by the Minister of Municipal Affairs and Housing to eliminate scientific and local expertise, and override local government decisions.[5] In November, 2020, an MZO was created to force development on the provincially significant Lower Duffins Creek wetlands complex, resulting in lawsuits from environmental groups, underway at the time of writing.[6] Further, while weakly understood by the public or government agents, the Duffins Creek watershed is subject to Treaty responsibilities with the Williams Treaties First Nations, signed by the Crown in the 18th and 19th centuries with The Chippewas of Beausoleil, Georgina Island and Rama and the Mississaugas of Alderville, Curve Lake, Hiawatha, and Scugog Island First Nations. They stand together to ensure their rights and relationships

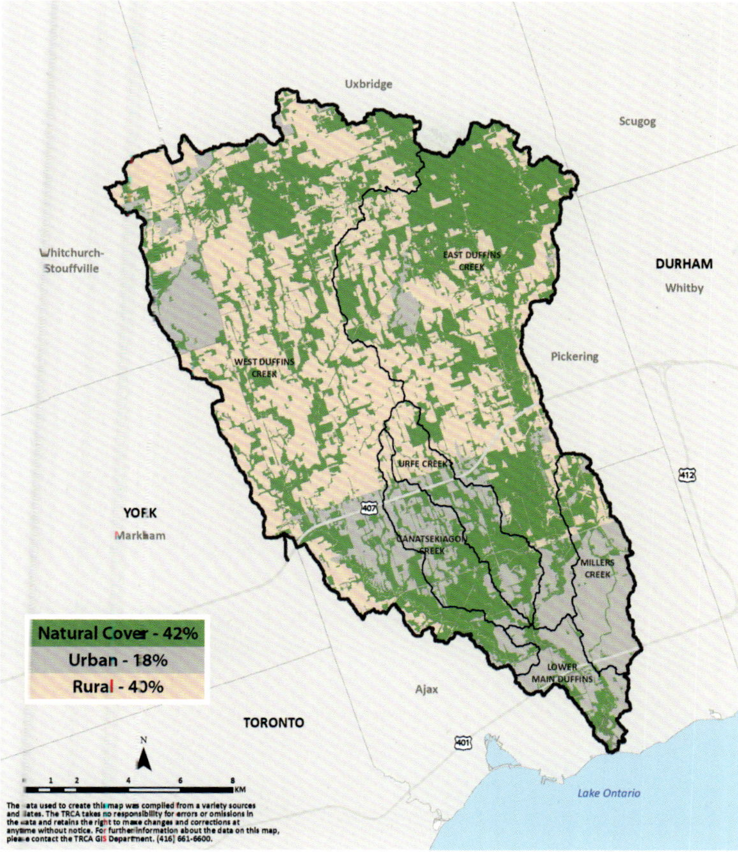

FIG.1 Duffins Creek Watershed Map. TRCA

to the land within the treaty areas are protected, stating "Protection, conservation, and sustainable collaborative management are a priority for the Williams Treaties First Nations."[7]

The Provincial Policy Statements (PPS) issued under the Ontario Planning Act declare matters of importance to the Province and provide policy direction for all planning matters. Regarding Indigenous engagement, the PPS, 2020 states:

The Province recognizes the importance of consulting with Aboriginal communities on planning matters that may affect their section 35 Aboriginal or treaty rights. Planning authorities are encouraged to build constructive, cooperative relationships through meaningful engagement with Indigenous communities to facilitate knowledge-sharing in land-use planning processes and inform decision-making.[8]

Without making this a requirement, or providing clear direction to guide this work, those responsible for implementing this policy are hesitant to act to avoid legal and political consequences. Policy 4.3 of the PPS 2020 also states: "This PPS shall be implemented in a manner that is consistent with the recognition and affirmation of existing Aboriginal and treaty rights in Section 35 of the Constitution Act, 1982." But in the case of the Duffins Creek MZO, the Williams Treaty First Nations state they were not consulted at all. Additionally, the Province-wide Bill 76, United Nations Declaration of the Rights of Indigenous Peoples (UNDRIP) Act, 2019, was considered for adoption by the Province and is now deferred to the Standing Committee of General Government at its second reading. This is no small measure, as the adoption of Bill 76 would dictate that the principles of UNDRIP (2007) are adopted into all Ontario laws. The widespread support by Members of Provincial Parliament for this Act at the second reading was promising and would require the enforcement of UNDRIP Article 19: "States shall consult and cooperate in good faith with the Indigenous peoples concerned through their own representative institutions in order to obtain their free, prior, and informed consent before adopting and implementing legislative or administrative measures that may affect them."[9]

At the recent federal government event, Toward the Creation of a Canadian Water Agency Regional Freshwater Forum – Ontario (Feb. 9, 2021), speaker Dawn Martin-Hill, of Six Nations First Nation, and McMaster University, offers insight into this, describing the success of transdisciplinary Indigenous-led conservation on her reserve

Right now, from biological, chemical engineers, to pediatricians, and so on, …we're all working in a transdisciplinary way. One of the things is we ask different questions, and we look at different data sets of what we might want, and what the Elders want us to look at. … it's not just about sharing data, it's about co-creating that data that makes sense to First Nations. And then secondly, we have people who understand how to clean up the water without being intrusive and invasive, but using Traditional Knowledge and Ways of Knowing to do that. Those things aren't even entertained by mainstream restoration strategies, and that needs to change as well. … Most First Nations would agree that we're not even at the table, let alone co-creating ways to improve the quality of our source water.[10]

Part II: Narratives

We offer the following experiences from working in the Duffins Creek watershed as examples of considerations and efforts in working towards landscape connectivity on First Nations Treaty lands. For Indigenous research, in the words of Shawn Wilson: "Part of the importance of developing an Indigenous research paradigm is that we can use the methods and forms of expression that we judge to be valid for ourselves."[11] Narratives, or storytelling, is used across Indigenous cultures as an effective and meaningful way of sharing knowledge, while also building relationships. "Stories allow listeners to draw their own conclusions and to gain life lessons from a more personal perspective. By getting away from abstractions and rules, stories allow us to see others' life experiences through our own eyes."[12]

Reviving an Indigenous Presence at Duffins Creek

Aanii (ah-knee) everyone, my Spirit name is Giniw (gee-knew), or in English, Golden Eagle. My English name is Gary Pritchard, and I come from Curve Lake First Nation which is north of Peterborough, Ontario. I am a member of the Otter Clan and a conservation ecologist. The traditional homelands of the Michi Saagiig (Mississauga Anishinaabeg) encompass a vast area of what is now known as southern Ontario. The Michi Saagiig are known as "the people of the big river mouths" and were also known as the "Salmon People" who occupied and fished the north shore of Lake Ontario where the various tributaries emptied into the lake. We were highly mobile thanks to the tributaries that fed Lake Ontario. We depended on the coastal wetlands and waterways for our survival. We would harvest fish and other foods using our knowledge systems and governance on the waterways prior to colonization. As an example, we knew that Atlantic salmon could only be harvested until the leaves along the water's edge would grow to the size of a fox's ear. Thus, allowing the fish who came after we were done harvesting ample time to rest and spawn. It was through this common understanding, those who needed food would always be provided from nature if they worked within the confines of our established natural law.

In 2018, the Williams Treaty Settlement was completed. After almost a century of our ancestors of both the Chippewas and Mississauga communities being denied access to the lands, harvesting rights, and culture, our way of life was finally resolved, however what had changed was not the communities, but the landscape. You cannot have reconciliation[13] and healing without a connection to the land. What better way to understand the landscape and ecosystem health for settler-based communities than through a report card system, similar to that observed in the watershed reporting for Duffins Creek. To address the aforementioned threats to the Duffins Creek wetlands, in the November 11, 2020 letter to the Mayor of Pickering, from Chief Kelly LaRocca, Portfolio Chief for the Williams Treaties First Nations, she stated, on behalf of all of the Chiefs:

Our ancestors have sought to protect these wetlands since the Gunshot Treaty of 1788 – there is a long history of our people serving as stewards of these lands. We hereby put the City on notice that the said wetlands are an Indigenous Protected Conserved Area (IPCA). Destroying this land and water source is sending a message to First Nations. The message is that there is no respect, no regard for First Nations treaty rights, or any type of Reconciliation[10] and that the City, and Province for that matter, feel that they have no obligation to consult with First Nations, even when the Courts have stated otherwise. In honoring the

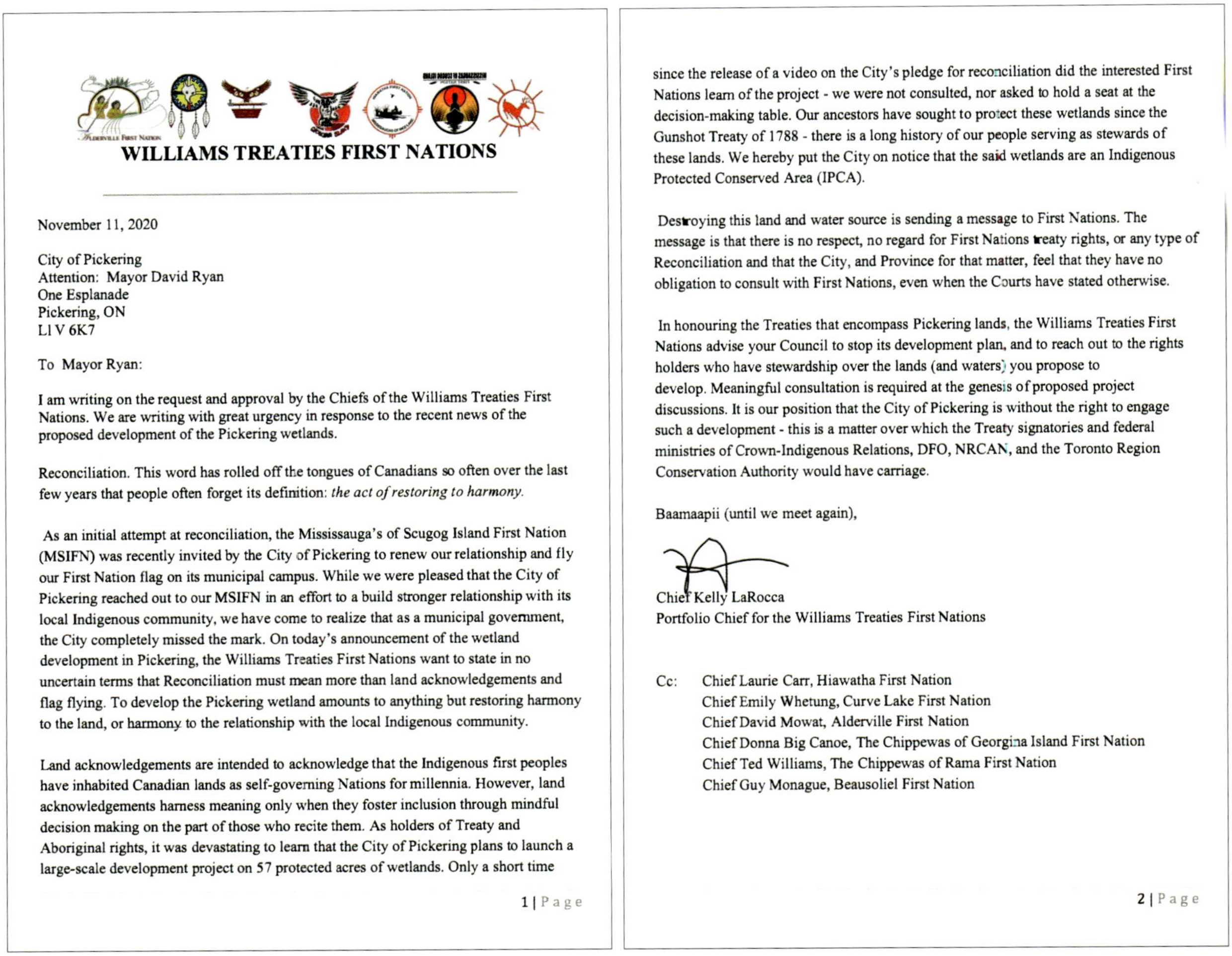

WILLIAMS TREATIES FIRST NATIONS

November 11, 2020

City of Pickering
Attention: Mayor David Ryan
One Esplanade
Pickering, ON
L1V 6K7

To Mayor Ryan:

I am writing on the request and approval by the Chiefs of the Williams Treaties First Nations. We are writing with great urgency in response to the recent news of the proposed development of the Pickering wetlands.

Reconciliation. This word has rolled off the tongues of Canadians so often over the last few years that people often forget its definition: *the act of restoring to harmony.*

As an initial attempt at reconciliation, the Mississauga's of Scugog Island First Nation (MSIFN) was recently invited by the City of Pickering to renew our relationship and fly our First Nation flag on its municipal campus. While we were pleased that the City of Pickering reached out to our MSIFN in an effort to a build stronger relationship with its local Indigenous community, we have come to realize that as a municipal government, the City completely missed the mark. On today's announcement of the wetland development in Pickering, the Williams Treaties First Nations want to state in no uncertain terms that Reconciliation must mean more than land acknowledgements and flag flying. To develop the Pickering wetland amounts to anything but restoring harmony to the land, or harmony to the relationship with the local Indigenous community.

Land acknowledgements are intended to acknowledge that the Indigenous first peoples have inhabited Canadian lands as self-governing Nations for millennia. However, land acknowledgements harness meaning only when they foster inclusion through mindful decision making on the part of those who recite them. As holders of Treaty and Aboriginal rights, it was devastating to learn that the City of Pickering plans to launch a large-scale development project on 57 protected acres of wetlands. Only a short time

1 | Page

since the release of a video on the City's pledge for reconciliation did the interested First Nations learn of the project - we were not consulted, nor asked to hold a seat at the decision-making table. Our ancestors have sought to protect these wetlands since the Gunshot Treaty of 1788 - there is a long history of our people serving as stewards of these lands. We hereby put the City on notice that the said wetlands are an Indigenous Protected Conserved Area (IPCA).

Destroying this land and water source is sending a message to First Nations. The message is that there is no respect, no regard for First Nations treaty rights, or any type of Reconciliation and that the City, and Province for that matter, feel that they have no obligation to consult with First Nations, even when the Courts have stated otherwise.

In honouring the Treaties that encompass Pickering lands, the Williams Treaties First Nations advise your Council to stop its development plan, and to reach out to the rights holders who have stewardship over the lands (and waters) you propose to develop. Meaningful consultation is required at the genesis of proposed project discussions. It is our position that the City of Pickering is without the right to engage such a development - this is a matter over which the Treaty signatories and federal ministries of Crown-Indigenous Relations, DFO, NRCAN, and the Toronto Region Conservation Authority would have carriage.

Baamaapii (until we meet again),

Chief Kelly LaRocca
Portfolio Chief for the Williams Treaties First Nations

Cc: Chief Laurie Carr, Hiawatha First Nation
Chief Emily Whetung, Curve Lake First Nation
Chief David Mowat, Alderville First Nation
Chief Donna Big Canoe, The Chippewas of Georgina Island First Nation
Chief Ted Williams, The Chippewas of Rama First Nation
Chief Guy Monague, Beausoliel First Nation

2 | Page

FIG.2 Letter to the City of Pickering from the Williams Treaty First Nations, page 1.

Treaties that encompass Pickering lands, the Williams Treaties First Nations advise your Council to stop its development plan, and to reach out to the rights holders who have stewardship over the lands (and waters) you propose to develop. Meaningful consultation is required at the genesis of proposed project discussions. It is our position that the City of Pickering is without the right to engage such a development – this is a matter over which the Treaty signatories and federal ministries of Crown-Indigenous Relations, DFO, NRCAN, and the Toronto Region Conservation Authority would have carriage[14] [FIG. 2].

I wanted to share this with everyone who reads this, that growing up and harvesting within my territory in the '90s and early 2000s was challenging on many levels. Members of my family could still feel the racism and fear of Settler law when we tried to harvest for either personal or community use. I remember in 1996, my cousins and I started to have our own boats to go out and explore our waters. An Elder once said as we pulled from the docks, "Keep to the reserve islands, that way those wardens or cottagers can't lie about what you are doing and get you arrested."

Arrested for what? Fishing within the delineated settler-based harvest season? That day has always remained in the front of my mind. As I have grown to understand, review, and ultimately create harvest limits and policy, I am left wondering if we are managing ourselves to extinction. Why do we challenge Indigenous gathering practices or ecosystem management when settler-based policy limits species' success, biodiversity, and ecosystem productivity?

1. Harvesting on the tributaries of the north shores of Lake Ontario, came with a similar set of challenges:
2. recreational anglers did not know Indigenous peoples had rights to harvest the tributaries which lead to violence,
3. municipal and provincial regulators and enforcement did not have an education in Indigenous rights to harvest which lead to conflict, and no one clearly understood their obligations set forth within the treaty.

Without Settler populations clearly understanding their obligations to Indigenous rights and honoring treaties, we will continue to have conflict and even violence against those who challenge Settler policy. As stated in the Gunshot Treaty, where this example of Duffins Creek takes place, there are clear First Nations rights to wetlands, water, and the rights to healthy environments to provide food and a future for all peoples. It is a shame that settlers manage the landscape with such lack of compassion or understanding of interconnectedness [FIG. 3].

Planning and Design at the Headwaters of Duffins Creek

My name is Sheila Boudreau, and I am a woman of mixed ancestry: Acadian (the first families to settle what is now known as Canada from France, c.1639), Mi'kmaq (ancestors who married early Acadians), and Celtic (British, of Irish and Welsh descent). I grew up in Ontario in the countryside of Halton Hills, followed by the urban edge of Guelph adjacent to a conservation area, and moved to the east end of Toronto over two decades ago (specifically, the treaty lands of the Williams Treaty First Nations and the Mississaugas of the Credit First Nation). I have been fortunate in my career to reflect on my ancestry and my professional responsibility to do better, to work towards reconciliation, involve Indigenous voices in my work, and to support Indigenous-led initiatives. When I became the manager of the landscape architecture team at TRCA, I encouraged my staff and colleagues to consider ways to improve Indigenous relations, and we sought opportunities to honor Indigenous cultures on the plans and designs we were responsible for. The Goodwood Resource Management Trail Plan was one example where we were intent on doing this, and where I led the

FIG.3 Building a Teaching Lodge in Williams Treaty Territory. Gary Pritchard

public realm planning and design, a project that was developed to connect local, regional, and trans-Canadian-trail systems.

An early visit to the Goodwood property made it evident to the design team that there was a strong settler history on the land, with fieldstone ruins of old foundations and walls, and an original rusted metal well hand-pump in a naturalized meadow area (possibly used for livestock). The site also includes a healthy ecosystem with an interior forest habitat for rare species, standing at the running cold water of the East Duffins Creek. Aware of the importance of water as being sacred to First Nations, I was inspired to highlight the creek area as a likely preferred location for Indigenous placemaking, to help to also tell the story of the First Peoples of the area. The final Trail Plan stressed the need to engage the Indigenous communities whose Traditional Territories include Goodwood, to work on plans and designs as the Trail Plan project progresses [FIG. 4].

As a sessional instructor with Toronto Metropolitan University and the University of Toronto, I was also intent on decolonizing the practice of teaching urban and regional planning and landscape architecture through land-based experiences that involved Indigenous Peoples. I organized a day trip for my students and invited urban Indigenous youth of *Nikibii Dawadinna Giigwag* ("Flooded Valley Healing," Anishinaabemowin), and the Anishinabeg Elder co-leading this program to join us (building on my strong relationship with the program as a co-founder). It was important to me that the trip was conducted in a way that honors Indigenous protocols and cultural practices, throughout the day. Before

getting on the bus, from my left hand, I offered the Elder a small, red fabric holding tobacco (the most sacred of Traditional medicines, as this is associated with communicating with The Creator). I asked her if she would consider sharing Traditional Teachings with my students and me that day, and by accepted the tobacco bundle, she showed that she accepted this request. We all embarked on the bus to head off to the site, excited for the opportunity to work together on culturally appropriate ideas for the project.

The day included smudging with Traditional medicines (tobacco, cedar, sage, and sweetgrass) and prayers, and a water ceremony at East Duffins Creek. The Elder shared Traditional Teachings shared about honoring the land, giving thanks to the water, and talked about the special harvesting of cedar as a sacred medicine from a healthy forest. All of the students voiced that they were deeply thankful for the opportunity to learn from an Elder, and to be on the land and near the water while doing so. No longer with TRCA, I am confident that as this project progresses, the intentions to improve understanding and awareness of Treaty responsibilities related to the Goodwood project will proceed in a good way.

FIG.4 East Duffins Creek, Goodwood Resource Management Tract. Sheila Boudreau

In thinking more broadly, natural area trails with connections to urban environments offer significant opportunities for Indigenous placemaking. For another project that involved significant engagement with local and regional governments, the *Trail Strategy for the Greater Toronto Region,*[15] I was asked to advise on the land acknowledgment for the opening acknowledgments, and to suggest locations for references throughout the strategy document regarding engaging Indigenous Peoples to include their voices and ideas. Text found later in the Trail Strategy document states that trail planners and proponents should aim to: "Collaborate with Indigenous communities to develop cultural heritage programs...(and) community engagement programs that respect and share traditional Indigenous ways and beliefs." As Chief LaRocca (with the Williams Treaty First Nations Chiefs) stated in the letter mentioned above, "land acknowledgments harness meaning only when they foster inclusion through mindful decision making on the part of those who recite them."[16] This consideration should be deeply reflected on by everyone who plays a role in improving or protecting land, water for all creatures, and in a way that respects and honors the original Peoples of those lands.

Conclusion

These are difficult issues regarding Ontario's troubled relationship with First Nations and are clear indications of the irreparable damages that results when governance for conservation fails to respect Indigenous interests. *The Water Declaration of the First Nations of Ontario,* created in 2008 by the Chiefs of Ontario (item 33 of 42) states:

When our First Nations negotiated and concluded treaties with the Crown, we were exercising our right of self-determination as nations. Our Treaties are recognized under international law and are a source of rights. As Treaty Nations, Canada has a legal obligation to engage us in a dialogue to determine their role in relation to the wellbeing of Mother Earth.[17]

Canadian education has failed to prepare its citizens to understand Treaties and inherent Indigenous rights, even at the highest levels of government. And while educators and elected officials alike refer to "honoring the Treaties," there is little substance shared about what this means. For government representatives legally responsible for decisions related to land and water, it appears negligent for them to claim they were unaware or uninformed about the Treaties when faced with Indigenous resistance to development.

A central question should be: What successes can we learn from Indigenous-led conservation efforts that can help improve land-based work for the betterment of all our relations, for the next seven generations? In fact, this was essentially the question posed at a forum held by the Government of Canada to discuss the proposed Canada

Water Agency, and also emphasized in a recent global report which states: "Indigenous-led approaches have highlighted innovative ways to design conservation reserves, environmental policy instruments, wildlife monitoring and management programs."[18] With a deep commitment and concerted effort from Peoples across cultural divides, focusing on conservation and landscape connectivity, it is possible that we can adapt from independent Treaty Peoples, to a place where all we have come to stand together.

Endnotes

1. Andrew F. Bennett, *Linkages in the Landscape: The Role of Corridors and Connectivity in Wildlife Conservation.* (IUCN, January 2003), https://doi.org/10.2305/iucn.ch.2004.fr.1.en.
2. Jessica Currie, James Snider, and Emily Giles, "Living Planet Report Canada: Wildlife At Risk," World Wildlife Fund Canada, 2020, https://wwf.ca/living-planet-report-canada-2020/.
3. IUCN, "IUCN Director General's Statement on International Day of the World's Indigenous Peoples 2019," August 9, 2019. https://www.iucn.org/news/secretariat/201908/iucn-director-generals-statement-international-day-worlds-indigenous-peoples-2019.
4. Government of Canada, "One With Nature: A Renewed Approach to Land and Freshwater Conservation in Canada. A Report of Canada's Federal, Provincial and Territorial Departments Responsible for Parks, Protected Areas, Conservation, Wildlife and Biodiversity," 2018, https://static1.squarespace.com/static/57e007452e69cf9a7af0a033/t/5c9cd18671c10bc304619547/1553781159734/Pathway-Report-Final-EN.pdf.
5. Tim Gray, "You May Have Never Heard of a Minister's Zoning Order and That Used to Be OK–but Not Anymore," Environmental Defense, August 28, 2020, https://environmentaldefence.ca/2020/08/28/may-never-heard-ministers-zoning-order-used-ok-not-anymore/.
6. Ontario Nature, "Environmental Groups Sue to Keep Ontario Wetlands Protected," November 30, 2020, https://ontarionature.org/news-release/mzo-lawsuit/.
7. Chief Kelly LaRocca, "Chief Kelly LaRocca, Portfolio Chief for the Williams Treaties First Nations to Mayor of Pickering Ontario," November 11, 2020, https://ehq-production-canada.s3.ca-central-1.amazonaws.com/f7cacf2da047e2a201fa2dd83961fa0715e431ba/original/1605815287/Williams_Treaties_First_Nations.pdf_44cfad97a77640907358d59313f8271a?X-Amz-Algorithm=AWS4-HMAC-SHA256&X-Amz-Credential=AKIAI3JCUKKD4ZO4WUUA%2F20210709%2Fca-central-1%2Fs3%2Faws4_request&X-Amz-Date=20210709T201939Z&X-Amz-Expires=300&X-Amz-SignedHeaders=host&X-Amz-Signature=7eaf5f6a31b420b9e45954ad7f94f43c2a25bb81ebb28b36131301d0efe62de9.
8. Ontario Ministry of Municipal Affairs and Housing, "Provincial Policy Statement, 2020–Under the Planning Act. 2020," 2020, https://www.ontario.ca/page/provincial-policy-statement-2020.
9. United Nations, "United Nations Declaration of the Rights of Indigenous Peoples," 2007, https://www.un.org/development/desa/indigenouspeoples/declaration-on-the-rights-of-indigenous-peoples.html.
10. Dawn Martin-Hill, "Toward the Creation of a Canadian Water Agency Regional Freshwater Forum–Ontario" (Forum transcript shared with author, February 9, 2021).
11. Shawn Wilson, *Research is Ceremony: Indigenous Research Methods* (Halifax: Fernwood Publishing, 2008).
12. Wilson, *Research is Ceremony.*
13. Truth and Reconciliation Commission of Canada, "Honoring the Truth, Reconciling for the Future: Summary of the Final Report of the Truth and Reconciliation Commission of Canada," 2015, http://www.trc.ca/assets/pdf/Honouring_the_Truth_Reconciling_for_the_Future_July_23_2015.pdf.
14. LaRocca, "Chief Kelly LaRocca."
15. Toronto Region Conservation Authority, "Trail Strategy for the Greater Toronto Region: Growing Our Legacy," 2018, https://trca.ca/conservation/lands/trail-strategy/.
16. LaRocca, "Chief Kelly LaRocca."
17. Special Chiefs Assembly in Toronto, "Water Declaration of the First Nations in Ontario (Resolution 08/87)," October, 2008, http://www.temagamifirstnation.ca/wp-content/uploads/2017/10/coo-water-declaration.pdf.
18. Stephen T. Garnett et al., "A Spatial Overview of the Global Importance of Indigenous Lands for Conservation," *Nature Sustainability* 1, no. 7 (2018): 369–74. https://doi.org/10.1038/s41893-018-0100-6.

4.4

Blue Gold

Agricultural Infrastructure & Climate Change in the Sahel

Matthew Poot

While much of the built work created by the landscape profession is typically situated within smaller scales of individual projects or slightly larger urban parks and designs for the public realm, there is a strong history of engaging with the large-scale via regional masterplans and landscape analyses. Landscape architects like Frederick Law Olmstead and Ian McHarg figure strongly in the development of landscape-based approaches towards urban development that embody a sensitivity to the ecological context and connection with underlying natural processes. This proposal engages with these traditions of landscape practice, seeking to connect the more abstracted processes of analysis with the tangibility of site-specific interventions that also reflect the needs of the community in which they are situated. It focuses on agricultural infrastructure within Mali as a means of demonstrating how a landscape-based approach is able to connect socio-political and environmental phenomenon acting across territorial scales (e.g. geopolitics and climate change) with the practical and contextual aspects of design at the site level (e.g. community engagement and planting strategies). The central questions driving this work ask how the landscape profession can address the impacts of climate change in areas where the profession is currently absent, and what benefits landscape-based approaches might provide over engineered solutions and conventional tactics used within the field of international development. The area discussed here was selected because it crystalizes many of the key issues when examining tensions between human activity and hydrological resources in dryland regions. The proposal itself was selected as winner of a competition in 2020 focused on solutions for landscape regeneration and improving climate resilience for vulnerable communities in lesser developed countries.[1]

XL: A Territorial Perspective

Derived from the Arabic word for "shore," the Sahel refers to the semi-arid zone stretching across the width of the continent between the Sahara Desert to the North, and the Savannah plains to the south [FIG. 1]. Receiving

OPPOSITE PAGE The yearly flood reveals landscape patterns which provide the basis for urban form across the Inner Niger Delta, where floodwaters rise up to six meters over a period of weeks around October each year in sharp contrast to mostly arid conditions. Agricultural practices take advantage of the slow ebb of these flood waters over the following months and further into the long dry season. Yann Arthus-Bertrand

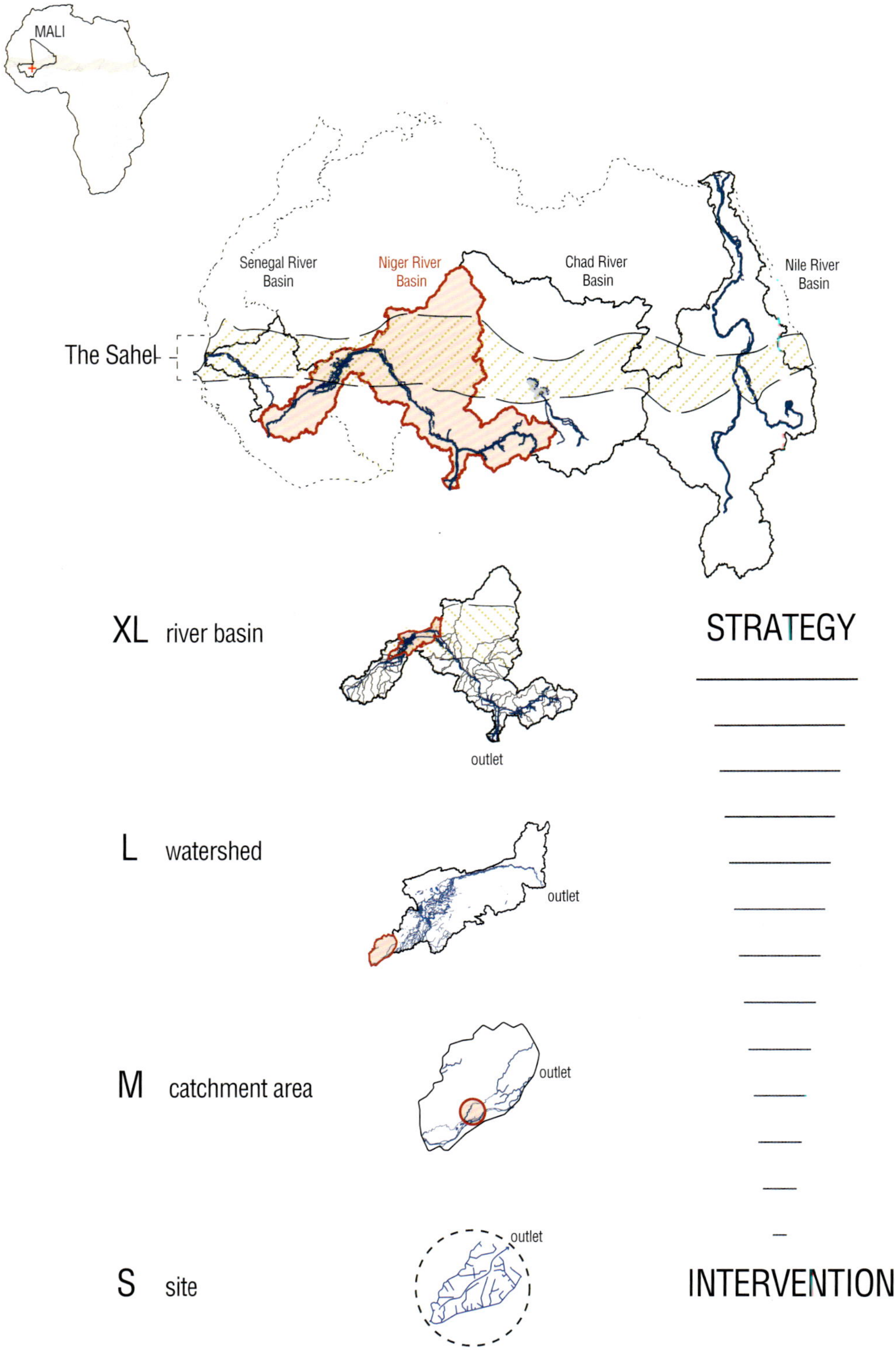
MALI
The Sahel
Senegal River Basin
Niger River Basin
Chad River Basin
Nile River Basin
XL river basin
outlet
L watershed
outlet
M catchment area
outlet
S site
outlet
STRATEGY
INTERVENTION

200–600 millimeters of precipitation annually during a short rainy season, the Sahel is an expanse of territory spanning the African continent defined by climate rather than lines of political jurisdiction. Within its shifting borders lies the Inner Niger Delta, a massive inland wetland that butts against the Sahara Desert, with its northernmost point near the historic city of Timbuktu. The patterns of seasonal rains and river flow drive the rhythm of life in human settlements and their larger ecological surroundings across the region. This is reflected not only through the adaptation of organisms within the Inner Niger Delta, but in the evolution of ethnic groups distinguished by relationships with specific elements of this dynamic system. The Bambara and Rimaibe peoples practice sedentary agriculture growing dryland crops or cultivating rice, while nomadic Fulani herders move their cattle across the Delta with the seasonal rains. Bozo and Bamboro communities have their livelihoods centered upon fishing within the Delta, and the neighboring desert communities of the Tuareg historically engaged in longer distance trading. The traditional practices of these groups have come under intense pressure from modernization, competition over increasingly limited resources from upstream resource use (e.g. hydro-electric dams and irrigation) and distortion of economic opportunities between rural communities and more distant urban centers where political power is concentrated.

The disparity between rural and urban communities in Mali has been a large factor in political instability, with two military coups in the past ten years; the first in 2012 and most recent in September of 2020. At the root of these political uprisings is popular discontent with pervasive corruption, extreme poverty, and lack of opportunity.[2] Though these grievances are not limited to rural areas it is no mere coincidence that the coup in 2012 followed a dry year with crop failures in 2011 and that the conflict began in Northern Mali where climatic changes are placing extreme pressure on already stressed water resources of the Delta. Political conflict in other arid regions of Sudan (Darfur) and Syria (Jazira) also display similar properties to the struggles in Mali, not as a direct result of a specific drought event but situations where severe degradation of water resources and deepening rural poverty contribute to existing political divisions and instability.[3,4] These trends make an argument for addressing the fundamental needs of rural communities directly, rather than symptomatic security-focused measures which follow conflict.

Engaging with the territorial scale brings connections between these kinds of social and environmental factors to light, enabling observation of critical patterns that are difficult to discern from the scale of the site, and even correcting for biases of localized observations. For example, the weather system of the Intertropical Convergence Zone (ITCZ) is responsible for the wet seasons that define the Sahel. Research has linked the severe drought experienced across the Sahel during the late 1970s and early 1980s with changes in ocean surface temperatures rather than

FIG. 1 Working across scales: Spanning across a continent, the drylands of the Sahel include four major watersheds where water resources are under intense pressure. This landscape-based framework connects the specificity required for work at site scale with the broader analysis needed to capture complex natural and social phenomena that act across a territorial scale. Matthew Poot

overgrazing and intensification in land use which were long assumed to be the primary factors based on localized observations of landscape change.[5] Further research at this scale also indicates a future of more erratic precipitation patterns correlated to ocean warming pushing the ITCZ southwards.[6] Without engaging with this territorial perspective, it becomes difficult to imagine projects which can properly anticipate and address the effects of climate change into the future with any reliability. Looking further into the relationship between these processes and physical form also provides a means for unifying work across scales of time and place.

For this proposal, hydrological structures have been used as a physical framework to move from strategic issues occurring across the four major watersheds of the Sahel, through individual river sheds and into localized catchment areas that can engage with the details of context specific to a given place [FIG. 2]. As part of the larger dialogue on landscape urbanism vis-a-vis infrastructural systems, Pierre Belanger has argued for this approach of "sliding across scales" to engage fully between the territory and the site.[7] This methodology has been used here to identify points of tension between the operational logics of biophysical systems and cultural traditions embedded in the landscape, against the superimposed order of modern infrastructure systems extended across territorial scales.

L: Regional Context

The agricultural complex of the Office du Niger (ON) located just upstream of the Inner Niger Delta in Mali represents just such a point of tension. The ON is both a political institution and a physical area of intervention that are the legacy of the 1919 vision of Émile Bélime, a French engineer in the colonial services which controlled Mali until 1960. Bélime's plans identified fossilized branches of the Niger River leading into derelict alluvial floodplains and called for these areas to be brought into production through forced relocation labor of Delta communities. A barrage along the river would raise water levels enough to restore flow and irrigate up to one million hectares.[8] This program articulated the extension of urban influence into the rural periphery, with the explicit purpose of providing a secure supply of cotton and rubber to the French industry. Despite opposition from other colonial administrators who sought to develop agriculture in more appropriate locations, these plans went ahead with the completion of the Markala barrage in 1946, leaving a system requiring massive foreign investment just to maintain basic operationality.[9] Although independence was gained from France in 1960, the top-down form of centralized administration has remained in place. Cotton and rubber have been abandoned in favor of other water-intensive and drought susceptible foreign crop species. Asian rice cultivars promise higher yields than local varieties endemic to the Delta, and sugarcane is grown to meet the needs of the

domestic market nationally.

Yet, these crops and the performance of this infrastructure system are at odds with the prevailing logics of the Delta just downstream. There we find an incredibly rich wetland ecosystem providing critical overwintering habitat for millions of migratory birds and waterfowl, a lush contrast to the extremities of the Sahara Desert directly adjacent. This critical resource supports its 1.5 million human inhabitants and supplies the rest of land-locked Mali with 50–100 thousand tons of fish annually and over 40 percent of its domestic rice supply.[10] The existence of the Delta arises from its extremely flat topography, where the course of the Niger River drops only 20 meters over a distance of 160 kilometers.[11] This shallow slope inundates anywhere from 8,000 square kilometers, as seen during the drought of 1984, to the highest recorded area of 36,000 square kilometers in 1957.[12] Although 2018 and 2020 have been two of the wettest periods recorded in the past 50 years,[13] they would only have

FIG.2 Landscape patterns created through traditional forms of land cultivation in the Inner Niger Delta. Yann Arthus-Bertrand

been considered average in the years from 1918 to 1968[14] as precipitation levels decline overall. Occupying the high-ground, architectural forms and settlements in the Delta reflect a landscape-based logic rooted in these climatic patterns, complemented by a highly managed agricultural landscape that has developed over many centuries [FIG. 3]. Fishing practices, river trading, movement of livestock into the receding delta for grazing, along with crop varieties and growing techniques endemic to this area are all tailored to this annual ebb and flow. The results of these relationships provide examples of what John T. Lyle calls "Deep Form," where the physical shapes and structures are reflective of underlying ecological process.[15]

In contrast, the modus operandi of the current food production system has little to no active relationship with the basic operational logic of the area and its dynamic hydrological rhythms. It is shallow form *par excellence*, dominated by monoculture agriculture, excluding animal herders accustomed to moving their herds through the lands, and separated from the "nature" enclosed within nearby forest reserves. The amount of water delivered to the ON upstream of the Delta remains consistent from year to year, regardless of the huge variations in precipitation, and in accordance with the flow rates delimited by the geometry of the gravity-fed canal system.

M/S: The Scale of Site

This proposal targets these irrigation infrastructures as a strategic forum of intervention because they offer potential for systemic transformation rather than symptomatic responses. The area of the Macina-Ke district within the ON is used as a case study which exemplifies both the challenges and opportunities of this agenda and replicates much of the land within the ON that employs a strategy of mono-cultural rice production [FIG. 4]. Sliding across scales from the river basin down into the Machine-Ke district, which forms a sort of miniature anthropogenic watershed functioning on the gravity-driven premise of water supplied from raised canals along the perimeter delivered inwards to the fields through secondary and tertiary canals before flowing into the inverse network of drainage trenches.

Utilizing the existing canal networks as part of the architecture for intervention, this proposal adds to its functional program to develop the range of ecological activity and economic potential supported by the infrastructure system itself. The basic techniques and technologies employed within the ON leave a wide opening for improvements that do not require dismantling and rebuilding of the current infrastructure yet can make them responsive to downstream needs and more resilient to external shocks and stresses.

The new program suggests a perimeter of high-yield rice for export while increasing the range of crops grown to include dryland staples of

FIG.3 TOP RIGHT The arid climate of the Sahel is broken by a short rainy season between June and September. In Mali, these rains flow North into the Delta where they support an intensely productive landscape over the following months as waters slowly recede until March, with low areas holding on to water longer as isolated lakes. Landsat imagery, U.S. Geological Survey, 2020

FIG.4 BOTTOM RIGHT Static Infrasctructure: The Macina-Ke district is one of the oldest irrigated areas within the Office du Niger. Even during the driest year of the driest period in the past century (1984), the intensive water use of this infrastructure system was maintained regardless of downstream needs or more effective and efficient production alternatives. Landsat imagery, U.S. Geological Survey, 2020

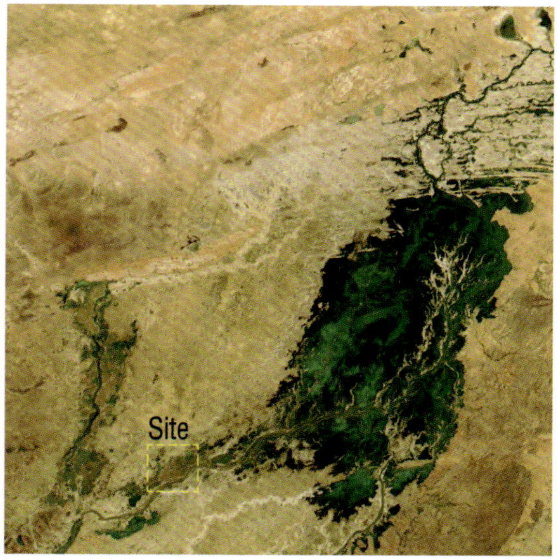

NOVEMBER 1984: THE GREAT DROUGHT

NOVEMBER 2020: A WET YEAR

WET // DRY

millet and sorghum, along with more drought-tolerant but lower yielding African rice strains [FIG. 5]. This allows the possibility for a response to changing levels of water flow and precipitation to guarantee output even in dry years, increasing the district's resilience to environmental shocks and improving its core mandate of providing reliable food supplies in an increasingly unpredictable climate. In these ways, the system begins to shift from a static to a more dynamic program. This strategy can be supported by the existing data infrastructure of the OPIDIN flood monitoring, currently used to give several weeks advance notice of expected flood levels across the Delta.[16] Making the agricultural programing of the ON flexible would allow this tool to work for agriculture within irrigated areas as well, creating opportunities to adjust the start of the planting season or change crop varieties in the case of extremely dry years.

Like many areas within the ON, the Macina-Ke district has several low-lying spots within flattened irrigated areas which retain standing water throughout the year, suggesting opportunity for intervention since they cannot be used for agriculture. Introducing greater ecological function through creation of wetland pockets to help address environmental issues of land degradation, biodiversity, and habitat loss in the nearby Delta. Focusing on these unused low areas submerged through the year can provide opportunity for establishing wetland habitat for nesting currently under pressure downstream in the Delta. The surrounding rice paddies are already used as foraging grounds by nearby wetland bird species that feed on insects and pests that farmers struggle to control.[17] By planting appropriate trees and wetland plant species, this relationship can be established into a positive feedback cycle where birds can thrive within agricultural areas while providing a valuable service to farmers through integrated pest management. Establishing wetland pockets can also work to create income opportunities for locals involved in conservation schemes that require long term involvement and oversight at a local level.

Using water otherwise lost through seepage, the supply canals act as a lattice for an economic planting strategy which uses selected tree species such as Acacia, Baobab, and Doum Palm along the canals. The paths along the drainage system can also be used as a network for livestock to move through the area, planted with a selection of groundcover, woody shrubs, and tree species which are geared towards producing fodder and fruits while functioning simultaneously as a series of shelterbelts and erosion control measures. The array of products traditionally associated with these trees have the commercial potential to provide an array of benefits for locals through additional income from building materials, firewood, medicinal products, and more. An

FIG.5 Introducing complexity into simple systems transforms a rigid infrastructure system into one which is more dynamic, resilient, and contextually appropriate. Modulating the agricultural program to reflect the dynamic climate is supported by agroforestry programs and ecological rehabilitation. Matthew Poot

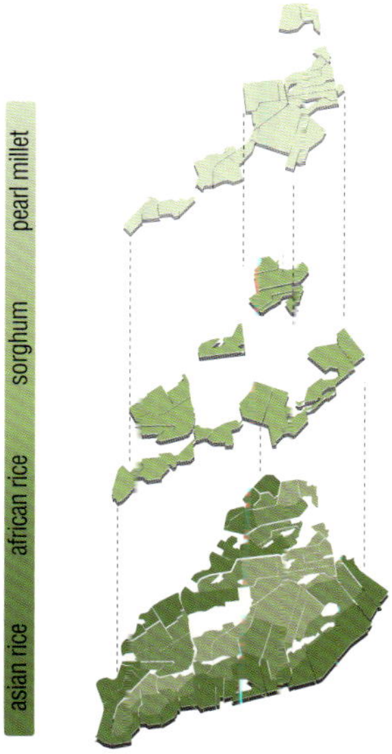

DRIER

areas farthest from main supply canals grow dryland crops during drought ensuring stable production

DRY

secondary zone shifts between rice during wet years and drought tolerant crops in drier conditions

WET

outer perimiter is maintained for water-intensive rice growing, inner areas also growing rice in wet years

FLEXIBLE AGRICULTURE

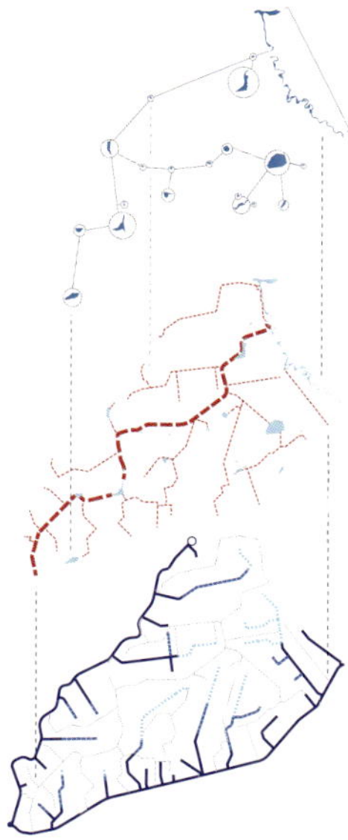

WETLAND POCKETS

transforming 203 hectares of waterlogged areas into ecological hotspots that also benefit farmers

DRAINAGE CANALS

connective ecological network linking wetland areas with fruiting and nitrogen fixing tree species

IRRIGATION CANALS

socio-economic agroforestry aimed at delivering opportunities for local communities and industry

MULTIFUNCTIONAL PROGRAMMING

DYNAMIC INFRASTRUCTURE

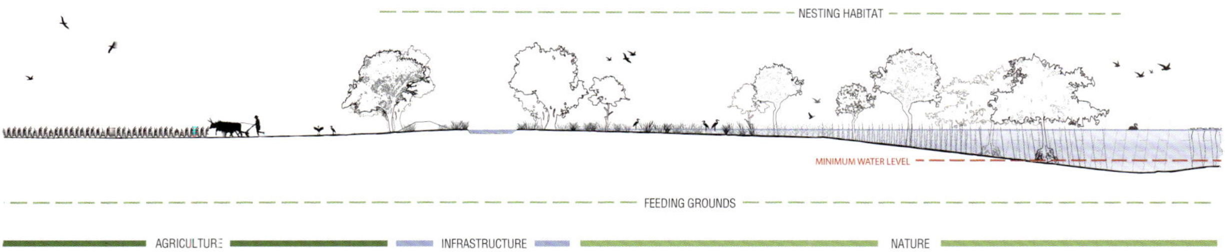

aesthetic program is added by associating each of these three species planted along the supply canals with one of the three corresponding growing sectors outlined in the final site plan, clearly demarcating the infrastructural zones across the landscape.

Deepening Shallow Form

The design strategy behind these interventions seeks to leverage the significant investments embedded in the existing infrastructure systems and establish social and ecological feedback loops. Increasing the complexity of land use supported by irrigation systems leads to a wider variety of economic activities in the same space, offering local communities the ability to create opportunities from a wider base of resources than currently present. Unlike crops alien to dryland regions such as sugar cane, these additional activities are rooted in local traditions and relevant industries capable of providing benefits for those who labor with them, rather than exporting profit to distant urban centers and foreign investors. The proposed agroforestry and ecological rehabilitation schemes would also involve creation of plant nurseries and permanent rural employment supporting secondary industries from timber, medicinal products, and a variety of food products. The connection between agriculture and ecology at a fundamental level also provides benefits relating to preservation of biodiversity which can be harder to quantify but are no less real or significant.

The role of the landscape architect here is not to simply create designs and implement them as pre-determined visions. Initial concepts such as this proposal can be developed, but then need to be taken further through consultation and engagement to refine them more precisely and develop concrete paths of action together with local partners, relevant agencies, and actors. Utilizing structures in the landscape provides a frame of reference to situate these actors according to their focus areas of expertise, establishing a platform that connects overlapping issues across scales to encourage greater collaboration. The connection of regional analysis to the interventions at community level is essential to this process, and crucial to addressing system-level challenges like climate change, regional conflict, and rural poverty with measures which are both equitable and effective. Neither a solely local nor national/regional focus alone can deliver the appropriate solutions that balance complexity of strategic challenges with practical needs specific to a given place.

Endnotes

1. For more information about details surrounding the competition you can visit www.climatecolab.org. Further work to pursue this proposal has been paused during the Covid-19 pandemic and will hopefully continue in the near future.
2. Claire Felter and Nathalie Bussemaker, "What to Know About the Crisis in Mali," *Council on Foreign Relations*, August 12, 2020, https://www.cfr.org/in-brief/what-know-about-crisis-mali.
3. Younes Abouyoub, "Climate: The Forgotten Culprit. The Ecological Dimension of the Darfur Conflict," *Race, Gender & Class* 19., No. 1/2 (2012): 150–176.
4. Jan Selby, "Climate Change and the Syrian Civil War, Part II: The Jazira's Agrarian Crisis," *Geoforum* 101, (May 2019): 260–274.
5. Alessandra Gianini, "Climate Change Comes to the Sahel," *Nature Climate Change* 5: 720–721, https://theconversation.com/climate-change-is-not-a-key-cause-of-conflict-finds-new-study-94331.
6. Seyni Salack, Cornelia Klein, Alessandra Giannini, Benoit Sarr, Omonlola N. Worou, Nouhoun Belko, Jan Bliefernicht and Harald Kunstman, "Global Warming Induced Hybrid Rainy Seasons in the Sahel," *Environmental Research Letters* 11, No. 10 (October 2016).
7. Pierre Bélanger, "Landscape Infrastructure: Urbanism Beyond Engineering" (PhD dissertation, University of Wageningen, 2013), 376.
8. Jean Filipovich, "Destined to Fail: Forced Settlement at the Office du Niger, 1926–45," *The Journal of African History* 42, No. 2 (2001): 239–260.
9. Filipovich, "Destined to Fail."
10. United States Department of Agriculture, "Rice, Milled Production (Mali)", Foreign Agricultural Service, last modified December 27, 2020, https://ipad.fas.usda.gov/cropexplorer/.
11. Alexander Arnaud, "Vulnerability of Biodiversity in the Inner Niger Delta to Water Resources Management Under Climate Variability and Change," Masters Thesis Report, Howest University of Applied Sciences, 2012.
12. Leo Zwarts (RIZA), Pieter van Beukering (IVM), Bakary Kone (Wetlands International), Eddy Wymenga (A&W), *The Niger, a Lifeline. Effective Water Management in the Upper Niger Basin,* eds. Zwarts, L., P. van Beukering, B. Kone & E. Wymenga (Mali/the Netherlands, 2005).
13. Earth Observatory, NASA, "An Inland Delta Flooded," accessed January 7, 2021, https://earthobservatory.nasa.gov/images/147692/an-inland-delta-flooded.
14. Leo Zwarts, "Will the Inner Niger Delta Shrivel Up Due to Climate Change and Water Use Upstream?," *A&W Rapport* 1537, Altenburg & Wymenga Ecological Consultants, Feanwâlden, 2010.
15. John Tillman Lyle, "Can Floating Seeds Make Deep Forms?," *Landscape Journal* 10, no. 1 (1991): 37–47.
16. Developed by Wetlands International and the national water ministry in Mali, OPIDIN functions as an early warning system for farmers, fishermen, and villages of the Inner Niger Delta. Precipitation and river flow data is collected far upstream at various stations along the Niger River and its tributaries, giving several weeks advance notice of the year's expected flood levels. This service is currently used to help give settlements in the Delta advanced notice of extremely high or low water levels weeks ahead of time to help avoid property loss during flooding and to prepare farmers and fishermen for low-water levels of drought.
17. Eddy Wymenga and Leo Zwarts, "Use of Rice Fields by Birds in West Africa," *Waterbirds: The International Journal of Waterbird Biology* 33, Special Publication 1 (2010): 97–104.

5 NEW MODELS OF PRACTICE

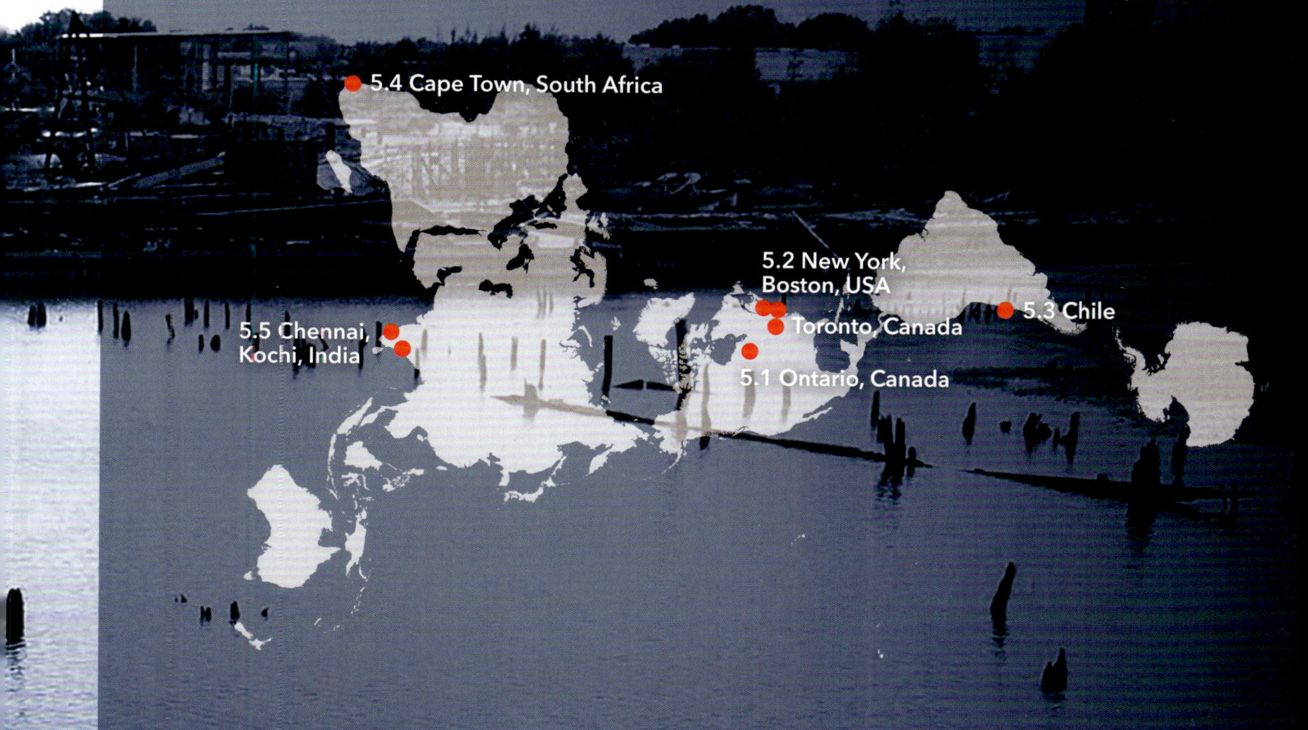

New Models of Practice presents five cases of groups or individuals who built models of practice and research that are informed by landscape, collaboration, and nature-based solutions. The practices operate in different cultural, political, and environmental contexts, using distinct facets of design and planning to approach socio-environmental conflicts. The chapters highlight the critical role of partnership in contested landscapes, the possibility of transdisciplinary dialogue through public art, the success of a landscape-informed response to regressive public policy, and the socio-economic benefits of resilient urban design.

PAN-O-GOLD

5.1

Codesign, Collaboration, and Systems Change

Reflections on Innovative Cross-Cultural and Interdisciplinary Practice Centered on Action in Landscapes of Conflict

Shelagh McCartney, Nina-Marie Lister, Jeffrey Herskovits

Canada has an urbanizing population concentrated in cities along its southern border and waterways.[1] However, this population, and the country's economy, remain heavily reliant on extractive resource industries[2] located in the geographically distant Near North and Far North.[3] Physically separated, land in the north is also distinct in tenure with nearly 90 percent being "Crown" or state-owned land, distinct from the majority private ownership of land in southern urban centers.[4] Southern populations are physically separated from northern, Crown lands which are out of sight—inaccessible, and therefore illegible as landscapes. This disconnection between industry and population centers generates landscapes of conflict and fragmentation due to the complex infrastructures that serve them [FIG. 1].

These contested landscapes have given rise to resistance, to movements focused on creating alternative futures for their land focused on interrelationships that will allow them to thrive into the future. Here, we reflect on our involvement in this resistance in places where complex ecosystems are at work and which are inherently relational: that is, relationships between creatures (human and non-human) and place, and the physical environment that sustains them. Our resistance uses a relational approach of interconnected systems—through engagement with transdisciplinary partners, and living landscapes, including wildlife—and we offer perspectives on ways in which academe can partner and ally in the co-creation of alternative futures through new methods of practice, teaching, and learning.

Resistance is not new to Canada's contested landscapes. What is new is the application of critical methodologies in place-making and place-keeping disciplines using a systems approach;[5] and the resultant emergence of cross-cultural, multi-sectoral, transdisciplinary partnerships forming in allyship, creating communities of practice. As settler scholars whose community-based and action-oriented research has taken place across these landscapes over the last decade, we offer reflections on the tensions arising from concurrent commitments to advocacy and scholarship. These reflections focus on the models of partnerships which

OPPOSITE PAGE Learning from elder at Nibinamik First Nation community cookout from traditional moose hunt as part of the Housing Needs Assessment project. Building strong and long relationships is basis for TDLs partnership model. L. Hintelmann for Together Design Lab (TDL)

The Together Design Lab (TDL) at Toronto Metropolitan University School of Urban and Regional Planning takes a collaborative approach to investigating and creating innovative solutions to housing issues within marginalized communities. Led by Dr. Shelagh McCartney, TDL recognizes the cultural, gendered, and classed implications of dominant housing systems, and relies on an immersive model of partnership between students, collaborators, and communities to understand the role of housing in shaping personal and community well-being. TDL looks to reimagine home environments through the values, goals, and aspirations of our partners. TDL works with many First Nation partners across Nishnawbe Aski Nation Territory (Northern Ontario) and with the Yellowknives Dene First Nation on Akaitcho Territory (Northwest Territories).

The Ecological Design Lab (EDL) is led by Professor Nina-Marie Lister at Toronto Metropolitan University School of Urban and Regional Planning, to test strategies, develop evidence-based next-generation practices, and find tangible solutions to sustainability and resilience, as we rethink, remake, reinvent, and renew our relationship to nature in the city. Creative, evidence-based thinking, community-collaborative planning and informed, inspired design are composite, requisite criteria for active and informed responses to complex socio-ecological problems. EDL projects include the potential siting of a vertical farm in the city of Toronto, developing a vision for the Emerald Crescent parks and open-space system in Edmonton, as well as the establishment of a National Wildlife Crossing Infrastructure database.

have underpinned our practices. We explore how, within sites of conflict, methods have been developed which counter existing relationships of power, challenge the weaponization of technical expertise from within institutional settings and discuss the need for ongoing reflexivity.

Critically, partnership, as we are discussing it, is not a single methodology or series of best practices fit for universal application. Instead, we offer a values-driven, relational, and place-based epistemological framework which requires ongoing mediation and renegotiation. This is complicated in practice by the historical, and ongoing, inequities which have created these landscapes of conflict. While these new complex relational partnerships form from shared objectives, partners are frequently differently positioned: with different lived experiences, ways of knowing, and levels of power. The implementation of partnership, here focused on co-creation of alternative futures for these landscapes, requires a praxis which simultaneously counters the macro-policies of oppression and fragmentation and micro-challenges of inequity and unspoken histories. As a result, in each of our applications, solutions require a systems approach[6] in which design outcomes are representative of the new understandings and knowledge formed through co-creation.

This framework of partnership can be situated within a larger shift towards participatory, critical, integrative-adaptive, and anti-colonial methodologies which support building equity in the built environment. However, the participatory researcher faces the above-mentioned challenges in gaining trust and countering power imbalances with community collaborators partnered with the scrutiny of their work as simply advocacy and dismissed as illegitimate within the academy.[7] Maintaining rigor within the complex negotiation of relationships and threat of landscape destruction is paramount to partnership success. Rigor should not be mistaken for value-free data, but instead be viewed as a commitment to methodological consistency and truth, which themselves can be used to record historical wrongdoings, visions for the future, and pathways towards landscape change.

While research paradigms have shifted towards action, teaching remains heavily focused on technical expertise, disciplinary silos, and formal evaluation. Our discussion of partnership frameworks here is limited by our understanding that this model is necessarily experiential; that the practice of co-creation is significantly more complicated than the theories. While institutions and individual scholars engaging in action-oriented research have the potential to create in Canada's contested landscapes, this power could be expanded through its greater inclusion in teaching. We both have endeavored to expand experiential opportunities for students—particularly through studio teaching—addressing structural barriers that remain by integrating our partnerships, and partners, into curriculum.

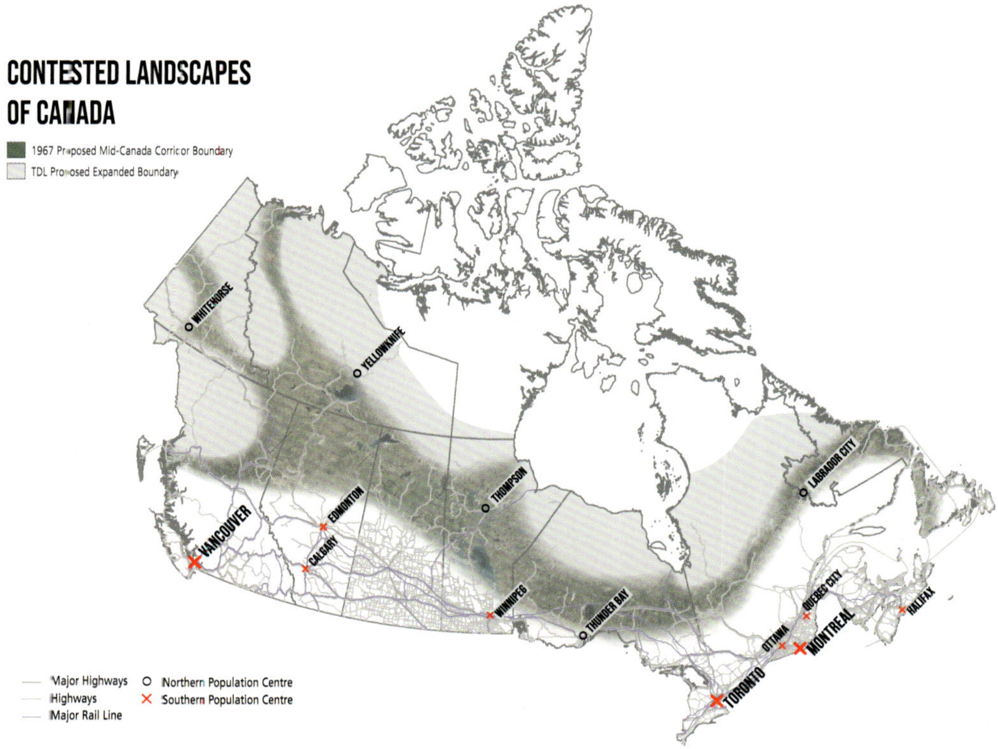

Landscape change and community-based partnerships are necessarily long-term projects based in the development of trusting, place-honoring relationships. University teaching is bounded by semesters and has a significant focus on individual assessment. Training students to integrate partnership into their practice requires the development of a set of skills which are outside of the traditional technical training of the place-making disciplines. We aim to model and teach the importance of using reflective practice as a tool to counter existing narratives of constraints in contested landscapes and disciplinary complicity in creating them. By using innovative and experiential teaching and training methods, we see potential to create a new generation of practitioners that embraces a landscape systems approach to partnership and thus practice.

Walking Together: Co-Designing Housing in Partnership With First Nations

Since 2014, Together Design Lab (TDL) has been working with Indigenous peoples to create community-based housing systems. Using a partnership-based approach, TDL has supported First Nations, Tribal Councils and Political Territorial Organizations in contested landscapes of northwestern Ontario and Northwest Territories. Central to these partnerships are the guiding Indigenous understandings of the interrelationships between housing, culture, and self-determination.[8] [FIG. 2] Together we develop designs, policies, and strategies aiming to reconnect broad systems of culture, climate, and geography with built form and community development.

FIG. 1 Contested Landscapes of Canada. The mid-Canada corridor is a geographically distinct region rich in natural resources but separated from Canada's urban centers Nicolas Kohek for Together Design Lab (TDL)

Home is at the center of each individual's physical, social, and emotional life. Canadian state colonialism has for generations made housing a site of conflict for Indigenous peoples across the country and forced assimilation by stripping the physical environment that communities live in of all connections to culture and place.[9] As a result, throughout the Near North, the settlements of First Nations peoples have come to resemble the homogeneous form found across suburban Canada, a grid-style housing environment imported from southern Canada that is inappropriate for the geography, climate, and culture of the region but reflective of a Canadian Standard, rather than a vernacular form that is connected to place.[10] Built on principles of economic efficiency, and the ongoing racist assumption that all Indigenous settlement is temporary, government housing programs and policies have led to the building of generations of inappropriate and inadequate homes. Misaligned with the climate, culture, and geography of its occupants, on-reserve housing has become a physical manifestation of Canadian colonialism which acts as a negative social determinant of health.[11]

FIG.2 250 Years of Assimilation: Documenting Canadian colonial policies and the grassroots resistance thereto on the landscape of housing in Eabametoong First Nation. Sarah Mater & Derek Ho for Together Design Lab (TDL)

While housing has been used as a tool of colonialism, it can, similarly, be used as a site of resistance. Housing, in this context, is not understood as a single unit of shelter, but instead as a system which creates community and contributes to the formation of landscapes of

well-being and cultural preservation. Through a process of co-creation which centers lived experience and place-based knowledge, we at TDL support communities and their members in imagining alternative futures for their landscapes.[12] [FIG. 3] Through interactive and immersive processes, a diversity of community members can be engaged in identifying how congruency can be created; where distinctions of culture, climate, and geography can be embraced and interrelationships to the natural world celebrated in the built form. For this to be possible, technical expertise cannot be used to sideline community members and instead must be used, through an iterative process of listening, learning, and sharing, to translate local goals and priorities into realities.

Imagining alternative futures is a deeply personal and vulnerable experience. Partnering with First Nations peoples in this emancipatory process as settler scholars presents specific challenges and risks given the history of exploitation. Beyond individual reflexivity, this practice requires a model of partnership and relationships rooted in trust and reciprocity. Entering into partnership cannot be a short-term project which simply repeats a transactional process of extracting local knowledge for personal gain; instead, it must involve mutual understandings and benefits. Each partner must be acknowledged as both a contributor and a benefactor, forming a reinforcing cycle of reciprocity. Given that existing housing frameworks are entrenched in colonial models of governance, outcomes must be identified beyond a single built project. To honor the sharing of community members, outcomes must be anti-colonial, building towards a sustainable system of community control. Our relational partnership of resistance counters existing relationships of power in the housing ecosystem.

While partnership frameworks create the opportunity for co-creation, the implementation of partnerships comes in the day-to-day activities undertaken to support housing systems change. Design activities require an epistemic shift towards the recognition of various forms of knowledge. While TDL is invited into partnerships because of disciplinary expertise, partnership requires that this skillset be deployed to enact community visions. Critical to this process is breaking down the technical and textual barriers and creating safe places wherein community members—from youth to Elders—feel comfortable exploring the concepts of landscape change [FIG. 4]. Imagining landscape change is not accomplished through a single toolkit of methods that provides an easily repeatable set of activities, but instead through the slower, more complex and unscalable process of listening deeply to unique aspirations of a particular community. Moving away from templates, prototypes and uniform understandings of northern landscapes and First Nations peoples, partnership requires a deep investment in understanding and action in particular environments.

TDL's community and place-based partnerships work to elevate voices which have been marginalized from Western discourse and allow for a reimagining of contested landscapes with wider contextual understandings. We train students to scale deeply, understanding that to reimagine place, through design thinking, Indigenous ways of knowing and social-science methods, partnership is required. Training students to integrate relational partnership into praxis involves modelling partnership and reflexive practice outside of traditional technical training. We recognize the voice and power of academic institutions and use this power to bring about change through partnerships and understand that systems change in contested landscapes is a long-term project.

FIG. 3 The Nishnawbe Aski Nation Environment, Energy & Climate Change Symposium gathered housing professionals from 49 First Nations to imagine alternative housing forms which would meet the needs of those least served by the current housing system. The diversity of regions, languages and people participating identified a variety of models of home which could create more appropriate living environments and improve well-being outcomes. Photo by A. Beaver for Together Design Lab (TDL)

Reconnecting Landscapes, People, and Wildlife Through Co-Creation

Since 2010, the Ecological Design Lab (EDL) has been engaged in co-creation of place-based solutions that (re)connect landscapes, people, and wildlife. Through design-based research and learning through collaborative praxis both with and within communities, the EDL has contributed to green infrastructure designs that, in the broadest sense, physically and functionally connect people to nature and, specifically, facilitate the safe passage of people and wildlife across roads.

Roads fragment landscapes, resulting in barriers to the safe movement of humans and animals; roads further fragment cultures from the places and landscapes that sustain them. Canada's growing urban regions and expanding road networks are associated with increasing wildlife-vehicle collisions, higher wildlife mortality and, in the long term, landscape fragmentation that results in habitat degradation and the global decline in biodiversity—along with a growing cultural gap between people and the ecosystems in which they live. There is strong evidence that purpose-designed wildlife crossing infrastructure (including overpasses, underpasses, and at-grade crossings) can dramatically reduce the risk of collisions and mediate negative environmental impacts.[13] Where the construction of wildlife crossing infrastructure has emerged, it has been slow, sparse, and ad hoc. Yet resolving these issues is not solely a technical or research challenge; it is also about working collaboratively and creatively across disciplines, within place-specific contexts, and building political, economic, and cultural consensus within communities of practice.

FIG.4 TOP Housing policy development in Bearskin Lake First Nation was a community-based process focused on creating an appropriate local housing governance structure. Community members, from young-to-old, worked together through a series of workshops in 2018 to understand how governance could be formed to ensure that all members of the community had more equitable access to appropriate housing. L. Hintelmann for Together Design Lab (TDL)

FIG.5 BOTTOM The Montana CoLab (2018) was an interdisciplinary design workshop that brought together professionals from engineering, landscape architecture, planning, and ecology to develop and pilot test an innovative design for wildlife crossings made from fiber-reinforced polymer (plastic). FRP materials are lighter in weight, less costly, and can be adapted for various types of wildlife and landscape habitat and to accommodate human use by bicycles and pedestrians. M. Brocki for Ecological Design Lab (EDL)

Reconnecting landscapes (between people and place, and wildlife and their habitats) is an interdisciplinary, socio-ecological challenge that lies outside the mandate of any single agency and remains unacknowledged in conventional systems of governance [FIG. 5]. Although the infrastructural design solutions to reducing fragmentation are known to work, there is an urgent and growing need for a coordinated, integrated approach to planning and design for widespread sustainable implementation of these infrastructures. This challenge cuts across scales and jurisdictions and requires a collaborative, transdisciplinary approach that connects researchers and practitioners to develop integrated, place-based solutions.[14] By engaging with these issues in an interdisciplinary and experiential learning format that links landscape design and road ecology with evidence-based policy and environmental planning, the EDL's CoLaboratory has created new opportunities for advanced design-based research and civic engagement. Importantly, this co-creative practice opens space for design-based professions to acknowledge and support healthy relationships between people, landscapes, and wildlife.

CoLaboratories (or CoLabs) are a community-expert collaborative working forum for hands-on design and planning to solve a systemic problem that is complex, multi-sectoral, and interdisciplinary. Held as a series of iterative community-based interprofessional workshops that are experiential, practice-oriented and problem-solving focused, CoLabs take place in an intensive one- to two-day format during which invited experts from different relevant disciplines, together with local community members, work to find common ground, equitably, using different ways of knowing and experiencing landscapes. The CoLabs are intended to develop a shared vision and, from this, to design practical, feasible solutions to a problem that no one single agency alone can solve.[15]

The CoLab praxis is grounded in theory, supported by research and refined in practice, in place and in community. The working format of the

CoLab resembles aspects of the design charrette tradition which have been incorporated into the "community design charrette"—a multi-day community design workshop for neighbourhood residents and local knowledge keepers, facilitated by professional planners, designers and municipal decision-makers.[16] However, the CoLab differs specifically in its emphasis on sequential iteration, shared learning, transdisciplinary knowledge generation, and the co-creation of outcomes. Continuous exchange, co-created in the working process, is key for producing formal knowledge that is also practicable and relevant to broader stakeholders.[17] In this way, the CoLab is not a self-contained activity but is grounded in a longer series of reflections, and the design workshop or charrette may function as the culmination of a longer process of discussions and negotiations, from which a preferred physical form or structure emerges through consensus and co-production.

Underlying the CoLab as method is design thinking which supports an inter- and transdisciplinary mode of knowledge production and which can illuminate process development, making design techniques accessible to non-designers. Design-based research is part of the lineage of systems-based research and practice approaches[18] and experiential learning-by-doing.[19] Realized through multiple modes of communication and expression, design thinking is highly visual, spatial, and analytical.[20] In this context, landscape-based transdisciplinary challenges (such as how to move people and wildlife safely across roads) can successfully facilitate collaborative knowledge production across academic disciplines, and with non-academic practitioners, local actors, community members, place-keepers, and governing agencies.

The CoLaboratory puts planning, engineering, and design professionals together with community leaders to share knowledge, assess barriers and opportunities, and co-create a resolution to this challenge. Methodological components of the CoLaboratories include: performing preliminary site and policy context research; compiling and analyzing technical data; mapping and visualization; cataloguing existing and case-precedent decision-making strategies; analyzing policy options and planning tools for each site; soft-systems mapping of policy contexts and planning tools (including overlaps, boundaries, and constraints); developing preliminary design solutions and implementation strategies; and ideation, programming and exhibit and/or communications development for public engagement [FIG. 6]. In this way, the EDL's CoLabs offer a diversity of collaborative strategies for co-produced design solutions in contested landscapes—solutions that benefit both humans and wildlife, within their communities.

More Than a Deliverable: Building Partnership

Both TDL and EDL are grounded in active, community-based partnerships to advance and entrench positive structural change in contested environments through a landscape approach of systems change. Our reflections on the nature, characteristics, and approaches to partnership follow below; these relate to the overlapping methods and values that are foundational to our design-based research and praxes.

Create Common Language for Shared Understanding

Distinct sets of professional terms and technocratic language are used by departments, agencies, and fields of practice, which often inhibits collaboration with those from outside of the sphere. Text and language can be used to assert authority, maintain power structures, and reinforce disciplinary silos. Partnership requires the creation of a common vocabulary to advance shared meaning. This happens through active or mindful awareness, "unlearning" the jargon that is embedded and implicit in professional practice (and which excludes non-experts), and from this, generating an explicitly inclusionary language that invites all stakeholders to participate.

Build Bridges Between Silos

Involve everyone, including from different disciplines and sectors, from the beginning, especially those traditionally left out or to the end of processes. Partnership requires the involvement of all from conception through to implementation. Frameworks can limit working relationships between those with different or specific types of expertise—either through the validation of particular tools and methods, the order of engagement of various groups in projects, or to particular points of project delivery. Such limitations can affect the integration of expertise at each stage of the project and the ability for effective contribution from the very beginning at the stages when major design directions have been established. Interdisciplinary teams or bridge-building among disciplines can be kick-started by inviting team members who wear "more than one hat" to share knowledge and experience; e.g., planners who are also designers, or policy-makers, or scientists who work with artists.

Think Outside of Constraints

Capital projects are often guided by design standards and manuals that set baselines for performance, materials, and dimensions. In the case of wildlife crossings, design standards are often adapted on highway design manuals intended for vehicular traffic which do not address the unique considerations associated with this category of infrastructure. In the case of housing, building codes and normative housing models set baselines for funding and do not address the cultural appropriateness of solutions. A strong partnership framework invites a reimagining that work towards better well-being outcomes.

Process is a Deliverable

The process of building and maintaining partnership should be considered a deliverable that is given the time and care of other project milestones. While partnerships are based in action and changemaking, investment in the processes which cultivate and nurture partnerships by supporting long-standing reciprocal relationships is critical to success. Assuming that partnership will occur simply as a result of a shared objective ignores the harm that can be caused by inadvertently or implicitly reaffirming existing power relationships and conflict resulting from disciplinary orthodoxy. Ensuring that an iterative and reflexive process of partnership is occurring requires naming it and valuing it explicitly within project work plans.

Move Objectives From "Fail Safe" to Safe-to-Fail

Traditional models of project delivery have emphasized control and static outcomes that leave little room to adapt to changing conditions over time, and which do not incentivize learning, or allow recognition of mistakes that can provide insights into improvements (see e.g., "safe-to-fail" learning examples introduced by Lister, 2007,21 and expanded by Ahern, 2012.22 A system wherein adaptation and change through learning and flexibility are not prioritized will simply reproduce existing outcomes and ignore the emergent findings of co-creation. Inclusive processes and partnerships risk being undermined if they are ultimately coerced into the reproduction of outcomes reflective of the status quo. Instead, project outcomes should embed learning and adaptation into an iterative cycle of course-correction through monitoring and evaluation of learned feedback.

Increase Confidence in New Designs and Approaches

Publicly funded projects can be hindered in their ability to implement innovative and culturally appropriate solutions. These are often determined to be expendable in the course of value engineering or precluded by restrictions that require the pursuit of the lowest-cost-bid. External proofs-of-concept, generated via prototyping efforts undertaken independently or in partnership with a public agency or community, can advance the state of practice by demonstrating the art of the possible, for example: capturing the public imagination through compelling stories of place, or the coexistence with wildlife as a valued and important community asset, or the traditional knowledge of community members embedded in project goal setting.

FIG.6 As interdisciplinary design workshops, CoLabs typically result in a wide range of visual, spatial, analytical, and communication materials to help elucidate design options for new types of infrastructures in challenging environments and to address complex socio-ecological conditions. Products range from mapping to data communication to poetry and art to share the stories of wildlife and people in the landscapes they share. NM. Lister for Ecological Design Lab (EDL)

Looking to the Future

Partnerships allow an important opportunity to focus on scaling deep. Embodying cross-cultural, multi-sectoral, transdisciplinary allyship through research-based knowledge transfer offers unique opportunities to create long-term communities of practice. Praxis undertaken together can make multi-scalar ecosystems change and co-create alternative futures. In this way, the problem and the approach are understood as relational. Partnerships facilitate cross-cultural and transdisciplinary understandings that catalyze the possibility for greater allyship across disciplines, communities, and place. In this way, partnerships help establish the potential to co-create space for action-based research and praxis.

The power and potential of carefully nurtured partnerships is to enable experimental co-creation opportunities for students and community members to advance long-term structural change. There is a clear and urgent need for increased teaching and training opportunities focused on broad scalar systems and landscape approaches that link iterative engagement of theory and practice within community as a place-based locus for integrating knowledge. Experiential learning in particular has an important role in helping to overcome traditional academic and professional disciplinary barriers and in bridging diverse knowledge types needed for addressing complex problems.

Ultimately, our collaborations aim to teach students to integrate partnership and multi-scalar thinking into praxis using experiential learning with real partners across real contested landscapes. In so doing, we situate co-design, co-creation, and co-production as explicit curriculum learning outcomes in terms of both methods and principles. Modeling such relationships, even in temporary and partial ways, through experiential learning opportunities provides valuable insights for students into alternative practice and importantly enables a dialogue with students on the topic of partnership. Although for the academy itself to challenge the power structures being defined through this model of partnership, we must shift the focus from individual expertise to a collective web of skills and relations made possible through experiential learning.

Endnotes

1. "Canada's Population Estimates: Subprovincial Areas, Population Growth in Canada's Large Urban Regions Slows, but Still Outpaces That of Other Regions," The Daily, Statistics Canada, released January 14, 2021, https //www150.statcan.gc.ca/n1/daily-quotidien/210114/dq210114a-eng.htm.
2. "Minerals and the Economy," Government of Canada, last modified March 18, 2021, https://www.nrcan.gc.ca/our-natural-resources/minerals-mining/minerals-metals-facts/minerals-and-the-economy/20529.
3. Gilles Rhéaume, and Margaret Caron-Vuotari, *The Future of Mining in Canada's North* (Ottawa: The Conference Board of Canada, January 2013).
4. V.P. Neimanis, "Crown Land," The Canadian Encyclopedia, accessed June 29, 2021. https://www.thecanadianencyclopedia.ca/en/article/crown-land; and Ducks Unlimited Canada, "Land Owners," Our Work, accessed June 29, 2021, https://www.ducks.ca/our-work/landowners/.
5. Leanne Betasamosake Simpson, *As We Have Always Done: Indigenous Freedom Through Radical Resistance* (Minneapolis: University of Minnesota Press, 2017).
6. Donatella H Meadows, *Leverage Points: Places to Intervene in a System* (Hartland, VT: Sustainability Institute, 1999); and Donatella H. Meadows, *Thinking in Systems: A Primer* (White River Junction, VT: Chelsea Green Press, 2008).
7. Sheryl Reimer Kirkham and Joan M. Anderson, "The Advocate-Analyst Dialectic in Critical and Postcolonial Feminist Research: Reconciling Tensions Around Scientific Integrity," *Advances in Nursing Science* 33, no. 3 (July 2010), doi:10.1097/ANS.0b013e3181e4a7d3.
8. Royal Commission on Aboriginal Peoples, "Chapter 4. Housing," in *Report of the Royal Commission on Aboriginal Peoples, Volume 3* (Ottawa: Minister of Supply and Services, 1996).
9. Royal Commission on Aboriginal Peoples, "Chapter 4. Housing."; and Adele Perry, "From 'the hot bed of vice' to the 'good and well-ordered Christian home': First Nations Housing Reform in Nineteenth-Century British Columbia," *Ethnohistory* 50, no. 4 (2003), doi.org/10.1215/00141801-50-4-587.
10. Tom Carter, *Evolution of Northern Housing Policy* (Winnipeg: Institute of Urban Studies, 1993).
11. Shelagh McCartney, "Re-thinking Housing: From Physical Manifestation of Colonial Planning Policy to Community-Focused Networks," *Urban Planning* 1, no. 4 (2016) https://doi.org/10.17645/up.v1i4.737.
12. Shelagh McCartney et al., "Restructuring First Nation Housing Need Through Community Driven Metrics," *Ontario Planning Journal* 33, no. 6 (November/December 2018); and Shelagh McCartney and Michael McKay, "What is measured defines the crisis: Using community-based housing metrics to create culturally appropriate housing in Nishnawbe Aski Nation," *Plan Canada* 59, no. 3 (Winter 2019).
13. Matthew Bell, Damon Fick, Rob Ament, and Nina-Marie Lister, "The Use of Fiber-Reinforced Polymers in Wildlife Crossing Infrastructure," *Sustainability, MDBI, Open Access Journal* 12, no. 4 (February 2020). DOI:10.3390/su12041557.
14. Nina-Marie Lister, Marta Brocki, and Rob Ament, "Integrated Adaptive Design for Wildlife Movement under Climate Change," *Frontiers in Ecology and the Environment* 13, no. 9 (2015), doi:10.1890/150080.
15. Nina-Marie Lister, Marta Brocki, and Rob Ament, "Integrated Adaptive Design for Wildlife Movement under Climate Change," *Frontiers in Ecology and the Environment* 13, no. 9 (2015), doi:10.1890/150080; and Nik Luka, Nina-Marie Lister, and Bria Aird, "The case for transdisciplinary charrettes: Complementing citizen engagement with innovations in professional co-production," *Sustainability* (forthcoming 2021).
16. Bill Lennertz, "The Charette as an Agent for Change," in *New Urbanism: Comprehensive Report and Best Practices Guide, 3rd Edition* (Ithaca: New Urban Publications, 2003).
17. Joan Nassauer and Paul Opdam, "Design in Science: Extending the Landscape Ecology Paradigm," *Landscape Ecology* 23, no. 6 (July 2008), DOI:10.1007/s10980-008-9226-7.
18. Peter Checkland, *Systems Thinking, Systems Practice* (Chichester: John Wiley, 1981); and Peter Checkland and Jim Scholes, *Soft Systems Methodology in Action* (Chinchester: John Wiley, 1990).
19. Kai N. Lee, *Compass and Gyroscope: Integrating Science and Politics for the Environment* (Washington, D.C.: Island Press, 1993).
20. M. Elen Deming and Simon Swaffield, "Research Strategies in Landscape Architecture: Mapping the Terrain," *Journal of Landscape Architecture* 6, no. 1 (March 2011), DOI:10.1080/18626033.2011.9723445; Rim Razzouk and Valerie Shute, "What is Design Thinking and Why Is it Important?" *Review of Educational Research 82,* no. 3 (September 2012), doi.org/10.3102/0034654312457429; and Edward R. Tufte, *Envisioning Information* (Cheshire: Graphics Press, 1990).
21. Nina-Marie Lister, "Sustainable Large Parks: Ecological Design or Designer Ecology?", in *Large Parks*, eds. J. Czerniak and G. Hargreaves (Princeton: Princeton Architectural Press, 2007), 31–51.
22. Jack Ahern, "From Fail-Safe to Safe-to-Fail: Sustainability and Resilience in the New Urban World," *Landscape and Urban Planning* 100,no. 4 (April 2011): 341–343, https://doi.org/10.1016/j.landurbplan.2011.02.021.

5.2

Resensitizing Urban Waterways and Their Publics

Ecological Art in the Built and Unplanned Environment in the Work of Mare Liberum

Kendra Sullivan, Dylan Gauthier, Sunita Prasad

The environmental art collective Mare Liberum ("the free seas") was started in 2007 in the Gowanus area of *Lenapehoking*—the ancestral land of the Lenape peoples, currently called Brooklyn, New York. Taking our name from the 1609 tract by Hugo Grotius establishing universal access to the sea, the collective formed as a synergy of ideas and people with backgrounds in industrial design, conceptual art, geography, and activism. Hurricane Katrina and later Superstorm Sandy in NYC were catalysts for the collective's initial mission to engage in issues relating to water justice, public/participatory art, anti-gentrification work, and environmental-policy shaping. In our own backyard, the collective formed as a response to a shortage of public access to the city's waterways. The Gowanus Canal is a toxic mile and a half of saltwater, broken concrete bulkheads, and crumbling street buffers that cut through four ultra-gentrified neighborhoods. In the earliest days, ML aspired to turn prohibitions into possibilities on the banks of the Gowanus: we organized community boat-building and political-education workshops in our studio, wheat-pasted boat-building plans onto construction fences, turned discarded building materials into gunwales, converted police barricades into boat paddles, and ultimately built a fleet of dorries with which we navigated the physical and political complexities of the canal as a community.

The collective has gone on to develop substantial work around the Hudson River in New York, the Mystic River in Boston, the Olentangy River in Columbus, and the Canal St. Martin in Paris. ML's boat-building workshops and voyages enable artists, activists, civic engineers, and policy makers to engage in community-led environmental decision making. Our daylong public workshops begin with basic materials and boat-building instruction, break for lunch and discourse with experts and from adjacent fields including design, policy, parks management, and environmental science, and end on the water in a newly minted fleet. Building a seaworthy vessel from scratch is a radically transformative and empowering experience, one that transports participants beyond the quotidian experience of daily, urban life, resensitizing them to their

OPPOSITE PAGE Mare Liberum, *SeaChange: We All Live Downstream* – Circumnavigation of Manhattan. Sunita Prasad

environmental surrounds, and inspiring sustained engagement in the shaping and maintenance of place.

The Role of Art in Shaping Public Visibility

Focusing on new models of practice, in this chapter ML offers a snapshot of the participatory and experiential methodologies we employ to invite community assessment and creative activity as part of a holistic planning and design practice. As a theoretical framework, we draw on such sources as critic Nicholas Borriaud, who coined the term "relational aesthetics" to describe collaborative art practices based on human relationships and their social contexts—poet Audre Lorde, whose embodied theory harnessed the raw, counter-hegemonic power of art, erotics, and aesthetics; and philosopher Nelson Maldonado-Torres, who writes that "decolonial aesthetics very directly challenges, not only each basic coordinate of modernity/coloniality, but its most visceral foundations and overall scope."[1] While theory informs our practice, our practice informs our understanding of the politics of place making and policy shaping [FIG. 1].

Artists can lend visibility to unseen geographies and their work is often at the forefront of public understanding of place. Artist-led participatory planning around environmental policy issues could become a key feature in the production of more just and sustainable urban landscapes. New genre and expanded field public art—as in the work of Tania Bruguera, Suzanne Lacy, Mierle Laderman Ukeles, Rick Lowe, and Theaster Gates—bridges public dialogues around equity, communing, and environmental justice. For example, Tania Bruguera's *Immigrant Movement International* established a community space where practical knowledge is merged with creative knowledge through what the artist calls "arte útil" (useful art). The space, *Centro Corona,* continues to provide advocacy, programing, and support for immigrant justice. In ecological art, artists support public analysis and engagement with place through the creation of images, text, sound, experiential, pedagogical, and time-based work. For example, Torkwase Dyson's *Wynter Wells Drawing School for Environmental Liberation* develops a curriculum fusing "visual arts as well as theories of geography, infrastructure, and architecture to initiate dialogues about spatiality" in the era of climate change.[2] As another example: artist and "counter-cartographer" Lize Mogel's *Walking the Watershed* connects residents of New York City with the policy concerns of upstate localities from which they draw their drinking water. Such art practices expand a dialogue and create shared public priorities around water policy, public water, and infrastructure.

Social cohesion and a sense of interconnectedness, or "communities of sense,"[3] are key frameworks for environmentalism in the age of climate crisis. Making space for dialog, spotlighting the work of frontline actors, and resensitizing a public to overlooked sites is a precondition of culture

and systems change. These practices refine public understanding about the ways places are perceived, managed, and constructed through a combination of nature and culture, as well as policy and public use. Social scientist Lindsay Campbell et al., have written that artists take part in the creation and signaling of "social infrastructures," and contribute to networks of stakeholders: "Physical spaces must be enlivened by individuals, groups, and organizations in order to function as social infrastructures that create opportunities for people to feel part of collective life."[4] As attitudes and understandings of ecological crises evolve, challenges increasingly call for multi-scale analysis and action. The sensitization of a public to a site through collaborative art praxis lends itself to a critical approach to participatory landscape making in the age of climate change.

Mission and Approach of the Collective

Building on the idea of a "transformative activist stance," coined by developmental psychologist Eduardo Vianna, ML proposes that navigating a river is a form of environmental pedagogy that encourages individuals to merge with a purposeful collective identity. Our practice relies on four methodologies: Mobile Architecture (building boats and site-specific, temporary structures), Publics and Platforms (engaging local communities around their waterways, identifying social infrastructure), Collaborative Networks (working together in an open-source methodology), and Water as a Commons and a Public Space (access and useability, equity, health, and toxicity).

Confronting a literal lack of access, we frequently need to traverse the physical obstacles that city planning has placed between the public

FIG.1 Mare Liberum, *Liberum Kayak Construction Workshop*, 2010. Stephan von Muehlen

and the waterfront (for instance, in planning that prioritizes roads, high-rise development, or industrial access to these sites). But our work also engages with breaking the invisible mental and legal barriers to the water that exist in the cultures of many cities. Barrier-traversing becomes key to a project that is equally about narrativizing how cities are designed and built, how and where their inhabitants interface with nature, and how humans and non-humans use their waterways.

Art as Method: The Water Rites Projects

In 2014, we initiated the project Water Rites, conceived in response to Indigenous water defenders organizing against the pipelines, the Flint water crisis, and the crisis of the world's oceans and freshwater reserves. As a counter to forms of soft ecological, political, and social violence—or "slow violence" in the parlance of Rob Nixon—Water Rites aims at connecting activists, artists, designers and planners, and policymakers around specific sites of ongoing colonial violence through pollution, development, or neglect. The project also focuses on creating social infrastructure for what Donna Haraway refers to as *flourishing*, an ontological category that encompasses economic security, art, writing, culture, food access, and community. Each phase of Water Rites explores a different place, organizes research through community-led design, "unplanning," and experiential learning. Each phase proposed a site-specific, process-based approach to policy shaping, planning, and design, outlined below.

FIG.2 Mare Liberum, *SeaChange: We All Live Downstream* - Construction of Paper Boats, 2014.Patrick Kiley

The Hudson River (Sea Change: We All Live Downstream, 2014)

Sea Change: We All Live Downstream was commissioned by 350.org in the lead up to the People's Climate March. The project connected civic groups working on interconnected environmental justice issues such as sea-level rise, racialized wealth and power disparities, and legacies of displacement and neglect across the Hudson River Valley. The project kicked off with a month of community boat-building workshops in which we constructed a fleet of kraft paper canoes which were based on a regional paper canoe design created in the 1890s [FIG. 2]. Launching from Troy and stopping in thirteen towns over the 150-mile paddle down the Hudson, we organized fireside talks, screenings, performances, and discussions on themes related to fracking, nuclear power, and community-led strategies of adaptation and resilience [FIG. 3].

The spectacle of a flotilla of paper boats—precarious, fragile, improbable—served as a platform for local stakeholders to network, leverage resources, and connect their regionally-specific needs and messaging with national and international climate policy. In one instance, we hosted workshops with the Sane Energy project, a group of concerned neighbors fighting to shut down the Indian Point Nuclear Power Plant, which have since been successful in lobbying New York State to take the facility offline. Protests and resistance to "bomb trains" (pressurized rail cars carrying fracked gas), drew on the still-recent Lac-Mégantic rail disaster in Quebec and have since successfully diverted a fracked gas terminal plant project in Newburgh, New York that would have displaced waterfront communities and created new public health hazards for the town's largely Black and Brown population. In Newburgh, and elsewhere along the way, we assembled community stakeholders, residents, activists, and planners, to talk through strategy for securing community control of contested sites.

Arriving in New York City, we organized a circumnavigation of Manhattan with local boat clubs, led an on-water protest that brought small boat owners to rally with banners, a full marching band, and floats across from the UN [FIG. 4]. We also organized a press event at The Floating Library, then docked in the Hudson, featuring a traditional water ceremony with Indigenous water protectors from the Dakotas.

Beyond the project's currency as one that fused art, design, and activism, we could imagine such an extensive approach to place-knowing being picked up by urban planners or policy makers as a valid form of site-specific research. In a very short period of time, with a very small budget, the project produced extensive research around the diverse concerns of Hudson River Valley communities. The on-water voyage offered a sense of adventure, (self) discovery, and coalition building.

The Mystic River (Or, the Other Island, 2015)

In 2015, Mare Liberum was invited by Harvard University to produce *Or, the Other Island*, an exhibition and research program. The resulting project transformed the Carpenter Center for Visual Arts into a temporary hub. Over two weeks, the collective built punts—flat-bottom boats with a

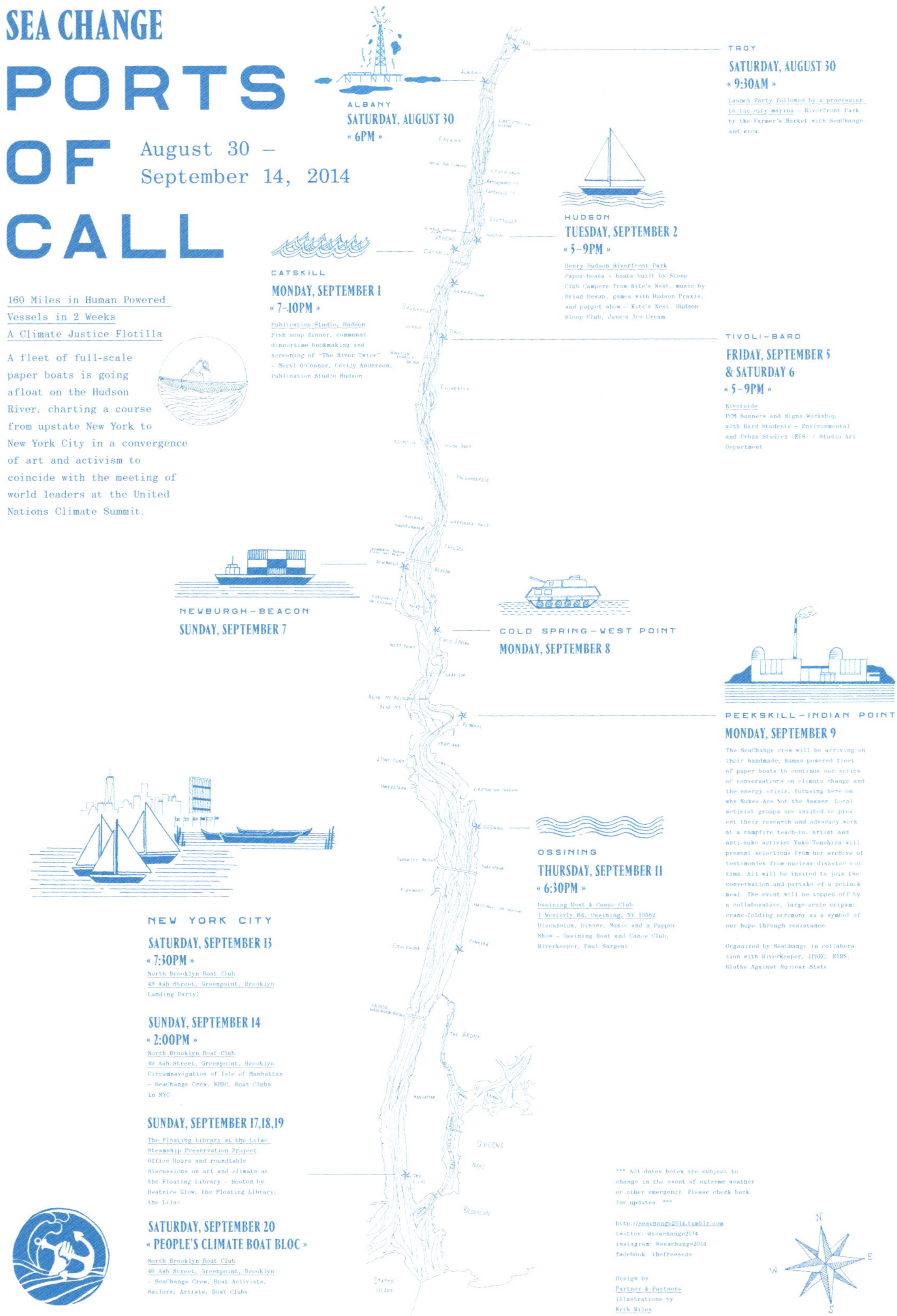
SEA CHANGE
PORTS OF CALL
August 30 – September 14, 2014
160 Miles in Human Powered Vessels in 2 Weeks
A Climate Justice Flotilla
A fleet of full-scale paper boats is going afloat on the Hudson River, charting a course from upstate New York to New York City in a convergence of art and activism to coincide with the meeting of world leaders at the United Nations Climate Summit.
TROY
SATURDAY, AUGUST 30
« 9:30AM »
Launch Party followed by a procession to the city marina – Riverfront Park by the Farmer's Market with SeaChange and crew.
ALBANY
SATURDAY, AUGUST 30
« 6PM »
HUDSON
TUESDAY, SEPTEMBER 2
« 5–9PM »
Henry Hudson Riverfront Park
Paper-boats + boats built by Sloop Club Campers from Kite's Nest, music by Brian Dewan, games with Hudson Praxis, and puppet show – Kite's Nest, Hudson Sloop Club, Jane's Ice Cream
CATSKILL
MONDAY, SEPTEMBER 1
« 7–10PM »
Publication Studio, Hudson
Fish soup dinner, communal dinnertime bookmaking and screening of "The River Twice" – Meryl O'Connor, Cecily Anderson, Publication Studio Hudson
TIVOLI–BARD
FRIDAY, SEPTEMBER 5 & SATURDAY 6
« 5–9PM »
Riverside
PCM Banners and Signs Workshop with Bard Students – Environmental and Urban Studies (EUS) / Studio Art Department
NEWBURGH–BEACON
SUNDAY, SEPTEMBER 7
COLD SPRING–WEST POINT
MONDAY, SEPTEMBER 8
PEEKSKILL–INDIAN POINT
MONDAY, SEPTEMBER 9
The SeaChange crew will be arriving on their handmade, human-powered fleet of paper boats to continue our series of conversations on climate change and the energy crisis, focusing here on why Nukes Are Not the Answer. Local activist groups are invited to present their research and advocacy work at a campfire teach-in. Artist and anti-nuke activist Yuko Tonohira will present selections from her archive of testimonies from nuclear disaster victims. All will be invited to join the conversation and partake of a potluck meal. The event will be topped off by a collaborative, large-scale origami crane-folding ceremony as a symbol of our hope through resistance.
Organized by SeaChange in collaboration with RiverKeeper, IPSEC, NIRS, Sloths Against Nuclear State
OSSINING
THURSDAY, SEPTEMBER 11
« 6:30PM »
Ossining Boat & Canoe Club
1 Westerly Rd, Ossining, NY 10562
Discussion, Dinner, Music and a Puppet Show – Ossining Boat and Canoe Club, Riverkeeper, Paul Sargent
NEW YORK CITY
SATURDAY, SEPTEMBER 13
« 7:30PM »
North Brooklyn Boat Club
49 Ash Street, Greenpoint, Brooklyn
Landing Party!
SUNDAY, SEPTEMBER 14
« 2:00PM »
North Brooklyn Boat Club
49 Ash Street, Greenpoint, Brooklyn
Circumnavigation of Isle of Manhattan – SeaChange Crew, NBBC, Boat Clubs in NYC
SUNDAY, SEPTEMBER 17,18,19
The Floating Library at the Lilac Steamship Preservation Project
Office Hours and roundtable discussions on art and climate at the Floating Library – Hosted by Beatrice Glow, the Floating Library, the Lilac
SATURDAY, SEPTEMBER 20
« PEOPLE'S CLIMATE BOAT BLOC »
North Brooklyn Boat Club
49 Ash Street, Greenpoint, Brooklyn
– SeaChange Crew, Boat Activists, Sailors, Artists, Boat Clubs
*** All dates below are subject to change in the event of extreme weather or other emergency. Please check back for updates. ***
http://seachange2014.tumblr.com
twitter: @seachange2014
instagram: #seachange2014
facebook: thefreeseas
Design by
Partner & Partners
Illustrations by
Erik Riley
N
E
S
W

square bow traditionally used to navigate shallow waterways and to transport cargo—designed and fabricated a table and benches to serve as a central conversation and planning area, built a pedal boat designed by Pierre Jeanneret, and transformed the iconic Le Corbusier ramp into a fountain, funneling captured rainwater back up to the roof through a system of ducts, scuppers, and spouts. We activated the gallery as a site for informal conversations around regional ecology, climate change, the global effects of plastics pollution, and neglect in relation to the City of Boston and its low-lying neighborhoods and waterways, and in particular, the Mystic River and its toxic legacies. Talks were led by landscape architects (Silvia Benedito and Pierre Bélanger), scientists (Max Liboiron, Sara Wylie of the Public Lab), and involved artists, students in the Department of Visual and Environmental Studies, and faculty members from a broad array of disciplines and departments.

We built and launched ten boats on the Mystic River. Public paddlers heard from local experts, including The Mystic River Watershed Association (MyRWA) and Clean Water Action. The Public Lab led a water temperature workshop to gauge whether wastewater from a local power plant was potentially affecting aquatic life. Trawling for microplastics with STS researcher Max Liboiron, and a performance on the life of the salt marsh by the artist collective Plotform (Jane D. Marsching and Andi Sutton) rounded out the voyage and connected participants to each other and to the landscape [FIG. 5]. The collaborative and participatory journey and resulting archive of experiences created the

FIG.3 LEFT Mare Liberum, *SeaChange: We All Live Downstream – Ports of Call*, (Map Designed by Partner & Partners). Mare Liberum

FIG.4 RIGHT Mare Liberum, *SeaChange: We All Live Downstream* – Circumnavigation of Manhattan: Joined by Rude Mechanical Orchestra and North Brooklyn Boat Club, 2014. Sunita Prasad

potential to shift policy around the use of, access to, and environmental situation of the Mystic River. Focusing our work on an under-recognized body of water and drawing a connecting line between communities along the Mystic and toxicity concerns that affect all local residents, the project catalyzed support for community members—both participants and visitors to the exhibition—to think about such seemingly global challenges as plastics pollution, ocean temperature rise, and the restoration of native ecologies (marshland) through a local frame.

Toronto (In Which We Draw A People's Map of the Don River Valley, 2020-present)

The initiative In Which We Draw A People's Map of the Don River Valley, co-presented in 2020-22 by Waterfront Toronto and Evergreen Brickworks on the Don River, centers on building river-specific boats and creating a map based AR/VR interface and website for the public to share knowledge on the changing site of the Don River in Toronto, Canada. Our temporary, participatory, public art project coincides with Toronto's massive Port Lands Flood Protection Project, which will, among other feats, reconnect the Don River to Lake Ontario. As the COVID-19 pandemic closed borders, making travel to Toronto and our normal in-situ mode of getting to know a locale impossible, Mare Liberum initiated a series of virtual events that would inform and enrich the project. The first was a public roundtable which brought together artists, curators, and policymakers to reflect on recent art and policy collaborations and the ways artists work through, inside of, and around institutional frameworks to reconfigure urban public space. A second event, a research sprint, brought together twelve artists, scholars, policymakers, environmental activists, and planners to outline a gray paper for those who wish to insert participatory art practices into community-based (un)planning. As we work, we are helping define for Waterfront Toronto, for instance, what is meant by "temporary public art" and how a public art project can find footing in its own time frame, especially since navigating the local, the Don, has become about responding improvisationally to the nonlocal realities of the pandemic. Our Don River project aims to "locate" and increase access to the Don River, while

FIG.5 Mare Liberum, Or, the Other Island - CCVA, Harvard, 2015. Dylan Gauthier

asking the public to envision the future of the river—and its role in their future—against the backdrop of a global pandemic and of one of the largest landscape infrastructure projects in North America.

Conclusion

It is not easy to quantify outcomes of most creative work. Artists are not policy makers, social workers, or scientists. Cultural production, however, shifts attitudes, shapes affect, and increases participation in civic life. Art is one way to rethink reality as it is sold to us, to reverse engineer the inevitable so that it is situated in and against complex histories. Arjun Appadurai, in *The Right to Research*, writes that research is the "generalizable capacity to make disciplined inquiries into those things we need to know, but do not know yet."[5] It is precisely in the openness of artistic approaches—the artist's ability to try, sometimes to fail, and to do so in public—that we can see helpful modeling of the what might be and the shaping of policy and design possibilities. In the words of theorist Jacques Rancière, art creates, alters, or disturbs aesthetics to inform the "social distribution of bodies."[6] In this way, aesthetics is one of the ways that society shapes itself, and artistic practice is primarily concerned with the shaping of aesthetics.

Art is often presented as a neutral or net-positive mode of civic and ecological engagement. But by incorporating participatory, reciprocal, accountable, community-based, dialogic, and democratic practice into the processes of urban design, artists have the opportunity to reinject engagement with political intention, answerability, and actionability. Art that is active, that is grounded in joy, and that makes boundary-breaking and trespassing—both disciplinary and physical—a subject, changes our relationship to the planned and designed city, and its rigid categories of use. Policymakers, urban planners, landscape architects, and urban designers might come to adopt the approach of expanded field public artists, and invite artists working through these methodologies to collaborate early in the design phases of public work.

Endnotes

1. Nelson Maldonado-Torres, "Outline of ten theses on coloniality and decoloniality," Foundation Frantz Fanon Website, posted 2016, accessed July 12, 2021, http://frantzfanonfoundation-fondationfrantzfanon.com/article2360.html.
2. Torkwase Dyson, "Wynter Wells Drawing School," Artist's Website, accessed July 12, 2021, https://www.torkwasedyson.com/wwdej.
3. Jacques Rancière, "Contemporary Art and the Politics of Aesthetics," in *Communities of Sense: Rethinking Aesthetics and Politics*, ed. Beth Hinterlinter, et al., (Durham: Duke University Press, 2009).
4. Lindsay K. Campbell, Erika S. Svendsen, Michelle Johnson, and Laura Landau, In press, "Activating Urban Environments as Social Infrastructure through Civic Stewardship," *Urban Geography* (May 4, 2021).
5. Arjun Appadurai, "The Right to Research," in *Globalisation, Societies and Education* 4, no. 2 (2006): 167–77.
6. Rancière, "Contemporary Art and the Politics of Aesthetics."

5.3

A Strategy-Driven Model for Sustainable Socio-Environmental Transformations in Chile

Flavio Sciaraffia

In 2019, the Chilean Ministry of Environment commissioned my office with a nationwide study to identify priority wetlands for conservation. Soon after, it included us as part of a multidisciplinary team to draft the minimum sustainability criteria of the Urban Wetland Law's bylaws—legislation that aims to protect urban wetlands and avoid further loss by enabling cities to enforce specific regulations. Other related projects followed, like developing urban wetlands conservation guidelines for city planning departments, as part of the law requirements, and supporting the implementation of the law. Traditionally, the public sector calls for specialist disciplines, like science and engineering, to design policy and develop studies or plans. However, these projects were developed by a firm led by a landscape architect. In an unlikely context where technocrats had not considered design a discipline capable of addressing critical socio-environmental challenges, the discipline of landscape architecture has influenced public policy at scale and high-level decision making. In the following I will explain how a design-led practice came to play an important role in issues that perhaps lay outside the profession's traditional playground. First, I will briefly examine the challenging context that precludes design-led practices to contribute to solving important socio-environmental challenges in Chile. Second, I will discuss the value proposition that allowed my office to be a relevant actor in addressing some of the challenges the country is currently facing. Lastly, I will reflect on the implementation of the value proposition by discussing two projects developed by my practice.

Context: The Technocratic Silo as a Barrier and Opportunity

Public institutions in Chile are geared towards specialization to address programmatic agendas. The hyper-specialization of professions fosters a natural association between a discipline and a field of knowledge. From the perspective of the public good and appropriate use of taxpayers' money, it is, therefore, correct and responsible to account for the best disciplinary fit between problem and solution. This builds the idea of "expertise" which

OPPOSITE PAGE Valdivia River and Adjacent Wetland Mosaic, City of Valdivia. GoogleEarth Pro

is especially beneficial for policymakers: by supporting their actions on expertise, they can provide a robust justification for decision-making and modulate their accountability against public scrutiny. In practice, this translates to a procurement system that outright disregards design disciplines by excluding them from the eligibility criteria in public tenders.

In this challenging context, our main client is an ensemble of technocratic institutions whose understanding of the physical environment and underlying processes is compartmentalized and siloed due to the bureaucratic nature of their organization. As a result, public institutions have specialist disciplines—science and engineering—on call to address sometimes complex issues that, in hindsight, would require a more comprehensive approach and collaboration across disciplines. In this scenario, how could a design-led practice compete with specialist disciplines? More importantly, what would be an appropriate value proposition that would make public institutions consider a generalist discipline to address their needs?

The Value Proposition: A Design-Led Practice with a Strategy-Driven Model

My practice is composed of professionals from several disciplines. On staff we have geographers, planners, data analysts, economists, and natural resources engineers. More than half of the professionals come from generalist disciplines (landscape architecture, geography, and regional planning). Trained in architecture, urban design, and landscape architecture, I am the firm's leader.

Our competitors are large consulting firms and university research centers populated with professionals from engineering, economics, or any combination of STEM[1] disciplines. This is the world of strategy consulting firms, an industry sector that rewards specialization and the figure of the expert professional with extensive experience. To compete in such a market, however, we offer a combination of robust analytical methods—which provide accountability in decision making—with strategy, design, and creativity. We refer to this as a strategy-driven model (SDM), which is a six-step framework to articulate landscapes and processes that respond to socio-environmental challenges in a prospective manner. The SDM draws from a corpus of landscape planning methodologies[2,3] developed over the last thirty-five years[4] and more recent adaptive management approaches in conservation planning[5] [FIG. 1].

Through a systematic review of projects commissioned by public institutions, we noticed that most of them focused on a single step of the SDM. For example, we found numerous analytical studies exploring specific, socio-environmental issues, but at the same time those studies didn't provide alternatives to address or solve them. Conversely, we discovered planning proposals that weren't rooted in analysis or even

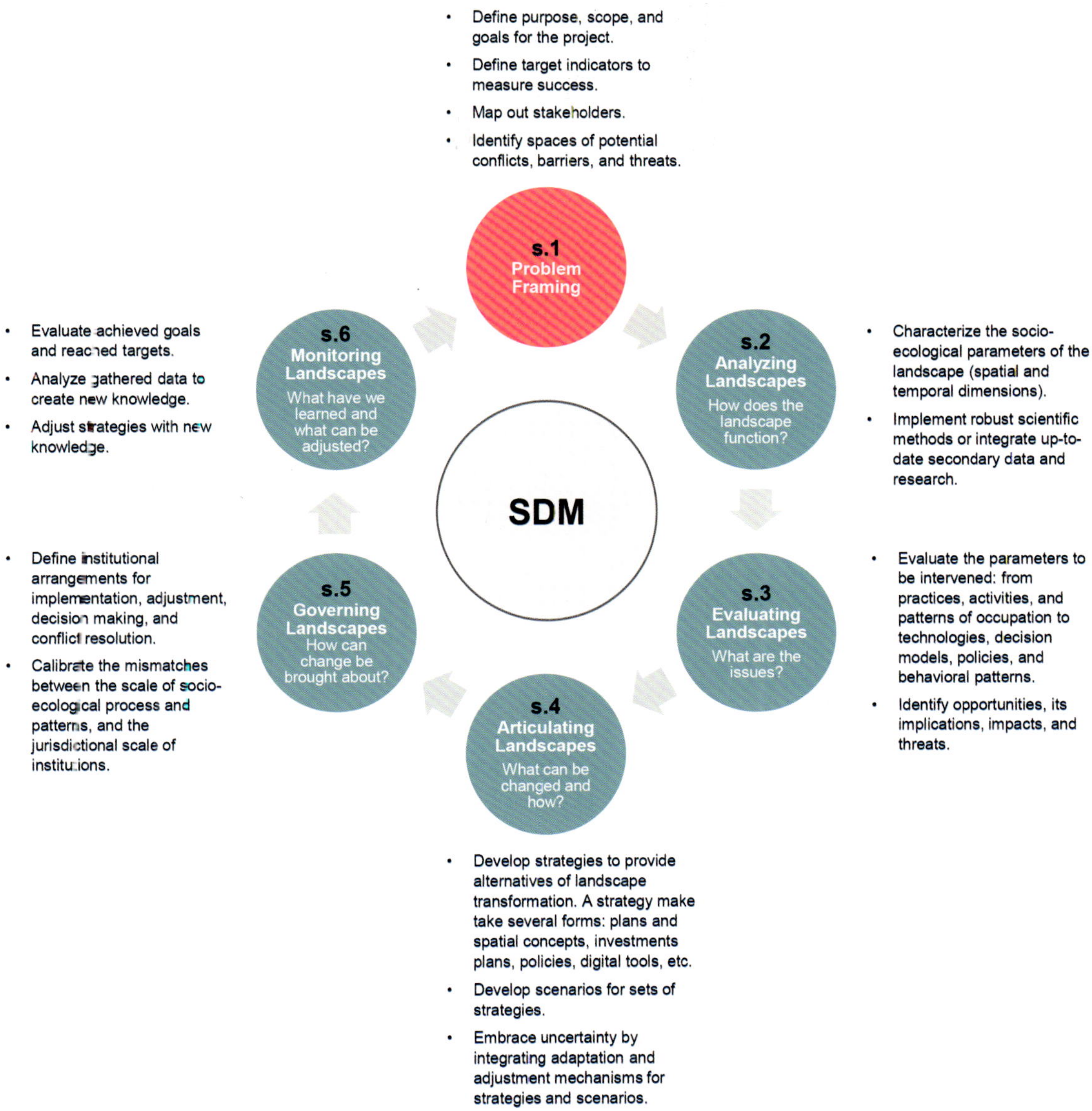

secondary scientific data—only assumptions—rendering them too risky to be implemented by authorities. Most critically, we detected a plethora of policies and public programs that never saw implementation because they lacked an adequate institutional framework for it. In sum, a constellation of isolated projects with good intentions—some repeated several times—that ended up archived and eventually lost after each government administration. After this extensive review, we figured that an appropriate value proposition was perhaps a project methodology that could to some extent articulate the entire SDM framework.

FIG.1 The strategy-driven model (SDM): Note that each step can be framed as a guiding question. Flavio Sciaraffia

Our main innovation, however, is not the SDM, which is a model that builds over a bulk of existing methodologies, but the realization that a successful project is one that spills over the entire process—albeit conceptually—either by considering previous steps or by anticipating and enabling the steps following further ahead. Thus, the value proposition conceives each project within the entire framework, understanding that its products need to account for the full sequence of the SDM model—even if our client requires us to focus just on a single step. We thus started developing our project proposals with that rationale. Eventually they caught the eye of public institutions, and soon after we saw our projects working to solve a wide range of socio-environmental challenges: from development planning to conservation planning, and from urban and infrastructure planning to regional and resource planning.

The Strategy-Driven Model in Practice: Two Case Studies in Chile

The strategy-driven model provides a whole-system approach to address socio-environmental challenges. It secures the project viability, while articulating strategies that act over the landscape. The model can be implemented in a range of topics, dimensions, and challenges, and it is a framework that systematically adds value to the initial project scope defined by the client. In addition to the framework, the SDM integrates five principles[6] that need to be considered throughout its execution. First, the "multi-scale" principle, which allows the reconciling of the mismatches that occur between the scales of governance and the progression of spatial and temporal scales of territorial processes and patterns. Second, the consideration that landscape patterns and processes are conditioned by the jurisdictional and geographical limits on which they unfold; finding the "interlinkages across limits" secures capturing the complexity of landscapes. Third, the "integrative" principle which allows aligning stakeholders' interests and negotiating trade-offs to create synergies across the landscape. Fourth, "adaptive strategies" that are more adequate to respond to unexpected change and can integrate new knowledge to reduce future uncertainty and increase resilience of landscape articulations. The last principle is based on the understanding of challenges in their "spatial (or geographical) dimension." Spatially explicit analyses and strategies drive stakeholders towards shared goals, fostering consensus and, therefore, facilitating new landscape articulations.

In what follows, I present two projects that work as case-studies for the SDM. The reader is encouraged to associate the project process with the SDM framework in figure 2, as well as identifying how the principles are captured through the project activities.

FIG.2 Wetland conservation priority GIS application: The application takes the form of a geospatial model that allows stakeholders assigning relative weights to variables and indicators. Once the weights are set, the model yields a high-resolution grid (30x30 meters) at national scale with priority values for each cell. The model then evaluates the grid values overlapping with the wetlands in the inventory and assigns a final priority value for each wetland. The figure shows results for the southern edge of the country based on a scenario created by the Department of Aquatic Ecosystems of the Ministry of Environment. The map on the left is the priority grid. The maps in the first column show the priorities for each wetland in the example. The maps in the second column show the priority at the sub-basin scale. This is another functionality of the application and allows contrasting how variables and indicators behave at the wetland scale and the next hydrological scale above. Flavio Sciaraffia

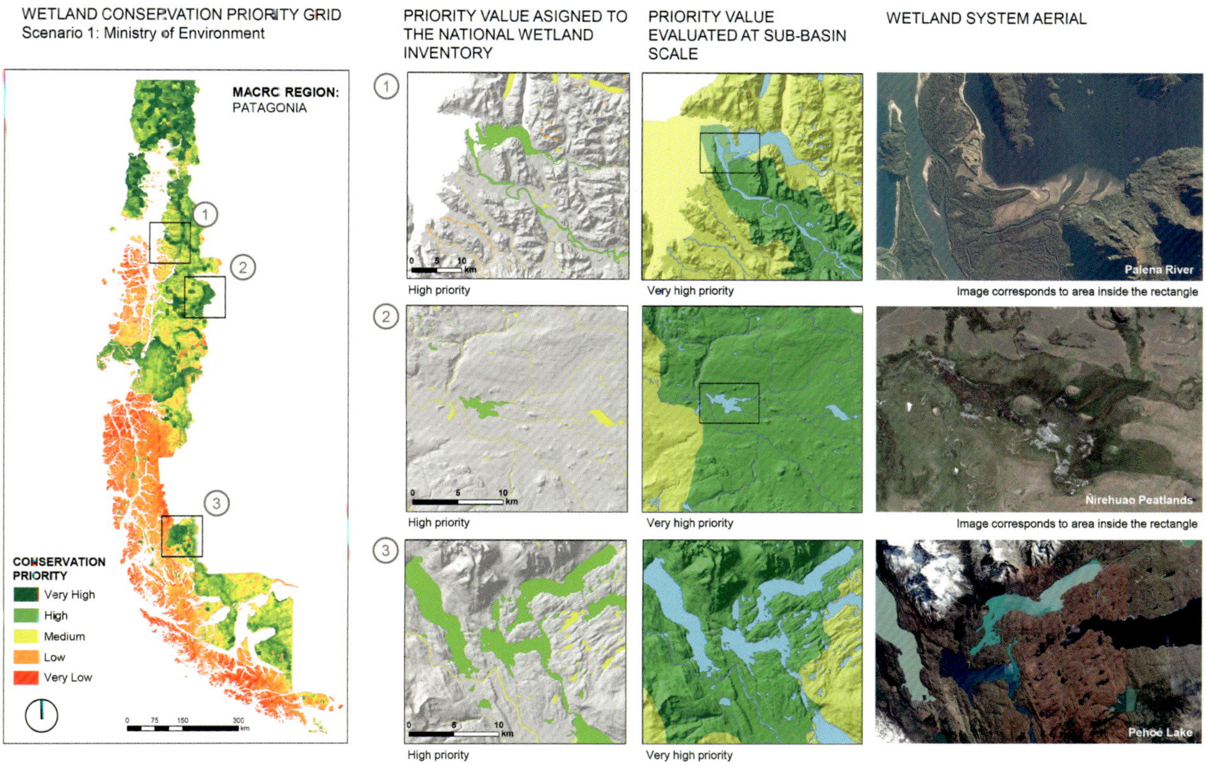

Case 1: Prioritizing National Wetlands Inventory for Conservation

Chile's National Wetland Inventory identifies over 5.6 million hectares of wetlands (7.4 percent of the country's gross area). Of these, 38 percent are under a protection category. Wetlands in its wide definition[7] are present along and across the country thanks to the Andes Mountains that draw rain from the ocean accumulating water in the form of snow and centenary glaciers. The interaction between drainage patterns, varied geomorphologic settings, and human activities gives way to a mosaic of coastal, continental, and artificial wetlands. Looking to meet national and international targets in biodiversity conservation,[8] the Ministry of Environment (MMA), our client, tasked us with prioritizing wetlands to guide conservation efforts. Prioritizing conservation is usually necessary because of conditions like limited resources, time, and political commitments. In this case, prioritization was also necessary because of a growing inventory of over 100,000 unique wetlands.

Initially, the client required a list of prioritized wetlands as the main product. We started with a comprehensive review of the state-of-the-art in wetland prioritization, encompassing national and international methodologies. Factoring in the recurrent updating of the inventory[9]—which denotes how dynamic wetlands and their management are—we proposed the development of a geospatial tool that could plug-in to the inventory and provide prioritization scenarios as needed. The tool is a GIS (Geographic Information System) application and was built using a visual programming interface. It prioritizes wetlands by evaluating spatial information from thirty variables packaged in five indicators that work as prioritization objectives: biodiversity conservation, water resources conservation, threats mitigation, carbon sequestration, and cultural ecosystem services [FIG. 2].

A new scenario can be generated by assigning relative weights to variables and indicators in the application. The objectives were defined with the client and capture specific institutional commitments and goals in wetland conservation. Several workshops were held with academic and public stakeholders to validate the objectives and variables, and to create alternative scenarios that resonate with each stakeholder's priorities. As government administrations change, and with it the MMA's programmatic agenda, the tool could accommodate incoming priorities, remaining relevant as different ministerial cabinets put forward their conservation agendas. By integrating the views of many stakeholders, the tool set the ground for a shared governance in wetland conservation, reducing the likelihood of conflict when deciding what—and what not—to conserve. A case in point during the project were the conflicting views between the MMA and the scientific community. For the former, priority was mostly based on the threats the wetland ecosystems were facing, whereas the latter considered that biodiversity conservation was the most important objective. Both views were able to converge in a scenario with shared priorities. We finalized the project by establishing a protocol to update the information on which the prioritization is made and by designing a flexible structure to integrate new objectives, if necessary, therefore equipping the tool with a built-in adaptation mechanism. Currently, the tool is in the process of being uploaded to the MMA's national biodiversity information system which houses data and applications to aid conservation efforts at different governance levels.

Case 2: Implementing the Urban Wetland Protection Law

In 2020, Chile passed a legislation to protect wetlands in urban contexts. This bill represents a general paradigm shift in conservation that has been applied in other contexts as well. It follows discussions in nature conservation which state that conservation does not mean an incompatibility between human activities and natural ecosystems,[10] proposing that it is the rational use—and not only the restriction of activities, uses, or access—that is the most effective conservation mechanism. Before this law, urban wetlands in Chile lacked legal recognition, making their conservation problematic.[11] Wetlands in urban environments are subject to an array of threats like draining, filling, and fragmentation because of land use change. At the same time, it is in cities where their benefits are more felt and needed by communities (providing ecosystem services like coastal protection, water purification and accumulation, food sources, biodiversity, and recreation). Thus, the law enables municipalities to identify and declare their urban wetlands, bestowing them with normative tools to conserve them. It also means that local governments acquire a series of responsibilities that will require new resources and capacities that are not often found in local environmental and planning departments. For example, the law requires the modification of municipal zoning plans to establish compatible uses and urbanistic conditions near declared wetlands; it also requires implementing a conservation management plan with specific measures based on identified threats. After our involvement in developing the bylaws of the legislation, the Ministry of Environment tasked us with designing a skill-delivering program—consisting of knowledge products, such as courses and guidelines—that could support and enable the implementation of the law by local governments.

In Chile, municipalities are the smallest unit of local government and where most traditional urban planning takes place. There are over three hundred municipalities with stark differences in resources and professional capacities. With the law already in force, we set the focus on defining a strong monitoring system that could accompany its implementation and aid the MMA in defining an appropriate support package for municipalities. We started by analyzing the current state of municipal management to assess whether local governments were adequately prepared or not to implement the law. Using public data, we developed an indicator system covering five dimensions of municipal management: environmental management, urban planning, civic participation, and public investment. For example, we examined how up-to-date local zoning plans were, if funded projects were successfully executed, and if there was an existence of participatory mechanisms, among other factors. Evaluating the indicator allowed us to carefully mediate between local realities and the expectations of the central government. The MMA realized that a one-size-fits-all approach to support the implementation was not possible because of the diverse municipal landscape. Using the indicator, we took a snapshot of the state of municipal management in 2020 and used the insights to design knowledge products for municipalities. We developed a series of self-guided online courses and guidelines covering basic and more advanced topics pertaining to urban wetlands. Topics included: the law and its implications to municipalities, procedural and normative aspects of the legislation, the state of urban wetlands in Chile, wetland hydrology and biology, threats to wetlands in urban environments, and wetland management, among others [FIG. 3].

To test the suitability of our monitoring system, we piloted one course dealing with the first steps of the law implementation, which involves the declaration of urban wetlands following a series of technical requirements per the bylaws. This includes the process of identifying

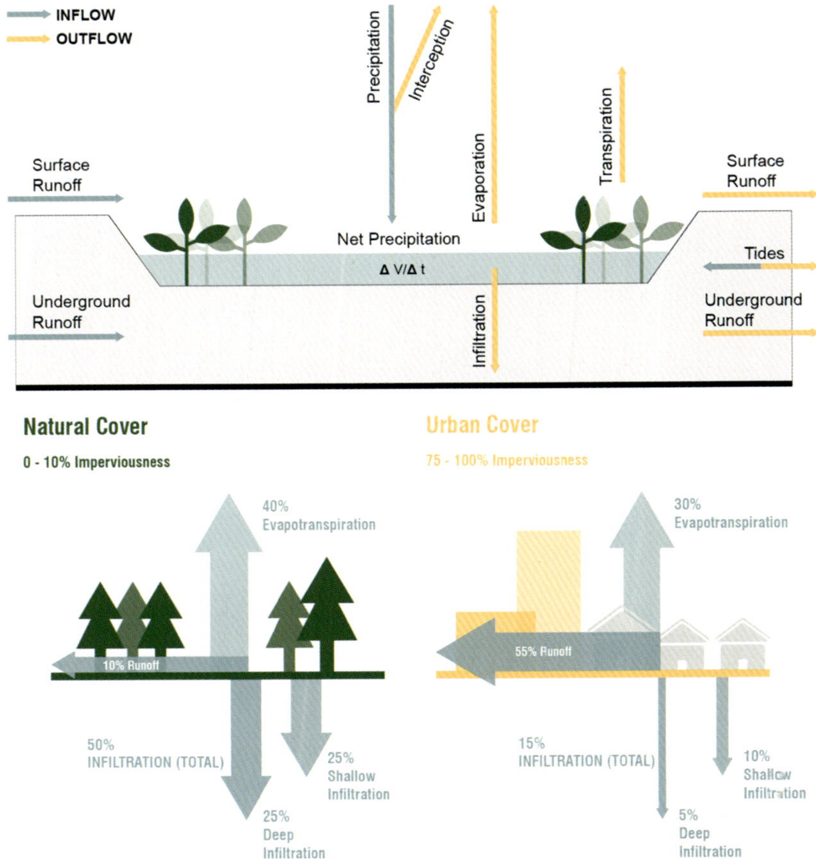

FIG.3 A sample of the information inside the knowledge products (guidelines and courses) designed to support the implementation of the Urban Wetland Law. Top: General model for the water balance of a wetland. Bottom: The impacts of urbanization in hydrological processes. Opposite page: Concept of drainage basin as a management scale for wetland conservation. Flavio Sciaraffia

and delineating wetlands, identifying threats and the benefits they provide for urban populations, and evaluating the ecological value of wetlands. Our team prepared this course and its materials over a period of six weeks in May 2021. More than half (#181 or 52 percent) of the country's municipalities subscribed and took the course, along with other regional level institutions. This proof-of-concept validated the usefulness of the monitoring system by providing practical insights in developing knowledge products. As part of the pilot, we also advised a selected group of municipalities in different aspects of law using the guidelines developed by us. Looking ahead, we expect that the yearly update of the indicator system enables a recurrent monitoring of municipal management, providing the inputs to adjust the MMA's skill-delivering program and support packages.

Lessons from the Implementation of the SDM in Chile

1. Landscape at the core of the strategy-driven model: In my practice we work under the assumption that the cultural project of humanity

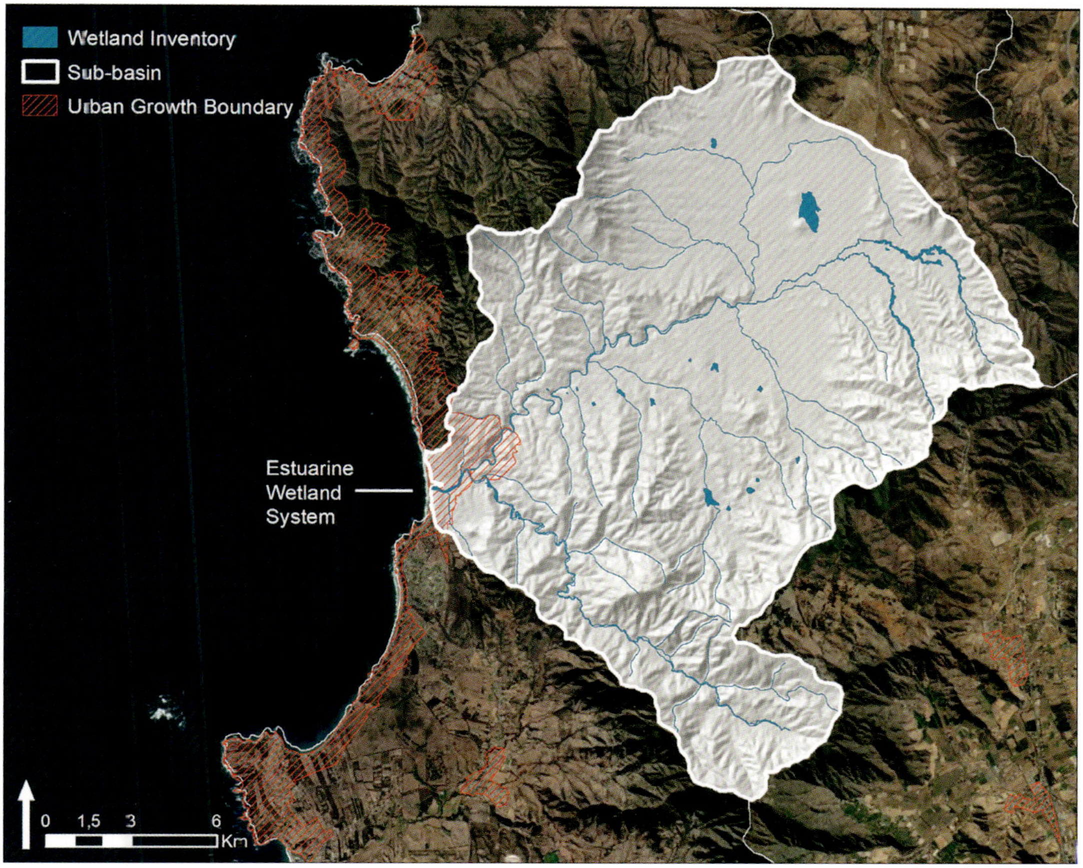

is enabled by a strong interdependence between societies and ecosystems, and that such entanglements are often disturbed by unsustainable landscape patterns of occupation and transformation. As such, our response focuses on articulating new landscapes—socio-environmental systems—where humans are agents of sustainability[12] as much as they are drivers of regressive landscape transformations. For this to happen, we believe it is critical to develop projects within a framework that allow explaining, evaluating, and/or changing the parameters and structures by which human societies give form to and modify landscapes. The SDM enables this for us. It allows exploring both the causes of problems and how to change regressive trajectories of landscape transformations.

2. Accountability and creativity in tandem: Scientific rigorousness and design coalesce in the SDM.[13] The former provides accountability, which is necessary for public decision-making; it has also given us credibility amid a professional space overcrowded with specialist practices. The latter provides us with flexibility and creativity to think of adaptable solutions and strategies.

3. Working for impacts at scale: As a principle of the SDM, working in a progression of scales is important because socio-environmental processes unfold at scales beyond a specific site. For us, and for most decision-makers in the public sector for that matter, the solution must be, unequivocally, at the scale(s) of the problem—both spatial and temporal. For designers, this means conceiving solutions under the concepts of strategy, scalability, flexibility, adaptation, and uncertainty. As a practice, we have decided to pull the strings that exert change at large landscape scales. Including other cases not discussed in this paper, the following projects stand out because of their impact:

- We defined the planning and sustainability criteria of the Urban Wetland Law under which over 460,000 hectares of urban wetlands could be integrated as green infrastructures in Chilean cities.
- We set up a template of municipal ordinance with actions, measures, and standards to guide municipalities in the management of their urban wetlands. This is national-level policy acting at a local scale.
- We provided a roadmap for the Ministry of Environment for an adequate rollout of the Urban Wetland Law by understanding the intricacies of municipal governance at national scale.
- We were responsible for developing a climate risk adaptation plan for the Metropolitan Region of Santiago, an area where 40 percent of the country's population live.

4. A viable model for design-led practices: The better part of two years passed before our model of practice was deemed attractive by the public sector—our main client. We feel the patience and persistence was worth it since it has allowed us to provide the much sought "expertise" with an expanded value proposition. So far, we have worked on diverse socio-environmental challenges across sectors, and at national, regional, and local scales. Projects on topics like climate change, biodiversity conservation, economic development, and policy making are part of our portfolio. Thus, we believe the SDM is a viable model for other design-led practices seeking similar objectives.

Endnotes

1. Science, technology, engineering, and mathematics.
2. André Botequilha Leitão and Jack Ahern, "Applying Landscape Ecological Concepts and Metrics in Sustainable Landscape Planning," *Landscape and Urban Planning* 59, no. 2 (January 2002): 66–70.
3. Jack Ahern, "Theories, Methods and Strategies for Sustainable Landscape Planning," in *From Landscape Research to Planning: Aspects of Integration, Education and Application*, ed. Tress et al. (Dordretch: Springer, 2006), 125–128.
4. The two previous references (Botequilha and Ahern, and J. Ahern) provide a summary of the main frameworks in the American tradition; in chronological order these are: (1) Landscape Planning by Julius Gy. Fabos (1985); (2) Framework Method for Landscape Planning by Carl Steinitz (1990); (3) Landscape Ecology by Richard T. T. Forman (1995); (4) Framework Method for Sustainable Landscape Ecological Planning by Jack Ahern, (1999); (5) Ecological Planning Model by Frederick Steiner (2000); (6) Sustainable Land Planning by André Botequilha and J. Ahern (2002).
5. Conservation Measures Partnership (CMP), *Open Standards for the Practice of Conservation Version 4.0.* (2020), 2-7, https://conservationstandards.org/download-cs/.
6. Jianguo Liu and William W. Taylor, "Coupling Landscape Ecology with Natural Resource Management: Paradigm shifts and New Approaches," in *Integrating Landscape Ecology into Natural Resource Management*, ed. Liu, Taylor. (Cambridge: Cambridge U. Press, 2002), 8–11.
7. As a contracting party of the Ramsar Convention, Chile adopted a similar definition for wetlands, which is generally wide: (...) "extensions of marshes, swamps, and peats, or surfaces covered with water, whether of natural or artificial regimes, permanent or temporaries, with water that is stagnant or flowing, fresh, brackish or salt, including extensions of marine water, the depth of which at low tide does not exceed six meters."
8. As a member of the Conference of The Parties (COP), Chile committed to the Aichi Biodiversity Goals of the Convention on Biological Diversity. Target 11 states that by 2020, at least 17 percent of terrestrial and inland water, and 10 percent of coastal and marine areas, should be conserved through protected areas. Chile has made significant efforts and even exceeded the original targets.
9. The National Wetland Inventory set up an updating protocol where different levels of governance, from local to regional, and national, can incorporate new information based on new wetland delimitation efforts, and corrections of existing ones. The inventory is updated yearly, with sometimes weekly and monthly updates in between.
10. Thomas Campagnaro, Tommaso Sitzia, Peter Bridgewater, Douglas Evans and Erle C. Ellis, "Half Earth or Whole Earth: What Can Natura 2000 Teach Us?" *BioScience* 69, no. 2 (February 2019): 119.
11. Chile has a Civil Law legal system, meaning that court decisions are based on the codified law and precedent is less important. For example, until 2020 the Environmental Evaluation System could not consider impacts on wetlands since this type of ecosystem wasn't codified in the text of the environmental law.
12. Jianguo Wu, "Landscape Ecology, Cross-Disciplinary, and Sustainability Science," *Landscape Ecology* 21 (2006): 3.
13. Joan I. Nassauer and Paul Opdam, "Design in Science: Extending the Landscape Ecology Paradigm," *Landscape Ecology* 23, no. 6 (2008): 636.

5.4

Learning Development by Doing

The Evolution of the Resilient Civic Design Collective

Lindsay Howe, Ben Mansfield

The built environment does not consist just of plans and material objects, but it reflects peoples' lives and livelihoods. Once constructed, it is exceedingly difficult to shift. Accordingly, identifying ethical, sustainable, and meaningful ways to develop the built environment is difficult, regardless of the context in which one operates. These challenges are particularly poignant in under-resourced areas like the townships of South Africa, where the apartheid system left deeply ingrained marks of inequality on both people and space. Deliberate strategies for the spatial segregation of races resulted in a legacy of peripheralization in places like Cape Town: monofunctional and impoverished settlements, in which the majority of the population resides, continue to characterize the landscape today.

These are the realities of many sites worldwide, and considering the urgency of climate change and resource scarcity, we cannot continue building according to the status-quo practices of previous generations. Many of us who studied fields like landscape architecture, architecture, or spatial planning feel a distinctive call to contribute to the kind of solutions that acknowledge the unevenness of the built environment, and the inherent unfairness of urban development.

To us, this meant shifting away from our original careers—Ben's, as a landscape architect, and Lindsay's, as an architect—into the field of "development," and towards much more socio-political thinking. Ben's first experience in South Africa was designing the urban agriculture concept, in response to food insecurity, for an informal settlement upgrading project by the ETH Zurich, entitled *Empower Shack*, beginning in 2011.[1] For Ben, the change from a design job to research-by-design endeavor was a conscious decision to explore how his experiences and values could best be directed to address global challenges of inequality and climate. At the same time, Lindsay was completing her master's thesis design for underutilized land in the former "buffer zones" of Johannesburg—areas that separated racially divided neighborhoods during apartheid—and planning to continue pursuing this topic for her dissertation. Our interests thus aligned, we began a decade-long (and counting) exchange

OPPOSITE PAGE South African post-apartheid spatial inequality. Johnny Miller, from his series "Unequal Scenes"

about the most meaningful way to apply our skill set. We concluded that we had to work with and for people, rather than imposing solutions from an exclusive, "expert" perspective—a long-dominant paradigm in the design professions.

Working in Cape Town provided an opportunity to test this theory. Through Ben's engagement with the community through the *Empower Shack* project, he was able to identify a need for small-scale agriculture and public spaces for people to meet. However, there was not a clear path forward for how to deliver this kind of project. He began to map underutilized plots of land around the area, and to mediate between people on the site and landowners of these plots, which was primarily the Western Cape Provincial Government (WCPG). He realized he was operating in a "terrain vague" of development, and would have to forge a new, innovative, and collaborative path forward.

Origins: Founding the Resilient Civic Design Collective

Thus, through passion and pragmatism, the Resilient Civic Design Collective (RCDC) was born. Rather than a traditional design office, with high fixed costs for personnel and facilities, RCDC embraced an agile, digital model of working. Based on any given project, an international "pool" of collective members could be engaged to collaborate with local, on-site partners. Conceived as a joint venture between South Africa and Switzerland, with the executive director located in Cape Town, RCDC was able to channel funding from well-resourced areas, like Zurich, towards local development efforts, capacity building, and knowledge transfer. RCDC aimed to be actively postcolonial in this regard—explicitly contesting the apartheid legacy in space, and in the structure of the organization itself.[2] It was not enough to deliver high-quality projects, we thought. We needed to base anything we did on listening, through an intensive engagement process, aiming for long-term impact and stakeholder empowerment. The ultimate goal was to remove ourselves as much as possible from the project objectives and

FIG.1 Intlanganiso school children critiquing Lukhanyo Hub designs produced by University of Cape Town, Department of Architecture; Simulated Studio Design Studio exhibition in 2017. Jeremy Jones, Director

FIG.2 Intlanganiso school children are learning about farming at the Lukhanyo Hub. Ben Mansfield

to establish a framework through participation that could continue far beyond the scope of a single project.

Ben began to concentrate his efforts on the site of the Intlanganiso Secondary School, by planning a center for urban agriculture and training as a social enterprise entitled Lukhanyo Hub. He raised funding and conceived a model for a neighborhood center on the unused land at the school in 2013. Our learning-by-doing process involves interviewing people, discussing their needs, and arranging events loosely following ethnographic research methods combined with South African engagement experts, such as 1:1 Agency of Engagement, Urban Works, and spatial planners from the City of Cape Town Spatial Planners.[3] Thus, the idea for "community gardening" and a hub for the school and the surrounding neighborhood was the result of incremental engagement with community leaders, teachers, school employees, local residents, government employees, and academic partnerships—such as studio design semesters with University of Cape Town architecture and urban planning students [FIG. 1].

Funding was raised from philanthropy, social corporate investment, government grants, and professional pro bono work. As a pilot project, a vegetable garden was built, and in parallel, an education and training program called the Lukhanyo Urban Farming Network (LUFN) was established to allow local residents to engage with others conducting urban agriculture throughout the surrounding area [FIG. 2–3].

FIG.3 Lukhanyo Hub, Phase 3: Visualization illustrating hub building and urban farming activities. Jack Carter Architects, London, UK

The RCDCollective Business Model

From this initial endeavor, RCDC developed into a social enterprise company registered in South Africa. Our stated mission was to leverage the complexity of the urban environment to generate sustainable, resilient developments with and for communities. Resilience, to us, meant working collectively to develop socially and environmentally responsive programming and infrastructure, which must also be sustained through a viable economic model. RCDC projects were thus informed by intensive and continuous engagement with the entire spectrum of stakeholders we could identify through empirical research.

The collective comprised a wide range of professionals, from social scientists and project managers to built-environment practitioners, developers, and environmental management specialists. We found each other through personal networks, projects, and shared frustrations with the current inequities and unsustainable building and planning practices. Each collective member from around the world found that when development went wrong, it had similar pitfalls—primarily, a reliance on "top-down" master plans that failed to incorporate the existing built environment and engage with an area's residents, resulting in superficial solutions rather than adaptive, sustainable projects. We each had our own sets of tools and approaches, drawing from collective members as needed.

Most of the contributions by us and our pool were conducted pro bono, for passion's sake or as a form of corporate social responsibility, because the work has consistently been rewarding. Funding was typically raised on a project basis, directly from clients. Due to low fixed overheads, it was possible to sustain this model for several years, from 2015–2020.

Evolving Our Mission and Methods: From RCDC to Integrated Sustainable Development Foundation

Our methodology is predicated upon facilitation—not dictation—and an intensive, lasting engagement process with stakeholders. A certain degree of "incrementalism" is key to this kind of development: creating frameworks that enable gradual, small changes, which can continually respond to the changing realities present on the ground. Resilience and sustainability mean creating systems that are flexible enough to meet the shifting needs of people and robust enough to persist in the face of new, unforeseen challenges such as climate change. This marks a departure from conventional, socially-oriented development projects. Many of these focus on the production of a building rather than analyzing the strategies people use to navigate their environment, and examining the successful elements that generate incremental but meaningful changes over time.

"Massive Small" Change

RCDC shared a philosophy—specifically, that many such small moments can eventually amount to a transformative movement—with the company Massive Small. Founded by urban design and development expert Kelvin Campbell and landscape architect and sustainability expert Andrew Campbell, Massive Small advocates for novel, democratic forms of sustainable development. Massive Small's philosophy describes how using simple structuring rules for urban development, based on the understanding of the city as a complex system, allows government institutions and people to make places that can better respond to current and future challenges. A well-managed, transparent, and synergistic collaboration between all sectors—civic, public, academic, not-for-profit, private—is needed, according to Massive Small, if we are to create healthy conditions for people, investors, and society as a whole.

Thus, RCDC and Massive Small aligned particularly around the idea that bottom-up initiatives can actually enable top-down policy change, and working at this interstice poses our best chance to create thriving cities. In 2021, Ben and Massive Small are developing the platform for formal collaboration to increase the visibility and impact of our mutual interests, joining our respective projects, research, and advocacy work. This collaboration of the Campbells' theoretical platform with Ben's concrete project work and the collective thus also marks the transformation of both initiatives into a new model of practice.

Integrated Sustainable Development Foundation

A nonprofit entity Integrated Sustainable Development (ISD), overseen by a highly experienced Chairman, Professor Stefan Allesch-Taylor and board with members from Africa and Europe, will fundraise and manage the appointment of local and international entities to deliver projects aligned to its focus areas. ISD will work closely with all sectors, including government agencies, and partner with academic institutions to facilitate the development of inclusive, resilient, and sustainable urban developments in under-resourced areas.

Lukanyo Hub: Our Flagship Project

An example of RCDC work that reflects these modes of thought and practice is the aforementioned Lukhanyo Hub project in the township of Khayelitsha. Located approximately 25 kilometers southeast of downtown Cape Town, Khayelitsha is one of South Africa's largest and fastest growing townships [FIG. 4]. Khayelitsha, meaning "new home" in isiXhosa, was formally established in 1985 as a Black neighborhood by the apartheid government, and experienced rapid urbanization after the first democratic elections in 1994.[4] Residents of the township have limited access to schools and skills development. Beyond extensive housing backlogs, such that 70 percent of the local population lives in self-constructed shacks, there is a lack of utilities, sanitary facilities, and access to clean running water as well

as transportation. The situation is exacerbated by the fact that youths are a disproportionately large segment of the population: according to Statistics South Africa's 2011 census, fewer than seven percent of its residents are over 50 years old, while 40 percent of its residents are under 19 years old.[5]

Land in South African townships is notoriously fraught with challenges related to service delivery, pressures of rapid urbanization, and limited socioeconomic development. However, an untapped potential is the underutilized land that resulted from the lack of services that were provided for educational facilities in Black areas under the apartheid regime.[6] While comparable education spaces in white areas included sport facilities and programs like libraries and science labs, this land was often simply left barren in Black or Colored neighborhoods. Today, this government-owned land has great potential to provide space for civic and community functions.

FIG.4 The site of the Lukhanyo Hub in Khayelitsha before the construction of the first project phase. Mike Bell, R&L Architects, Cape Town, South Africa

FIG.5 The expanding Lukhanyo Hub after the implementation of high-quality sports facilities. Mike Bell, R&L Architects, Cape Town, South Africa

Envisioning Lukhanyo Hub

The idea for the Lukhanyo Hub originated when multiple actors from the public, private, and institutional sectors began to plan a community space in Khayelitsha on land owned by the Western Cape Education Department (WCED). Ben established the non-profit company *Lukhanyo Hub NPC* (LH

NPC) to deliver a basic site design, implement sports and recreation facilities, construct a micro-farm and training center, and identify the process to evolve their existing facilities into a fully integrated community hub. The "hub" concept revolves around creating a self-sustaining center, aiming to empower the local community through education and skills training.

Following the initial success of the urban agriculture project, further cycles of needs analysis were conducted. Academics were interviewed in order to learn from similar projects and to utilize theoretical frameworks about collaborative and communicative planning.[7] The network of government departments expanded in order to align with and later inform public policy. A spatial planner for the Khayelitsha district and eventually the Provincial Minister for Human Settlements even approached the project and offered to partner with the team, to explore options for unlocking the potential of unused government land for public benefit, in particular as a response to issues of food security, improving education and health outcomes, and creating safer public space—a critical problem in townships like Khayelitsha.

The engagement and analysis concluded in a vision for Lukhanyo Hub, envisioning it as a neighborhood hub addressing the needs of the school and surrounding neighborhood residents with space for sports, educational and training facilities, public health programs, and micro-enterprises. The programs, the physical infrastructure for them, as well as an economic model have since been developed [FIG. 5]. This "infrastructure" is conceived as a modular concept in which high-quality components can be built incrementally, allowing expansion when conditions (and budgets) allow. The construction budget (around 700,000 USD) for the high-quality sports facilities was secured from a government innovation fund through facilitation from Ben together with the school principal. The hub's on-site manager, Jeremy Jones, actively facilitates developments supporting the school principal and liaising with government and neighbourhood residents.

"Upscaling" the Hub Into a Pilot Project for Replication

The cross-sectoral partnerships established during this initial phase between the school management, government departments, academics, NGOs, and local community leaders provided a robust foundation for several technological innovations and economic models that are now being "upscaled." For example, after implementing the urban agriculture component, the landscape architecture firm OKRA—operating pro bono as well as with funding from the Dutch government for international development work—began collaborating with the local NGO Isidima and other RCDC collective pool members on improved water resilience systems for the site. Working together, the team designed a system [FIG. 6] that ensured water supply for the school and urban agriculture—even during the drought conditions rapidly becoming the new normal for Cape Town—and reduced their monthly operational costs sixfold. The money saved was utilized, among other purposes, to employ a full-time plumber for system maintenance. We now aim to replicate this water resilience technology throughout Khayelitsha, in other townships areas across Cape Town, and beyond [FIG. 7].

RCDC's work on Lukhanyo Hub was formally recognized by the WCPG, when it was designated an official pilot project for designing underutilized parcels of land at schools across the province. It was even embedded into planning policy, as case study analysis of the project was included in the WCPG's official development guide, The Living Cape Framework.[8] The WCPG also established a multi-departmental task team to support the further development of the project. In conclusion, Lukhanyo Hub illustrates how Massive Small principles can be applied by linking bottom-up needs analysis with top-down policymaking. Bringing the full identified range of stakeholders together in engagement sessions was the heart of RCDC's mission, values, and methodology, and it will continue to drive our future as ISD. Our pipeline of live projects include: a neighborhood center in Lamu, Kenya working with Kids in Motion Foundation; developing the testing and development of incon.ai, an AI-construction tool to improve construction quality, develop

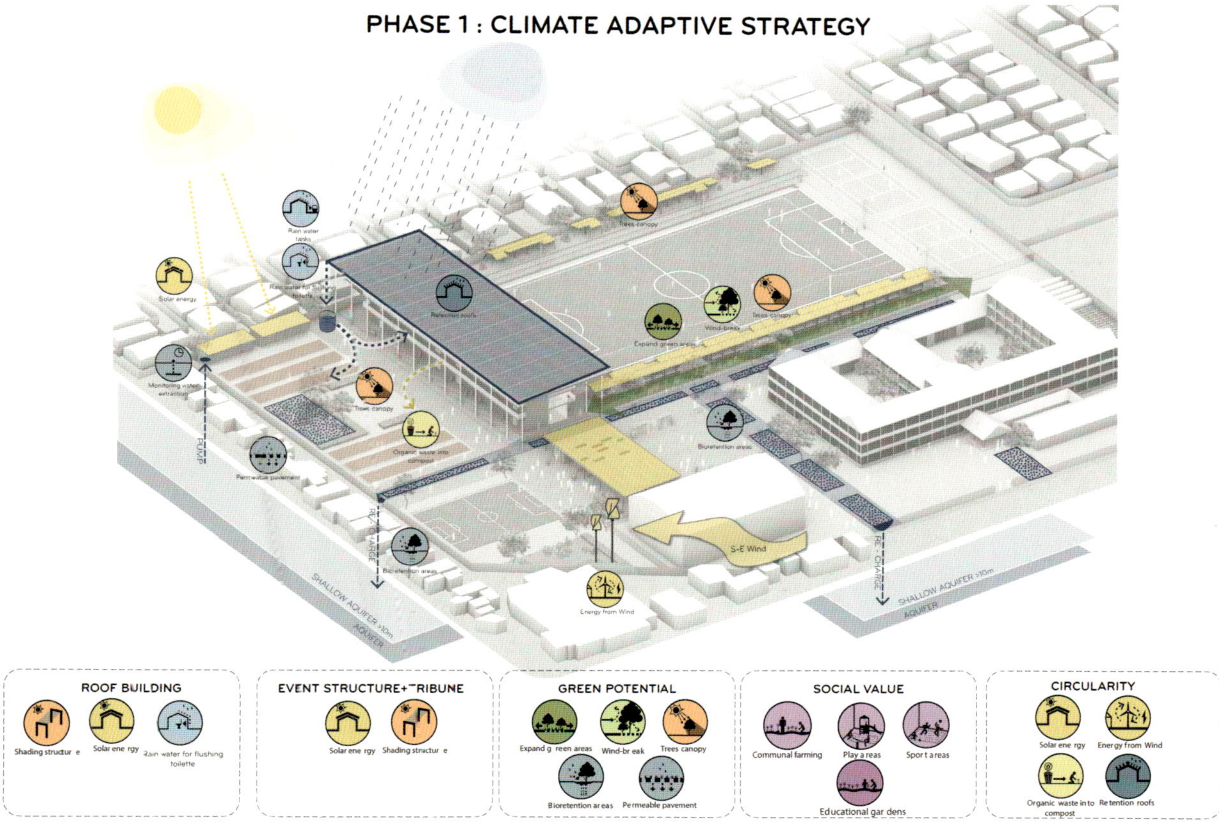

skills and increase site safety in under-resourced areas, created by Instructive Construction AG, an ETH Zurich spin-off company; a vision and feasibility study for a site in Lusaka, Zambia; a film project focused on the utilization of unused land at schools; developing a township urban-farm-based food brand; C40 Resilient Cities – South Africa competition entry submitted; implementation of an early childhood and training center at Lukhanyo Hub; developing a regenerative agriculture farm as part of an urban development in Kenya.

Looking Forward Together

The disruption caused by future climate change and rapid urbanisation in Africa—most affecting the vulnerable in society—can be mitigated through collaborative design that prioritizes people and environmental stewardship. We believe we can change the way we make cities by following several key concepts: (1) grounding our work in inclusion and accountability; (2) targeting adaptivity of economy, environment, and society; (3) promoting urban resilience in the form of a polycentric model for neighborhood development; and (4) pioneering innovative technologies.

FIG.6 Application of the Climate Adaptation Toolkit at Lukhanyo Hub, developed by OKRA Landscape Architects. OKRA Landscape Architects, Utrecht, Netherlands

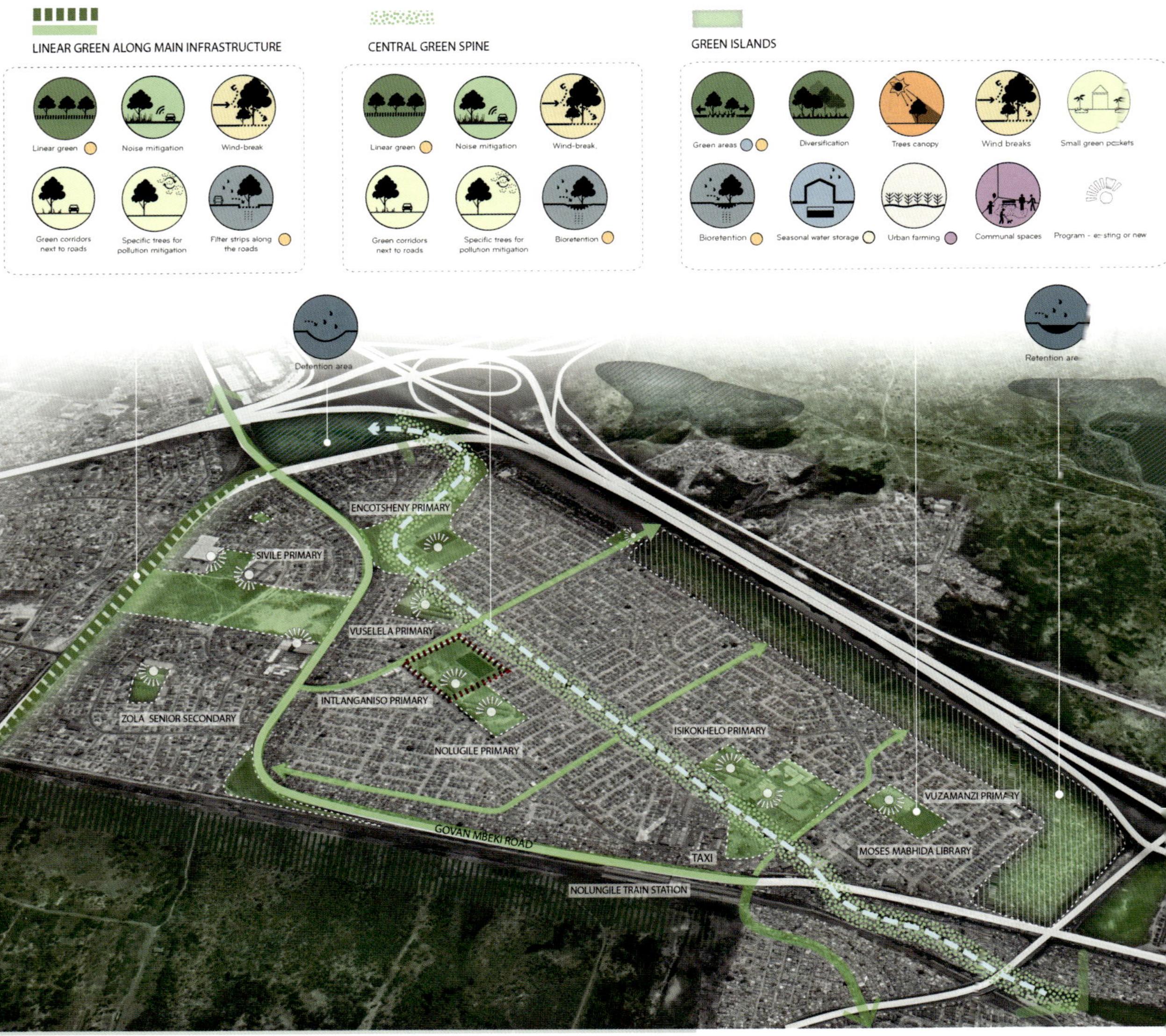

FIG.7 Proposal for a green structure in Khayelitsha applying OKRA's Climate Adaptivity toolkit on a larger scale. OKRA Landscape Architects, Utrecht, Netherlands

In contexts like South Africa, development projects have typically been "imposed" onto underprivileged populations without a two-way dialogue about their needs and expectations. Our process, instead, relies on working with local leadership to identify and empower key voices within a target neighborhood, informing our work through all stages, from program conception to design development and construction implementation. This is done through workshops between stakeholders throughout the development process, allowing for continuous feedback to all impacted parties. The process also allows the future users to shape outcomes according to their specific needs, increasing the chance our projects have to make a lasting, positive impact.

The entire history of our work in South Africa and beyond has been a process of learning by doing, of sharing, of listening and changing. As we are presented with new challenges, we must be prepared to meet them with new practices and technologies, by building on the lasting relationships we forge through mutual trust and benefit. This idea of incremental, but continual, progress has shaped RCDC since its onset, and will continue to drive our future models of practice.

Endnotes

1. Empower Shack was a research-based project conducted by the ETH Zurich's *Urban-Think Tank*, focused on conceptualizing solutions to improve living conditions in Cape Town's "informal settlements." This term typically refers to areas in which shack dwellings have been constructed by people themselves, often upon land where the occupants have no limited or no legal tenure. See: Ananya Roy, "Urban Informality: Toward an Epistemology of Planning," *Journal of the American Planning Association*, Vol. 71, No. 2 (2005): 147–158.
2. For an introduction to the debates about postcolonialism that shaped the discourse in geography and built environment studies, see: Brenda SA Yeoh, "Postcolonial Cities," *Progress in Human Geography*, Vol. 25, No. 3 (2001): 456–468. See also: Gillian Hart, "Geography and development: development/s beyond neoliberalism? Power, culture, political economy," *Progress in Human Geography*, Vol. 26, No. 6 (2002): 812–822.
3. Uwe Flick, *An Introduction to Qualitative Research* (London: Sage, 2009).
4. Gail Super, "Violence and Democracy in Khayelitsha. Governing Crime through the 'Community'," *Stability: International Journal of Security & Development*, Vol. 4, No. 1 (2015): 1–20.
5. For detailed current population statistics, see Table 13 in: Nesbert Zinyakatira, "Population Data," Western Cape Government Department of Health, WCG Circular H 102/2020 (2020): 19. Available online: https://www.westerncape.gov.za/assets/departments/health/h_102_2020_covid-19_population_data.pdf
6. For maps of the underutilized spaces identified and the location of Lukhanyo Hub, see: Edgar Pieterse, Pippa Green, Bella Knemeyer, Alison Pulker and Alma Viviers, *The Integration Syndicate: Shifting Cape Town's Socio-Spatial Debate* (Cape Town: African Centre for Cities, 2018): 136–143.
7. For a basic introduction to collaborative planning, see: Heather Campbell and Robert Marshall, "Ethical Frameworks and Planning Theory," *International Journal of Urban and Regional Research,* Vol. 23, No. 3 (1999): 464–478 and Vanessa Watson, "Deep Difference: Diversity, Planning and Ethics," *Planning Theory*, Vol. 5, No. 1 (2006): 31–50.
8. The Living Cape Framework is a document outlining a proposal for how to make existing human settlements more equitable and resilient. See: Zoleka Jacobs, "The Living Cape: A Human Settlements Framework," Western Cape Government Department of Human Settlements, 3. Available online: https://www.westerncape.gov.za/general-publication/living-cape-human-settlements-framework

5.5

Collaborative and Strategic Approaches to Build Urban Resilience in India

Sourav Kumar Biswas, Praveen Raj, Shreya Krishnan, Manushi Ashok Jain, Balaji Balaganesan, Suriya KP, Sujhatha Arulkumar, Aditi Subramanian, Logeshwaran Subramanian, Pankti Sanganee (Sponge Collaborative)

Sponge Collaborative is a collective of young professionals working between Boston, Bengaluru, Chennai, and Delhi to produce and test new models of resilient urban development. Our team was built upon the International Landscape Collaborative's (ILC) theoretical agenda of the landscape approach.[1] The landscape approach is a guiding principle to navigate complex socio-ecological systems[2] and inform strategies for designed interventions at various scales that can reconcile socio-economic needs with environmental justice and global sustainability. We recognize the need to contextualize the landscape approach in diverse cultures and produce relevant case studies grounded in the experience of developing economies that face the greatest risks from climate change.[3] The same places stand to benefit the most from nature-based solutions as a cost-effective and resilient approach towards climate adaptation and service delivery by leveraging landscape systems. To respond to this challenge and opportunity, we have formed a research-oriented practice in India that derives insights through practice while learning from and building ILC's research agenda. This essay compiles reflections from our foray into India's urban planning discourse through early successes in Chennai and Kochi since its founding in 2018.

Through team collaborations across time zones and local stakeholder engagement, the Sponge Collaborative has developed visions and frameworks for the coastal cities of Chennai and Kochi. We promote the idea of the framework rather than masterplans to guide the implementation of infrastructure in a strategic manner to build resilient urban systems over time. Through publications and presentations, the collaborative also disseminates the idea of a multi-scalar approach that links site-scale interventions to basin-wide resilience. Using our experience, we reflect upon the unique political challenges and propose alternate institutional collaborations that can facilitate the mainstreaming of the landscape approach in urban water management and metropolitan infrastructure planning.

OPPOSITE PAGE Aerial photograph of the Karikkamuri neighborhood in Kochi, Kerala, India. Entekochi Urban Design competition by GiZ India, 2020

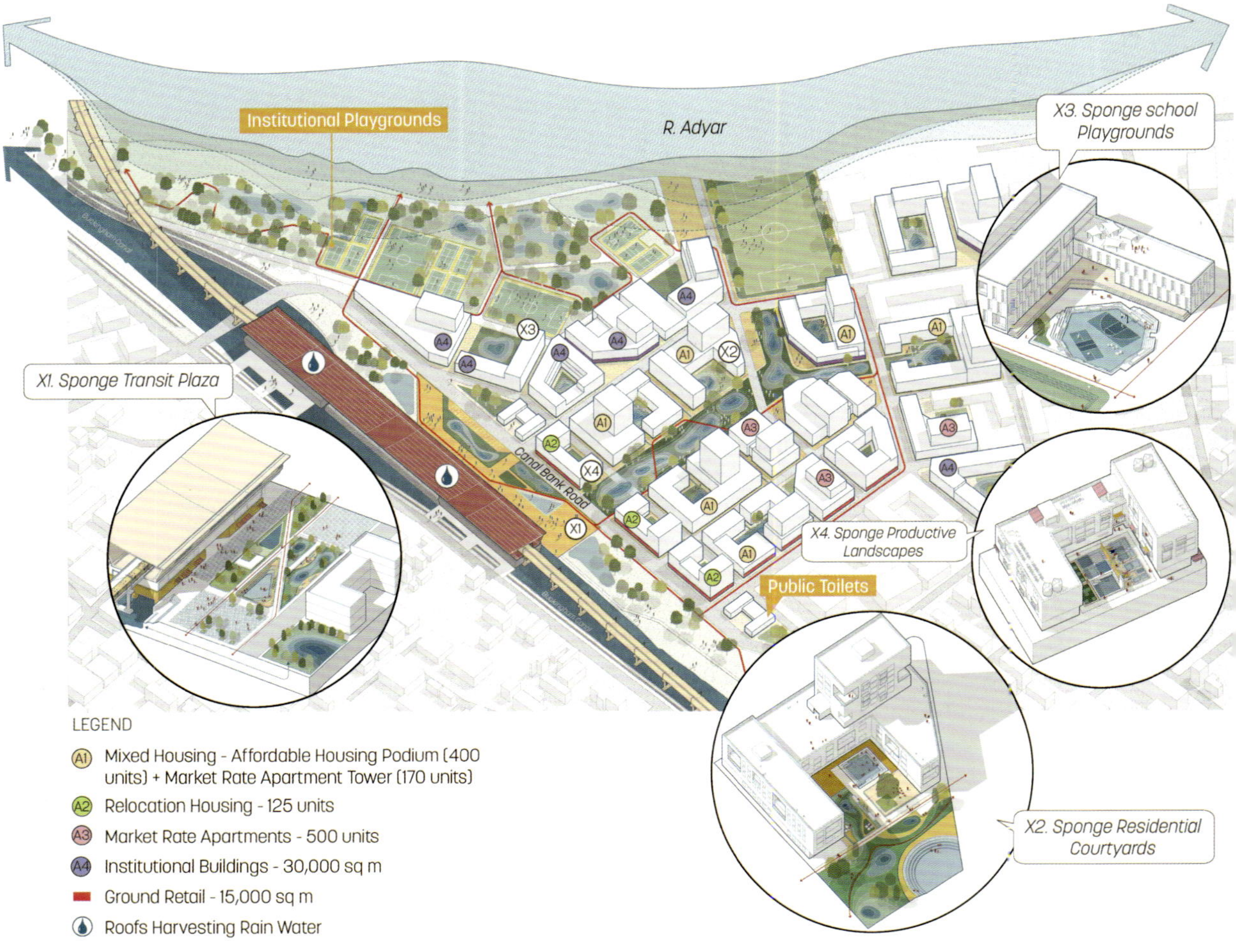

FIG. 1 Vision for a transit-oriented development with integrated blue-green infrastructure submitted by Sponge Collaborative for the Eyes on the Canal Competition organized by GIZ under the "Cities Fit for Climate Change" initiative. Sponge Collaborative, Eyes on the Canal competition entry, 2018

The spark that catalyzed the formation of Sponge Collaborative was an open ideas competition to rejuvenate part of the Buckingham Canal and its adjoining urban neighborhoods in Chennai, India. The Eyes on the Canal competition was organized in 2018 by Deutsche Gesellschaft für Internationale Zusammenarbeit (GIZ)—an international development agency affiliated with the German government focused on technical capacity building. Two colleagues at Sasaki—Sourav Kumar Biswas, a landscape planner and ILC founding member, and Praveen Raj, an urban designer with roots in Chennai—saw an opportunity to inject new ideas to the urban planning discourse in India. In their winning competition entry, the five-member team including three young architects from Chennai promoted integrated planning and water-sensitive urban design principles [FIG. 1]. An important differentiating factor in our proposal was a vision for the canal that spoke to the larger issues facing the region and could be scaled up to turn the urbanized river basins into "Sponge Basins." Our vision to build the resilience and livability of the Buckingham Canal site considered the health of the larger Adyar River basin—one of five river basins within the Chennai metropolitan area.

The Sponge Collaborative grew from five to ten members in 2020, when we won another open design competition to improve Kochi's Mullassery Canal precinct in an integrated manner. The Entekochi Urban Design Competition was also organized by GIZ under the Climate Smart Cities initiative. We used this competition to connect an integrated urban development vision not just to land-water linkages but mobility systems and community solid-waste management. The next stage of both competitions allowed us to engage several technical, community, and political stakeholders while devising pilot projects for implementation [FIG. 2]. In the following sections we describe the nature of our interactions and lessons for professional engagement from Chennai and Kochi.

FIG. 2 Following our competition win, the Sponge Collaborative team presented the Sponge Framework and pilot projects to various stakeholders in Kochi including the mayor, district collector, municipal engineers, and local community representatives. Sponge Collaborative

The Need for Nature-Based Solutions and Blue-Green Infrastructure in India

Chennai and Kochi are one of 52 urban regions in India with a population of greater than one million that are currently going through unprecedented expansion and rapid urbanization. This has created new ecological conditions that place greater environmental demands on land-water resources in both cities. Existing institutional frameworks and planning protocols are ill-equipped to formulate development patterns that can achieve sustainable development goals in the face of rapid change and increasing climate-change-induced risks from drought and flooding.

The landscape approach to urban infrastructure brings a holistic-systems view to the design, planning, and implementation of stormwater, flood-mitigation, and mobility infrastructure. The landscape approach specifically leverages green-blue systems like urban forests, water bodies, riparian, and coastal areas as nature-based solutions to flood-mitigation and water-resource management. However, the dominant paradigm of water-resource management in Indian cities like Chennai and Kochi exclusively relies entirely upon a historic network of gray infrastructure such as channels, culverts, and canals. As urban landscapes are concretized and cloudbursts—i.e. large amounts of rain falling in a short amount of time—become more common, the designed capacity of the gray-infrastructure network is no longer sufficient and fails regularly during the monsoons.

We recognize that the stormwater and drainage sector represents a sizable portion of central government development schemes and municipal budget allocations in contrast to sectors like parks and public spaces. While the sectoral interest for these funds is purely towards flood mitigation, we believe there is an opportunity to tap into this stream to design and build blue-green stormwater infrastructure that achieves this purpose while also improving the resilience and livability of urban areas. Given the strong interest in infrastructure by India's policymakers, bureaucrats, and politicians, the Sponge Collaborative uses design thinking and strategic planning to devise multi-functional infrastructural typologies that unlock multiple co-benefits. Funding allocated for the stormwater and drainage sector is then unlocked to make a positive impact on public health, common spaces, and urban ecology.

Sponge Collaborative makes the case for strategic planning in Indian city-regions where blue-green infrastructure and nature-based solutions can bring about multiple co-benefits for local communities and stakeholders while greatly reducing the need for expensive gray infrastructure investments. This is particularly relevant in emerging cities or peri-urban areas that have the natural capital to support nature-based solutions at scale and do not have the technical or fiscal capacity to implement and maintain gray infrastructure solutions like centralized sewage treatment plants and extensive stormwater networks.

In both Chennai and Kochi, we engage with an ecosystem of stakeholders consisting primarily of municipal engineers, city or district-level bureaucrats, and city-level elected representatives. Urban development in India has traditionally been delivered by experts who are rooted in the engineering disciplines, distinct from the social science and spatial design spheres, as a result of colonial legacies of knowledge production and dissemination. Consequently, there is a lack of multidisciplinary perspectives and staffing in municipal governments across India. The municipal corporations of Chennai and Kochi, for example, which are responsible for approving development permits, have no urban planning or urban design professionals on their staff. This means that infrastructure investment and phasing decisions are often made by engineers and bureaucrats without consulting urban planning or landscape professionals.[4] Against this background, our presentations were targeted at the municipal engineers of the Chennai and Kochi Municipal Corporation, with the goal of explaining a landscape approach and how it differs from the existing, technocratic approaches to infrastructure delivery.

Making the Case for Sponge Basins in Chennai

Chennai is a rapidly growing megacity and metropolitan region with a population of around 10 million. For the past few years, Chennai has faced a recurring cycle of floods and droughts that culminated in the severe water crisis of 2018. However, this cycle was set in motion over the past two decades as Chennai's built-up area more than doubled—sprawling over farmlands, forest, wetlands, and low-lying areas. The region is home to hundreds of water bodies and porous landscapes that were uniquely adapted to receive heavy monsoon rains and help water flow into the rivers and oceans via streams or percolate into the aquifer. As urban development indiscriminately concreted over these landscapes and waterways, the

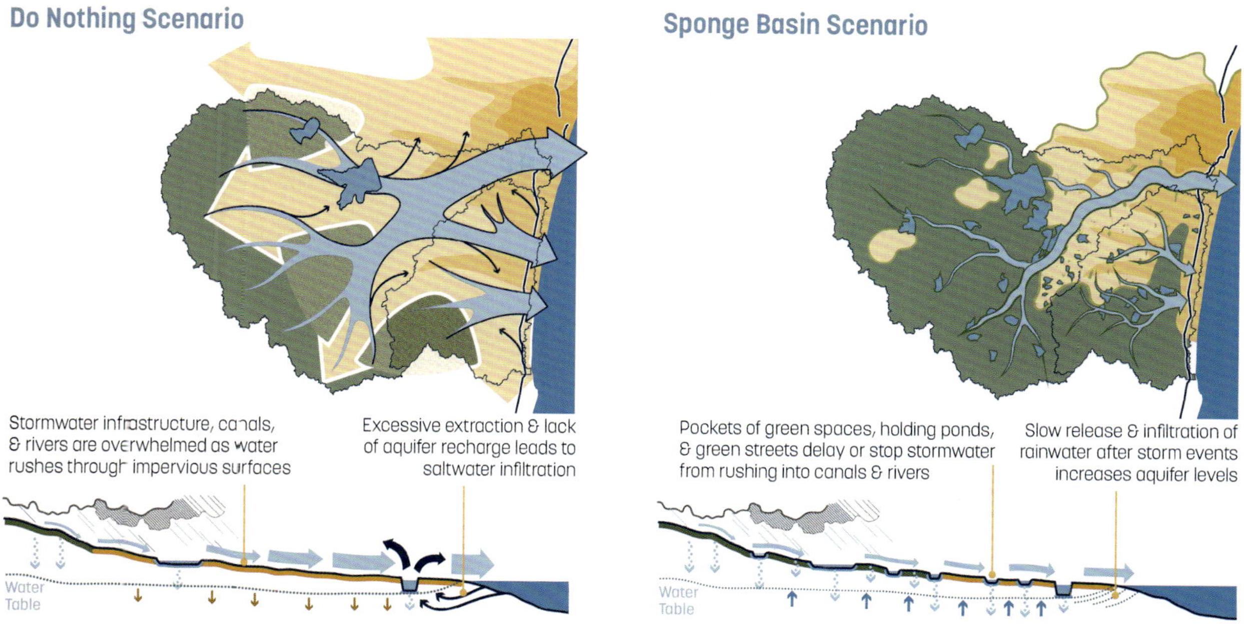

imperviousness of urban-land cover generated more runoff from rainfall that easily overwhelmed Chennai's outdated stormwater systems, channelized rivers, and canals. Today, Chennai is facing exponentially increasing risks from drought and flood as climate change makes rainfall more erratic and cloudbursts more common [FIG. 3].

Our vision for the canal positioned the protection of the region's green-blue system against rampant development as a priority and then illustrated a scalable network of blue-green infrastructure interventions that replicated the hydrological functions of natural systems within a constrained urban fabric. The Sponge Basin concept integrates strategic basin planning with nature-based solutions principles of *"protect"* (functioning natural ecosystems like wetlands and forests), *"restore"* (degrading ecosystems like polluted water bodies), *"enhance"* (ecosystems like riparian or coastal edges facing erosion), and *"construct"* (hybrid infrastructure that replicate natural functions).

During our presentations to municipal representatives, we stressed upon improving technical and strategic capacity to cultivate urban resilience incrementally through coordinated investments towards blue-green systems. While this approach is more intuitive to designers, planners and development professionals, the pathway to integrate these principles into the practice of planning and infrastructure investments was not apparent to Chennai's municipal engineers and implementation agencies. To address this gap, we published *The Sponge Handbook: Chennai*[5] specifically to convince a technocratic audience and inspire the next generation of planners in India. The handbook is a comprehensive and visual catalog of blue-green infrastructure embedded within a planning

FIG. 3 Unmanaged urban sprawl reduces the ability of landscapes to mitigate flooding during cloudbursts. These drawings contextualize the project site within the larger basin and highlights the challenge of building basin-wide resilience that is rapidly concretizing. Sponge Collaborative, Sponge Handbook: Chennai, GIZ India, 2019

and implementation guide for the Indian context. This document was made freely available on the ILC website and has been digitally viewed and downloaded thousands of times and presented at various academic and institutional forums. The handbook is our Collaborative's first prototype to help mainstream nature-based solutions in flood mitigation and stormwater management and to promote a strategic framework approach for urban planning in India.

At a strategic level, cities need to supplement existing gray infrastructure by leveraging existing blue-green systems like wetlands, ponds, parks, and urban forests and constructing hybrid blue-green infrastructure that mimics the hydrological function of natural systems within urban streets and open spaces. The handbook illustrated how institutions from regional to local scales could implement this approach inspired by China's Sponge City Program, Singapore's ABC Water Programme, and Copenhagen's Cloudburst Management Plan.[6]

In Chennai, we came across multiple state government ministries who are divided along sectoral silos but have a role to play in realizing the principles of "Sponge Basins." We found planning or sectoral bodies rarely examine infrastructure investments within their respective basins. This led us to draw a stakeholder matrix that recognizes the multi-scalar jurisdictions required to manage land-water resources in a holistic manner and describes alliances between institutions and civil society needed to guide development at the regional scale and implement blue-green infrastructure within wards—the smallest urban administrative units.[7]

Finally, we curated compelling visuals and sequential diagrams to explain how small, short-term projects can be woven into the urban fabric over time to create a resilient blue-green network of infrastructure—or what we called "Sponge Network"—at the neighborhood scale. We embedded the Sponge Network within a strategic framework so infrastructure investments can be coupled with placemaking, housing, and transit to create livable neighborhoods that are more resilient to flooding. All our visions were strategically phased within a timeline of investments towards buildings, streets, open spaces, and water bodies that improved the public realm but functioned as a resilient network during cloudbursts.

Building a Sponge Infrastructure in Kochi

We refined our multi-sectoral approach in Kochi where we had more success in getting stakeholder buy-in and moving towards implementable pilot projects. Our winning competition entry presented a clear narrative about the multi-sectoral benefits of nature-based solutions, and then highlighted well-being as a co-benefit by focusing on a three-pronged framework plan and toolkit for ecology, mobility, and community [FIG. 4].

The Kochi metropolitan area is home to an estimated three million people living on low-lying land with calm backwaters, networked canals, and rich biodiversity. Over the last couple decades, Kochi and its adjoining areas have seen tremendous growth at the expense of its lush green cover and the concretization of its natural waterways. In 2018, Kochi experienced historic levels of flooding with the competition project site regularly flooding every monsoon. Following our competition win, we engaged with the Mayor of the Kochi Municipal Corporation (the elected head of the city government), the High Court (the top judicial authority in the state), and the District Collector (the top bureaucrat in the district administration). Flood mitigation was a top priority for all government stakeholders in Kochi. We used this to our advantage by proposing a "Sponge Framework" for the Mullassery Canal precinct building off their preliminary awareness of and enthusiasm for the Sponge City Initiative in China. We presented our approach to decision-makers as being a binary between "the landscape approach to stormwater management," vs. "the existing gray infrastructure approach," thus emphasizing the transformational potential for blue-green infrastructure and positioning Kochi as being at the forefront of innovation. While there were a few dissenting voices from key government departments in charge of flood mitigation and disaster management, which continues to focus on engineering-heavy solutions such as canal dredging and gray-infrastructure solutions, we were able to gain successful buy-in from critical stakeholders such as the Mayor and District Collector.

The Sponge Framework offers a feasible and relatively low-cost alternative for flood mitigation with strategic pilot projects that was packaged in the form of a detailed project report to the High Court on the Mayor's recommendation [FIG. 5]. The Court will be evaluating the cost-benefits of our blue-green-infrastructure proposal to a gray-infrastructure engineering proposal. In our drawings and report narrative, we firstly stressed the resilience of a stormwater-management approach that opens multiple pathways for runoff via a network of sponge streets and open spaces that delay or store rainwater during cloudbursts. Secondly, we highlighted the co-benefits that well-designed streets and open spaces, built within a holistic framework, bring in terms of biodiversity, livelihoods, neighborhood vitality, community safety, and sustainable mobility. In doing so, we hope to secure the political will and unlock funding to implement what could be India's most comprehensively integrated blue-green streetscape and the first blue-green streetscape in south India.[8]

Lessons From Our Engagement for Alternative Models of Practice

Sponge Collaborative is driven by the belief that designers and planners bring valuable insights and solutions to India's manifold urban challenges. We are also driven by our desire to drive strategic investments that can

ADAPT
Landscape Toolkits

	Protect	Restore	Enhance	Construct
Green Systems	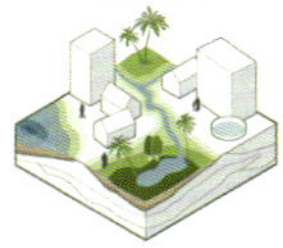 L-A1 Urban Forests/ Groves/Tree Mapping	 L-B1 Soils/Degraded forests	 L-C1 Parks/Maidans	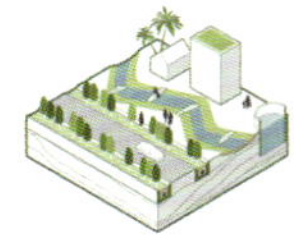 L-D1 Green roofs/ Constructed wetlands
Surface Water	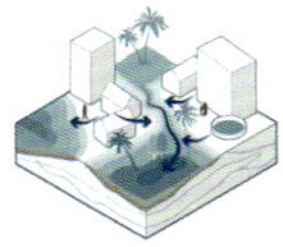 L-A2 Lakes/Water bodies/ Monitoring	 L-B2 Canal day-streaming/ Edge restoration	 L-C2 Coastal edge against erosion	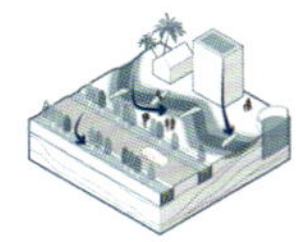 L-D2 Bioswales/Curbside rain gardens
Ground Water	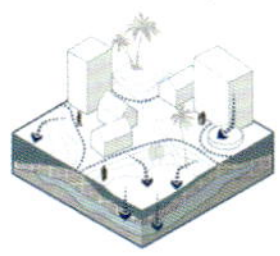 L-A3 Aquifer recharge zones/Aquifer Mapping	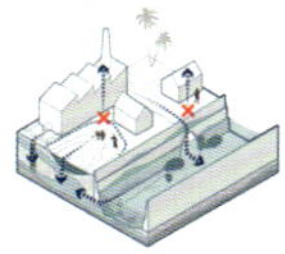 L-B3 Polluted/ Depleted aquifers	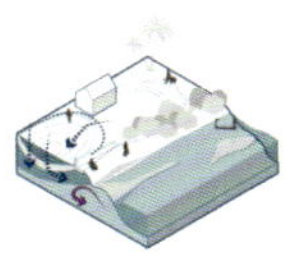 L-C3 Coastal aquifers against saltwater intrusion	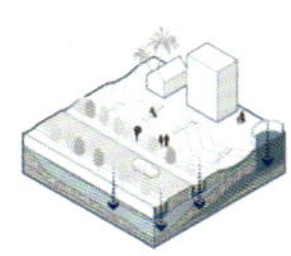 L-D3 Infiltration ponds/ Rainwater harvesting

CONNECT
Mobility Toolkits

	Access	Include	Activate	Generate
Arterial roads	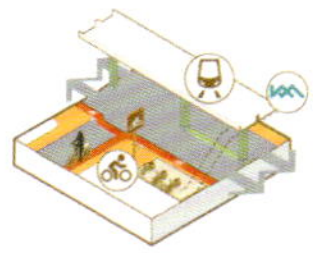 M-A1 Sidewalk/Cycle lane/Public Bike-Sharing	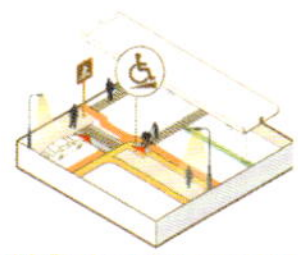 M-A2 Pedestrian crossings/ Tactile pavers/Ramps	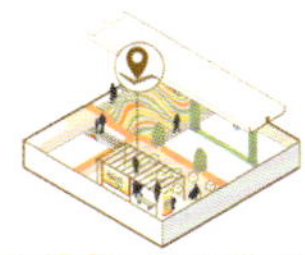 M-A3 Pop-up pavilions/ Cultural trails/Crosswalk art	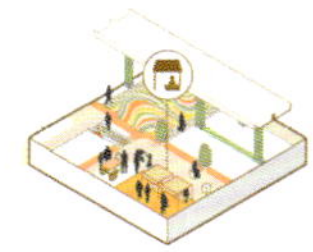 M-A4 Designated and temporary vending zones
Neighbourhood roads	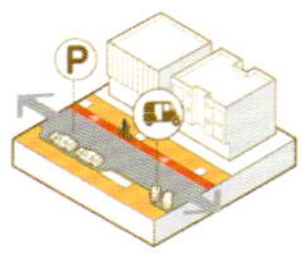 M-B1 Sidewalk/Cycle lane/ Rickshaw stand/Parking	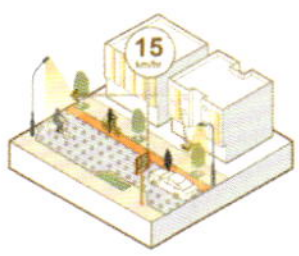 M-B2 Shared zones/Eyes on the Street/Street lighting	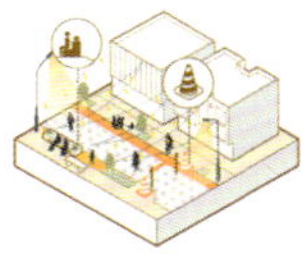 M-B3 Park lets/Temporary street closures/Seating	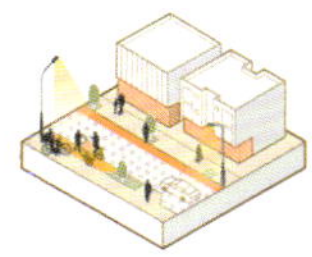 M-B4 Active street edges/ Vending zones
Open spaces	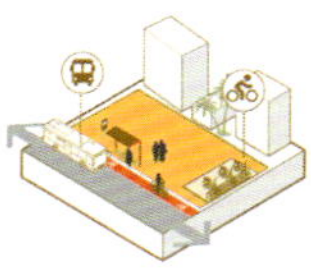 M-C1 Bus stop/Sidewalk, cycle lane/Cycle parking	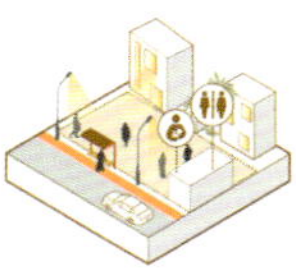 M-C2 Community toilets/ Feeding rooms/Street lights	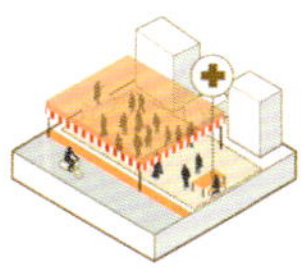 M-C3 Community event spaces/ Public service camps	 M-C4 Pop-up markets/ Vendor spaces

EMPOWER
Community Toolkits

	Inform	Engage	Collaborate	Support
Household	 E-A1 Building awareness	 E-A2 Community led initiatives	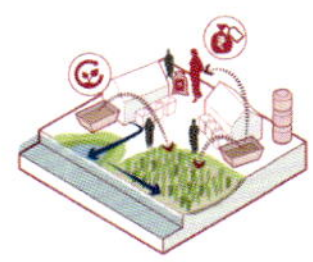 E-A3 Catalysing lifestyle changes	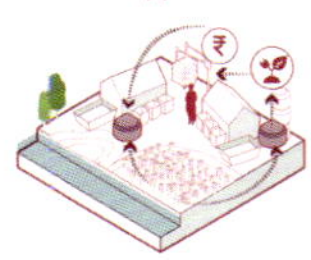 E-A4 Waste as resource
Neighbourhood	 E-B1 Community awareness	 E-B2 Building local knowledge	 E-B3 Community stewardship	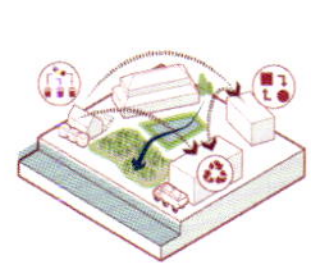 E-B4 Capturing positive network effects
City	 E-C1 Creating systemic awareness	 E-C2 Participatory governance/ community stakeholders	 E-C3 Knowledge exchange	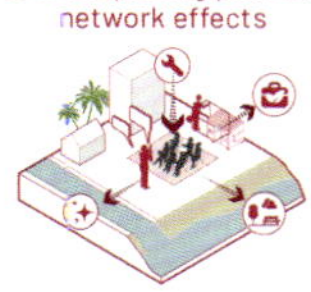 E-C4 Capacity building and funding/Infrastructure delivery

be scaled up for systemic impact. The challenges raised by climate change and India's trajectory of urbanization require multi-sectoral paradigm shifts informed by enlightened multi-disciplinary initiatives. We hope to build an alternative practice that builds upon the following lessons we have learnt so far:

1. **Mainstreaming multi-scalar ecological sensitivity and systems thinking to make urbanization sustainable:** Urban planning in India needs to begin with a deep acknowledgment of land-water linkages that sustain cities and the ways in which they are disrupted by urbanization. Municipalities and metropolitan development authorities should recognize how unplanned expansion threatens landscapes, aggravates flooding or drought, and compromises livability. Coordinated infrastructure investments that build urban resilience at the city scale will only be effective if regional planning protects, restores, or enhances natural systems. Our practice will emphatically address urban development at multiple scales—from the street to the region.

2. **Embedding visions within a framework to coordinate investments and build urban resilience incrementally:** Designers are trained to produce compelling visualizations that make principles more tangible for local communities and decision-makers. We consider visualizations as a political tool and wield them strategically. However, we found it important to embed these visions within a framework of actions. Any specific project or site can be overruled due to unforeseen circumstances, but once an influential stakeholder or group agrees upon the principles of the framework, the planning process will eventually yield transformative outcomes over time. In our engagements, we always prioritize making the case for a framework rather than proposing a static masterplan.

3. **Engaging with decision makers and collaborators in non-traditional spaces and forums to change minds:** Designers and planners need to find creative ways to be present in the same room as technical, financial, and bureaucratic decision makers. Design thinking and integrated planning are valuable ways to approach wicked problems that are typically confronted in siloes by more technical or policy-oriented professionals. Moving beyond the circle of our peers and like-minded allies, we should be comfortable being the only design thinkers in the room. This puts us in a unique position to change minds and create new forms of multi-disciplinary collaborations with ecologists, economists, engineers, social scientists, and local communities that are needed to ground ideas and make them implementable.

4. **Breaking disciplinary and institutional silos to build hybrid infrastructure with greater co-benefits:** New infrastructure paradigms

FIG.4 ADAPT+CONNECT+EMPOWER presented toolkits to improve urban ecology, mobility, and community and applied them as systems framework to improve the Mullassery Canal precinct in a holistic manner. Sponge Collaborative, Ente Kochi Urban Design Competition, 2020

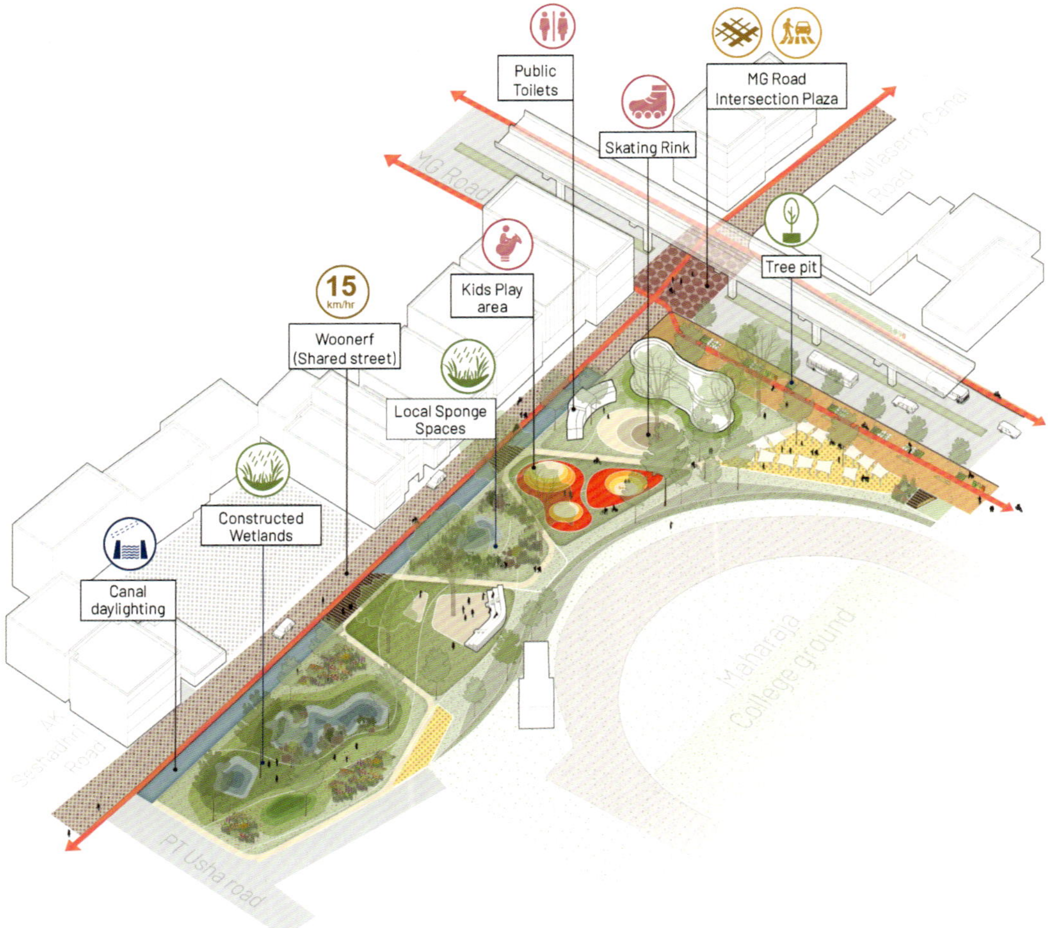

FIG.5 A detailed plan for a strategic site within the precinct identified pilot projects for implementation. A public space that improves community wellness, urban ecology, and pedestrian mobility is interwoven with blue-green infrastructure that delays and temporarily stores stormwater to mitigate flooding. Sponge Collaborative, Framework for Mullassery Canal (unpublished, 2021)

demand new forms of collaborations, models of financing, and protocols for implementation and maintenance. Implementing our Sponge Basin principles requires scientific understanding and datasets of the basin hydrology, geology, and topography at regional and site-specific scales. Designers need to be supported by enlightened engineers to carry through visions to feasible implementable projects. We need holistic economists to help us redefine what is bankable and run new forms of cost-benefit analysis that evaluates the life cycle of the project, the associated co-benefits, and inherent value of biodiversity. Sponge Collaborative hopes to inspire a critical mass of professionals in India who can produce datasets, write policies, and implement projects that make cities more resilient.

Investing in transparent and democratized processes to elevate emerging voices and innovation: Two open ideas competitions afforded our young collective to engage decision makers and broadcast innovative ideas to the broader community. Urban development and infrastructure projects are mostly steered by large consulting or engineering firms who compete within restrictive procurement practices. This practice rewards experience implementing outdated infrastructure standards rather than incentivizing collaborations that can lead to more innovative and resilient solutions. Sponge Collaborative is committed to growing the pie for integrated urban planning by freely sharing our work and encouraging young and mid-career designers and planners to use our strategies in their own cities, universities, and practices.

Endnotes

1. The agenda of the ILC responds to the immediacy of the climate crisis and the description of the Anthropocene as defined by: Paul J. Crutzen, "The 'Anthropocene,'" in *Earth System Science in the Anthropocene*, ed. Eckart Ehlers and Thomas Krafft (Berlin, Heidelberg: Springer, 2006), 13–18.
2. In recognizing the pervasive and perverse impact by sprawling urbanization, extractive industrialization, and environmental degradation, socio-ecological systems offer a framework for approaching the management of natural resources and landscapes that are heavily modified by and sustained by new social configurations. We understand socio-ecological systems as defined by Fikret Berkes, Carl Folke, and Johan Colding, *Linking Social and Ecological Systems: Management Practices and Social Mechanisms for Building Resilience* (Cambridge, UK: Cambridge University Press, 2000).
3. Flavio Sciaraffia et al., "Framing a Landscape Approach for Territorial Development in the Age of the Anthropocene," in *From the South: Global Perspectives on Landscape and Territory*, ed. Flavio Sciaraffia et al. (Santiago, Chile: Ediciones Universidad del Desarrollo, 2019), 14–23.
4. See Aparajith Ramnath, *The Birth of an Indian Profession: Engineers, Industry and the State 1900–47* (New Delhi: Oxford University Press, 2017) to understand the role of the colonial state in embedding engineers in the planning, operations and maintenance of municipal public works. For responsibilities of municipal governance vis-a-vis the state government with regards to urban planning and operations and maintenance in India, see Om Prakash Mathur, "Local Government Organization and Finance: Urban India," in *Local Governance in Developing Countries*, ed. Anwar Shah (Washington D.C.: World Bank, 2006), 169–204.
5. Sourav K. Biswas et al., *Sponge Handbook: Chennai* (New Delhi, India: GIZ India, 2019).
6. Hao Wang et al., "A New Strategy for Integrated Urban Water Management in China: Sponge City," *Science China Technological Sciences* 61, no. 3 (March 1, 2018): 317–29, for Sponge Cities in China; and Kuei-Hsien Liao, "The Socio-Ecological Practice of Building Blue-Green Infrastructure in High-Density Cities: What Does the ABC Waters Program in Singapore Tell Us?," *Socio-Ecological Practice Research* 1, no. 1 (March 1, 2019): 67–81, for the Singapore ABC Waters program; For the Copenhagen Cloudburst Masterplan, see "Good Practice Guide: Climate Change Adaptation in Delta Cities" (London; New York; Rio de Janeiro: C40 Cities Climate Leadership Group, 2016), 13, http://c40-production-images.s3.amazonaws.com/good_practice_briefings/images/5_C40_GPG_CDC.original.pdf.
7. Annapurna Shaw, "Metropolitan City Growth and Management in Post-Liberalized India," *Eurasian Geography and Economics* 53, no. 1 (January 1, 2012): 44–62, for an understanding of how Chennai and Kochi have developed since 1991 under neoliberal development paradigms.
8. For an example of an exploratory policy report by other Indian municipal corporations on introduction of blue-green infrastructure in India, see "Future Proofing Indian Cities: Madurai Action Plan for Blue-Green Infrastructure," (Chennai, India: Climate and Development Knowledge Network, 2014) http://www.asiapacific.atkinsglobal.com/~/media/Files/A/Atkins-Corporate/group/services-documents/future-proofing-cities/FPIC_Madurai%20Action%20Plan_1214.pdf; Also see
9. Smita Rawoot et al. "Mumbai Case Study: Product of Research on Enhancing Blue-Green Environmental and Social Performance," in *High Density Urban Environments* (Mumbai, India: Ramboll Foundation, 2015) https://ramboll.com/-/media/files/rgr/lcl/bgi_final-report_mit_mumbai_20160403.pdf?la=en
10. However, we have been unable to find detailed documentation of successful on-ground blue-green infrastructure initiatives in Indian cities. Interviews have gleaned that there has been a potential BGI pilot implemented on JM Road in Pune.

EDITORS

Shelagh McCartney

Dr. Shelagh McCartney is a licenced architect and urbanist specializing in marginalized community development and housing. She received her Bachelor degrees Environmental Studies and Professional Architecture from the University of Waterloo, and as a Fulbright scholar, Master of Design Studies and Doctorate of Design from Harvard Graduate School of Design. An Associate Professor at the School of Urban and Regional Planning at Toronto Metropolitan University in Toronto, Canada, McCartney has 10 years of housing experience in partnership with First Nations communities in Canada working with youth and elders. She is Director of Together Design Lab, an innovative research and design lab exploring platforms that focus on contemporary, interdisciplinary approaches to community and open territory design. McCartney is a Fellow of the Royal Architectural Institute of Canada.

Samantha Solano

Samantha Solano is a landscape architect and Assistant Professor of Landscape Architecture at the University of Massachusetts, Amherst. Her research and design methodologies are centered on using critical mapping as a means to reveal the unrecognized, unformalized, and unrepresented narratives hidden throughout landscape as it relates to equity, ecology, and design. She is the founding principal of JUXTOPOS a research practice focused on revealing these illegible landscapes and is the co-founder of the Visualizing Equity in Landscape Architecture Project (VELA). She holds a Master in Landscape Architecture from the Harvard University Graduate School of Design and is a member of the International Landscape Collaborative ILC.

Sonja Vangjeli

Sonja Vangjeli is a Landscape Architect and Design Project Manager at Waterfront Toronto, where she oversees design and implementation of large-scale public realm projects that aim to integrate nature-based solutions with urban infrastructure. Interested in the potential of urban landscapes as vital ecological infrastructure she works on urban design strategies that balance development priorities with site identity, heritage conservation, and landscape performance. Sonja has international experience as Landscape Designer with West 8 and Sasaki and as Researcher with the Zofnass Program for Sustainable Infrastructure. She is an alumna of the Harvard University Graduate School of Design (MLA) and University of Waterloo School of Architecture (MArch) and is a member of the International Landscape Collaborative ILC.

Hannes Zander

Hannes Zander is a Swiss landscape architect and researcher. He is currently working as PhD Fellow at The Oslo School of Architecture and Design where he is studying plans of urban growth and development in the context of an environmentally degraded and structurally weak region in rural China. Previously, he has been working as managing director of the research institute Ecological Urbanism Collaboration at Peking University, as research associate for the Sustainable Exuma project at Harvard University, and as practicing landscape architect for design firms in the U.S. and Europe. Hannes is holding a Master in Landscape Architecture degree from the Harvard University Graduate School of Design and is co-founder of the International Landscape Collaborative ILC.

CONTRIBUTORS

Yann Arthus-Bertrand is a renowned French environmentalist, photographer, journalist, and activist. He directed several films about the impact of humans on the planet and founded the international environmental organization GoodPlanet Foundation.

Sujhatha Arulkumar is an architect, urban designer, and researcher at Sponge Collaborative in Chennai, India.

Shannon Baker is an urban designer and landscape architect working as project director at Waterfront Toronto, Parks and Public Realm for the Port Lands Flood Protection project.

Balaji Balaganesan is an architect, urban designer, and product developer working at Sponge Collaborative in Chennai, India.

Antonia Besa is an architect at PAUR Paisaje Urbano in Santiago, Chile.

Sourav Kumar Biswas is a regional planner and geo-spatial analyst at GeoAdaptive in Boston. He is also principal advisor at Sponge Collaborative and co-founder of the International Landscape Collaborative.

Sheila Boudreau is an instructor at Toronto Metropolitan University and the University of Toronto, as well as founder of SpruceLab Inc. in Toronto.

Keith Bowers is a landscape architect and restoration ecologist. He is the founder and president of Biohabitats where he has applied his expertise to more than 600 projects throughout North America.

Matthew A. J. Brown is a landscape architect and co-founder of Brackish Design Studio in Atlantic Canada.

Robert Burley is a Canadian photographer whose work explores the relationship between nature and cities, architecture and the urban landscape.

Edward Burtynsky is a renowned Canadian photographer and artist known for his large format photographs of industrial landscapes representing industrialization and its impacts on nature and the human existence.

Malihah Chamani is an Iranian landscape architect and doctoral candidate at the Professorship of Landscape Architecture and Regional Open Space at the Technical University Munich.

Hexing Chang is a planner, landscape architect, and researcher at Turenscape in Beijing.

Adriana Chávez is an adjunct assistant professor at the Columbia University Graduate School of Architecture, Planning, and Preservation and co-founder of ORU, Office for Urban Resilience, based in Mexico City.

Sandra Cooke is a landscape architect and co-founder of Brackish Design Studio in Atlantic Canada.

Marine Cusa is a French marine biologist exploring, testing, and promoting methods to combat illegal fishing practices and seafood fraud. She is completing her PhD at the University of Salford in the UK.

Alberto de Salvatierra is the founding director of the Center for Civilization and assistant professor of urbanism and data in architecture at the University of Calgary School of Architecture, Planning, and Landscape.

Jennifer A. Dowdell is a senior landscape ecological planner and designer at Biohabitats based in the Chesapeake Bay bioregional hub in Baltimore.

Tamsin Faragher is a landscape architect working as the City of Cape Town's Principal Resilience Officer.

Berta Flaquer is a Spanish architect currently finishing her PhD in urban studies at Luleå University in Northern Sweden.

Dylan Gauthier is a Brooklyn-based artist, designer, curator, and educator. He is co-founder of the art collective Mare Liberum and teaches art, design, and systems at Parsons, The New School.

Jeffrey Herskovits is an urban planner and working as a researcher with Together Design Lab at Toronto Metropolitan University in Toronto, Canada.

Hans Hortig is a landscape architect working with Architecture of Territory at ETH Zurich and is co-founder of the cartographic studio maps&more.

Lindsey Howe is appointed professor of architecture and society at the University of Liechtenstein and lecturer at the ETH Zurich Institute of Landscape and Urban Studies.

Vid Ingelevics works as a visual artist, writer, independent curator, and educator, and is associate professor at Toronto Metropolitan University School of Image Arts.

Manushi Ashok Jain is an architect who works as director of campus planning, urban design, and architecture at Sponge Collaborative based in Chennai, India.

Justin Kollar is a PhD candidate and a research fellow at the Leventhal Center for Advanced Urbanism at MIT, the Massachusetts Institute of Technology.

Suriya KP is an architect with the Sponge Collaborative based in Erode, Tamil Nadu, India.

Shreya Krishnan is the director of community planning, strategic design, and sustainable development at Sponge Collaborative based in Delhi, India.

Gini Lee is a landscape architect, interior designer, and pastoralist. She is professor at the University of Melbourne and an adjunct professor at RMIT University as well as the University of Adelaide in Australia.

Nina-Marie Lister is an ecologist and landscape planner and professor in the School of Urban and Regional Planning at Toronto Metropolitan University in Toronto.

Ben Mansfield is a landscape architect based in Zurich, Switzerland. He is the managing director of the Integrated Sustainable Foundation, working on urban developments in South Africa, Zambia, and Kenya.

Thomas Nideroest is a Swiss landscape architect and researcher working with Sasaki in Boston. He is co-founder of the International Landscape Collaborative.

Matthew Poot is a Canadian landscape architect working with Link Arkitektur in Oslo, Norway, and as consultant for the City Region Food Systems program within the UNFAO in several cities across Africa and Asia.

Sunita Prasad is a New York City-based artist and filmmaker. She is a member of the collective Mare Liberum, the video art co-operative Temp.Files, and Brown Girls Doc Mafia.

Gary Pritchard ~ Giniw (Golden Eagle) is a conservation ecologist and Indigenous engagement/placemaking specialist from Curve Lake First Nation, Ontario, Canada.

Mirwais Rahimi is an Afghan architect, planner, and social scientist currently finishing his PhD at the Doctoral School Bordeaux Montaigne Humanities in Bordeaux, France.

Praveen Raj is an urban designer, planner, housing expert, and architect. He is the director of masterplanning, urban design, and housing at Sponge Collaborative based in Bengaluru, India.

Víctor Rico is an architect and urban designer. He is co-founder of ORU, Oficina de Resiliencia Urbana, based in Mexico City.

Pankti Sanganee is an urban designer at Sasaki Associates in Boston and works on hydrology and landscape strategies within established urban environments at Sponge Collaborative.

Flavio Sciaraffia is an architect, urban designer, and landscape architect specialized in strategic sustainable planning. He is partner at the Chilean office of GeoAdaptive in Santiago, co-founder of the International Landscape Collaborative, and was the chief editor of the group's first book *From the South*.

Eli Ristin Skum is a veterinary scientist with a focus on preventive health care in West-Finnmark, Sápmi, Northern Norway.

Julia Smachylo is an urban planner and designer. She is assistant professor of landscape architecture at the University of Connecticut.

Aliza Sovani is a Canadian landscape architect and interdisciplinary design and planning professional currently based in Toulouse, France. She is co-founder and director of lili media & design, an environmentally focused creative agency.

Aditi Subramanian is an architect and urbanist with Sponge Collaborative, currently pursuing a master's degree in urban design at the University of California, Berkeley.

Logeshwaran Subramanian is the principal architect and sole proprietor of RADIIX Design Studio based in Tiruppur, Tamil Nadu, India and working with Sponge Collaborative.

Kendra Sullivan is a Brooklyn-based writer, publisher, and artist. She is a member of the art and boat-building collective Mare Liberum.

Elena Tudela is a PhD student in architecture at the Faculty of Architecture at UNAM where she serves as professor of the Environmental Urban Department. She is co-founder of ORU, Oficina de Resiliencia Urbana, based in Mexico City.

Kjerstin Uhre is an associate professor in landscape architecture at UiT The Arctic University of Norway and partner at Dahl & Uhre architects in Tromsø.

Ryan Walker is a lens-based artist in Toronto and an educator in the BFA Photography Programs at Toronto Metropolitan University and Sheridan College.

Dong Wang is a landscape architect and researcher at Turenscape in Beijing.

Jane Welsh is the project manager of the environmental planning unit of Toronto City Planning and current chair of the Canadian Society of Landscape Architects Committee on Climate Adaptation.

ADDITIONAL IMAGE CREDITS

Background map on book cover and global index (p.6-7):
produced by Hannes Zander.

Sources: Global glaciers and ice caps, with data from: RGI Consortium (2017). Randolph Glacier Inventory - A Dataset of Global Glacier Outlines: Version 6.0: Technical Report, Global Land Ice Measurements from Space, Colorado, USA. Digital Media, https://doi.org/10.7265/N5-RGI-60; Northern hemisphere permafrost, with data from: Obu, Jaroslav, Sebastian Westermann, Andreas Kääb, Annett Bartsch (2018). Northern Hemisphere Permafrost Extent and Ground Temperature Map, 2000-2016 (continuous coverage, >90%; discontinuous coverage, 50-90%; sporadic coverage, 10-50%; isolated patches, 0-10% coverage). Alfred Wegener Institute, Helmholtz Centre for Polar and Marine Research, Bremerhaven, PANGAEA, https://doi.org/10.1594/PANGAEA.888600; Vegetation cover, with data from: JAXA Japan Aerospace Exploration Agency, Earth Observation Research Center, ALOS Advanced Land Observing Satellite (2017). 1km-Resolution Forest/Non-Forest Map 2017, https://www.eorc.jaxa.jp/ALOS.

CREDITS FOR SECTION DIVIDER PAGES:

1. Robert Burley (p. 32-33)
2. Alberto de Salvatierra (p. 90-91)
3. Berta Flaquer (p. 146-47)
4. Marine Cusa (192-93)
5. Mare Liberum (240-41)

Photograph on page 300 by Robert Burley.
Forks of Rouge River and Little Rouge Creek, Rouge National Urban Park, Greater Toronto Area, 2013.

§ NOTE ON TORONTO METROPOLITAN UNIVERSITY RENAMING

In August 2021, Ryerson University announced that it would begin a renaming process to address the legacy of Egerton Ryerson for a more inclusive future (https://www.ryerson.ca/next-chapter/). The Standing Strong (Mash Koh Wee Kah Pooh Win) Task Force recommendation (2021) to rename the university report states: "For as long as the university is named after Egerton Ryerson, our narrative will be centred on his legacy. Given that our namesake is increasingly recognized as a symbol of colonialism, our identity as an institution can no longer be disentangled from separate schools, segregation, the genocide of Indigenous Peoples and cultural erasure. With a new name, the Toronto Metropolitan University can boldly move forward, guided by our institutional values and principles of commemoration."

The Truth and Reconciliation Commission of Canada released its summary report in 2015 that includes 94 Calls-to-Action for Canada to address the "cultural genocide" of Indigenous Peoples through segregation as enacted with the residential school policy and achieve true reconciliation. Reconciliation is not an Indigenous problem, it's a Canadian problem and every Canadian needs to be aware of this very dark (but not distant history as the last school closed in 1996) period of history, understand that it has caused an intergenerational and ongoing impact and find ways and means to support reconciliation.